Civil War Women

The Diaries of Belle Strickland and Cora Harris Watson

Holly Springs, Mississippi
July 25, 1864 - June 22, 1868

Commentary by
Robert Milton Winter, Ph.D.,

with photos from the
Chesley Thorne Smith Collection

MILLSAPS-WILSON LIBRARY
MILLSAPS COLLEGE
JACKSON, MS 39210-0001

CIVIL WAR WOMEN
Copyright 2001 by Thomas•Berryhill Press
ISBN 0-9648638-8-X

This book may not be reproduced in whole or in part without permission.

Address for information
Thomas•Berryhill Press
Box 178
Lafayette, CA 94549

Printed in the United States of America

Cover: Strickland Place
Painting by Herndon Davis, noted painter of early American homes. Originally commissioned for the Memphis *Commercial Appeal* (April 13, 1941).

For Chesley

CONTENTS

Acknowledgements vii

Foreword ix

Introduction xii

I. Belle Begins a Journal 1

II. Hiding from the Yankees 5

III. We are Living on Cornbread and Butter 25

IV. He was Much Taken with the Lady that Sang 41

V. To the Foundry for Some Tacks 59

VI. Eddie and Johnny Went to Sell Eddie's Yankee Horse 77

VII. Caring for the Sick 87

VIII. Helping Poor Soldiers' Families 101

IX. A Popular Merchant Slain 119

X. Miss Lizzie Expands Her Educational Efforts 129

XI. Elizabeth Watson and Fenelon Hall 139

XII. President Johnson Impeached 159

XIII. Decorating the Soldiers' Graves 175

XIV. A Difficult Era in a Proud Community 191

Epilogue 215

Endnotes 223

Index 295

Acknowledgements

Projects of this sort, while requiring solitude in the study, are never lonely undertakings. Friendships are born, and a researcher's gratitude for the interest and help of others grows with the turning of each page.

It was Mrs. Chesley Thorne Smith, while busy caring for her husband, the Hon. L. A. Smith in his long illness, who took time to bring the Belle Strickland and Cora Watson diaries to my attention, and who generously opened to me her huge collection of Holly Springs memorabilia and photographs. Chesley has the wonderful gift of memory-both in range of recall and accuracy of detail. She is one of the few collectors who not only *has* the items that a researcher needs, but who also has everything *organized*, so that she can put her hands on them immediately!

The original typescript of the diary was made many years ago as a classroom project at Holly Springs High School by Miss Josephine Wyatt. Miss Wyatt's ability to read the old fashioned handwriting was unerring, and she performed a great service.

To Dr. Hubert McAlexander, a son of this city and professor of English at the University of Georgia-THE expert on Holly Springs history-I owe a pleasant debt, for Hubert has always been more than ready to share his knowledge and offer insight on many questions-even those that he had to go to a good deal of trouble to answer. He also lent many of the photographs that enliven these pages. Always the mentor, Hubert has imparted much of his own "know-how" to me in the craft of searching out and writing local history.

The friendly and helpful staffs of the Marshall County Library and Marshall County Historical Museum are due great praise, for it was these good ladies who cheerfully searched out a score of obscure books and references for me over the course of this undertaking.

I also thank William Stebbins, of Florida, who preserved Belle's mother Jane Strickland's letters to her husband, and the Rev'd Dr. Albert H. Freundt Jr., who gave me letters from Sophia Boyd Hays, who passed through Holly Springs in her Civil War journeys, and whose comments amplify scenes recorded in Belle's and Cora's diaries.

This book owes all its attractive features, minor editing and design to the expert work of Tom Adams, owner of the Thomas-Berryhill Press, and his assistants, in Lafayette, California. Tom has deep Holly Springs roots, and though he did not grow up here, he should surely consider himself a citizen of our community.

Finally, the forbearance and encouragement of the Holly Springs Presbyterian Church cannot be forgotten. It was these good people-my pastoral flock and adopted family-who made it possible for this and several similar efforts to see fruition. They lead me to hope, as my seminary president, the Rev'd Dr. T. Hartley Hall IV, of Virginia, said some years ago of a colleague who came to the College Church at Hampden-Sydney: "that truly this minister has found a congregation where his eccentricities may be considered virtues."

Foreword

As a small child I liked to sit in my little chair (which had been my grandfather's chair two generations earlier), and listen to the conversations of my grandmother with her afternoon visitors. In this way I learned about the old families of Holly Springs including those of my playmates. There were also fascinating stories of the Civil War in this firsthand information. My impressions of that war came in this manner rather than from textbooks.

My favorite visitor was Aunt Belle. (The custom in those days was to give a close friend of one's family the affectionate title of "Aunt" attached to her first name.) I dearly loved Aunt Belle and she seemed fond of me. One Easter she gave me a little yellow chicken, which I immediately named "Belle." My little chicken grew up to be a rooster and folks laughed about a big strutting rooster named Belle. And when for Christmas I received a beautiful baby doll with a bisque head and open-shut eyes she was given the name "Belle."

After I was older, Aunt Belle took me to spend the night at Buddie's (her older brother's) home in the country at Hudsonville.[1] His wife was Miss Rena. (Another custom was to call a married woman by her first name with the title Miss.) The mother of their two granddaughters had died, so that Lorena and Mary Thomson lived with their grandparents. Mary Thomson took me horseback riding, letting me ride the gentler horse and use her prize saddle with the great big horn. We rode through the woods and over the hills. But the thing that I remember most vividly is the big spring that ran off as a brook with the butter being kept cool in the clear spring water.

These memories lead to the main object, Belle's diary. In all the years of these associations I never heard of the diary until after the deaths of my grandmother and Aunt Belle and until I was married with children of my own. Aunt Belle's half-sister, Perle, lived in the Strickland house with Belle's half-brother, Frank. After Perle was sixty years old she married Mr. Gerard Badow. When Mr. Badow was left alone and decided to move to another town he gave the diary to Charles N. Dean, to whom I am grateful for letting me copy it.[2]

Belle begins the diary by saying that "Papa has given me this book for a Journal, and I have promised to write in it every day until he comes again." No mention is made of where or why he has gone. But a glance at the date gives the clue, since it was a Civil War year. However to understand why she and her siblings were not left at home needs explanation. Belle's mother (born in 1835) had died, June 29, 1863,[3] so the children were left in the care of a neighbor, Catherine Davis (Mrs. J. W. C.) Watson, while Papa was off to war. You also need to know that Mrs. Watson's daughter, Elizabeth Davis ("Miss Lizzie"),[4] had started a school in the Watson home. Helping as a teacher was Cora Harris (Mrs. William T.) Watson, who had married a Watson son. He was killed in the First Battle of Franklin, Tenn., and "Miss Cora," as she is called in the diary, had come to live with her husband's family. Cora Watson also kept a diary, and discusses many of the same incidents and events as did the young child Belle. It is interesting to compare the perspectives the adult and the child give of Civil War incidents, national affairs, and events in the history of Holly Springs.

Later in the diary, Belle again lives at home in the Strickland Place. In 1867, Major Strickland married Jane Leak, daughter of

x

Forward

Colonel Francis Terry Leak, the wealthiest planter in Tippah County, who lived just over the Marshall County line, near the village of Salem. Belle calls the second Mrs. Strickland "Mama" in the diary.[5]

    I was able to identify some of the people mentioned in the journal, but Dr. Hubert McAlexander has helped me with many others.

— Chesley Thorne Smith

Introduction

Keeping a journal was widely recommended in the nineteenth century as an improving exercise. Thus, Belle Strickland of Holly Springs, as well as the others in her class at school, were encouraged to write in their journals each day. Adults, such as Cora Watson, also practiced the art, and where diaries survive, they give rare insight into daily life. A few disciplined persons continued to make entries in their secret books throughout their lives. While many are scarcely more than chronicles of the mundane doings of long-forgotten individuals, or copybooks for snippets of verse, some diaries serve as windows through which the observer may look back upon a fading past.

Belle's diary allows an unusual opportunity to review the American Civil War and Reconstruction from a child's perspective. Here one finds observations of deep pathos concerning casualties of battle mingled with youthful reports that she had practiced her required hour at the piano. Still, Belle was not too young to be a dedicated Confederate partisan. With regard to the slaves who lived in and around the homes of their owners, her writing reveals that she had learned to express both the paternalistic affection and unfeeling bigotry that adults around her so tragically displayed in their everyday actions.

Interest is added to nine year-old Belle's diary from the entries in another journal kept in the same period by Cora Watson, then twenty-one, and the widowed daughter-in-law of Judge and Mrs. J. W. C. Watson. Comments from Cora Watson's diary are interspersed with Belle's journal in these pages. The Watson diary, kept in 1864-65, records scenes in both Holly Springs and Covington, Tenn. Her granddaughter Cary Johnson used the journal as the basis for a master's thesis at Louisiana State University in 1929.[1]

Belle Strickland, born March 1, 1855, to William Mathew and Martha Mildred Thomson Strickland, was reared at Strickland Place, her family home on what was then called Depot or Church St. (now Van Dorn Ave.) in Holly Springs, Miss.[2] The Strickland home, long a landmark and symbol of the heritage of the family which lived there, was a vernacular plantation house with an inviting double-deck porch and small, square columns. It had a spindled gallery rail, surmounted by a gable roof across the front. The house faced the town's main street-leading to the busy station that saw the coming and going of trains on the Mississippi Central Railroad.

In pioneer days, the Strickland Place lay on the town's southern boundary. Behind it were woods-miles of hills and valleys that the early white pioneers found covered with trees of every variety, through which ran meandering streams from hundreds of gushing springs. These flowed to the Tallahatchie River, which ran east-west between Holly Springs and Oxford. The land was cleared for cotton, but on the long sloping hillside behind the Strickland house site, a large wooded area remains, called either "Strickland's" or "McCarroll's" Woods because of the two families who lived side by side at the forest's northern edge. These woods, which once extended from the Strickland Place east to the railroad, have gradually yielded to the town's expansion, were the scene of Civil War adventures and have furnished a playground for generations of Holly Springs children.

Introduction

As with all early Holly Springs houses, timbers for the Strickland Place were hewed by hand near the site. No nails were used in the framing, and the structural members were mortised and pinned with wooden pegs. All the lumber was heart pine, and bricks for the foundation and chimneys were handmade. The house itself was entirely of wood; the kitchen and outbuildings were built later of brick. It was a large home. There were six eighteen by twenty foot rooms on the first floor, and two rooms of the same dimension on the second. The grounds were fronted by tall hedges, with the house set well back from the street. Unusual cylindrical plastered pillars formed gateposts, such as one might see at the entrance to a French country estate, and a serpentine brick walk edged with boxwood led to the porch. In later years, the lawn was almost obscured by lush vegetation that Belle's younger sister Perle allowed to flourish. The house had many interesting antiques, including items used by Major Strickland in the Civil War.[3]

An interesting account came down through the family concerning the furnishings of the house, a story involving Belle's mother, Mildred Strickland. It was related to Olga Reed Pruitt by Perle Strickland Badow, for Mrs. Pruitt's book of anecdotes, *It Happened Here: True Stories of Holly Springs*.

"*Story of the Big Bed*"

William Matthew Strickland shivered in the winter darkness as he groped for the blankets. Expertly and from long practice he tugged at the cocooned form of Mildred, his wife, as she slept serenely beside him, wrapped in all the bed covers. The same thing had happened last night and the night before. It would happen tomorrow night and the next night for Mildred was a hopeless cover puller. Nothing could stop her. Sleeping without cover wasn't the only thing. The bed itself was too short. Ever since he had married Mildred Thomson and come to live in this house that had been built beside an Indian trail in 18[3]8,[4] he'd had to jack-knife his 6-foot-4 form into this normal sized bed. Cold and disgruntled, he decided that he was done with his nightly tugging with his sleeping wife for his share of the bed covers. And there in the darkness he made his plans. He would have a bed made that would accommodate his long frame, as well as two sets of covers, one set for Mildred and one for himself. He knew a firm in Cincinnati that made such beds. He ordered the bed next day. When it was delivered it was found to measure 6 x 7 feet inside, 7 x 8 outside and was more than 10 feet high and made of rosewood. It still occupies the same spot in the front bedroom, a monument to the wife who had a proclivity for pulling the covers. And people come to see it and wonder mildly why anyone would want such a bed, not knowing about the two sets of covers.[5]

There was a tradition that the Strickland Place had been spared under unusual circumstances during the Civil War. According to Perle Strickland Badow, the tale unfolded this way:

"Between Friends"

This house would have been destroyed early in the Civil War but for the friendships that existed between North and South. Major William Strickland was at the front and Miss Carrie Newton of Connecticut was visiting his wife. The two ladies were entertaining one of Miss Newton's friends, a Federal soldier, when a Confederate raiding party appeared. The ladies quickly rushed the visitor upstairs, out on the roof of the back porch and under the eave of the upper story. Although they carefully searched the house, the raiders did not find the Yankee soldier. Some time later, when the town fell into Federal hands, officers of Gen. Grant's staff appeared to inspect this house relative to turning it into a hospital for infectious diseases. Upon hearing that the building had been approved and knowing it would be destroyed when the Federal army was done with it, Miss Newton's friend went to his commanding officer and related the manner of his escape from the Confederate raiding party. He urged that the house be spared as a gesture of appreciation. His plea was heard. Strickland Place was not taken for a hospital and the home stands today, the first two-story frame house erected in Holly Springs.[6]

Belle's family was prominent in the society of Holly Springs, a proud little community which sprang up in the flush times which rippled across North Mississippi when the land was opened to

Introduction

white settlers. Her father, William Mathew Strickland (1823-1903), was born to a prominent family near Raleigh, N.C. W. M. Strickland's father was Squire Mathew Strickland, said to be descended from England's Sir John Strickland. His mother was descended from the Earl of Warwick.

W. M. Strickland was one of Marshall County's early settlers, coming first to Chulahoma on the western edge, where he worked in his brother's store. He later moved to Holly Springs and read law under J. W. C. Watson and Judge James F. Trotter. Admitted to the local bar, he formed a partnership with Judge Jeremiah Watkins Clapp in 1849 and later with James T. Fant and Arthur Fant. In that year, Henry Craft, another of the town's attorneys, wrote of Strickland in his diary: "He has the principles and feelings of a gentleman and is one of those in whose discretion and honor I feel perfect confidence. . . . I like him very much because he is a high minded, right hearted man."[7]

For half a century, W. M. Strickland's name was associated with civic and business ventures in the community. When the Civil War broke out he was among the first to enlist.[8] He joined the Jeff Davis Rifles, which included many of the town's leading men, and in keeping with preferment often given to the well-born,[9] Strickland, who began as a sergeant, attained the rank of major by war's end. Long an adherent of the Baptist Church (his name appears as a trustee when the congregation erected its second house of worship in 1855), Strickland was, in his later years, "a comrade, mentor, and advisor" to the town's younger men, especially graduates of St. Thomas Hall,[10] one of the town's early schools.[11] Before and after the war he was active in theatrical associations which staged elaborate plays in the town's Masonic Hall.[12] He died at Holly Springs, March 4, 1908, and is buried in Hill Crest Cemetery.

The other characters in the story will be introduced in their turn, but almost all, like Strickland, took advantage of the wide opportunity that the growing frontier provided, to make a name and leave an impress on local society.

CIVIL WAR WOMEN

The American Civil War was a time of great disruption for Mississippi and her people-a time of devastation from which Holly Springs and the state have never fully recovered. The diaries of Belle Strickland and Cora Watson show how the members of two families-bound up in the war as provocateurs and partisans-nonetheless found order in the midst of chaos and were able to reach out in praiseworthy acts of compassion and in the development of a remarkable educational effort. They remind us that no one can embrace any cause quite so purely as we think, but their example shows how two allied families in a small Southern town were able to wrest dignity and purpose from the vicissitudes of war and to face an uncertain future with trustful serenity and impressive service to others. Most of their graves are unmarked in the cemetery, but their legacy lives on in Holly Springs!

— *R. Milton Winter*

I. Belle Begins a Journal

Before going away to war, Belle's father gave her an elegant leather bound volume with blank pages to use as a diary. On the first page it carries this inscription in Major Strickland's hand: *"Presented to Belle, for her Journal, by her Father, 25 July 1864."* The little book, seven inches square, was stamped with the name William M. Strickland. Belle kept her diary from July 1864 to July 1887. Now, 137 years later, the earlier portion comes to life. In the opening pages, we find nine-year-old Belle with the J. W. C. Watson family, which lived one block from the Strickland home.

> **Monday, July 25th 1864.** *Papa has given me this book for a journal, and I have promised to write in it every day until he comes again. He went away Sunday morning before day. I have missed him very much since he went away. I am sorry that he can't stay with us all the time. Minnie[1] says that he is gone to Canton to get her a ball. There was a report of the Yankees today, and all the soldiers had to run, and I was glad that he was not here. Miss Cora commenced a worsted quilt, and did not want to finish it, so she gave it to me. I went to work on it this morning, and I sewed on it all day until this evening. It was reported that the Yankees were coming, and I put it up. Eddie[2] went out to Mrs. Martin's[3] soon this morning before day. Mr. Molloy[4] spent the day with Mrs. McCully. Buddie went to Walker's Mill seven miles out of*

town with Johnny McCarroll.⁵ He said he would come back either this evening or tomorrow morning. We heard from Mr. Watson today, and he will be at Meridian⁶ tonight, and we think he will be here Thursday. Miss Nannie Dickinson⁷ and Miss Julia Little called today. Mrs. McCulley gave Mr. Molloy a silk handkerchief and a cake of soap and a pair of gloves and two shirts. Miss Cora cut out Minnie a doll and Miss Lizzie has been making it all day.*

"There was Another Report of Yankees"

After General U. S. Grant's plans for capturing Vicksburg by land from the north were spoiled by Confederate General Earl Van Dorn's early morning raid at Holly Springs, Saturday, December 20, 1862, the city was not considered valuable enough strategically by either army to maintain a regular occupation force. Holly Springs, however, did suffer numerous raids. Historians do not agree on the number, but it is clear that the town changed hands many times. The Magnolia Hotel on the north side of the square was headquarters for the officers of whichever army happened to occupy what was sarcastically called "The Independent Republic of Holly Springs."⁸ It is said that the ladies of the town, fearful to venture onto the square if Yankees were present, would climb the tower of the unfinished Presbyterian Church to see whose flag was flying in the center of town. For years, an odd record, tabulated on the columns of the Hugh Craft Place on Memphis St., bore witness to the many changes of authority which occurred during this period, giving the dates of fifty incursions by U. S. soldiers. John M. Mickle said that this "illustrated the methodical turn of the owner."⁹

Tuesday, July 26th 1864. This morning there was another report of the Yankees and they said that they were in sight, and we all got up and commenced to hide our things. Mr. Molloy and all

---

• Belle's journal entries are set in italic type.

the soldiers had to run;[10] *and Miss Amelia McCarroll*[11] *came over and said that they were running cars to Scales depot, and were coming to occupy this town, and scared us all nearly to death. But Miss Amelia went round to Mr. Craft's and saw Mr. Joe Scales, and he told her it was not so, and that relieved us very much. Miss Lizzie sewed on Minnie's doll all day today, but still has not finished it. It is made very nice. Buddie came home from the mill this evening, and it was reported that the Yankees were coming again, and he ran with the mule. Mr. Molloy stayed all day with Miss Alexander. He has only one more day to stay. Miss Amelia McCarroll and Miss Nannie Dickinson are going as far as Grenada with him. Miss Cora had a chill this evening.*[12] *Mr. Molloy came home and brought us some apples.*

CIVIL WAR WOMEN

II. Hiding from the Yankees

Local citizens, especially those in the Confederate army, or with roles in its government, repeatedly had to hide from Federal troops. As a senator in the Confederate Congress, J. W. C. Watson was a prime target. His friend J. W. Clapp, also of Holly Springs and a member of the Confederate House of Representatives, had to resort to almost comic measures to escape detection.[1] Clapp's imposing residence stood three blocks north of the Watson home.[2]

On one occasion in 1863, when returning from Richmond, Clapp reached Holly Springs with great difficulty. With U. S. troops in possession of the Pontotoc Road, he moved through the fields and woods at right angles to the road. According to his journal, he stopped at one house where he obtained breakfast, and then proceeded

> with a view of giving information to our troops, but found myself in the predicament of the man who fled from the lion and a bear met him, for I was challenged by one of our pickets, who had his gun drawn on me and took me for a spy, and was as he said in the act of shooting me.

Clapp persuaded the young man to take him to his commander, who accepted Clapp's credentials and apologized for the picket's conduct. Clapp arrived home safely, only to discover that Holly Springs was occupied by soldiers. When he entered the city he was recognized by U. S. officers and men were sent to arrest him. Clapp told his diary:

> I took refuge in the house of a near neighbor, Mr. Nelson,[3] who helped me up into the loft and covered the entrance with a piece of furniture. The day was warm and the heat of my hiding place almost unendurable, but upon reflection I concluded that it was more tolerable than a Yankee prison and submitted to the roasting until the danger was over.

On another occasion, Clapp told what happened after he returned home after a long absence on a mule named "Beck."

> The 'Yanks' were engaged in a fight with our troops in the street fronting my house when we were at dinner and the first intimation we had was the report of firearms and the clatter of horses' feet. I, of course, lost my appetite and without sticking upon 'the order of my going,' left by the back door as the nearest place of concealment, made my way into an adjoining lot where the weeds were very thick and tall and lay there panting with heat and thirst until near sunset, and the next morning about sunrise whilst I was still in bed, my son Will came dashing into the room with the exclamation- 'The Yankees are in the yard and have got Beck!' Of course I lost no time in getting out of bed, but what to do was the question. My clothes were on a chair at the bedside, but I had no time to put them on. A servant girl stuck my boots up the chimney and put my watch in her bosom and my wife disposed in some way of my hat and clothes, and as I could not venture outside, I made my way to the attic or garret in my night apparel, and in looking anxiously about for a hiding place it occurred to me to get inside one of the large iron capitals that finished the columns to my front porch. Here I was completely concealed, but could hear the Yankees riding on the pavement in the front yard and talking, and supposing they knew I was at home and had come on purpose to capture me, and would set the house on fire if I did not make my appearance, my feelings at the time may better be imagined than described. Will, however, very adroitly managed to get rid of them and save Beck, and I was after a while able to leave my place of concealment."[4]

Men of lesser rank, such as Mr. Malloy, also had to hide from the soldiers.

Wednesday, July 27th 1864. *Old Mr. Thomson[5] passed by and told Mr. Molloy that the Yankees were coming, and he had to run before he got his breakfast, and stayed away all day. [He] left word for Miss Lizzie to pack up his things, but she did not commence until he came back. Miss Cora had a fever all night, and stayed in bed all day until late this evening. Mr. Paine[6] came and told us the news, and while he was here Mrs. Basset came, and soon after Mr. Paine went away, Miss Emily Phillips came. Miss Julia Little made Mr. Molloy a beautiful tobacco pouch. This evening Mr. Molloy came home and Miss Lizzie packed his things. Miss Nannie Dickinson made him a tobacco pouch too. Miss Lizzie finished Minnie's baby this evening. It is a real Confederate doll. We all thought it was very pretty when it was finished. Minnie was mightily delighted with it. Buddie stayed all night with Aunt Mollie[7] tonight. Eddie has not come back yet.*

"Visiting Christ Church"

Belle's father favored the Baptist Church, but she and the other children visited the town's other churches from time to time. Belle was fascinated by the ritual of Episcopal and Roman Catholic churches, and took every opportunity to visit their services. She was not alone in her interest. Emma Finley, also Presbyterian, who lived near Holly Springs on a plantation called "Woodland," was present when the Episcopalians first occupied their elegant new church, September 19, 1858. She told her diary:

> Sunday we went to hear the first sermon in the new Episcopal church. It is beautifully frescoed, & ornamented both within & without;- a fit place in which to sing praise to the Most High. Mr. Ingraham is a very pleasant preacher- could not judge of his power from the one sermon. I trust he may do much good. [8]

The new church, with buttressed walls, Gothic battlements, and a tall spire was beautiful. Dr. Willis M. Lea, a parishioner, wrote to his cousin Dr. Ellis Malone in North Carolina, January 1, 1859, that "the new Episcopal Church would pass well in any city."[9]

Thursday, July 28th 1864. Mr. Molloy left this morning soon. It was reported that the Yankees were at Mr. Cannon's and we all were very glad that Mr. Molloy was not here. I sewed on my quilt and made two blocks today. I laid down on the bed with Miss Cora, and Miss Cora read some to me in her scrapbook, and I was very much amused with the "Arkansas Traveler." I went to the Episcopal church[10] with Hattie Dancy. Miss Cora heard from home this evening. Mr. Watson came while I was at church. He jumped over the fence to tell them all howdy.[11] And when church turned out they told me that Mr. Watson had come, and I came home as fast as I could. At first Minnie would not go to him. She calls him "Grandpa." She said last night, "I am tired yookin at you, I want to do to bed." Minnie calls the baby that Miss Lizzie made her "Mollie Dixie." Mr. Watson heard her the other day singing:

"I yuv my Papa dat I do,
"And I hope Papa yuv me too"

"J. W. C. Watson–Uncompromising Puritan"

John William Clark Watson (1808-1890) was described by his biographer as "an uncompromising Puritan."[12] An elder of his church at Holly Springs for forty-four years, he would not travel on the Sabbath. Jefferson Davis once wrote him about criticism because Davis had declared a day of repentance, fasting, and prayer- apparently at Watson's behest. Some Confederates did not believe repentance was necessary and that such displays might send the wrong signal to the enemy. Still, many admired Watson and his family. Helen Craft Anderson, whose forebears were closely allied with the Watsons, preserved these memories of the Watson family, so prominent in Holly Springs, especially in the life of its educational institutions and Presbyterian Church:

> I dimly recall that as a small child, I fell through the sleeper of the unfinished house which is known now as the 'Old Watson Building,' which was being built for the residence of Judge J. W. C. Watson, a fine old Virginia gentleman and Christian who became one of Mississippi's distinguished citizens. I spent many pleasant days and hours here with this lovely family in my childhood and girlhood; it was a home typical of all that is best in life, culture, refinement, hospitality, and religion.[13]

Born to John and Elizabeth Finch Watson in Albemarle County, Va., J. W. C. Watson married Catherine Frances Davis, daughter of Staige Davis of Charlottesville, Va., September 8, 1831. He was a graduate in law from the University of Virginia, practiced a few years at Abingdon in his native state, and about 1839 went to the frontier, coming to Holly Springs in 1845. Like many of the town's leaders, Watson was a Whig before the war, opposing secession as long as possible. But when Lincoln called for troops to subdue the South, Watson said he could not "go against blood and kindred." He was a Confederate Senator for Mississippi from November 12, 1863 until the fall of Richmond. The Watsons were a family in mourning. They had six children-two sons died in the Civil War.[14]

After the war, Watson edited the Holly Springs *South* and served in the state legislature, where he sponsored a bill establishing the Mississippi Railroad Commission. He then successfully defended the legislation before the U. S. Supreme Court, the high point of his legal career. Watson was a member of a committee sent to call upon President Ulysses S. Grant to counter the activities of Republicans in the Congress. He was circuit court judge (1876-82), and in 1878, the University of Mississippi awarded him an honorary Doctor of Laws degree. But Watson had weaknesses. His friend F. A. Tyler was a big smoker with tobacco fumes "strong enough to run an elevator," and as the story goes, Watson, a total abstainer from tobacco, used to like to sit by the hour close to Tyler and be heartily smoked![15]

These days were not among the easiest of Watson's life, but as may be inferred from Belle's second notation below, he did not violate his rule against travel on the Sabbath.[16]

Friday, July 29th 1864. This morning Buddie wrote a letter to Papa for the first time. I spent the day at Mr. Clark's[17] today. This evening I went to church with Hattie Dancy. Tonight Mr. Watson went out in the country because he was afraid of the Yankees.

Saturday, July 30th 1864. This morning it was reported that the Yankees were right in town and Mr. Watson ran and hid but it turned out to be two Yankees who said that they were deserters. This evening Mr. Watson went to Okolona. Miss Nannie Dickinson came and said that her Father had sent for her and was very anxious for Miss Cora to go with her, but Miss Cora has not decided yet whether she will go or not.

"Mr. Paine Said that the Yankees Were Expected"

Belle was greatly interested in her Sunday school class. Her teacher was Miss Clementine Clapp, daughter of her father's law partner. The Rev'd Henry H. Paine, the Presbyterian minister, was a Confederate partisan,[18] and much troubled by the U. S. occupation of Holly Springs. Federal soldiers had desecrated his church in 1862, perhaps because there were Confederate leaders in the congregation. Paine, like his colleague John N. Waddel, of LaGrange, Tenn.,[19] sometimes found it expedient not to conduct services during the war, rather than risk arrest for what they did or did not say when addressing the Almighty.

Waddel gave this account of attempts to silence his preaching:

Hiding from the Yankess

LaGrange was visited on some three or four different occasions by raiding parties, but it was not permanently occupied until the close of the year 1862, when after the fall of Corinth the Northern army was massed in heavy force on the Memphis and Charleston R.R., covering a stretch of country some ten miles in length, and even more planting themselves in force at various points, to the terror and distress of the inhabitants. The town from that time was never free from a garrison, more or less numerous and troublesome, until the close of the war. I remained in the place with my family. . .and was subjected to very great aggravations and annoyances. I was forced to give up my house as the head-quarters of the notorious Gen. John A. Logan, who allowed me two back rooms for my own use, and another for my daughters, while he occupied the parlor for his own use, and my study was the office of his chief of staff. . . .He remained there three weeks, and while he did not subject me to any insult or outrage, yet he and his aide kept the house and the yard crowded with squads of private soldiers by day, and they were frequently engaged in Bacchanalian revels at night. The consequence of all this was that when the General with his troops evacuated the premises, the rooms occupied by them presented the appearance of having been occupied by any class of tenants but that of gentlemen. . . .The federal soldiers who were left in LaGrange. . .tore down the College building and used the bricks to build huts, and chimneys to their tents, until there was hardly a vestige left, or trace of the LaGrange College to indicate the spot where it once stood. On a certain Saturday morning, as I was seated in my room, I had placed in my hands by an orderly a communication from [the] Provost-marshal, who was in command at that time in LaGrange:

Dec. 13, 1862,

Rev. J. N. Waddel,

Sir: Until you have identified yourself as a citizen of the United States, by renewing your allegiance to the government and constitution thereof, you will discontinue your labors as a minister of the gospel in this place. You have hitherto used all the means in your power to aid this wicked rebellion, and your labors have been successful in creating suffering and death amid a once happy people. Instead of being a humble follower of our Savior, endeavoring to save a dying world from their sins, you have stirred dissentions [sic], created estrangements in families, and urged vile treason toward the best government that God ever created upon earth. . . .I trust you have seen the error of your ways, and that you will acknowledge the justice of these plain-spoken words.

> Respectfully, your obedient servant,
> F.F. Peats, Major and Provost-Marshal

The soldiers attended the LaGrange Presbyterian Church, and Waddel determined that the authorities planned to compel the oath-taking publicly or to arrest him before the congregation, so that he declined to preach the following Sunday.[20]

Henry Paine may have had similar fears.

Sunday, July 31st 1864. We went to Sunday school. Miss Clemmie Clapp heard my class.[21] I wish Miss Mary Paine[22] would come. She has not been there for seven or eight months. When we came home and started to church[23] we met all the people coming from church because Mr. Paine said that the Yankees were expected and he would not preach. We did not think that they would come and went to the Episcopal Church. This evening Buddie stayed over at Aunt Mollie's and I stayed at home and read and learned the hymn that begins, "The sun that lights the world shall fade." Miss Cora decided that she would go to Somerville. We all will miss her very much.

"Cora Watson Crosses Enemy Lines"

Cora Watson spent a month in the summer of 1864 visiting her foster-father, Judge Harris in Covington, Tenn., sixty miles northwest of Holly Springs. It was on this visit that she began keeping her diary.[24] Meanwhile, as they journeyed into Federally-controlled territory above Holly Springs, Cora and her fellow traveler Nannie Dickinson, were subjected to just the sort of encounter they had feared.[25] But the Union soldiers showed a kind of gallantry toward the women, realizing that up until the war's outbreak, women would never have attempted a journey of this sort without male chaperons.

Monday, August 1st 1864. *This morning Miss Cora went away. She expected that she would go at six o'clock but Miss Nannie Dickinson did not come until eleven o'clock. It was reported that the Yankees were coming. It had been reported so often that very few people believed it, but in the evening they came sure enough and caught three of our soldiers but we did not know any of them. Two officers came here to supper and told us that they met Miss Cora about seven miles from town and there had been a little skirmish just before they met her. She and the other ladies were very much frightened but Lieutenant Bennett made a corporal go with them past the column.*[26]

"Mars Rides the Mississippi Central"

Holly Springs gained its wealth not just from cotton but by building a railroad which hauled the cotton. As the South's largest agricultural region without good access to either water or rail transportation, Marshall County's need for a railroad was acute, and once constructed, its beneficial effects were felt immediately. Wealthy men found their worth increased, and even more cotton was produced. The spate of mansion and church building which ensued at Holly Springs was but one of the tangible results.[27] The Mississippi Central Railroad, completed in 1859, in which the Watsons and all their friends invested, was badly damaged in the Civil War. The line was broken first by the Union army and then the Confederates, as the course of war directed. The only difference in the destruction was that the Southerners took orders from railroad president Walter Goodman, and thus its wreckage was less complete than the North's. All bridges and most track above Oxford were ruined.[28]

Tuesday, August 2nd 1864. *This morning a good many infantry came in. They said that the cars*[29] *[would come] either this evening or tomorrow morning. Guards were put all round the house and they treated us very kindly. Mrs. Watson invited some* *of them to come in to dinner and four of them did so. Miss Bettie Hull*[30] *and Miss Bettie Thomas came over to see us and told us how some of our soldiers got away last night. Five of the guards came in to supper and some of them seemed to be right clever men. They came in after supper and talked 'till ten o'clock. I forgot to tell about the Yankees killing one of Eddie's pigs.*[31] *Mrs. Watson had the rest put in the wood house and says that she is going to keep them up until the Yankees go away.*[32] *The cow did not come up tonight and Mrs. Watson was very uneasy about her.*[33]

"Troop Movements Described"

Belle was fascinated by the soldiers who marched through Holly Springs. Most were Union troops. By this time the town had become used to the sight. Maria Brodie Mason, a Nashville heiress and wife of Carrington Mason, a prominent Confederate leader,[34] told how people locked their doors, closed the shutters, and stole timid views of the blue-coated soldiers marching by. As Grant massed troops for his assault on Vicksburg, she wrote that:

> It was a sore sight to Southern eyes, but numbers, style, and elegance of equipment in comparison with the shabbiness of the Confederate cavalry offered a fascination which could not be resisted. The blue grass paddocks of Kentucky and Tennessee had supplied the officers with the finest of thoroughbreds and the splendid uniforms and gay flags presented more the effect of a pageant than an army. The next day the infantry began to arrive. My home stood at the end of the street on which they came into town, so that they turned to the west in front of the house, marched one square, then turned south again into the Oxford Road, so I believe I saw every regiment in the army, for although the sight was heartbreaking, it was magnificent. First would pass by the regimental band playing always 'The Girl I Left Behind Me'; then marching four abreast in handsome new uniforms, came the infantry and as the music of one regiment died away, the next could be heard in the distance, and so on and on for three days they came, as we thought, a great

blue monster, going to swallow up the devoted victims of the Confederacy. The wagon train was five days long.[35]

Wednesday, August 3rd 1864. *This morning the Yankee cars came in and brought in soldiers and goods too. The infantry came in. This evening I went over to Aunt Mollie's and saw a great many soldiers pass by. They went out of town by Mr. Mason's.*[36] *This morning the cow came back and Mrs. Watson had her put up in the wood house with the pigs.*[37]

"Entertaining the Yankees"

Civilians were compelled to yield their homes for military use. During preparations for the Vicksburg campaign, General Grant occupied the Holly Springs home of Col. Harvey W. Walter, and General C. S. Hamilton had rooms in the Strickland Place.[38] This practice continued throughout the war and beyond. Sometimes relationships were cordial, and it was not unknown for owners to volunteer their homes to the use of the army as a means of preserving them. Indeed by such self-serving generosity whole towns were spared. A letter exists in Harvey W. Walter's hand, inviting Grant and his wife to make Walter Place their home while in Holly Springs.[39] No doubt all guests were not as pleasant as those who stayed with Belle's Aunt Mollie Hudson, but there were some cordial associations.

Friday, August 5th 1864. *This morning I went over to Aunt Mollie's with Lucy after some apples for Mrs. Watson. Aunt Mollie has a captain staying with her. He treats her very kindly and pets Fonta*[40] *a great deal. He says that she reminds him of his little children at home. He has the sore eyes and says that he hopes to get a discharge and go home. He lives in Minnesota. When I came back from Aunt Mollie's I played with Minnie 'till dinner*[41] *and then I read in "Robinson Crusoe." A Negro brigade came in and I looked at them through the shutters. A wagon train passed* *'till ten o'clock at night. There were two hundred wagons and two droves of cattle. We heard the brass band way in the night.*[42] *Uncle Stephen*[43] *got home this evening. He left Mr. Watson at Okolona Tuesday, and he came home part of the way with General Chalmers*[44] *and his troops. They are gone towards Abbeville. At Okolona Uncle Stephen saw General Forrest walking about on two crutches and he says that he heard him tell General Chalmers to save his men and not to fight the Yankees if there were too many of them.*

Saturday, August 6th 1864. *Aunt Mollie came over to see us and Miss Bettie Hull was here too. Aunt Mollie's captain went away today and she was very sorry. He cried when he told her good bye and promised to write to her if he got home.*[45] *I sewed on my quilt. This evening Miss Mollie Craft came round to tell us good bye. She is going to Kentucky to see her mother. All the young ladies from Mrs. Hull's came over. Three Yankees came in tonight and talked some time. They gave us a paper that came from Memphis this morning and tells about the fight at Petersburg where we gained the victory. We are much afraid they will get Atlanta, though.*

"Methodist Church Commandeered by Federal Chaplain"

In parts of the South occupied by U. S. soldiers, northern Methodist personnel commandeered "disloyal" Southern pulpits under a policy authorized by Secretary of the Army Edwin M. Stanton and prosecuted by Bishop Edward R. Ames. Stanton authorized several denominations to this activity, but Methodists were the only ones to vigorously pursue it. It resulted in great resentment among both white Southern preachers and people.[46]

Sunday, August 7th 1864. *There was no Sunday school today and there was no preaching except at the Methodist church and a Yankee chaplain preached.*[47] *Buddie is still staying at Aunt*

Mollie's. *This morning two or three thousand of cavalry passed by and twenty-two pieces of artillery and about two regiments of infantry. All going South.*

"Soldiers Conscripted from Methodist Congregation in Covington, Tenn."

Cora Watson told of a contrasting incident during her visit to Covington, Tenn. The local Methodist Church was surrounded by Confederates who rounded up men for the army. By her account:

Wednesday, October 5, 1864

Conscripting has been going on in town this week. Monday night the Methodist church was surrounded, and as the congregation came out of the doors, all men subject to the conscript laws were compelled to resume their seats until the others got out and were then carried along by the soldiers. An officer, Capt. Dawson of Dyersburg, and several men with lanterns stood at the door, and every window was guarded. A good many notorious shirkers of duty were nabbed.[48] *

"Mammy Had Gone"

John B. Boles wrote that "For every beloved house-servant who sided with the master when Union troops came near during the Civil War, there were one or more who led the black exodus to freedom." Boles ventured that "their greater knowledge of their master's foibles, and their increased familiarity with liberty, only resulted in a greater hunger for freedom."[49] The departure of slaves was a wrenching experience for masters, not least for economic reasons, and, as word spread of the Emancipation Proclamation, Southerners (especially those behind enemy lines) feared loss of their property in labor. "Mammy" and Wash, slaves of the Hudsons, were typical of many blacks who fled. To the insult of the slaves'

• Cora Watson's journal entries are set in san-serif type and indented.

departure was added the injury of pillage by soldiers. These acts were not uncommon, though perhaps not as one-sided as Southern apologists averred.[50]

> **Monday, August 8th 1864.** *This morning Mrs. Watson was right sick and did not come down until dinnertime. This evening Aunt Mollie came over and told us Mammy[51] had gone. Her husband Wash had gone to the Yankees. He sent for her and made some threats if she did not come. She was very much distressed when she took leave of Aunt Mollie and the children. [Mammy] said if Wash went into the army she would come back.[52] A good many other Negroes went today.[53] I went over to Aunt Mollie's and it looked so lonesome without Mammy that I cried.[54] Two Yankees came over to Aunt Mollie's and wanted to buy a chicken and Buddie told them that he did not have any. They asked a great many questions and looked all about the place as if he was searching and knocked like it a bit when she came home and we told her about it.[55]*

"A Slave Exodus at Somerville, Tenn."

Cora Watson, writing August 26, 1864, at Covington, Tenn., recorded similar events in Somerville, Tenn., midway between Holly Springs and Covington. The slaves, flush with the hopes of freedom, were leaving their owners. Some drifted back and eventually began working for wages.

> *Received by Johnnie a note from Hannah, one from Bee and one from Nannie. From them I obtain news of a raid of the Yankees and Negroes into Somerville on Tuesday last which 'was worse than the famous Hayhawkers raid of Jan. 3rd, 1863.' They broke open all stores and strewed their contents over the streets and behaved in a most insulting manner to the citizens. Over a hundred Negroes left from Mr. Dickinson's, all from Messrs. Moore, Stanley and Greenway, Dr. McClellan and Mrs. Wilfong. These are indeed exciting times.[56]*

"The Best Set of Yankees that We Ever Saw"

Southerners were loath to admit it, but many times their property was safeguarded by Federal troops. After the 12th Iowa Regiment left Holly Springs, people were afraid for their safety, as well as their possessions.

> *Tuesday, August 9th 1864. This morning I was waked up by the music and when I went to the window we saw two or three regiments of Negroes passing by.*[57] *Then came a long wagon train. Mrs. Watson counted two hundred wagons. One of the guards named Mr. lback [came] in to see us and sat all the morning. Mrs. Watson and Miss Lizzie like him very much. I practiced some and began to make a dress for Minnie's doll. Our guards went away this evening. We were very sorry. It was the 12th Iowa Regiment and it was the best set of Yankees that we ever saw. All of us were afraid to undress and go to bed.*

"Surly Servants and a Visit with the Rev'd Mr. Pickett"

The ladies were beginning to chafe under the extended camps of the soldiers, the surliness of their newly emancipated slaves, as well as the petty thievery of the troops. A bit of refinement came as local clergy visited in the homes of Holly Springs. With most of the town's men off at war, ministers assumed a place of greater importance and were called upon for advice on many subjects, including politics. Though the Watsons were unreservedly Presbyterian, they received the Rev'd James Thomas Pickett, D.D., of Christ Church, on the most intimate terms.[58] The leading members of Christ Church Parish were possessed of secessionist sentiments identical to those of Major Strickland and the Watsons. Indeed, six of the eleven generals Holly Springs furnished to the Confederacy were members of Christ Church, and the diocesan convention which severed ties to Protestant Episcopal Church (U.S.) was held at Holly Springs in April 1861.[59] Pickett had become rector of Christ Church in 1862, two years after the tragic death, December 18, 1860, of the beloved, the Rev'd Joseph Holt Ingraham, LL.D., the former rector, whose tragic death stunned the nation. Ingraham, a popular author, was fatally injured in the church's vestry on a Saturday evening when he accidentally dropped a pistol he carried due to rumors of a prowler.[60] Pickett was a Confederate chaplain, and was respected by almost everyone in Holly Springs.[61]

Wednesday, August 10th 1864. We had a quiet night and when we woke up this morning we found a new set of guards. They are of the 100 and 22nd Illinois Regiment. One of the 3rd Iowa came in out of the rain and sat a long time. Mr. Paine came. While he was here and after Mr. Paine went away, Mr. Pickett came. When they were all gone Aunt Mollie came and stayed 'till after dinner and I went home with her. The Yankees are camped in our wood lot and Aunt Mollie says that they pester her very much by going in her orchard and coming for milk. Since Mammy went away, Aunt Mollie has to cook for herself,[62] because old Lizzie won't do it,[63] and she [doesn't] like to send Belle and Alfred[64] down in the kitchen where the Yankees are.[65] This evening we were standing at the gate and we saw a guard up at Mrs. Hull's corner. Mrs. Watson said that she wished that he would come down and talk some, so Minnie ran up to him and said, "Mamma says, 'Turn dar'" ["Come there"], and when he didn't come she ran back and took hold of his hand and led him down to our gate. He talked a while and seemed to be a right nice man.[66] We have had several showers today.

Thursday, August 11th 1864. This morning I went over to Aunt Mollie's and helped her to pick up apples. She had them knocked down because the Yankees got them. When I came home I read some in "Junker Scholt." I practiced some and sewed on my quilt some. This evening I read some fairy stories 'till Aunt Mollie came. And I went home with her and stayed all night with her.

"Miss Lizzie Heard Me a Lesson"

The Watson family, finding its income reduced by the war, was forced to put its women to work. Moreover, as the South's young men-as well as many of its male teachers-marched off to war, women were summoned to fill the breach. Before the war, Holly Springs had been a regional educational center with between four and five hundred students enrolled in four schools: for boys, St. Thomas Hall (a school of the Episcopal diocese) and Chalmers Institute (strongly allied with the Presbyterians), and for girls, the Holly Springs Female Institute (also with Presbyterian ties) and Franklin Female College (which had a Methodist allegiance). All the Holly Springs schools closed when the war began, and remained closed for the duration of hostilities. "Home schools" for neighborhood children were the result, as a few individuals carried forth their resolve that the young should be taught. The fact that this could be done at all during such times gives some measure of the convictions held by these persons-many of them Presbyterians imbued with Scotland's love of learning. Thus, Elizabeth Watson, with the assistance of her sister-in-law Cora, began instructing the sons of their household, with Belle and her brother, who were boarding with the family, as well as two or three children who lived nearby. The effort was undertaken *ad hoc*, but it grew into a more disciplined course of study, and finally, into a respected Presbyterian college. Belle's words betray the speech patterns of her English and Scots-Irish ancestors, for whom such expressions were not ungrammatical.[67]

Friday, August 12th 1864. This morning when I came home from Aunt Mollie's I practiced some and then Miss Lizzie heard me a lesson and then I sewed some on my quilt. A whole division of Yankee cavalry passed through here returning from the south and going toward Salem. This evening I practiced some and sewed some too. Mammy[68] was in town today. She came back for her things.

Saturday, August 13th 1864. I practiced a good deal today and sewed on my quilt some. This evening Miss Stella Craft[69] came up. We are having a quiet time now. This morning I borrowed an instruction book from Miss Bettie Hull.[70]

"Keeping the Sabbath"

Persons living in the twenty-first century often attribute better church attendance to their ancestors, but records indicate that people in earlier times also missed services for various reasons.[71] The chief impediment was weather. This was understandable for families that lived on the outer boundaries of a parish, but even townsfolk, lacking sidewalks, missed worship when rain turned streets to mud. Belle and Buddie sanctified the Sabbath,[72] memorizing Sunday school lessons and learning hymns by heart, a salutary practice made necessary because songbooks were not provided in the churches.[73]

Sunday, August 14th 1864. There was no Sunday school and none of us went to church.[74] I read in the Bible and several other books. Miss Lizzie heard my Sunday school lesson. This evening I learned the hymn that begins, "I lay my sins on Jesus." Buddie came over a little while this morning and said his Sunday school lesson. . . .

"Mrs. Watson Stayed with Mrs. Walthall Last Night"

Although Holly Springs had several physicians (two of whom possessed medical degrees) women nursed the sick, the young of their households, as well as other women in the neighborhood. Catherine Watson found herself called upon for such assistance, sitting with Sarah Southall Wilkinson (Mrs. Barret White) Walthall, mother of the much-admired Holly Springs Major General and later U. S. Senator, Edward Cary Walthall.

Monday, August 15th 1864. *I was with Miss Lizzie all the morning helping her make some jelly for Mrs. Walthall. After we got it made it wouldn't harden. Mrs. Watson stayed with Mrs. Walthall last night. She is very sick and thinks that she can't live but a few days.*[75] *In the evening we tried some more gelatin to see if it would harden but it did not succeed any better than the first, so we conclude that jelly can't be made in the summer without ice.*[76]

"Spending the Day"

Southerners made a great practice of visiting. Visitors would come for the day, the week, or the month. Some came and never went home. David Hackett Fischer writes that there was a class of impoverished gentlemen in England and America "who made 'visiting' their profession."[77] Belle's visit to Mrs. Clark, the wife of her teacher, was only for a day, and Belle and Rosa Clark, schoolmates, amused themselves playing the piano and singing.

Tuesday, August 16th 1864. *This morning I went over to Mrs. Clark's and spent the day. We had a very pleasant time. Rosa*[78] *played some on the piano and we sang together. After I came home in the evening Mary McCroskie*[79] *came to see if we had heard from Miss Cora and Miss Nannie Dickinson but we had not since the first day they left. We heard that the Yankees were going away. This morning they went all around searching for salt. They got 40 bushels from Mr. Nelson's and two barrels from Mrs. Anderson's. They pretended that the Provost Marshall had ordered them but he hadn't given any such orders and the men were arrested. Mrs. Watson was so uneasy about Eddie that she wanted to send Henry*[80] *down to Mrs. Martin's to see about him, but Mr. Crump*[81] *and Mr. Read said it wasn't safe.*

Wednesday, August 17th 1864. *This morning I helped Hannah[82] wash up the dishes. Fonta and the baby came over and I played with them and the other children. We had a great many showers today and I went over to Aunt Mollie's and got caught in one. I went up to Miss Lucilla Read's[83] to take my tuition and Buddie's. Miss Lizzie read "The Forty Thieves" to me.*

III. We are Living on Cornbread and Butter

By 1863 food had become scarce for soldier and citizen alike.[1] Holly Springs newspaperman and historian John Mickle remembered how people made do with substitutes:

> Roasting ears were grated on large tin graters, like nutmeg graters, and used for bread. Toasted dried corn was ground and used for coffee, and tea was made from sassafras leaves. Most families kept a cow and had milk and butter. . . .People ate meat when they could get it. I saw my first orange after the war-they sold for twenty-five cents apiece in Memphis.[2]

In spite of privations, the Watsons never refused a soldier's request, often inviting some of the more promising men to the family table-such was the etiquette of "Southern hospitality." But Cora Watson remembered better days. On February 9, 1865, she wrote that:

> Mrs. Smith, Mr. Anderson, and Carrie came about eleven and spent the day. Our dinner was quite stylish for these hard times-a nice turkey, with gooseberry sauce, a baked ham, cold beef, tongue, stewed fruit, sweet and sour pickles, batter-bread, hard and light biscuits, and butter, with tea and coffee. Yet looking back to the dinners of our years ago makes this one seem poor.

Others made do with less. W. Irwin McGowan, who lived in the Spring Creek community southeast of Waterford in southern Marshall County, remembered the desperation following Van Dorn's raid. His older brothers had joined the army, and Irwin, the thirteen-year-old son of the house, felt the responsibility of providing food for his widowed mother and the others that remained on the place. He told of one bitter experience:

> Our food supply was almost exhausted. For days we had eaten nothing but the small sweet potatoes the soldiers had overlooked and the hominy which we made from a hidden supply of corn soaked in lye leached from the ashes of our wood fires. One day mother called me and said, 'Irwin, we must have a meal. All the children are getting sick from eating nothing but potatoes and hominy.' We had a scant supply of corn left and the gristmill stood idle. In happier days it was our custom to grind one day each week, supplying the needs of the plantation and neighborhood.[3] We hitched a strong team to each end of a long pole and, driving them round and round, ground the corn between the two great millstones. But now we had no teams left to use. However, I began to make my plans and to send word around that there would be a grinding at McGowan's mill on Monday. On the appointed day, I arose before sun up and harnessed Kit-Mother's saddle mare, the only animal left on the place, with a patched up harness and waited at the mill in suspense. Finally a boy came, driving a team of oxen that resembled nothing so much as the seven lean kine which Pharaoh in his dreams saw come up from the river Nile.[4] They were the most miserable little fleabitten beasts that you ever saw. The boy took in the situation with a pessimism devoid of surprise. After a brief consultation, he agreed to help me for his need of meal was as great as mine and we went to work to do the only thing possible. He hitched his oxen with their patched gear to one end of the pole and I fastened Kit to the other. Kit was a splendid saddle mare. She had taken first prize at the Fair in Holly Springs the first year of the war. Mother always rode her but she had never been harnessed to anything before. She was thin and emaciated from long hiding in the woods and short rations, but her spirit remained unbroken. The boy called to his oxen and with much urging succeeded in starting them off. I led Kit and for a few minutes all went well but, watching closely, I saw the light of comprehension gradually begin to dawn in her eyes. I could read her thoughts as clearly as you ever read a man's eyes from the expression of his countenance. It took her a few seconds to realize the insult that had been put upon her but when she did her anger rose

uncontrolled and carried everything before it. I have never doubted I verily heard her eyes snap, as with a leap she freed herself from the rotten harness and in fury started for the house. Judy, the cook, saw her coming and called out, 'Misses, there won't be no meal today. Here comes ole Kit with all them strings and straps ahanging to her.' But before she could say more, Mother's calm voice replied (and after fifty years my father repeated her words as proudly as if he were showing his children a medal of honor), 'Yes, there will be. I sent Irwin for meal and he will bring me some.' Just then I was far from being so confident. As a last resort, we raised the stones to make the work as light as possible and put one of the oxen in Kit's place. Leaving the owner of the beasts to drive his team, I climbed to the left of the mill to examine the results. Never in the whole four miserable years was I so absolutely discouraged when I looked down and saw the tiny stream of meal hardly larger than a knitting needle and began to figure what my toll would be. Utterly hopeless I threw myself down on the floor and cried. Not for long, however, for soon I heard a hail and looking out I saw two grown men riding a pair of splendid mules. They were soldiers home on furlough and, hearing of the grinding, had come for meal for their families. The situation was soon explained and they willingly agreed to take out the oxen and put in their mules. They were still only two to do the work of four but the mules were strong and the soldiers agreed to grind as long as the mules held out and then divide whatever we made. Hopeful once more, I tightened the stones and we went to work again. Before the mules were exhausted, other neighbors began to participate and by making frequent changes we ground all day. When the first pint of my toll of meal was measured out, I seized it thankfully and made a dash for the house that Judy might cook it for dinner.[5]

The situation was only a little better in Holly Springs.

Thursday, August 18th 1864. . . .*Mrs. Gray came after some meat and bread, and after she went away Mr. Paine came.*[6] *A woman came here that was at Mrs. Martin's Friday and said that Eddie and Johnny had gone down to the river bottom with Mrs. Martin's cattle and [that] all the men of that neighborhood are camped down there.*[7] *We are living on cornbread and butter.*[8]

"Hiding the Animals"

Cora Watson recorded in her journal at Covington, Tenn., August 13, 1864, that the people there also took steps to hide their animals.

Soon this morning Amp and George Branscome passed, driving Mr. Lloyd's and Uncle Alfred's stock to Pa's farm to keep them away from the Yankees. Told Mr. Tucker that a few days ago the Yankees, led by one of Mr. Lloyd's own runaway Negroes, went to his house and carried off every servant he had and behaved very badly besides. I can imagine the alarm and excitement it occasioned in the neighborhood and particularly at Uncle Alfred's. They must have started the stock off in the night.

"Till Late in the Evening"

Southern nomenclature often needs explanation-terms, such as "dinner," which in Belle's day referred to the midday meal ("supper" was the day's final repast) and "evening" which referred just not to the hours of twilight and "early candle-lighting" but included the afternoon, as well. It was a vestige of the planter culture of Virginia, whereby those of the privileged classes liked to give the impression that time was theirs to while away. Work was done in the forenoon; "evening" was given to leisure.[9]

***Friday, August 19th 1864.** Mrs. Watson stayed all night at Mrs. Walthall's and she is a great deal better. It rained all day today and I sewed 'till late in the evening and then I went down stairs to help Hannah churn and stayed down there until nearly dark. Mrs. Watson got Henry to go down to Mrs. Martin's after Eddie and he is going to start tomorrow. I made Mrs. Watson's butter up for her. I practiced some and Miss Lizzie heard me a music lesson. I haven't read any today.*

"Several Gentlemen Got Up from the South Today"

Holly Springs lay behind enemy lines, and with the tracks of the Mississippi Central torn up and Union sentries at every crossroads, travel was difficult and dangerous.[10] Every train that started over the line watched carefully for burned bridges and wrecked track, with news of Yankee raiding parties constantly in the crew's ears.[11] Dr. J. N. Waddel, who often preached in Holly Springs and Oxford, told about difficulties of travel between the two towns in this period:

> I must be indulged in an attempt to describe our mode of transportation from Oxford to Holly Springs, as it will give the reader some conception of the utter demolition of everything like the facilities and conveniences of passage and locomotion that had resulted from the war, and which before the war had been in successful operation in that region of the country. The distance between the towns of Oxford and Holly Springs is thirty miles by rail. Over the first thirteen miles we rode on a flat car, quite a company of us together, drawn by a very small engine. This placed us on the south bank of the Tallahatchie River. There we were reduced to locomotion on our feet, crossing on a flat ferryboat, as the railroad [bridge] had been destroyed,[12] and on the north side of the river we found the track again with a flat-car standing waiting for us, drawn by a single mule! On this, at the rate of five miles per hour, we performed the remainder of the trip, reaching Holly Springs about 2 o'clock p.m., having been on the way some six hours, a space ordinarily requiring but little more than one by steam.[13]

Saturday, August 20th 1864. This morning I fell down the back steps and hurt myself right badly. I sewed a good deal and practiced and took a music lesson. Henry started to Mrs. Martin's after Eddie today after it stopped raining. I went up to Mrs. Craft's and they told me that Miss Carrie[14] *was coming and Miss Fannie*[15] *and the children. Miss Bettie Hull came over here this evening. Several gentlemen got up from the south today. They were waiting for the Yankees to get away. Mr. John Bradley*[16] *came in too soon and they caught him and took him up north because he is a member of the legislature. Mrs. Watson got a letter from Miss Cora today.*

"Noah's Flood and the Tallahatchie Bottom"

The family attended divine service and heard their minister preach from Genesis 6:5-the Almighty's indictment of humanity in the era leading up to the destruction of earth by flood-Noah and his family were the only ones saved-a righteous remnant. This verse, a classic text of Presbyterian orthodoxy, was used along with Isaiah 64:6 and Romans 3:10 to validate the Calvinist doctrine of human depravity. Such a sour theme must have given some satisfaction to a congregation in the depressed situation in which Holly Springs found itself.[17] Meanwhile, Forrest's troops came up from the abyss, determined to make an assault upon the U. S. garrisons at Memphis. He rode with two thousand out of Oxford on the evening of August 18. Swinging to the west, they crossed the Tallahatchie at Panola and headed north. Heavy rains caused rivers and streams to run full. Undaunted, Forrest charged his men into Memphis before daybreak on August 21. (This was the famous raid, known to generations of children, in which Forrest's brother is said to have ridden his horse into the lobby of the Gayoso Hotel in pursuit of General Hurlbut, the Union commander.) Forrest did not have sufficient strength to hold the city and, after rounding up prisoners, withdrew along the same route by which he came.[18] It was truly an event of "Noahic" proportions!

> **Sunday, August 21st 1864.** *We went up to the church but there was no Sunday school. Mr. Paine preached on the text "And God saw that the wickedness of man was great in the earth and that every imagination of the thoughts of his heart was only evil continually." As we were coming home from church I told Miss Lizzie, "Suppose Eddie is at home when we get there?" and she said, "Oh, there is no hope of that," but just then Hannah said, "Tell Miss Lizzie Master Eddie is come."[19] We came home then*

just as fast as we could. He looks very well though he has been sleeping out in the mud holes of Tallahatchie bottom.[20] This evening I learned the hymn, "I was a wandering sheep." Several gentlemen came in to see what news Eddie brought. He said that Forrest crossed the river last week at Polona[21] going on toward Memphis. This morning firing was heard in that direction and we all think that we have got the city.

"A Fire on the Square"

Although Holly Springs was not burned during the Civil War, the town square did suffer war-related destruction, along with several houses and other buildings in the city, including the iron foundry and railroad shops on the eastern edge of town.[22] The first raid by Union troops came early in 1862, when General William T. Sherman followed retreating Confederates down the Mississippi Central from Grand Junction. His advance troops entered the city June 17, 1862 and three days later occupied the town and destroyed the railroad bridges. They also wrecked the Jones, McIlwain Foundry. It was converted into a hospital to care for the wounded and subsequently burned. Robert B. Alexander, a local citizen, lamented to his diary on July 2 of that year, "Yankees [are] in H. Springs stealing and pilfering as usual." Grant amassed weapons, ammunition, food, and supplies for his Vicksburg assault. He then marched south, leaving only a few troops to guard the supplies which filled every barn, warehouse, public building, store, and church in the city. But worse was to come. A newspaper gave this account of Confederate General Van Dorn's raid at daybreak, December 20, 1862, during which 2,500 cavalrymen penetrated, guerilla-style, deep inside enemy lines:

> The rapidity with which the tents of the enemy were vacated was marvelous; and impelled by burning torches and rapid discharges of side arms, the Yankees took no time to prepare their toilets, but rushed out into the cool atmosphere of a December morning clothed

very similarly to Joseph when the lady Potiphar attempted to detain him.[23] The scene was wild, exciting, tumultuous. Yankees running, tents burning, torches flaming, Confederates shouting, guns popping, sabres clanking; Abolitionists begging for mercy, 'rebels' shouting exultingly, women *en dishabille*, clapping their hands, frantic with joy crying 'kill them'-a heterogeneous mass of excited, frantic, frightened human beings presenting an indescribable picture, more adapted for the pencil of Hogarth than the pen of a newspaper correspondent.[24]

Helen Craft, later a pupil in Miss Elizabeth Watson's school, lived a block south of the square, just below the Presbyterian Church. By her account:

My sister and I were sleeping in one of the lower rooms. We were awakened about 3:30 by an excited clatter of swords overhead and voices in the adjoining hall and knew that something unusual was taking place. . . .Soon after our yard servant knocked on our window to say, 'the whole town is on fire.'[25]

Fires were set at the warehouses and supply depots; the railroad shops were destroyed, and the entire east side of the square was burned. The Masonic Hall in which the women of the town had gathered to make clothes and roll bandages at the outbreak of the war and which, after Holly Springs had been seized by Federal soldiers, had been used for an ammunition storehouse, was blown up. Eyewitnesses testified that when the explosion took place, the entire three-story building was lifted, intact into the air before it burst into pieces. The mother of Memphis mayor E. H. Crump, who lived next door, feared that the Presbyterian Church, filled to the rooftop with gunpowder, would be blown up.[26] By four o'clock, reported J. G. Deupree, trooper of the 1st Mississippi Cavalry, and a participant in the raid, "all Federal property, save what could be appropriated had been destroyed, the prisoners had been paroled, and Van Dorn resumed his march northward."[27] The action was minor in comparison to other battles of the Civil War, but magnified in the memory of local citizens and was recounted by novelists Sherwood Bonner and William Faulkner. Meanwhile-his supplies destroyed-Grant fell back on Holly Springs, and from there returned to Memphis, from which he decided to go down the Mississippi River for his third and final assault on Vicksburg. It was an anxious night in Holly Springs, as Union soldiers returned, their plans defeated, and they threatened the town with the torch.

The situation seemed once again as angry two and a half years later.

> **Monday, August 22nd 1864.** *Last night after we all had got to sleep we were waked up by a man going along the street hollering "Fire! Fire! The whole town is on fire." And we all jumped up and dressed and when we went out we saw the whole side of the square on fire. We went nearly to it. We saw that clean from Doctor Litchfield's store up to Mr. Scruggs[28] was in a blaze. Mr. House[29] got the men to bring water and they stopped the fire at Mr. Scruggs'.[30] It looked beautiful and we looked at it a while and came home and went to bed.[31] Today we heard that five or six thousand went from Moscow down south and we think that they sent a scouting party who set the square on fire. This morning there was a report of the Yankees and this evening there was another. Mrs. Watson and Miss Lizzie went up to see Miss Carrie Craft. This evening I went to Mr. Clark's and stayed 'till night. We were very afraid thinking that the Yankees might come in and burn the town. And we slept in our clothes.*

"Holly Springs Mourns its Dead"

Holly Springs poured men into the Confederate army. Casualties were heavy, with many dead and others maimed for life. The communion roll of the Presbyterian Church listed six killed in battle, including a son and nephew of the church's pastor, the Rev'd Henry Paine. Those lost were William Connelly, Cyrus A. Johnson (elected in 1860 as one of the church's first deacons), David B. Paine, Henry R. Paine, William L. Sims, and William T. Watson, son of

Senator and Mrs. Watson. Johnson had served with the Home Guards, and was highly thought of in the community.[32]

Tuesday, August 23rd 1864. Mollie Smith[33] and Lena and Jimmy Gray[34] come over to see me and stayed 'till dinnertime and then this evening Aunt Mollie came and brought Fonta with her. I forgot to say that Mr. Lewis Anderson was buried last Saturday. We heard yesterday that General Benton was killed, [along with] Mr. Cyrus Johnson and several others from this place. Forrest got in to Memphis last Sunday but we don't know the particulars.[35]

"The Yankees Came Sure Enough"

Belle was amazingly grown-up for the nine-year-old she was as she kept her diary in war-ravaged Holly Springs. This entry shows how all strove to maintain a semblance of normalcy. Young Edward Watson saw matters more seriously and took steps to protect his pony-one of a few animals left in the neighborhood, and needed for transportation. However, events of the next few days would cause the remnants of Belle's childhood innocence to wither.

Wednesday, August 24th 1864. Mrs. Watson stayed all night with Mrs. Walthall and Miss Susan and Miss Lucy Hull[36] stayed all night with us. There was a report of the Yankees and Eddie took his pony up to Mr. Govan's.[37] The Yankees came sure enough in a little while. I practiced and took a lesson. I went over to Mrs. Dancy's[38] and enjoyed myself very much. This evening I went over to Aunt Mollie's.

"Mrs. Hull Raided and the Courthouse Burned"

Troops of both armies occasionally molested the citizens of Marshall County, so that one begins to wonder which army exacted more pain from the community. The first such raid came in July 1862, when Sherman raided a house belonging to William F.

Mason, treasurer of the Mississippi Central Railroad. By Olga Reed Pruitt's account:

> The raiding party came from the south and stopped to ask some questions of an old Negro before entering the town. 'Who is the richest man in town?' they asked. 'Mr. William Mason,' the old man answered promptly and innocently. That was the information they wanted so they sought out this house, the home of William Mason and his family. The house was easily recognized. One of the largest in the city, it was almost square, but had the arched doors and windows usually defined as Gothic. Pushing their way inside, the soldiers ransacked the place, the completeness of their destruction being exceeded only by their fiendish ruthlessness. With their bayonets, they gleefully punched out the eyes in portraits done in oils. They tore the keys out of the piano. They piled the china on the walk and with their guns, shattered the fragile pieces. They made raucous sport out of dashing priceless cups and saucers against the walls. As a parting indignity, a bayonet was thrust through the front door. [The scar may still be seen.][39]

Belle describes a raid by Union troops. Her Aunt Mollie Hudson suffered loss in the melee.

> ***Saturday, August 27th 1864.*** *There has been so much confusion since Wednesday that I have not written in my journal at all...Wednesday night I stayed with Aunt Mollie, Thursday about dinnertime the Yankees came in on their way from the south. They treated Mr. Dagg very badly and have done very badly at Miss Lida Anderson's*[40] *too and took everything Mrs. McWilliams*[41] *had and took all of Aunt Mollie's meat.*[42] *They did not do anything at our house. They were the meanest set we had ever seen. We had a quiet time Thursday night but in the morning we were waked up by hearing that they were searching at Mrs. Hull's.*[43] *We jumped up and dressed as quickly as we could and before we were dressed we heard the ladies over there screaming very loud. Then five or six more came out and got on their horses and galloped away. Almost directly Mr. Crump came with the guards. Then we went up there and heard what they had done. Eight or*

nine men rushed in the house and while some stayed downstairs the rest went upstairs. When they came to the young ladies' room, one opened the door and put his head in, and when he saw they were not dressed he said, "Shame on you for sleeping so late." Then he stepped back one or two minutes, but before they could dress he was back and began to break open the trunks. Miss Susan went to get out of his way, [but] he caught hold of her dress and said, "You stay here," and she pulled away from him so hard that she fell down. This made her so angry that she said that she wasn't afraid anymore and thought if he touched her again, she would scratch his eyes out. She and Miss Bettie Thomas and Miss Bettie and Miss Lucy Hull began to scream and Mrs. Hull downstairs joined in, hollering, "Murder! Murder!"[44] so the robbers said they will bring the whole Yankee nation on us. Then they went out and got on their horses and went away as fast as they could. They took off all of Brodie's[45] clothes and a good many of Mrs. Hull's spoons.[46] They told Mrs. Hull, "Hush, you old fool," and said if she did not stop her noise they would ram a chunk down her and burn her house. Some of the officers told Mrs. Crump they would find out these men and punish them, but he said it was no use. After breakfast we went over to Aunt Mollie's and [were] very much troubled. The Yankees have searched her house four or five times and had taken thirty pieces of meat from her and cursed her and said they would burn her house. When we came home we heard that the 12th Iowa had come in town and would be put out on provost guard and we all were very glad for we thought we would be quiet, but before they could be put out the courthouse caught on fire and burned up.[47] We all are very sorry that the old town clock is gone. A good many stragglers came here and some of them stole three pieces of Mrs. Watson's meat. Two others came and took Mrs. Watson's wagon.[48] All this was done before the guards were put out and [we were] glad enough to see them when they came. After that all was quiet. At night one of the guards came in and ate supper with us. He sat and talked a long time. This morning three came to breakfast. Ed invited them, because one of them gave him a horse. I forgot to say that yesterday they came here after a mattress and told Mrs. Watson a wounded Confederate soldier [was] there, and she gave him one. Mrs. Watson sent the wounded soldiers some dinner and told them that they must give the Confederate a good share.[49]

"The McConnico Home Burned"

Some of the U.S. soldiers (as did Confederates on other occasions) acted unlawfully. "Guards" appointed by the Federal authorities had to restore order - in this case putting out fires the soldiers had angrily set. One Holly Springs residence destroyed by soldiers belonged to the McConnicos.[50] Having been residents of the city only a short time, Andrew McConnico had moved his family in covered wagons from Vaiden, Miss. in 1856, where he had overseen construction of the Mississippi Central Railroad. In Holly Springs, the line's headquarters, McConnico was corporate secretary and auditor for the company. As befits a man of his station, he was elected an elder the local Presbyterian Church in 1860-an unusual honor for one whose entrance into the community had been so recent. After the war the McConnicos moved away, never to return.[51]

> **Sunday, August 28th 1864.** *The Yankees went away this morning. There was church but we did not go. This evening some of our soldiers came in town and we were very glad to see them. I forgot to say that this morning we were waked by the servants saying that the Yankees were going to burn the town and we got up and dressed as quick as we could. When we went down to the gate we saw a house on fire and I thought that they would burn the town sure enough and tied all of my things up in a bundle. It was Mr. McConnico's house that was on fire. They tried to burn Mrs. Minor's[52] house and several others but the guards put out the fire.[53] Our guards were just as kind as they could be and stayed*

with us until the last minute. When they were going out the Major of the 12th Iowa went around and got up all the stragglers and did not leave one.⁵⁴ This evening I took a long nap because I [was awakened] so early this morning and afterwards learned the hymn that begins, "There is a path that leads to God." I read in the Bible and in a little book called "Missionary Tales."⁵⁵

"Hospitality for Soldiers"

Hospitality was considered a positive duty in the Southern catalog of virtues-an obligation inculcated in each generation since the days of Virginia's Cavaliers. Accordingly, the Watsons extended hospitality to both Confederate and Federal soldiers-although perhaps from different motives in each case. Nonetheless, it accrued to the benefit of the household, no matter which side happened to be in charge, to curry the favor of the military authorities. The effort was a sacrifice with food and other provisions in short supply. Maria Mason recalled the scene as defeated Confederates took refuge in Holly Springs:

> The Confederate Army, under the leadership of General Earl Van Dorn, had on the 3rd, 4th, and 5th of October 1862, been thrown against the fortifications of Corinth, Miss., a place of great strategic value, being at the junction of two important railroads and the scene of the Battle of Shiloh. The Confederate forces had met with a terrible defeat, Gen. Price having lost 1/3 of his command of 7,000 men. The army was completely demoralized, and disregarding all discipline, they straggled cold, hungry and dispirited into the neighboring towns and farm houses. They came in to Holly Springs. . .by twos and threes, [during] all of a cold, rainy October day, many of them barefooted and in their shirt sleeves. Some had begged pieces of rag carpet from the farmers' wives, and cutting a hole in the middle through which they thrust their heads, thus combined, tent, overcoat, and umbrella. The people made great fires in their houses and laid them along on the floors; it was the best they could do, the blankets had long ago been sent to the boys in the army. . .⁵⁶

The Hull sisters played and sang for the soldiers, and seem to have made an impression upon their admirers.

Monday, August 29th 1864. *Our soldiers were here all day. It is so pleasant to see them after having been with the Yankees so long. It is the 3rd Kentucky Regiment. They are so far away from home that they can't get good clothes and are right ragged and dirty but are very good soldiers. Some were here for breakfast, dinner, and supper.[57] After supper Miss Betty and Miss Susan and Miss Carrie Smith[58] came over and played and sang for them.[59] They seemed to enjoy the music very much indeed but before they had heard half enough there was an alarm of the Yankees and they had to leave.[60] We found out afterwards that it was a false report, but it was too late for the ladies to play anymore.[61]*

IV. He was Much Taken with the Lady that Sang

Legend credits a piano for saving Holly Springs. By one account, in the aftermath of Van Dorn's raid, Maria Mason descended her stairway to find a Federal soldier playing the Steinway in her parlor. The rosewood piano, her prized possession-a wedding gift from William F. Mason, her father-in-law, and said to have been presented to her by Henry E. Steinway himself-was said to be the finest musical instrument in North Mississippi. The music swung into her own song, "Whispering Wind," dedicated to her by Hermann Adolf Wollenhaupt, the composer and her music teacher in New York.[1] Upon questioning, the soldier revealed that he knew the composition because he, too, had studied under the famous pianist. The soldier was Col. Benjamin Harrison Grierson, and it is believed that it was by his order that the town was spared.[2]

> *Tuesday, August 30th 1864.* *This morning one of the soldiers came back to tell us goodbye. He said he was very sorry the music was interrupted. He said that he was very much taken with the music, but he was much more taken with the lady that sang. That was Miss Bettie. The regiment went back south today. Tonight Mr. Farris and Adjutant Ritter stayed all night with us. They had been up to LaGrange on a scout and did not go with the regiment. The Yankees are there still.*

"To See Mr. Cox's House"

John Mickle recalled the building of great mansions in Holly Springs.

> Prosperity had come to planters and townsmen of Marshall County and Holly Springs by the mid-fifties and a building program was started to supplant the modest houses that served while their fortunes were being acquired, with stately homes. This program crystallized into the completion of a few fine houses in and around Holly Springs, when the Civil War broke it up. In town, on Salem Avenue there were built the Judge J. W. Clapp home, now occupied by Lester G. Fant, the Robert McGowan house now occupied by S. R. Crawford [the house known today as 'Montrose,' the home of the Holly Springs Garden Club], the Will Henry Cox [sic] place; the Dr. Charles Bonner place, now the Belk place, the Wynne place, now occupied by John Sowell [today's 'Wakefield,' home of Judge and Mrs. D. Rook Moore III], and the Dr. Pointer place (the old oil mill lot).

The Coxe Place was and is one of Holly Springs' most interesting homes. Mickle wrote that

> The Cox place on Salem avenue was the most pretentious of those completed. The acreage was larger than it is today, the grounds were landscaped and the large stable and outhouses were in keeping with the mansion. The house is of Gothic style with large rooms and high ceilings. The marble mantels for the fireplaces were made to order in Italy. It contained the first bathroom with running water in the city, and had its own gas plant for lighting the houses and stable. The stable was destroyed by fire. Mr. Cox died soon after the war and Col. Dixon Comfort Topp of Grenada county bought it and moved here. . . .The house cost $60,000 to build in ante-bellum days, a much larger sum than now.

The elaborate wrought iron gates at the entrance to the yard were manufactured by Wood & Perrot of Boston, Mass. The house, with its unique Gothic architecture, drew many visitors. When newly completed in 1859, Emma Finley wrote of it and the Clapp mansion,[3] just up the street: "We. . .drove round by the Clapp's & Coxe's- beautiful houses they are- wouldn't object to possessing similar ones."⁴ Similarly, on January 1, 1859, Dr. W. M. Lea had written to his brother in North Carolina, describing Clapp's house as "a splendid mansion" and said that Will Coxe had put up another one. Indeed, said Lea, "There is much building going on here-several large buildings on the square-Masonic Hall very large, 3 story-several stores and other buildings under contract besides depot buildings etc. etc."⁵

> *Wednesday, August 31st 1864. I went to see Rosa and Dora⁶ Clark and while I was there it began to rain and I stayed all the morning. This evening I went over to Aunt Mollie's. I walked with Aunt Mollie and Miss Sally McCarroll and Bettie up to Mr. Cox's to see his house.⁷ The Yankees took up some of the tiles out of his porch and it will soon be ruined. . . .⁸*

"Miss Lizzie Commenced School This Morning"

One cannot say whether Elizabeth Watson's educational efforts were an implicit or explicit expression of her Presbyterian beliefs, but she seems to have been well qualified for the task. In 1849, Henry Craft judged her "the most intellectual girl of her age that I have ever known, and noted that "her society is very different from that of most young ladies." He remarked that "to fine natural abilities she added considerable information acquired by reading, and she converses with the ease and at the same time with the force and elegance of a well educated gentleman." He concluded that she was "altogether the most interesting young lady in the place."⁹ September 1, 1864 marks a red letter day in the educational history of Holly Springs, and indeed, of Mississippi, for it was the organized beginning of a school operated in the Watson home, which eventuated some years later in the North Mississippi Presbyterian College (after 1903 called Mississippi Synodical College). Previously, Elizabeth Watson had taught Belle and the neighborhood children on an informal basis-the town's male teachers being off in the war and its Female Institute having been taken by the

Confederates as a hospital for soldiers (it was burned by local citizens after its use as an infirmary for infectious diseases).[10] But now the school which met in her home took shape according to the regular academic calendar, and as such, it became the only operational educational institution in Holly Springs during this period.

> *Thursday, September 1st 1864. Mrs. Watson was sick last night with the toothache.[11] We heard from Miss Cora she said that her father begs her to stay with him and we all feel very badly about it. We want to see her very much. Miss Lizzie commenced school this morning. I am very glad to begin my lessons again. Mr. Munford brought up all of the old mail from Oxford last night, and this evening Mr. Paine came up and brought Mrs. Watson six or seven letters from Jimmy.[12]*

"We Said Two Lessons"

Curriculum was limited in the early days of Miss Lizzie's school, for no doubt the effort and its conception grew gradually in the teacher's and the public's mind. Textbooks were not available, and so Elizabeth Watson made do with what she had. Women had taken subordinate roles in schools up to this point, and the children also had to become accustomed to going to school after the disruption that war had imposed on local habits of school attendance. Visitors appeared, and that was enough to end lessons for one day.

> **Friday, September 2nd 1864.** *We said two lessons and Mrs. Smith and Miss Carrie came and spent the day, and after while Buddie came running in and said that Mr. Frank Smith[13] was out at the gate and all of us jumped up and ran out there to see him. He looks very well. This evening Mrs. Martin came and stayed all night with us. I have not been right well for a day or two.*

"Buddie and Eddie are Very Much Taken with Blow-Guns"

Even in the stern days of the Civil War, all was not labor and sorrow. Toys were few during this time, but Buddie Strickland and Eddie Watson found ways to amuse themselves with blowguns, reminiscent of the paint-ball games played by boys in the present![14]

Saturday, September 3rd 1864. Mrs. Watson put on a sock for me to knit for Buddie. I almost finished the rib. Uncle Stephen came with the mules today. Mrs. Martin stayed all day with us and this evening Henry drove her out home in the wagon, and Miss Lizzie and Miss Stella Craft rode out home with her and stayed 'till after dark. Buddie and Eddie are very much taken with blow-guns. They make them out of small gas pipes[15] and blow mud in them.

Sunday, September 4th 1864. Last night we were playing and Mal belonging to Mrs. Hull[16] fell off the porch on my head. It hurt me very much and today I felt very badly and couldn't go to church or Sunday school, but laid down nearly all day. I read some in the Bible but did not get my hymn. Miss Lizzie had an opportunity to write to Miss Cora this evening.[17]

Monday, September 5th 1864. The first thing I thought about this morning was that my head didn't ache and I was very glad. I went in school and said all my lessons.

"Senator Watson Returns from Richmond"

A recess in the Confederate Congress made possible a visit by J. W. C. Watson. As a leader in the government, his presence in the community made him a much sought after person for news about the war and its prospects.

Saturday, September 11th 1864. I find that I cannot write in my journal every day while I go to school but I hope that I will be able to write every Saturday what has happened in the week. Tuesday evening Uncle Hudson and Mr. Watson came. Uncle Hudson brought me a ring and ball and brought Minnie a little basket and ball that Papa sent us. Papa made the ring out of a peach stone and the basket out of a plum stone. We were all very glad when Mr. Watson came. A great many people have been coming to talk about the news. The Yankees have got Atlanta and everybody feels very badly about it, but Mr. Watson says that he [doesn't] think they will keep it long. We have heard also that General Morgan was killed. A woman in East Tennessee got him to come to her house and then in the night she went and brought the Yankees to get him. He wouldn't surrender and they shot him through the heart. . .Aunt Mollie said that she is going down south with Uncle Hudson when he comes again. She won't go this time because she wants to stay to get her winter clothes, but I am afraid that will be hard to do, and the Yankees will not let anybody get anything out of Memphis.[18] *Mr. Watson is going to Grenada Monday and I wrote three pages to Papa to send by him.*

"I have no Copy-Book Now"

Paper for school was used sparingly even in prosperous times-slates being the preferred surface for practice-writing and sums.[19] But in earlier times, Holly Springs youth were exposed to a well-rounded curriculum. T. B. Mason, a local merchant, had advertised in 1847 "a full set of text books," including the famous readers by Presbyterian minister William H. McGuffey, of Ohio, which taught generations of American youngsters not only the skills and reading but instructed them in the canons of Christian virtue. These were used by Holly Springs' Chalmers Institute until 1879.[20] Because the children had no copybooks, Miss Lizzie improvised, requiring them to write in their journals. Thus we have Belle's account of Holly Springs during the Civil War.

He was Much Taken with the Lady that Sang

Meanwhile, Mrs. Martin played the role of refugee. The South was full of them.

> **Wednesday, October 12th 1864.** *It has been so long since I wrote last in my journal. I have been so busy with my lessons and music and writing letters Saturday that I have not had time to write. I have no copybook now, and so, Miss Lizzie has told me to write in school. Since I wrote last I have commenced taking music lessons from Miss Carrie Smith. I began on the 21st of September and I like it very much. I wrote to Papa twice and Miss Cora once and Katie Coffman once. Papa sent me a homespun dress that I wrote to ask him for and Auntie has made it for me.[21] Mr. Watson is at Columbus now. We are looking for him tomorrow. Mrs. Martin got home from Memphis a few days ago and is staying with us now. She got out a few things[22] because she told General Washburn[23] that the Yankees had burned her house.[24]*

"Sending Mail by the Confederate Post"

In these wartime days, the Confederate postal service had virtually ceased. People relied on friends, relatives, and passing military companies to deliver communications.[25] Meanwhile, Eddie toiled over Latin, a sure sign that Elizabeth Watson intended to do right by the boy while his father was away. He would be reared a gentleman-and a learned one at that!

> **Thursday, October 13th 1864.** *Day before yesterday I finished a letter that I began Saturday to Papa. I sent it to Miss Mollie McConnoco to take down South[26] and mail it for me. Yesterday a letter came from Papa to Buddie which is the first we have had for a long time.[27] Eddie went in his Latin day before yesterday. Johnny Martin[28] went out to his Cousin Rebecca's this morning. This evening I went over to Aunt Mollie's to bring our walnuts home and then I helped Ellen and Lucy to hull them. Aunt Mollie came over and stayed a little while. While she was here a lady came by*

the name of Mrs. Raiford. When Auntie went away she asked me to go up to Doctor Gholson's[29] home with her. Tonight after supper we were all in the sitting room and Mr. Watson came in, and we were all very glad to see him . . . .

"Right Hard Lessons"

It appears that at first Miss Lizzie's school was not as demanding as schools before the war. In November 1840 the following subjects were taught in the Holly Springs Female Collegiate Institute: *Junior Class*-alphabet, spelling, reading, first lessons in arithmetic and geography; *Middle Class*-maps and globes, English grammar, history of the United States, mythology-Jewish, Grecian, and Roman antiquities; and *Senior Class*-exercises in English syntax, orthography, reading of poetry and prose with definitions, epistolary composition, botany, natural philosophy, chemistry, geology, physiology, geography of the Near East, with maps and globes, ancient history and geography with the ancient atlas, modern history, the higher ranks of arithmetic; algebra, geometry problems, further delineation of maps, rhetoric, logic, mental and moral philosophy.[30] Religious subjects were also included: J. W. C. Watson was lecturer on the evidences of Christianity, giving a course similar to the one he taught at LaGrange Synodical College. But as will be seen from Belle's diary entries, a broad range of subjects and skills were introduced in Elizabeth Watson's school, especially considering that Belle was being instructed at or near fourth-grade level.

> ***Friday, October 14th 1864.*** *This evening I took two pages in the instruction book and am nearly up with Jennie Mickle. Miss Carrie came home with me to knit on her gloves. I went over to see Aunt Laura[31] and stayed 'till nearly dark. When I came home Miss Carrie Craft was here. Mrs. Watson is having all of her sugar cane hauled to the mill to make molasses out of it. Tonight*

Eddie and Buddie brought some home and I tasted it and it was very good . . . .*³²*

"Fannie Fort Came after Some Patterns"

Dresses were made from patterns, and continued to be made this way for several generations, until ready to wear women's clothing became popular in the South. In 1859, Emma Finley gave these descriptions of sewing: "It was 'stitch, stitch, stitch' Tuesday and Wed. Gus going to town for some of the '<u>fixings.</u>' Wed. evening we took the carriage, for Dr. Caruthers' residence- accompanied by a trunk and innumerable boxes & bundles- & found them just taking the last stitches there. It is so tiresome & takes one half from the merriment to have to work so hard, then dress & stand up four or five hours."³³ Even in peacetime, getting something to wear was a chore. During this period, Belle wore homespun, which her father bought for her-cotton being in short supply at home.

Saturday, October 15th 1864. Fannie Fort³⁴ came down after some patterns for her Aunt Carrie.³⁵ I played a long time this morning outdoors with Lucy and Sue, Aunt Jennie's two children.³⁶ I got a letter from Papa today.

"This Morning I got up right Early"

Early rising was seen as a virtue. Virtuous or not, in this era before electric lights, most went to bed and got up earlier than is customary today.

Sunday, October 16th 1864. Two soldiers were here last night and one stayed all night. This morning I got up right early to get my lessons. We went to Sunday school and church. When I came home I read some in the Bible. This evening I got the hymn that begins, "Remember thy Creator now." And then I went to church. It was a right good sermon on the parable of the prodigal son.

When I came back I read some in "Pilgrim's Progress." Minnie has been right sick, and tonight Mrs. Watson gave her some medicine[37] that the doctor gave her for her and she is good deal better this morning.

"A Gentleman and a Soldier"

Many Southerners-brash men from privileged homes, went into the contest without knowing the sacrifice that war demands. Hodding Carter captured their bravado in this account: "The men and boys of Holly Springs and Marshall County were as ready to fight as any in the South and as confident that since one Southerner could whip 20 Yankees, the war would be a lark that might even end before they could enjoy it."[38] Sons of wealth joined the various companies which were mustered at the Holly Springs depot, all hoping they could "teach the abolitionists a lesson." Willis Lea, son of a Holly Springs physician, served in the Jeff Davis Rifles, among whose officers were Belle's father, W. M. Strickland.[39] Many of these boys were better Christians than soldiers, and quite a few lost their lives.

Monday, October 17th 1864. *I got up very early this morning to study my grammar. We went in school and got on very well with our lesson. This evening I took my music lesson and knew it very well. Miss Carrie came home with me to knit on her gloves. We heard that Mr. Willis Lea was killed near Winchester in Virginia. While Miss Carrie was here Jennie Mickle[40] came to see me. We played until nearly dark.*

"After Some Chestnuts"

Apples, walnuts, chestnuts, and pecans were valued by all, but even more in wartime, because foodstuffs had been pillaged by the armies. Just now, the chestnuts that Belle, Eddie and Elizabeth Watson sought were probably needed to help sustain life.

Tuesday, October 18th 1864. I got up this morning and practiced an hour before breakfast. Soon after Eddie got done with his lesson Miss Lizzie and he and myself took a long walk after some chestnuts. [We] stayed until nearly dark, but didn't get anything. We rambled all over the woods that belonged to Mr. McCarroll.[41] Mr. Willis Lea was a good Christian. There are not many that everyone is so sorry for as they are for him. He was the best young gentleman that lived in the neighborhood and was a good soldier. Everybody in town liked him. He had a good many friends.[42]

"Reading about Scotland"

Most white Holly Springs citizens could trace their lineage to either Scotland, England, or both. Sir Walter Scott's novels had spurred in a resurgence of interest in Scotland, and stimulated many to fresh appreciation of that country's history. The names given to the old houses and plantations in and around Holly Springs, as well as the Gothic Revival architecture of several of the houses and churches, testify to the persistence of the town's Scottish memories, as well as its romantic revival by novelists such as Scott.

Wednesday, October 19th 1864. I didn't study any last night because I was so tired but I got up this morning tolerably early but did not have time to practice any. We are reading about Scotland and the battles with the English.[43] We read this morning about the death of the King Robert III. The state [Mississippi] is in a terrible condition now. I went to take my music lesson this evening and Miss Carrie came again. After supper Miss Carrie and Miss Sallie Mott[44] and Mr. Frank Smith came up and stayed 'till bedtime. This evening I heard that Rosa and Dora Clark were coming home and I was very glad.

"A Disciplinary Case"

Often the reader forgets that Belle is nine years old. Although her mother's death, her father's service in the army, and the stresses of war had forced Belle and her brother to grow up faster than most children, they were still children-and on this day, at least, behaved childishly. The incident gives a clue to the way youngsters of the era were disciplined. Ever the teacher, Elizabeth Watson missed no opportunity for didactic exercises.

> *Thursday, October 20th 1864.* Mr. Anderson[45] paid us a visit in the school today and heard us read and spell. Something happened today that I don't like to write about but I hope it won't happen again soon. Buddie and I got into a dispute and fighting. Miss Lizzie told me to stay upstairs and not come down 'till tomorrow and told Buddie not to go off the lot. This evening I came down and practiced. Mrs. Martin got back tonight. While I was upstairs I read some places in the Bible which Miss Lizzie showed me. I also learned some verses that she showed me. One of them was this: "Wherefore my beloved brethren let every man be swift to hear, slow to speak, slow to wrath: For the wrath of man worketh not the righteousness of God."[46] Another was: "He that hath no rule over his own spirit is like a city that is broken down, and without walls."[47] The chapters which I read were about Jesus and told how patient He was when people reviled Him and treated Him badly. In my fight with Buddie the inkstand was upset and a good many blots got on my journal. They make me think about my bad behavior.

"Miss Carrie Gave Me a Right Hard Lesson for Monday"

Caroline Hatch ("Miss Carrie") Smith, one of Belle's music teachers, later married James Crump, son of William Crump, who lived out of Holly Springs over Salem Bridge on a place named Tuckahoe.[48]

> *Friday, October 21st 1864.* Eddie went away and we did not say all of our lessons. I went to take my music lessons but Miss

Carrie was not at home, and I went over to Mrs. Hull's and took it. Miss Carrie gave me a right hard lesson for Monday. It is right pretty too. There was a report of the Yankees but it was all false. Everybody ran out of town because they thought that it was certainly so.

"Letter Writing, a Feminine Art"

One of the aims of female education was to produce dedicated correspondents for the family. Holly Springs ladies of the privileged class gave much effort to letter writing, and most women, feeling it was their duty to keep the ties of family and friendship strong, exchanged mail with a large number of relatives and acquaintances-all this in addition to social entertainment of every kind. Belle seems to have been particularly devoted to these tasks.

Saturday, October 22nd 1864. I wrote to Papa today and Minnie and Fonta sent a rose bud to him, and I put them in the letter. . . .This evening I went up to see Tillie Paine[49] and stayed until nearly dark.

"This Day Belongs to God Alone"

Sunday certainly did. Kept as the "Christian Sabbath," Holly Springs observed Sundays with an hour of Sunday school, an hour and a half at Morning Service, and another hour and a half at the Evening Service. Notices were placed in the newspapers giving times of Sunday school classes, and noting whether the minister would conduct divine service. (On Sundays when their church had no preaching, worshipers would attend one of the other churches. The custom continues in some Mississippi communities to this day.)

Sunday, October 23rd 1864. This morning I got up and studied my lesson. After breakfast we went to Sunday school and church. When I came I read some in "Pilgrim's Progress" and finished the book. Then I learned the hymn that begins "This day belongs to God alone." And then we went to church.

"A Protracted Meeting"

Presbyterian revival meetings of this era were decidedly different from those in more evangelistic churches. Though they adhered to a highly rationalistic creed and professed belief in a predestinating God, Southern Presbyterians did promote a kind of revivalism-a type of religious exercise unknown among their kinsmen in the Reformed Churches of Europe. Samuel S. Hill Jr. has written that because of this, Southern Presbyterianism "has lain a few degrees to the left of the central stream of its heritage."[50] By the mid-nineteenth century, Presbyterian revivalism had become institutionalized. Like Methodists and Baptists, and even some Episcopalians, Presbyterians preached evangelistically, though the Presbyterians phrased their appeals in a more restrained manner than did ministers of the more popular churches. But revivalistic Presbyterians were left with a disquieting question: Given their belief that children born to Christian parents were numbered with the people of God and baptized, how then was it that they must yet repent and be converted under the preaching of an evangelist? The dilemma was not decisively addressed for decades until, at length, a more conservative theology took root and a system of confirmation was instituted in place of efforts toward conversion through evangelistic appeals. Henry Paine, known in the community as an artful preacher,[51] was a firm believer in revivals. In September 1859, he had been appointed by the North Mississippi Presbytery to preach a sermon before that body "On the Best Means of Promoting Revivals." Paine and his congregation also supported the revivalistic efforts of other churches. Robert B. Alexander, a member of the local Methodist Church, reported on a meeting in his congregation in the spring of 1854, during which the preacher "called for mourning," arousing much feeling. "The house was crowded," Alexander wrote, with "a great many Presbyterians."

Meanwhile, Presbyterians reported that healthful indications were emanating from their churches. The Mississippi Synod's narrative on religion in 1864 reported that while "it should create no surprise if the Church should still rock beneath the ground swell of the terrific revolution through which the whole country has just passed...the divine blessing has clearly rested upon the labor of our pastors, and though few large revivals have attracted the public eye, steady and large accessions have been made to the communion of the Church."[52]

> ***Monday, October 24th 1864.*** *Mr. Paine had church and we went. He said that he was going to have it again tomorrow and tomorrow night. This evening I went and took my music lesson and when I came back from there I went to see Rosa and Dora Clark.*[53] *They got home last night and they came home with me and stayed until nearly dark. When they went home I walked nearly home with them.*[54]

"Six Candles Would Light the Room"

Prior to the advent of gas and electric lights, "evening" services were usually held in the late afternoon. Candles were not only expensive, but their use was considered (at least by Presbyterians) a frivolous waste.[55] In rural churches where members had to travel a long way, the second service of the day was usually held after an extended lunch hour, during which the congregation might retire to a nearby member's house for entertainment.[56] In cities, where travel was more convenient, the custom of having the second service at a later hour became more and more accepted, so that by mid-century the use of candles was becoming common. A notation in the Holly Springs Presbyterian Church's session-book during the 1840s refers to a meeting convened "at early candle lighting." Belle's journal lets the reader know that the town kept up its proprieties as best it could, in spite of the privations of war. Earlier, her mother had appealed to Major Strickland to "Send me a box of candles if you can."[57]

> Tuesday, October 25th 1864. Mr. Paine had church and we went. . . .Mr. Paine said that he was going to have church tonight and that he thought that six candles would light the room. Mr. Frank Smith came up to tell us goodbye. He has been at home on a wounded furlough. He is going back to Virginia to his command. We are all very sorry that he has to go back. Mrs. Martin started to Memphis to try to get Miss Eliza[58] out home. She expects to ride all day and all night.[59]

"I am Getting so Bad in Writing"

Belle was frustrated that she was not more proficient in forming her letters. Penmanship was stressed in those days, and boys and girls took pride in writing a beautiful script. To those living in an era when handwriting is neglected, it appears that those of Belle's day who excelled at calligraphy left behind beautiful manuscripts in the form of letters, journals, account ledgers, and notations of every kind. The scarcity of paper and pens made practice in these useful arts difficult even for the willing.

> Wednesday, October 26th 1864. Mr. Paine had church again today and we went. Mr. Watson came home this evening and he was very tired. Miss Lizzie and I went to church with Buddie. It was a very good sermon, so good that I didn't go to sleep. I am getting so bad in writing that I don't know what is the matter. I don't write as well as I did a few weeks ago but I hope that I will soon write [much better]. Anyway, I want to.

"Mr. Watson Has Not Succeeded in Getting a Wagon Yet"

The autumn of 1864 revealed that in Mississippi even so august a personage as the state's Confederate Senator was reduced to barter in quest of a wagon. But the occupation forces had confiscated nearly everything. The few luxuries were reserved for children, and Belle's sister Minnie was the recipient of one such fancy in a period when most little girls had to settle for "homemade."

Thursday, October 27th 1864. *We got a letter from Miss Cora this morning and she said that she was going to come home the last of this month or the first of the next and we were very glad to hear it. Two gentlemen stayed here this evening. One was a soldier. After we got Miss Cora's letter we went to church. The soldier took a letter to Tennessee for Miss Lizzie. Mr. Watson has not succeeded in getting a wagon yet. He is trading for one now.*

Friday, October 28th 1864. *We went to church today. I went to take music this evening. I have got a right hard piece. While I was practicing Mr. Carrier came. We were impatient for him to open the box but he could not do it 'till morning. He stooped down and whispered to me and told me to dream about "Minnie's doll."*

"Something for Mr. Watson to Take with Him"

Packing was a community project. Not only did clothes have to be folded for the journey, but foodstuffs had to be prepared, as roadside refreshments were few. Church services on this Sabbath were omitted, for the Presbyterian catechism recognized that exceptions-could be permitted-for "works of necessity and mercy."[60] The women's feverish activity was undertaken to ready Senator Watson to attend the second Confederate Congress that convened in Richmond, November 7, 1864.[61] Young James Watson accompanied his father to begin another term at the Virginia Military Institute.

Saturday, October 29th 1864. *Mr. Carrier opened the box this morning and got out the things. Minnie's doll is the prettiest I most ever saw. Mrs. Watson was out in the kitchen all day making something for Mr. Watson to take with him and some cakes* *and candy for Jimmie.*[62] *We didn't go to church today because we were so busy. Mollie Smith came over to borrow my Sunday school book and she stayed a little while. Mr. Watson stayed at home all day and people were constantly coming in to see him. He expects to go away Monday and Mrs. Watson is packing up his things. Miss Carrie and Miss Stella and Miss Helen Craft came up to help Mrs. Watson pack.*[63]

"An Inquiry Meeting"

Inquiry meetings were arranged in connection with protracted meetings to arouse the souls of the enlightened. Old School Presbyterians conducted these affairs as sedate, rationalistic presentations of doctrine as compared to the machinations of more evangelistic communions-the "mourner's bench," the "anxious seat," and the "sawdust trail." Still, Henry Paine's protracted meeting seems to have borne fruit-at least, Belle's entry for October 31 shows that he was pressing his cause into a second week![64]

Sunday, October 30th 1864. *Mr. Paine had an inquiry meeting instead of Sunday school and I went. Mr. Paine had church and we went. It was a right large congregation. Mr. Paine had another inquiry meeting, and Buddie and Eddie and I went. Mr. Paine had church again tonight and we went.*

V. To the Foundry for Some Tacks

The Jones, McInwain Foundry, established about 1843 (which made Holly Springs a target in the Civil War), and employing two hundred workers, is said to have been the South's largest casting foundry. It was located a mile and a half north of town. The foundry, Holly Springs' only ante-bellum industry, made column capitals which grace the old mansions of the city, as well as ornamental ironwork for the French Quarter in New Orleans.[1] Four days after Fort Sumter, the foundry purchased land on the northeast side of the city on the railroad. J. W. C. Watson handled the sale. Here tradition says they manufactured the first small arms for the Confederacy. Sherwood Bonner gave this description of ceremonies that marked the foundry's conversion into an armaments factory:

> Crowds. . .were outside the building, and as many as were allowed to enter were within. Standing there amid the din and whir of the machinery, while the sooty-faced workmen hurried hither and thither and the great furnace roared and reddened, [we found] the hour pregnant with significance. As the melted ore poured forth, a woman's hand held under it the great iron ladle and emptied it into the mold with the solemnity of a priestess assisting at a holy rite. Every woman and child followed in turn. It was our consecration to the cause-an hour that I cannot remember now without a thrill of emotion akin to that which thrilled me to the very centre of my being as I clasped my hands around the iron handle and felt in that moment I sealed my devotion to the South.[2]

After Holly Springs was captured, the foundry was used as a hospital. It was devastated by various military engagements, so that by 1864, as Belle's note reveals, little more than rudimentary blacksmithing was carried on at the once-important Confederate munitions supplier. Today, not even a historical marker remains to mark the site of one of Mississippi's first manufacturing concerns. Meanwhile, Mr. Paine's evangelistic services broke the monotony of an autumn where empty cotton fields meant there was little else to do.[3]

> **Monday, October 31st 1864.** *Mr. Watson got off this morning and took Miss Eliza Martin with him as far as Oxford and Mr. Carrier went too. I went to the inquiry meeting again today and went to church. Miss Lizzie and Mrs. Watson went with me to church. I went out to the Foundry with Ellen and Lucy after some tacks for Mrs. Watson to tack down her carpet with. Eddie brought some grapes home to us.*

> **Tuesday, November 1st 1864.** *Miss Carrie Smith went to Memphis this morning. We all went to church and it was a right good sermon. . . .We children made a pretty playhouse out in the yard, and I played in there until nearly dark. Mrs. Martin came back and stayed all night with us.*

"A Present from Major Strickland"

Belle took pleasure in small presents her father sent. Nuts and fruits were delicacies in those days, and delighted children in the way that electronic toys would today.

> **Wednesday, November 2nd 1864.** *It was so rainy that we couldn't go to church. . . .I went over to Aunt Mollie's this evening after some apples and chinquapins that Papa sent us. . . .*[4]

Thursday, November 3rd 1864. *We did not go to church either. . . .Miss Lizzie began to trim my hat and trimmed it very prettily. It took her 'till dark to finish it nearly. Aunt Mollie came over this evening. I finished my book tonight that I was reading. The name of it is "The Young Marooners." I think it was the prettiest book I ever read in my life.*

"Visiting the McCarrolls"

Since both the Strickland and Watson homes have been demolished, the closest tangible reminder of Belle's era is "McCarroll Place," which stands next door to the site of the Strickland house (where the new St Joseph's Catholic Church is now). The McCarrolls lived in a pleasant, rambling cottage, which occupied a large yard. John R. McCarroll, Marshall County's "unbeatable sheriff"[5] for thirty years, and his family played unwilling host to Union soldiers in the summer of 1862. Privates were quartered in tents on the grounds. Bullet holes may still be seen in the walls of the detached kitchen-the result of soldiers' target practice. Inside the cottage, the men hid rifles and bayonets in the library in an open space where two log houses were joined. Years later, when French doors were set between the parlor and the library, the store of rusted guns and a bayonet were found between the walls. Brick and timber stacked for construction of a new and larger home, were taken by the soldiers. Silver buried for safekeeping was never retrieved. During Van Dorn's raid, a wounded Union soldier crawled into the shelter of the front bedroom and died on the floor. After vainly searching for some identification, Mrs. McCarroll had her servants secretly bury the man on the grounds, after which the family lived in fear of reprisal should the troops return and discover one of their men buried on the place. The site of the unmarked grave in the woods behind the house remains a scene of melancholy repose.[6]

Friday, November 4th 1864. *I went over to Mrs. McCarroll's this morning to get Miss Mary to make a black body[7] for me and* *then I went to church. After I came back I went over there and stayed all day. . . .*

Saturday, November 5th 1864. I went to Miss Mary McCarroll's to try my body on. It fitted very well. I practiced my half an hour then went to church. I then went over to Miss Mary's to take her some buttons.

"Hymns They Sang"

Belle's memorization of hymns belies a change among religious folk, whereby hymns supplanted the use of psalms set to music as the church's chief medium of praise. Presbyterians held to psalms longer than anyone else, but due to the Methodists who enthusiastically embraced the hymnody of the Wesleys, by the mid-nineteenth century almost all sang hymns. That said, it is noteworthy that only two of the eleven hymns Belle names are still in the Southern hymn repertory today, for despite affection for "old hymns," the favorite hymns of church folk have changed several times since the 1860s! Hymns which were sung in the churches Belle attended emphasized the order and stability of life under the guidance of God. Never heard in the white-controlled churches (although blacks regularly worshiped with whites in this period) were the spirituals that emerged from the African American experience. The Rev'd Henry Paine, who was a hymnwright,[8] held to high standards of music, and his blessing upon the use of instruments to accompany the church's praises marked him as a progressive, when many opposed organs in Presbyterian churches. In 1857, Paine asked his elders to purchase for the congregation, a book "to promote the diffusion of a knowledge of sound music," and Paine, with Holly Springs elder J. W. Clapp, was appointed to study the new Southern Presbyterian *Psalms and Hymns* (1867), and report on it to the presbytery.[9]

Sunday, November 6th 1864. Mr. Paine didn't have Sunday school this morning but had an inquiry meeting instead. We all went to church and it was a very good sermon. I went to the inquiry meeting again this evening. Then I learned the hymn that begins, "Oh, for a heart to praise my God." I forgot to say that Uncle Hudson got home Saturday night and brought me a flower from Papa and some papers.

"Troop Movements Cancel Church Services"

Clergy in towns along the path of enemy troop movements-particularly those regarded as "firebrands"-faced a recurrent problem, lest they be arrested by military officials who disliked their preaching. Henry Paine was known to preach on themes dear to Confederates. Thus, when U. S. troops were in or near Holly Springs, he often declined to preach-lest his church be occupied again and this time treated more maliciously than before. The Crafts, who lived next door to the church were loyal Presbyterians.

*Monday, November 7th 1864. I got up right early this morning and played with Minnie. Eddie and Buddie went after Miss Cora this morning. I practiced my half an hour and then went to church. We got there just as Mr. Paine was dismissing the church. When we came out we went to Mrs. Craft's and stayed a little while. Then I went down to Mrs. Clark's and enjoyed myself very much.
. . .*

"A Letter to Major Strickland"

The Watsons and Stricklands were intimates. Not only did the Watsons readily offer the care of their home to Major Strickland's children after their mother's death, but the members of the household seemed to enjoy the free relations of close friendship. This letter from Elizabeth Watson to W. M. Strickland, an example of the incidental correspondence that went back and forth from Holly Springs to Strickland's military locations, gives information about events in a month when Belle's pen was silent.

Holly Springs, Nov. 28th, 1864.

Dear Mr. Strickland,

Ma regrets very much that she forgot to send the buckskin by Mr. Hudson and hopes it will still reach you in time for your pants to be made before you are in want of them. The present opportunity of sending the package is afforded by a Mr. Eggleston, a son of a connection of Cora's, who being to all appearances in the last stages of a decline, is on his way to spend the winter with an aunt, a Mrs. Edward Baptist of South Ala. He speaks however, of stopping with some relatives of his own name in Yalobusha Co. and so, may have to mail this, and in that case, there is no telling when it will reach you.

We hear so many rumors of Yankees below us that I fear there must be truth in some of them, but still I trust the scamps may be turned back before they reach Canton or injure the R. R. or do serious harm in any way.

The children continue perfectly well and Minnie, believe, is even fatter than when you saw her. Willie[10] and Belle have staid with their Aunt Mollie a good deal since the death of her dear little boy. Tonight, Willie is with her and Belle is, by special invitation, staying with Rosa and Dora Clark.

Our school has not yet been resumed though I hope it will be in a day or two. Eddie is not yet right well, however, and the unsettled company state of our household caused by the arrival of Cora and her cousin has been freshly aroused, just as it was subsiding, by the coming yesterday evening of Sue Harris and her children.[11]

Col. Harris' mother has recently died and the charge of his little son, Mason, has consequently devolved on Sue.[12] She has him with her now. He is an overgrown fellow, being larger than Ed though only four months older than Willie, but seems very amiable and well disposed. For his mother's sake, I feel interested in him. Sue says nothing will ever induce her to become a refugee again, and as her place is completely ruined, she is already looking about for a boarding house or for one which she can furnish with what she can collect of her furniture so that she can go to housekeeping.

Gen. Adams and staff are still here though for what purpose is utterly inconceivable to everybody. The Memphis trade is for the present effectually locked up on the Yankee side. When the trap closed it caught several of our ladies-Mrs. Mott, Carrie Smith and Betsy Hull. Lida Anderson just did get out and it is fortunate she did for Mr. A. was most nervously impatient during all the time she was gone.

We heard from Pa by Jimmie Crump, who left him in Richmond on the 15th inst. and reached here the 24th. He (Pa) was well and in fine spirits, but gave us no encouragement to look for his speedy return.

Willie is looking forward with the greatest pleasure to his Christmas trip and I sincerely hope that neither Yankees nor anything else will interfere with it. Belle has begun taking music lessons from Mr. Tepe and likes him very much. I am sure the liking will be mutual. Minnie very often talks of you and of what you did during your recent visit, and very often she gets a piece of paper "to write to her papa," and after she has scribbled some parallel lines that really do look like something like writing, she says she has told you to "tum to shee her." She is perfectly delighted at having Sue's baby in the house and said of her own accord that she would call him "little buddie." He is just the age that Mollie's was, and like him very fat and fair and good humored, so it is no wonder she was reminded of him.[13]

Mollie seems now to be quite well. She is deeply distressed, but still resigned, and I trust that He who has wounded will heal her bruised spirit and will make her trial the means of her eternal good. Mal Butler, too, has just been called on to mourn the loss of her youngest. It was buried yesterday. So it is that in one way or another God seems to be bringing all "under the rod." Oh that His dispensation may be sanctified to each and all of us!

Ma joins me in love and so I know would the children if they were at home.

Yours truly, Lizzie W.

We are all sincerely obliged for the papers you so kindly send. They are a <u>treat</u>.

"A Holiday Tableau"

Having come to live with her in-laws after her husband's death, Cora Watson entered fully into the life of her adopted community. She observed that all was not heavy and sad in Holly Springs, despite the dreadful events that followed a long series of Southern defeats. By her philosophy, people could still indulge in laughter-for a good cause! She recorded that the ladies of the town, along with some Confederate soldiers (a good many of them "nice officers") were rehearsing a tableau in the Episcopal Church to be presented the following Friday. Tickets would raise money for poor soldiers' wives.[14]

Wednesday, December 28, 1864. *Lida and Carrie came by from a rehearsal of the tableaux which are to be enacted on Friday night. The girls have a great deal of fun meeting to rehearse-the soldiers and officers about town being always at the tableau rooms. General Martin and staff arrived in town a day or two ago, and I expect there are a good many nice officers here. Mrs. Carrington Mason is directress, and Lida amused us very much by giving an account of the way Mrs. Mason wanted the Peri at the gate of Heaven represented. Lou Hamner[15] was the Peri, and Mrs. Mason insisted on sending down and having the little wooden gate brought up from the Presbyterian church to stand for the gate of Heaven, before which Lou Hamner was to be disconsolately kneeling, when she could very easily have opened it and gone in. Lida told her that would never do, that everybody would laugh at it; and it didn't suit her anyway, for she was too much of an Episcopalian to believe the Presbyterian church gate was the gate of Heaven. So they have decided to change it in such a way as to make it a very pretty scene.*[16]

Mr. John C. Walker is to be doorkeeper, the price of admittance is $5.00 in Confederate money, $1.00 in greenbacks, or .50 in silver, and the proceeds to go to the assistance of poor soldiers' wives in the county. Mr. Pickett is to call out the scenes. I told Mrs. Smith that she must caution him to be careful and not call 'A scene from the Bride of Lameroon,' 'A scene from the bride of the lamb in the moon,' as Dr. Wilkerson did in our tableaux at Somerville. Cousin Sue came down and took dinner with us, and this evening 'pompadoured' and 'waterfalled' her hair, and she, Belle, Mason and Eddie have gone to the tableaux. . . .

Saturday, December 31, 1864. Cousin Sue and the children didn't enjoy the tableaux much. Captain Fort and his company were there and behaved very 'rowdyishly.' Mrs. Venable dropped in this evening and told us a good deal of bad news. Willie Crump writes his father that Hood's army is diminished by half by the campaign and completely demoralized. . . . People seem to believe that our army under Hood is falling back to Corinth. And 'they say' that Sherman is in possession of Savannah.

"We went to Sunday School, but There was None"

The importance of Sunday schools to American churches cannot be overestimated. Because of the great emphasis that was placed upon it, as well as the larger size of families in the nineteenth century, the number attending then seems huge to contemporary statisticians. Children of the Holly Springs Presbyterian Church placed their offerings in a "missionary box," which was sent to a "heathen child" in India. There was catechetical recitation, as well as study of Sunday school papers, such as *The Children's Friend*. One cannot be sure for what reason the Presbyterian Sabbath school did not meet on this day-whether because of the New Year, the war's alarms, or the absence of a teacher. Meanwhile, the Watsons made room for a Confederate soldier, who boarded for several days.[17]

Sunday, January 1st 1865. I have neglected my journal so long that I cannot make up for it. . . . .I know that I cannot keep it up regularly but I will write in it occasionally. We went to Sunday school today but there was none. I stayed with Rosa and Dora last night. We went to church this morning. When I came home today from church I read some. I forgot to say that this morning when I came downstairs a wounded soldier came in and he told Mrs. Watson that he was trying to get to his uncle's. He said that his uncle's name was Franklin and his name was Moore. This evening I learned the hymn that begins, "Where shall I be when I shall go?"

"The New Year Dawns Bright. . .Only the Voice of Man is in Discord"

Cora Watson also made an entry in her journal on New Year's Day 1865:

Sunday, January 1, 1865. The new year dawns bright and beautiful; all nature seems glad, and only the voice of man is in discord. Still we hear the clash of arms, and see the glittering bayonets reflected in pools of human blood. Oh! may this calm, lovely new year's day be typical of the time here at hand, when 'The drums shall throb no longer,' and 'The kindly earth shall slumber lapt in universal law.' All went to church.

"Reading the Bible Through"

A New Year's resolution encouraged the American Bible Society was to read the Bible cover to cover in the space of a year. Reading plans were distributed on small cards that could be used as bookmarks. It can be assumed that more began than finished, but worn Bibles from this era indicate that there were those who completed the project successfully many times over. Belle at least made a beginning.

Monday, January 2nd 1865. I began to read the Bible through last night.[18] *Read three chapters every day and five on Sunday.*

There was a report of the Yankees this morning and everybody was running in every direction but it was all false. . . .

Tuesday, January 3rd 1865. *Miss Lizzie commenced school today but not regular school. . . . Auntie and Fonta came over today and stayed until right late. Miss Sally Hamner came over just as Auntie started. Miss Julia Little came, too. . . .*

Wednesday, January 4th 1865. *We went up to Cousin Sue's this morning and [stayed] two or three hours. She said that the baby was sick last night. . . . Miss Lizzie gave us holiday today. I played out of doors again today with Sue.*

Thursday, January 5th 1865. *We went in school this morning but did not say all of our lessons. I practiced my hour and Cousin Sue came up. I played out of doors with Sue and Minnie and Hannah all the rest of the day.*

"Melting Lead"

Melting lead was a pastime for boys, often with explosive results. The soft metal could be shaped into useful objects, and in an era before plastic, it was used to craft toy soldiers.

Friday, January 6th 1865. *We went in school again this morning. . . . I wrote to Papa this evening and Eddie stayed in there with me, and melted some lead to make some bars of lead.*

Saturday, January 7th 1865. *I copied my letter this morning and Eddie began his. I did not practice my hour this morning. Eddie didn't finish his letter but I did. The soldier is here still. He sent a courier to Early Grove this morning.*

"Wars and Rumors of Wars"

Cora Watson's diary included these comments for the same day. This and other entries reveal how rumor-plagued the South was in the last days of the Civil War. Most lines of communication had been cut, and people did not know what to believe. Confederates held to every shred of hope, believing what they wanted to hear.

Sunday, January 7, 1865. Mrs. Venable[19] came in this evening. Tells us there is rumor of another attack on Richmond repulsed by Lee-also another of the death of Jefferson Davis. This caps the climax of our misfortunes. Mr. Paine came soon after Mrs. Venable. He thinks, as we all do, that this is the darkest hour of the war. Sherman in Savannah, Hood's army retreating, demoralized and with thinned ranks from the disastrous campaign in Georgia and Middle Tennessee, which was from the beginning to end a series of defeats-together with Lincoln's occupation of the U. S. presidential chair and his vigorous prosecution of the war-are a combination which is almost disheartening. There is an incident in the Battle of Franklin which is very affecting. General Cockrell, commanding a brigade of Missourians, was shot through both legs and one arm, but with the other arm guided his horse from the field. Colonel Gates of the same brigade was shot through both arms, but his horse was so accustomed to follow that of General Cockrell on the field of battle that it did so on this occasion, bearing the veteran hero, his arms dangling uselessly at his sides, safely from the field. It was in this battle that the gallant General Pat Cleburne fell. After the engagement, his body was found in the second line of the enemy's entrenchments.[20]

"A Cold Church"

In keeping with prevailing custom, no provision was made to heat the new Holly Springs Presbyterian Church when it was built in 1860. Heating was rare in American churches until after 1840 when the hot air furnace was invented. Presbyterians-true to their conservative reputation-resisted furnaces in their churches on the grounds that they were an unconscionable luxury. But the provision of heat in the new Christ Church in 1859 had been a selling point-perhaps even more inviting than its pipe organ. Belle does not say why there was no Sunday school for a month or six weeks, but given the date of her remark, one may guess that weather played a part in the situation.

> ***Sunday, January 8th 1865.*** *We went to Sunday school but there was none. We went to church today and Mr. Paine said that there would be no Sunday school for a month or six weeks. This evening I learned the hymn that begins, "The pearl that worldlings covet" and read some more in the Bible.*

> ***Monday, January 9th 1865.*** *We woke up this morning and it was right cloudy. It rained a good deal last night. . .Mr. Moore went away yesterday. His cousin came after him. His name was Franklin.*

> ***Tuesday, January 10th 1865.*** *We got up this morning and it was snowing. It snowed all day but was so wet that the snow did not stay on the ground. We went in school this morning. I stayed in the house all day. Nobody came.*

"I Need Not Say Any Grammar or Geography until Buddie Comes Back"

Coeducational teaching came to Holly Springs with the Civil War. Until this time the sexes had been segregated in school, but in this war fought to preserve the status quo, the role of blacks and women was vastly transformed. One local change, introduced by Miss Lizzie's school, was the teaching of boys and girls together-a change not immediately continued after the war's conclusion.

> ***Wednesday, January 11th 1865.*** *We went in school today and read and spelled and wrote and ciphered. Miss Lizzie says that I*

need not say any Grammar or Geography until Buddie comes back. We heard that Mr. Clark had come home and I went down to see him, but he had not come.

"Mrs. Watson and Miss Cora and Miss Lizzie Played with Us"

Sometimes a harsh picture is painted of Victorian child rearing. Belle lets us know that adults could be playful, even as they saw to the serious business of teaching the young.

Thursday, January 12th 1865. Yates Freeman[21] stayed all night with us last night and Johnny Martin. We had very much fun indeed. Mrs. Watson and Miss Cora and Miss Lizzie played with us. We went in school today. . . ..Mr. House got home today and we heard that he did not get anything. . . .[22]

"Borrowing the Sifter"

Basic household items were in short supply. Cora Watson reported this exasperating situation.

Thursday, January 12, 1865. Took a notion to pay Cousin Sue a visit. Found her sitting down on the floor sifting meal. She has no sifter; but borrows one once a week and sifts enough flour to last a week. War times!

"Miss Lizzie Began the Roman History Last Night"

Material goods were short, but Miss Lizzie saw to it that the children learned their Roman history. This was because Confederates saw much in the history of Rome that seemed to parallel their cause.

Friday, January 13th 1865. We went in school this morning and said nearly all of our lessons. . . .I made some wreaths of arbor vitea and made one for Minnie's doll. I worked all the evening 'till nearly dark. Miss Lizzie began the Roman history last night.

"Purchasing Goods from Mr. House"

As Cora Watson told her diary on October 25, 1864, while in Covington, Tenn., she despised those who traded with "Yankees." "This evening two men just in from Memphis with three or four wagons laden with goods[23] stopped and asked permission to stay all night out of the rain.[24] It was granted-and they came in the sitting room and commenced talking with us. They belong to the worst class of Southern men-who trade regularly with the Yankees, perjuring themselves every day. One of them, a Dr. K. of Durhamville, was a very genteel looking and rather handsome man." Cora disliked having to trade with those who did business with the Yankees, but sometimes compromise was necessary. On August 26, 1864 she had written: "Mr. R_____ has a cunning, sleek, money-loving face. While his superiors are fighting and dying for our country every day, he is staying at home speculating. I felt the supremest contempt for him. But there are only two ways for me to get anything to wear-to compromise my principles and perjure my soul by going and swearing allegiance to a government which from the inmost depths of my heart I hate, or to be polite and smiling to a speculator and get him to do me the favor to get them-of the two evils I choose the lesser." Now, from Holly Springs, she wrote about the family's neighbor, the illustrious blockade runner, James Jarrell House:

Friday, January 13, 1865. Hear today that Jos. E. Johnston is reinstated in command of the 'Army of Tennessee' (or, more properly, of Mississippi). This is good news. Hood's career has been unfortunate. . . .Soon after Sister took in school, Betsy came over to tell us that Mr. House had a store in town, with all sorts of nice things for sale for Confederate money. I went in and told Sister, and the children persuaded her to let Eddie (who had finished reciting) go down and see what he had. He and Johnnie went. They came back with an account of the rush to buy, which quite amused me. Johnnie bought a pound of candy for $5.00 and 'treated us.' Eddie and Johnnie went back soon to get some more, but found the merchants had shut up shop, having sold almost enough to break them. Tomorrow they will sell for 'Yankee currency.'

"Eddie Wrote to His Pa this Morning"

Edward Minor Watson (1851-1887), son of J. W. C. and Catherine Davis Watson, grew up to become President Grover Cleveland's Assistant U. S. Attorney General. After the war, "Eddie" and his friends gathered outside Maury Institute and North Mississippi Presbyterian College-the institutions which grew out of Miss Lizzie's little school. John Mickle, who grew up with him, recalled that "a long wooden bench stood outside of the sidewalk under the trees, which the boys called 'The Roost,' and here gathered such choice spirits in their youth as Brodie Hull, Billie Smith, Jim and Ed Watson, Yates and Russell Freeman, Tom Nelson, Lee and Alex Chism and Mason Dancy, along College street, and doubtless Jim Greer, Will Strickland and John McCarroll just over on 'Depot' street." As Mickle said, "They were a jolly bunch. . ."[25]

Saturday, January 14th 1865. Eddie wrote to his Pa this morning. I had company all day and. . . .I went and took my music lessons. I went up to Cousin Sue's and stayed until nearly dark. Lucy came home with me. She is staying up there in the day but comes home at night. When we were nearly home we met Ellen and went back with her, and then when we were coming back again we met Miss Cora and Eddie and Miss Lizzie.

"A Political Sermon"

Belle was old enough to listen to and appreciate sermons, and Cora Watson's diary lets us know why this particular homily occasioned favorable comment from Confederate sympathizers.

Sunday, January 15th 1865. *We went to church and it was a very good sermon. I read in the Bible until church this evening. I did not learn my hymn.*

"Henry Paine Buoys His Congregation's Spirits"

Presbyterian ministers generally did not comment on current issues, especially when these were charged with political fervor. But Henry Paine fanned the flames. One of the favorite themes of clergy in this period was that the South was faring badly because of its hubris-if the people would only repent, the tide would turn in battle.[26]

Sunday, January 15, 1865. *Mr. Paine says it is his firm conviction that this is the last year of the war. He thinks neither the South nor the North can sustain themselves longer than through this year, and he thinks if the people will only humble themselves and pray earnestly for God's blessing on our cause, and if the soldiers will only resolutely do their duty a little longer, the victory will be ours. This, he says, is a dark hour for us in this part of the country. Hood's army, broken, crushed, dispirited, thrown back from Tennessee on our state; and our position here between the opposing armies very unfortunate. Many persons think that Holly Springs will be occupied by the Yankees, and there is a rumor in town that Thomas is leading his army down from Nashville to Memphis preparatory to an advance through this country. Mr. Paine says we are undoubtedly on the eve of another bloody and fearful campaign, and our state is to be the seat of war. We ought earnestly to pray for success for our arms and for strength to endure the trials through which we may be called on to pass. Sister read aloud tonight in Bickersteth's 'Treatise on Prayer.'*

VI. Eddie and Johnny went to Sell Eddie's Yankee Horse

Horse trading was a manly art, and the boys were practicing their skills. Horses were in critically short supply, and the boys obtained a bale of cotton in barter for the animal. As Cora Watson reported on Saturday, January 14: "Eddie swapped his Yankee horse today for a pretty black pony, four years old, and $100 in South Carolina money, which he sold for $30.00 in greenbacks. A very good trade." The deal apparently fell through, for Belle records further negotiations in the matter.[1]

> *Monday, January 16th 1865.* *Eddie and Johnny Martin went down south to sell Eddie's Yankee horse. They expected to stay two or three days. I went in school and played out of doors yesterday evening.*

"Bartering for Cotton"

Before the Civil War, Ralph Waldo Emerson wrote that cotton threads held the Union together; certainly, as Shields McIlwain remarked, "Cotton was now holding the Civil War together."[2] Cotton was the South's only real currency, and by Cora Watson's account, Edward Watson made a good exchange for the horse he had obtained from the Union soldier:

Monday, January 16, 1865. *Mr. Margrove brought back Eddie's Yankee horse this morning, and took his pony and money. He says the horse is stiff. I am sorry for Eddie, as he was so delighted with his bargain. He and Johnnie are off now trying to exchange the Yankee for a bale of cotton.*[3] *Johnnie told Ed a boy from town made such an exchange a day or two ago, down on the Tallahatchie, and they set off this morning to do so, too.*

"Altering Old Finery into Fashionable Shapes"

Except when blockade runners came with fashionable goods, which they sold at exorbitant prices, Southern women had to "make do" with old clothes. Even those who primly eschewed high fashion for the sake of 'the Cause,' must have felt a bit dowdy in their well-worn costumes.

Tuesday, January 17, 1865. *Eddie and Johnnie got back tonight. Exchanged the Yankee for 300 pounds of cotton. . . .I have been working a little today, altering my old alpaca and a 'Gabrielle'-or 'Confederate wrapper.'*[4]

"Mr. Anderson is Taken Prisoner"

William Albert Anderson (1842-1923), was intimately associated with education in Holly Springs throughout his long and useful life. Born at Hudsonville to John H. and Lee Ann Ridley Haggard Anderson, the Andersons had come to Marshall County with the original white settlers in 1836. The family moved to Holly Springs in 1846, where John H. Anderson was a leading attorneys until he died in 1861. W. A. Anderson was educated at Chalmers Institute, after which he was graduated from the National Normal University in Lebanon, Ohio-an institution devoted to the education of teachers. After service in the Confederate army, he returned to Holly Springs and was headmaster of Chalmers[5] for ten years, after which he was principal of the city's public school for fifteen years. Anderson married Helen Craft, who was a pupil in Lizzie Watson's school, several years ahead of Belle. Years later, when the

Rev'd C. Z. Berryhill was minister of the Holly Springs Presbyterian Church where the Andersons were members, the ministerial family would sit on the front porch of the manse[6] greeting neighbors on summer evenings, and Mr. Berryhill would greet the pencil-thin Mr. Anderson with a jovial "hello," waiting until he was out of earshot to whisper to a niece: "There goes the shadow!" The Andersons lived in the house now called "Alicia" on W. Chulahoma Ave. John Mickle wrote that Anderson "was a most likeable man, and the most just and impartial teacher I ever knew."[7]

Tuesday, January 17th, 1865. I went in school today. Miss Helen Craft comes up every day and says her lessons but she did not come yesterday. I went down to Mrs. Clark's this evening. When I came back I went out to the wood with Hannah. Mr. Anderson is taken prisoner. Mrs. Watson and Miss Lizzie down there tonight.

"Up to Mrs. Craft's for Supper"

Hugh and Elizabeth Collier Craft were among the leading citizens of Holly Springs. He had come in 1836 to oversee land sales resulting from the Chickasaw Cession, and his land office remains a landmark in Holly Springs-it is now the Visitor's Welcome Center of the Holly Springs Tourism and Recreation Authority. The Crafts amassed wealth as investors in the Mississippi Central Railroad. The thick walls of their home, erected in 1851, were filled with charcoal, making it sturdy and draft-resistant.[8]

Wednesday, January 18th 1865. Eddie and Johnny came back last night and brought a bale of cotton with them. Cousin Sue Harris came and spent the day with us today. Mrs. Watson and Miss Cora and Miss Lizzie went up to Mrs. Craft's to supper tonight. We all stayed upstairs until they came back.

"I Had Some Right Hard Sums Today"

Mathematics seemed to be Belle's most challenging subject. Like generations of students before and since, she was vexed by having to add long columns of numbers.

Thursday, January 19th 1865. *Eddie is sick and cannot go in school. I went in school this morning. I had some very hard sums today and it took me a right long time to do them. I went up to Cousin Sue's this evening. Miss Cora is going to stay all night with her.*

"A Letter from Papa"

Belle was interested when Mrs. Watson received a letter from Major Strickland, for it no doubt concerned arrangements that he had made with Mrs. Watson for Belle and Buddy's care and schooling while he was away.

Friday, January 20th 1865. *I went in school this morning. Alfred came over and said that Uncle Hudson had come and Alfred brought a letter to Mrs. Watson from Papa. I went over there as soon as I got through with my lessons. I staid over there until nearly dark. I got on better with my arithmetic today.*

"An Ambitious Reading Project"

Even while they were occupied by an army, some Southerners of the educated class made an effort to cultivate the mind. On January 20, 1865, Cora Watson noted the commencement of this interesting project, with an ambitious goal: "Commenced reading tonight in Liddell's *History of Rome*. Sister and I have determined to read carefully this history and afterwards Arnold's *Roman History*. We have a plan to travel through Europe after the war, and we must prepare ourselves to appreciate what we see." Belle, too, was interested, as her notation for the following day indicates, but sadly, Cora and Lizzie's goal of travel in Europe was never realized.

> *Saturday, January 21st 1865.* I wrote to Miss Carrie Newton[9] this morning. Then I sewed some and sewed some more tonight and Miss Cora read some in the history of Rome.

"I Read a Heap in the Bible"

Belle's resolve to read the scriptures by a systematic plan had slipped, so she redeemed a rainy Sabbath attempting to catch up. The evening's entertainment was typical. Inez Berryhill Adams, who lived at the Holly Springs manse with her aunt and uncle, Presbyterian minister, the Rev'd and Mrs. C. Z. Berryhill from 1907 to 1912, recalled that "evenings saw us sitting in the parlor, talking. On cool evenings, a fire burned in the fireplace grate, and the oil lamps cast a warm glow. Conversation was our primary form of amusement; radio had not been invented, and Victrola music was considered vulgar. Occasionally, Aunt Essie played the piano, and we sang hymns."[10] The melodeon was a kind of reed organ, often found in parlors of this era.

> *Sunday, January 22nd 1865.* We did not go to church today because it was such a bad day. I read a heap in the Bible and read some in the Life of Solomon. I learned the hymn that begins, "Jesus, I my cross have taken," and then read some more in the Bible. Miss Lizzie played some on the melodeon this evening.

"A Sabbath Evening"

Sabbath evenings were spent at home, reading the Bible and other devotional books, singing hymns, and otherwise refraining from worldly activity. Cora Watson gives this account of the household's Sunday activities.

Sunday, January 22, 1865. *The family gathered around the fire, with Sister playing on the melodeon and the rest of us singing. Sister read aloud a chapter in Bickersteth's 'Treatise on Prayer' and one of Blent's Lectures on 'The Articles,' and Belle and Eddie learned and recited hymns.*

"We Read Some Tonight in a Magazine"

Magazines and other popular literature were hard to come by during the war, and old numbers were treasured as gold. In happier times during February 1859, Emma Finley told her diary that while her brother was busy clearing land on the farm, "we of the house have read Mabel Vaughn's *Fern Leaves* & are today enjoying the new *Harper*."[11]

Monday, January 23rd 1865. Eddie and I went in school today and said some of our lessons. A soldier was here this morning and took his dinner here. He brought Miss Cora a letter from her Papa in Tennessee. We read some tonight in a magazine. We read about three pieces before I went to sleep.

"Domestic Evenings in Holly Springs"

Family evenings before television consisted of reading, sewing, and conversation. Different ones would take turns reading aloud, while the others sewed, or listened quietly.

Tuesday, January 24th 1865. We went in school this morning. I commenced my doll dress today. . . .Miss Lizzie and Miss Cora read some and Mrs. Watson sewed.

Wednesday, January 25th 1865. We went in school today and said our lessons this morning. . . .I sewed on my doll dress this evening and sewed some tonight. Miss Cora wrote in her journal and Miss Lizzie read some in the history of Rome.

Thursday, January 26th 1865. *I went in school today and said my lessons. . . .I went over to Aunt Mollie's and stayed until nearly dark.*

"Political Rumblings"

As the Civil War drew to a close, the air was full of schemes by which the conflict might be resolved. Cora Watson excitedly recorded some of these ideas. Even Mr. Paine thought that peace was not far off. Meanwhile, the family enjoyed some delectables from Mr. House's recent efforts at blockade-running.

Tuesday, January 24, 1865. *Hear today that Jos. Johnston is not in command of the Army of Tennessee. There is great talk of foreign recognition and peace near at hand. It is said that France and England have given Mr. Lincoln until the fourth of March to adjust matters amicably and after that time, they say, they will only recognize him as President of the states which elected him. I trust it is so if it will bring us an independent peace. The Northern papers say an embassy-of which Vice-President Stephens and William Rives are members-has been sent from Richmond to Washington, and one-of which Frank Blair is a member-from Washington to Richmond. I pray that the crisis may be near at hand, for I firmly believe that our Cause is too just and holy to fail, and I am sick at heart of this dark, sanguinary war-time. But I am distressed to see the depressed and subjugated feeling which prevails. It may not be general throughout our Confederacy-I hope it is not-but it is universal here.*

Thursday, January 26, 1865. *There is so much talk of peace that we were anxious to talk with some gentlemen in whose judgment we could have confidence and sent for Mr. Paine to come down this evening. He says he thinks peace is not far off, yet does not seem to be decided as to how it is to come-only he is confident that it will not be as a result of our subjugation. It cannot come too soon then. . . .I bought a beautiful balmoral from Miss Stewart for $15, and have made it.*[12] *This evening I got Eddie to go down to Mr. House's-he having just returned from Memphis with a stock of goods-and buy me a pair of shoes, beautiful ones of glove kid, buttoned up and* trimmed with patent leather-very cheap, too, only $10. I sent $2 more down by Eddie and bought a treat for us all, especially the little ones. Mrs. Venable came in while we were enjoying it, and I had an opportunity to gratify Stell-whose kindness I would like to make some return for-by sending her some nuts and candy, which are such rarities that we enjoy them as we never did before.

"Mr. Anderson is on Parole"

Known to generations as "Uncle Ally," W. A. Anderson's pedagogical manner was not indulgent. Mason Jones, son of William A. and Margaret Mason Jones, recalled this incident involving future Memphis mayor and congressman Edward Hull Crump, who was reared in Holly Springs and attended the Holly Springs Public School under Anderson. Jones wrote that: "Anderson had been wounded in the Civil War leaving him with a stiff right arm. However else it handicapped him, it was useful for taking 'roundhouse swings' at students needing discipline." One year:

> the classroom was so overcrowded that Edward was assigned to a stool behind Uncle Ally's desk. Once, as the teacher pursued a subject with the class, the boy quietly moved his stool by the blackboard and began to draw pictures, attracting more attention to his artistry than Uncle Ally got for his teaching. Sensing that something was wrong, the master turned, and tiptoeing up behind the artist, swung at him, intending to unseat him from his perch. But the boy, seeing the blow coming, ducked quickly, and Uncle Ally's great swing knocked down the chimney to the stove. The room was filled with so much smoke and soot that school had to be dismissed.[13]

Friday, January 27th 1865. We went in school today. Mr. Anderson came last night. He was taken prisoner and is on parole. He came to see us today. While he was here an old woman came and said that she and her children had not had anything but bread to eat for three weeks and that she had no bread now. Mr. Anderson called Mrs. Watson out and gave her twenty dollars in greenbacks.[14] I went over to Auntie and stayed a little while.

Eddie and Johnny went to Sell Eddie's Yankee Horse

Saturday, January 28th 1865. *I practiced but a half-hour today because I wanted to write to Papa and Eddie wrote to Jim. I went over to Auntie's this evening. Uncle Hudson is going away Monday.*

"Mr. Crump Thinks We Are Whipped"

William Crump (1806-1873), elderly, opinionated, and a Unionist,[15] said what others were too proud to admit. The war would soon be over and the South would be prostrate. His remarks caused Cora Watson and her mother-in-law to do some soul searching. They imagined life in a re-united nation as "refugees in a foreign land" and discussed the idea of moving to some other country-a popular theme especially among distressed Confederates at this time. Ten thousand Southerners went into exile after 1865, establishing ex-Confederate colonies in Mexico, Brazil, and Venezuela. Others wandered to Canada, and from one European nation to another. A few even assisted Egyptian leaders in training their army. The exiles performed significant religious work-paving the way for missionary work by Southern denominations in South America.[16] Meanwhile, "Obedience to Confederate conscription laws is almost nil," wrote Harvey W. Walter of Holly Springs to J. W. C. Watson, December 28, 1864. This incident in Holly Springs illustrates the truth of Walter's observation.[17]

Saturday, January 28, 1865. *Col. Jesse Forrest, with his command of about 140 men, has been in town all day conscripting.[18] There have been a good many arrests made in town and in the neighborhood. Two of his men-one an officer, Capt. Jordan-and the other a Mr. Simms-came in, and asked for supper, and sat for some time. They, and I hope they represent the spirit of our soldiers generally, are hopeful and determined never to yield. . . .Mr. Crump came in and sat two or three hours this evening. He thinks we are completely whipped and scouted the idea of our ever gaining our independence. We all opposed him, and he and Mother had quite a con-*

troversy on the subject. Tonight after he left, we renewed the theme, and, admitting the possibility of our subjugation, decided that we could not remain here and discussed all the countries we thought we might like, to decide one to go to.[19] It is a dreary picture to imagine ourselves, refugees in a foreign land, with no fortune and obliged to support ourselves by toil. If we gain our Cause, we can remain here, where the languages and customs of the people are our own, regain what we have lost pecuniarily by the war-or, at least, manage to live easily and comfortably.[20]

VII. Caring for the Sick

In Civil War times, hospitality's definition was broadened to care for the sick, there being no hospitals except perhaps for the seriously wounded. At various times during the war the Holly Springs Female Academy, the Baptist and Catholic churches, as well as the courthouse had been used as hospitals. Both the female academy and courthouse had burned, and the Catholic Sisters of Charity had been evacuated. Now, under U. S. occupation, it fell upon townspeople who supported the Confederate cause to care for their own. This was not the first ill soldier the Watsons had befriended, nor would it be the last. The act was a "work of mercy" which filled a Sabbath devoid of traditional religious exercises.

> *Sunday, January 29th 1865.* We went to church today but there was none. I read some in the Bible this morning . . . .We got some verses in the Bible instead of a hymn. Colonel Huyett came here today and was very sick tonight.[1] We had to send for the doctor.

"Eddie Went Out in the Country"

Young Edward Watson, now about fourteen, was restive under feminine restraints. No doubt he wished he could enlist in the army.[2] Excuses of every sort were invented to pursue activities deemed more important than attending school, especially since his older brother had entered the Virginia Military Institute. One could hardly blame the boy. Belle's brother Buddie seems to have suffered from similar preoccupations in a corner of the world where even today books and learning seem to many boys to be a ladies' occupation.

> ***Monday, January 30th 1865.*** *I went in school today but Eddie went out in the country. I. . .went in and took my music lessons because Mr. Tepe told me Thursday to come this evening. He told me that he would not teach any more until the first of March. The reason that he is going away is because he has got a little baby out there in the country. We are looking for Buddie today but he did not come.*[3]

"Memories of Miss Lizzie's School Room"

Helen Craft Anderson Craft (1847-1931), recorded memories of her days as a pupil in the Watson home. As the youngest of Hugh and Elizabeth Collier Craft's seven surviving children, Helen Anderson was a leader in her town's cultural and religious life. A musician and author, she wrote eyewitness accounts of the Civil War and yellow fever of 1878 and served for many years as organ teacher at Mississippi Synodical College. She was a founder of the local Philharmonic Society, and operated the town's first public library.[4] She married the scholarly William Albert Anderson, the town's leading educator. The Thursday Club, a prominent literary organization, was organized in the Anderson home.[5] At her death, John Mickle wrote that "Mrs. Anderson possessed strong intellectual faculties, and was a woman of deep culture."[6] She recalled that "There were eight in our class, the 'Seniors,' and seven in the other classes . . . ." She noted that "we had one unusually brilliant member of our class, Kate Sherwood Bonner, who afterward was a friend and protégé of the poet Longfellow, and was making a name in literature. . .when her untimely death when only thirty-three years old, cut short her ambitious career."[7]

Tuesday, January 31st 1865. I went in school today and Eddie went up town for something. Miss Helen Craft came this morning. Mrs. Dancy and Miss Mary came while we were at dinner and brought Fanny with them. We had some company tonight but I played in the other room.

"Mrs. Lewis, Blockade Runner, Reports Talk of Peace"

Cora Watson saw a hopeful sign, then dismissed it, in this report from a woman who did business with merchants across the Union lines. Rumors abounded, but defeat loomed, and the Watsons had to know.

Tuesday, January 31, 1865. *Cousin Sue and I stopped in at the house of a Mrs. Lewis, who is a blockade-runner, but a strong Southern woman, and a person of a great deal of intelligence. She has just returned from Memphis. Says there is quite as much talk of peace among the Yankees as with us here, but they have no idea of peace on any other terms than reconstruction.*

Thursday, February 2, 1865. *Dr. Dancy tells us there is a rumor in town of an armistice of ninety days. I do trust it is true; even a cessation of hostilities for three months would be a joyful reprieve.*

"I helped Uncle Stephen Unload the Wagon"

"Uncle" Stephen was a slave, and children like Belle were happy to play at slave labor when it suited them. A trusted worker, Stephen Watson traveled long distances on business for the Watson family, even going behind enemy lines to bring goods from Memphis.

Wednesday, February 1st 1865. I went in school today and Eddie too. We are looking for Buddie this evening, but he didn't come. We reckon that he will come tomorrow evening. I played all this evening out in the yard with Sue until Uncle Stephen came with the corn and I went and helped unload the wagon. We had some more company tonight.[8]

"Further Reports from Memphis"

Sarah Dickens Martin and her children were intimates of the Watsons. Mrs. Martin, who had connections in the city, reported that the Federal authorities were firmly in control there and that they had effected those egalitarian social principles which Southerners dreaded. It represented to them, an end to their way of life. The report evoked deep expressions of resentment and resistance from Cora Watson. Her spirit of undefeatable Confederate nationalism was not uncommon among women of her class and rank.[9]

February 3, 1865. *Mrs. Martin came in today. She gives a horrid account of things in Memphis. Dana,[10] the commander-in-chief there, is a rank abolitionist, and will scarcely have any troops in the garrison other than Negroes, whom he parades over the streets all the time. He rules in Memphis with the greatest severity. Insults ladies and everyone else who applies to him for a permit. He is said to bear a striking personal-as well as moral-resemblance to 'his Satanic majesty,' and prides himself very much on the likeness. He wears his hair very long, and hanging in three plaits over his shoulders. I suggested an improvement in his coiffure, which was for him to stand two of the plaits out straight in front of his forehead. Mrs. Martin said it was impossible to walk the streets of Memphis without being elbowed off the sidewalks by Negroes-men and women-and stared at most impertinently by Yankee officers.[11] Though she exerted herself a great deal, she found it impossible to obtain an interview with Dana in order to secure a permit to bring out a very small amount of goods. At the picket post in coming out, a Yankee soldier put his hands all over her shoulders, bosom and around her waist to discover if she were smuggling out any contraband articles. How can a Southern woman submit to such outrage on her purity, such gross indignity and insult to her womanhood?[12] All these marks of petty tyranny, together with the deep wrongs we have received, swell my heart with the most implacable hatred, and strengthen my determination never to be willing to 'forgive and for-*

get' them. Rather war the rest of our lives, rather suffering, misery of any kind-than re-union with the Yankees.

Monday, February 3rd 1865. *Buddie got home Friday, but was not very well. He is better now. We all went in school today, but Miss Helen Craft did not come until we were nearly done with our lessons. It took me a long time to do my sums because one was so hard. Mason Harris is here now and Captain Airs.*

"A Rumor that General Lee has been made Commander-in-Chief"

Belle's pen is silent for almost two months, but Cora Watson dutifully records events in this crucial period of the South's history.

Saturday, February 4, 1865. *Mr. Hudson and Mr. Thomson came to see us this evening. Mr. T. says there is a rumor that General Robert E. Lee has been made Commander-in-Chief of our armies. If so, it will give universal satisfaction. I saw an article in the Richmond Sentinel a few days ago recommending it, and everybody has wished it for a long time. It is also said that California has seceded and put herself under the protection of Maximilian, and that Messrs. Stephens, Campbell and Hunter have returned from Washington without having affected any of our difficulties.*

"Emancipating the Slaves"

The wearing effects of war eventually convinced Confederates to contemplate the emancipation of their slaves. The Rev'd Benjamin Morgan Palmer, D.D.-long regarded as the South's most eloquent preacher-had stated in July 1858 in an address titled "Our Historic Mission" at LaGrange Synodical College that the Negro was condemned by God to a position of servitude. Three years later, in his famous Thanksgiving Day sermon in the First Presbyterian Church of New Orleans, November 29, 1860-credited by many with galvanizing Southern opinion for secession-Palmer asserted that the great duty of Southerners was to serve as "the constituted guardians of the slaves themselves," and that in order to save the slave "from a doom worse than death," he declared that the relation of slavery had to be preserved. It was a duty, he said, "which the church owed to the civilized world." Palmer had repeated the statement many times in the intervening years, and as late as the summer of 1864, the General Assembly of the Presbyterian Church in the Confederate States had adopted a statement declaring that "it was the plain duty of the Southern Presbyterian Church to conserve and perpetuate the institution of slavery."[13] But on January 11, 1865, General Lee had declared in favor of enlisting Negroes in the Confederate armies and recommended a "plan of gradual and general emancipation." Henry H. Paine declared his agreement with Lee's position. Cora Watson summarized her pastor's views:

Tuesday, February 7, 1865. *Mr. Paine thinks there is little hope of peace, unless there is some intervention of Foreign Powers that we know not of. Says there has been the most complete revolution of feeling among the people on the subject of emancipation[14] in the last six weeks.[15] That there is an unanimous sentiment in favor of it, if by so doing peace may be accomplished. The whole Christian world is against this institution, and we cannot expect their sympathy or aid while we retain it. Almost every person approves the idea of the employment of Negroes in our army, since if we do not use them the enemy will employ them against us.[16] We can soon learn to do without them, and, in the end, I have no doubt we will be better off rid of them. It will be harder for the Negroes themselves than for us. Thousands of the worthless, lazy creatures will starve to death, I expect. . . .[17]*

Saturday, February 11, 1865. *This evening saw two soldiers coming up the walk and sister, thinking them to be Capt. Connor and Selby, had asked them in the parlor. They called for me, and when I went in, to my utter astonishment I beheld Amp and Willie Ewell.[18] I brought them right into the sitting room and introduced them to the family. They are just from home this morning and on their way to Col. Cox's regiment, the 12th Confederate cavalry, of which Maj. Bates is major. They are just 17 and overflowing with patriotism* and enthusiastic ardor. Poor boys! I wonder how long it will be before they are disgusted with a soldier's life! We couldn't persuade them to stay at night. 'Oh, no!' They must get on to their command! It was then about sun-down. I expect they rode until bed-time and then camped. It won't be long before they'll be glad enough to stop at night in a comfortable bed. They were elegantly equipped, and had fine horses.

"Mr. Paine Called, Bringing Us a Number of 'Sentinels'"

Newspapers and magazines were eagerly exchanged. *The Richmond Sentinel*, published in the Confederacy's capital was the newspaper of record for most Southerners in this period.

Monday, February 13, 1865. *Mr. Paine called, bringing us a number of 'Sentinels.' He gave us some account of the 'Peace Mission.' Our commissioners had an interview with Lincoln and Seward on board of a Federal gunboat at Hampton Roads. The Yankees would listen to no terms but absolute submission, and of course that ended the matter.*

"She was Full of the Party Last Night"

John M. Mickle, then a boy, remembered parties given for "the army of occupation," when, for the sake of entertainment, both men of the South and the army in blue seem to have been able to put aside differences-if but for an evening. Holly Springs was famous for its balls, but as war clouds gathered, a committee of the Presbyterian session, including J. W. C. Watson, J. W. Clapp, and the Rev'd Henry Paine, drafted on March 19, 1860, "an explanation of the session's opposition to dancing and other worldly amusements." In 1861 the Presbyterian Synod of Mississippi condemned dancing, and the North Mississippi Presbytery followed suit in 1866.

Tuesday, February 21, 1865. *Betty Thomas came over today. She was full of the party she attended last night at Mrs. Henry Williamson's. All the girls were there, and a good many soldiers* besides the town boys who were home on furlough. Beaux are becoming so scarce that the girls have taken W.S., B.H., and A.G.[19] for escorts to-and partners at-the parties. Parties are becoming quite the order of the day. Last week there were two-one at Col. McGuirk's, the other at Mr. Govan's. Tonight there is to be one at Mr. Bradley's.[20]

"Demon Rum Condemned"

The use and abuse of alcohol was frowned upon by the righteous, as Cora Watson's remark here makes clear. Yet, Federal authorities were said to have encouraged the habit among Southern people. They refused to declare whiskey a contraband commodity, and allowed traffickers to pass through Union lines. Vast amounts of liquid corn were stored at various times on the Holly Springs square. Meanwhile, the parties seem not to have pleased some churchgoing adults of the community.

Thursday, February 23, 1865. *I was surprised and disappointed to discover in Major B's appearance this afternoon unmistakable appearances of recent dissipation. That has been the curse of the South, blighting so much promise, destroying so many fair lives. If the war might eradicate that evil, I would be willing to let it go on.*

Friday, February 24, 1865. *Heard today that we had evacuated Charleston. It may be a good policy to concentrate our forces, and I suppose Charleston is really a point of little importance to the Confederacy, but I am so sorry for the people there. They have maintained so determined and protracted a resistance to the Yankees, who anyway feel particular malice against them on account of the defeat at Fort Sumter, that I am afraid they will suffer severely now. . . . Cousin Sue came around this evening and sat until after ten. Gave us quite a spicy account of the party. Said there was a perfect jam and a mixed crowd. It was 'exclusives,' 'parvenues,' nobodies, strangers, soldiers, citizens, and blockade runners, mixing together indiscriminately. She said Betsy T. and Betsy H.[21] put on any quantity of airs. I think if the parties keep on our girls will become as demoralized as the girls we have been hearing of in Dixie. Mother told Major B. yesterday that she always liked to hear*

of the soldiers going to parties and enjoying themselves, but she
thought the parties were better for the soldiers than for the girls.

"Confederate Peace Mission Rebuffed"

Some Mississippians favored a negotiated peace, but the Watsons shared no such sentiments.

Saturday, February 25, 1865. *Received by Mr. E. A. Thomas-who is direct from Richmond-quite a batch of papers and letters. I think the contemptuous treatment of our peace commissioners by the Yankee officials was the best thing that could have happened to us-better than to have won a great battle. Reverses had dispirited our people and caused many of them to seriously contemplate reconstruction with favorable eyes. Now that the Yankee government had told us expressly on what terms they will permit us to return-the acceptation of the amended Constitution, the laying down of our arms, in short, perfect submission, there is no Southerner-who is not a miserable craven, and I have not heard of one-who can bend his neck to such a yoke. The papers are filled with accounts of meetings of different regiments in which they express their determination to die or to be free. On the night of the 7th inst. There was a mass meeting of ten thousand persons in Richmond, and the unanimous sentiment was 'liberty or death'-One of the papers says that a man who would whisper 'Reconstruction!' now would be hung to a lamp-post. The enthusiasm seems to be as great now as at the beginning of the war. We needed this insult to fire again the waning fire in some Southern heart.*

Monday, February 27, 1865. *Uncle Stephen came on home soon after we got here. Assigns as a reason for his long stay that he could not get a pass out of Memphis. Says he took breakfast with Hester Ann[22] one morning. Says she is living very comfortably. Saulsberry is pastor of a church-shepherd of a flock of black sheep.[23] Hester Ann takes in sewing and washing-where before she gained her freedom couldn't do her own washing.[24] Monk is dead-she took cold from going to school without her shoes. Ada is attending school[25]...Two soldiers came this evening and asked to be permitted to stay all night, and they are here now...They talk like young* men accustomed to good society, but they look dissipated and evidently have been drinking this evening. Gen. Dana displayed some strategy in endeavoring as he does to demoralize our men and thus render them inefficient soldiers.[26] He imposes restrictions on all trade except that of whiskey, and he grants permits for an unlimited quantity of that to come out of his lines. There has been more drunkenness in town since Dana took command in Memphis than at any other time since the commencement of the war. Sometimes the drunken soldiers are so disorderly, firing their pistols and otherwise behaving 'rowdishly,' that it is really dangerous to go on the streets in the evening. It was so the evening we went down to Cousin Sue's and Mr. House protected us home.[27] If there is anything that can make me feel our cause may fail, it is this behavior of our soldiers.[28]

Monday, March 6, 1865. Hear a rumor that Sherman's army is defeated and the ubiquitous Sherman killed. So he will surprise the inhabitants below by turning up there next!

Thursday, March 16, 1865. I sent to Mrs. Long's[29] today, and engaged her to bring me a bonnet from Memphis. She was very polite and obliging and said she would bring me a bonnet and anything else I wanted. Mr. Hoppy Thomson[30] called in this evening, and I asked him to sell $10 in gold for me, which he said he would do if he could, but has sent me no word yet. I am afraid I cannot send for my bonnet after all.

Friday, March 17, 1865. Mr. Thomson sold my gold ($10) for 235 today and I went down and gave the money to Mrs. Long.

Saturday, March 18, 1865. Mrs. Venable got home from the South last night-Miss Carrie says traveling in Dixie is horrible. She gives an amusing account of the mania for dry goods prevailing among the ladies. She could scarcely get away with any clothes. They buy half-worn dresses with the greatest eagerness, and give enormous prices for them, and she says she could have obtained almost any price for her new bonnet. . . .I have been reading during the last few days 'Madelune,' a story by Julia Kavanagh. It is one of the most simple, natural and beautiful stories I have ever read. . .it has inspired me with a new desire to do something for my country. If there was ever a time when women might do good, it seems to me that time is now. Madelune had an unpromising field to work in, and with one jot less of faith in God's goodness and of determined perseverance, she would never have established the hospital of Mont. St. Jean-yet we sit with our hands idly folded and say there is nothing we can do.

"I Have Not Written in My Journal for a Long Time"

After a lapse, Belle resumed her diary-keeping with this entry:

Monday, March 27th 1865. *I have not written in my journal for a long time and will begin today. We went in school today and said all of our lessons. Mr. Sam Pryor[31] was here and stayed about an hour. Miss Lizzie went out to see him. I am going over to Mrs. McCarroll's to see Bet maybe this evening. I stayed all night with Auntie last night and came home very late this morning.*

"More Cynicism from Mr. Crump"

William Crump was not popular with the Watsons. The elderly man's son had come home from the war, and Cora Watson thought his action dishonorable.

Monday, March 27, 1865. *Diana Holland[32] just came in. What an earnest, devotedly patriotic woman she is! Says she intends to tell Jimmie C. that she heard a young lady say that 'he had retired from the army with a Captain's rank and pay and gone to peddling goods.'- which is, in effect, what everybody says. I declare, old Mr. C. ought to be abolished. He is the greatest old croaker in town and is doing incalculable mischief by preaching submission and reconstruction to the people and spoiling his sons as soldiers, and bringing out whiskey to demoralize the soldiers who go about him. Dr. Dancy told us he heard him say not long ago our cause was hopeless and we should stop the war, and make the best terms we could with the Yankees. Dr. Dancy asked him what would become of their sons,* who were in the army. 'Oh,' he said, 'they can go off to Mexico, or somewhere, and take care of themselves'-heartless old wretch!

"Miss Lizzie Never Does Give Holiday."

Elizabeth Watson was a committed Calvinist who believed that idleness was a sin. Meanwhile, Belle helped Eddie Watson prepare shot for his rifle. The work was not only unladylike, but dangerous.

Tuesday, March 28th 1865. We went in school again today and always do, for Miss Lizzie never does give holiday. When she was sick and when everyone told her that she ought not do it, she taught school. We have not been having Sunday school for a long time, but it began last Sunday.[33] We are getting on very well with our studies now. We are looking for Mr. Watson home soon.[34] We got a letter from Papa yesterday, nearly every one of us. I intend to finish my doll dress this evening maybe. I have been helping Eddie make shot this evening.

"News from Major Strickland"

Cora Watson reported the receipt of intelligence from Belle's father. Naturally, all were interested in the news, even if it was depressing

Thursday, March 30, 1865. *Willie received a letter and Sister a package of papers from Maj. Strickland today. The news in the papers is not cheering. President Davis' message to Congress is rather despondent in its general tone, acknowledging a possibility of our failure. Congress adjourned on the 18th inst., so we may begin to expect Father in two or three weeks. Sherman has reached Fayetteville and is in communication with Wilmington. Sheridan has made a junction with Grant at the White House near Richmond. May God help us; we are fighting against fearful odds, and but that ours is the sacred cause of freedom, I should well nigh despair. If we seemed earnest and serious, engaged with all our might, every* *one, young and old, woman and child, doing all we could towards the accomplishment of our great end, I should think we were a nation worthy of liberty, and would hope in the face of the most serious misfortunes that success would ultimately crown our efforts. But it is far otherwise. Selfishness, hardness, indifference and levity, and the still more pernicious evils of skulking duty and desertion among the soldiers, croaking submission and reconstruction among some of the people at home make my heart sink within me. We are not half as good as a people as we were the first year of the war. Then nothing we had or could procure was too precious to devote to our country's cause. Our dearest and best friends were cheerfully sent forth to battle for our rights. Our means, our labor and our loved ones were all willingly offered on the altar of freedom, while prayers went up daily from a thousand altars for our guidance and success.*

VIII. Helping Poor Soldiers' Families

"Lee Surrenders-Lincoln Assassinated-John Wilkes Booth Captured and Slain"

Cora Watson's diary provides information for a five-week period when Belle is silent. It was a momentous spring in America's history, and in the history of Holly Springs. The tragic month began with an exercise in the absurd: writing 'April Fool's Day' notes for the slaves.

Monday, April 3, 1865. *Went walking in the garden after dinner. Frank accosted me with 'Miss Cora, have you got time to write a "Apul fool" letter for me dis evenin?' I told him I had nothing to do, and would write for him, and asked him whom it should be to. He said to Sallie Craft and, after a little hesitation, asked if I wouldn't write another to Cynthia Gholson. I told him I would, and then he wanted another written to Lou Nutall, so I'm in business this evening.*

"Major Crump Captured"

Raids, recalling those which disturbed the neighborhood the previous August, occurred once more. The effort seemed to have been to capture Major Brodie Crump, which was done with a minimum of violence. Cora Watson, having lost her husband to the war, was utterly opposed to the philosophy of "forgive and forget."

Wednesday, April 5, 1865. *We were roused unceremoniously this morning by Hannah exclaiming in excited tones in our ears, 'De town is full o' Yankees!' We sprang up, made hasty toilettes, and came down. None appeared on our street, however, until some time after breakfast when a squad went into Mrs. Hull's and captured Major Brodie Crump. Then they searched at Dr. Smith's, here, and on down this street, omitting only Mr. Walthall's and Mrs. Lane's.[1] They searched very lightly here, only opening the doors and looking in. I think there were not more than a hundred and twenty. They took everybody by surprise and captured eight soldiers. Major Crump was the only one we knew. They treated the citizens very civilly, stealing nothing that I heard of. Washburn's policy, we hear, is to be <u>conciliatory</u>, and he says, 'The American mind is so elastic we will soon forget all the past.' He greatly exaggerates the elasticity of the American mind if he thinks we Southern people can ever forget the wrongs and insults we have received from the Yankees. They seem more detestable coming as friends than enemies. This is the most provoking insult yet. We know there are claws in the velvet paw, and we would rather see them. No-'Add not unto your cruel hate your yet more cruel love.'*

"Rumors of the End"

With speculation rife as to the end of the Confederacy, Senator Watson's family was determined to do what they could to help their cause in its hour of need. Ironically, though the Civil War was famously fought to preserve the *status quo ante-bellum,* one of its unintended effects was to thrust women into a new kind of prominence and visibility through charitable work they undertook outside the home-all, of course, to aid the war effort. Quite out of its usual character, the Presbyterian Church was to be used for a 'political meeting,' in Cora Watson's words, "to arouse the people to feel and act for the cause." The effort revealed-not surprisingly-that some were supportive of continued effort for the Confederacy, while others were not.[2]

Saturday, April 8, 1865. Heard of some Yankee papers in town containing an announcement of the fall of Richmond, and account of the capture. Sent and got them. They tell of desperate fighting, often hand to hand in the trenches, of their being repeatedly repulsed, and once driven back a mile and a half, but each time being reinforced, and pushing our men back by superior numbers-and, after three days of gallant resistance, of the evacuation of our Capitol. We were almost overwhelmed by the news at first. But despair has its accompaniment of desperation, and we have determined to arouse ourselves and do something for our country. We have remained inactive so long, and now unless everyone does all in his-or-her power, all is lost. Mr. Hoppy Thompson came over after tea and sat until bed-time. He brings additional bad news-of the fall of Selma, and capture of valuable government books, and that Forrest was in Selma at the time of the capture. He had been misinformed as to the numbers of the enemy, being prepared for only 5,000 while 20,000 came on them. General Forrest, General Roddy and General Armstrong were in Selma (so says the paper) and escaped only with their escorts, each General receiving several sabre cuts, showing how narrowly they escaped. So we have additional reason for exertion. Our two generals, Lee and Forrest, on whom we depended most implicitly have been defeated, and if we give way to despondency now we are conquered.

Sunday, April 9, 1865. Sister and I have determined to set out tomorrow morning to endeavor to have a public meeting to arouse the people to feel and act for the cause.

"Mr. Pickett will Speak for Us"

It would be fifty years before women would address meetings with men present in Holly Springs. And although the first woman to be ordained a minister of the Presbyterian Church, U. S. was a former dean of the Mississippi Synodical College,[3] which grew out of the very meetings now being planned-that event- which took place one hundred years later in 1964-was too far in the future for anyone to contemplate. No one in Holly Springs on this occasion was prescient as to what changes the education of the town's children might lead.

Monday, April 10, 1865. *Early this morning Sister and I went over to Mrs. Minor's to consult as to the best means of getting up a meeting. Decided to have a meeting called for 3 o'clock tomorrow evening at the Presbyterian Church. Wanted Miss Diana to go around with us to talk to some of the people about it, but she was sick in bed, and we concluded to try Miss Reese Jones.[4] Told Miss Diana we should invite and expect Mr. Pickett[5] to come speak for us. Went down to see Miss Reese. Found her suffering a good deal with a sore eye, but she approved so much of the meeting that she came with us. We went up to Mr. Fort's to get his advice and assistance. He considered the enterprise a laudable one, and agreed to assist us to the extent of his power. We wish to obtain a response to Mr. Trenholm's call on the people for money-cotton, plate, jewels, etc.,- to be contributed to the treasury department to assist in paying our soldiers; and to reorganize our Aid society, to do all we can for the soldiers in the field and their families at home. Mr. Fort is to write notices of the meeting, and post them on the square and send one to Mr. Pickett to read in church. Though we were right tired, we had seen the good effects of talking with the people sufficiently to encourage us to set out again this evening. Went first to Mrs. Hull's. Encountered more difficulty there-in the person of Mrs. Hull-than anywhere we have been. Susan and Betsy Thomas were quite patriotic and agreed to do anything they could-to economize in their personal expenditures, and help to feed, clothe and educate the destitute families of soldiers, as we plan to do. Betsy Hull we did not see, but hear she is considerably demoralized. Met Ida C. and told her about the meeting, and told her she must come. 'Perhaps,' with the most affected manner, and passed on. I do not like her face. It has the beauty of the serpent. I know she is treacherous. We met Mrs. Carrington Mason and Lou Hamner and told them what enterprise we had on foot. They endorsed us heartily, though Mother tells us tonight that Mrs. Mason paid her a confidential visit this evening to say that, for private reasons, she could not be publicly connected with our society. Sister and I went to Mrs. Hamner's. Sallie was enthusiastic, 'perfectly delighted.'. . . She and Sister went* on down to see Miss Emily Polk,[6] and I came on to Mrs. Craft's. Met Mr. Paine. He feared he would not be able to attend, having been called into the country to marry Lewis Scruggs and Augusta Finley-would, however, endeavor to be present. At Mrs. Craft's the stream of patriotism runs low; Sister came after a while, and we went to Mrs. McCorkle's.[7] Mrs. McCorkle and Mrs. Nelms[8] expressed a great deal of patriotism, but would not agree to attend the meeting. Went on to Mr. House's to try to induce him to become the purchaser of some of our plate. He was not at home, but we met him, and he promised to come up and see Mother about it. Then we went down to Mrs. Fennell's.[9] They are patriotic, but recommend caution. That won't do-we want to let the Yankees know expressly that we are by no means subjugated. . . .Almost tired out tonight, but sent for Mr. Pickett to come around and talk with us. He thinks the meeting the best thing that could be done, will come, and assist in any way that he can. He talked earnestly and eloquently of our affairs, drawing encouragement for us from the examples furnished by history of Nations contending longer and against greater odds and finally becoming free, citing our own revolutionary struggle, the seven years' resistance of Greece against the Ottoman power, and the War of the Netherlands. We begged him to say that tomorrow to the people at the meeting, but he says he cannot speak. I am sure he will do whatever he can. Sister and I have been trying to write some resolutions, and mature some plans for proceeding in our meeting, tonight.

Tuesday, April 11, 1865. Sent for Mr. Fort and Judge Trotter at 8:30 this morning. They came, and took the conduct of the meeting now off our hands, we giving them our plan. Miss Diana and Miss Reese Jones came in after the gentlemen were gone. Miss Diana thought it might be a good thing to have the letter read in the meeting, and we sent for Dr. Dancy[10] and asked him to read it, but I think he talked like he was afraid the Yankees might hear of it. I wish the people who feel right would not act in so cowardly a manner. I am certain Dr. Dancy has the success of the Confederacy at heart. . . Sister went to see Mrs. Smith and Carrie. Carrie is sick, but Mrs. Smith told Sister to put their names down as members of the Aid Society. I have written circulars of the Society to be carried through the house. Sent for Betsy Hull to come over, and talked with her in regard to the object of the meeting, which seems to have been misunderstood by some of the people, who seemed to think we were going to form a conscription bureau to drive the men to the army. Called in Annie Smith, whom we saw passing, and explained the object of the meeting to her. Both girls promised to come. We were closely occupied until time to go to the church. . . .There were a good many persons present-not a crowd, however, very few except those we invited, and not all of them. Neither Mrs. McCorkle, Mrs. Nelms, nor anyone from Mr. Fennell's were present. Judge Trotter conducted the meeting,[11] which was opened with prayer by the Rev. Mr. Johnson.[12] Judge Trotter made a bold, earnest and patriotic appeal to the people to do or die for freedom, which was followed by a short, but pointed and forcible speech from Mr. Fort, in which two resolutions in relation to Mr. Trenholm's call were introduced. A committee is to be appointed to solicit contributions which Mr. Fort engages to forward to Mr. Trenholm. Mr. Fort read a stirring letter, written by Senator Ben Hill of Georgia to Miss Evans, and Mr. Paine made a short speech.

Wednesday, April 12, 1865. *A rainy day, the rain falling incessantly from morning to night. So we could do nothing today out of the house. However, it may be a fortunate thing for us, since it has given us time to consider as to our best means of usefulness. The paroled soldier has been here all day. He seems much impressed with our earnest desire to aid the cause, and says he will tell the ladies South about the spirit of the ladies here on the line. I am sorry the society could not meet to organize today.*

Thursday, April 13, 1865. *With lighter hearts than have beat in our bosoms for a long time, Sister and I set out this morning on an errand which we believed to be one of usefulness to our Cause. This evening we return weary and dispirited, not at any want of success in our day's work-that has equaled, if not exceeded our expectations-but, I will not anticipate, but go regularly through the day. We left home at about seven-thirty, and went to Mr. Fort's and offered our services to him as agents in town of the committee appointed to collect contributions for Mr. Trenholm. We thought it*

Helping Poor Soldiers' Families

would be better for ladies to do this in town for several reasons, and Mr. Fort fully concurred with us in this opinion, and gladly accepted our offer. We went first to see old Col. Lucas.[13] He was at home, and his daughter, Mrs. Cal Smith,[14] was with him. After some general conversation, Sister introduced the subject of our visit; but, although Col. Lucas was enthusiastically patriotic, he was actually unable to contribute anything to the support of the Confederacy. He had no money, plate, jewels, but finally gave us a gold-headed cane. The old man looks very feeble-as if he had one foot in the grave-and I [do] not think he would try to deceive us. I hope not. Mrs. Smith agreed to be one of the twenty or twenty-five to contribute $20.00 in gold, or plate or jewelry to that amount. They recommended Mr. Stillman to us; and we went there, but were told at the door that he was sick in bed, and we went across the street to Mr. Roberts. The ladies were at home and received us and our business kindly. The girls joined our society, and all promised to assist Mr. Trenholm, but could not say how far, Mr. Roberts not being at home. We thought there would be no impropriety in our seeing Mr. Stillman if Mrs. Roberts would go with us, which she readily agreed to do. We returned to Mr. Stillman's and saw him. He was in bed and looked badly. He gave a $100.00 Confederate note, and promised to do more when he got better. From there we went to Mr. Strickland's, the jeweler, whom we thought to be a 'blockade runner,' and therefore we wanted from him a liberal contribution. We were mistaken-in both our suppositions. He is a poor man, and I believe a worthy one. He did as well as he could, I think, giving a $50.00 Confederate note. Our next place was Mrs. Bracken's. Charlie Bracken has just returned from prison, and his mother has to buy a horse and outfit for him, besides having all the care of the whole family on herself, but she gave a $100.00 Confederate to the cause. Mrs. Lucas promised to become one of the twenty-five if she could. Said she would let us know in a few days. We crossed the street to Mr. E. A. Thomas'. There we found a good deal of patriotism. Mr. Thomas, as soon as we disclosed the object of our visit, handed me a $50.00 note (Confederate). Sister said, 'Mr. Thomas, we expected the gentlemen to give Confederate money by hundreds and thousands.' He looked a little blank, and took the note back, giving $100.00 in place *of it. He told us to get after some of these sick old fellows about town and tell him what they gave, and he would give more. Mrs. Thomas' silver was burned in their house, but she gave us the blackened and melted fragments of it,[15] and Miss Laura promised to look over her effects and see what she could give. We started to old Captain Chew's, but seeing Col. Goodrich and Dr. Gholson standing in front of Col. Goodrich's office, we stopped to present Mr. Trenholm's call to them. Col. Goodrich was quite facetious on the subject.[16] Asked us what Col. Lucas gave, and offered to buy the cane and told us to ask him how much he would take for his <u>blue cockade and sash</u>-that he was anxious to procure them. Recommended Capt. Chew to us, said he would undoubtedly have no money, but to tell him he would lend him as much Confederate greenback or gold as he was willing to give. Dr. Gholson promised us a contribution in Confederate money, but Col. Goodrich would only snap his eyes and <u>snuffle</u> out teasing things, and we left him.[17] Stopped at Miss Carrie's. She promised to give $20.00 in plate, and Stell offered her gold thimble and bracelet. Met Capt. Chew[18] coming. Presented Mr. Trenholm's call to him. Had invested all his money in Texas and had nothing, was sorry. Sister said she knew a gentleman who would lend him whatever he was willing to give. He asked who, and Sister told him Col. Goodrich. He promised to see him. Called to tell Cousin Sue we would take dinner with her, then went on to Mr. Govan's. Met old Mr. McCulley, but found him the hardest case we had met-he pleaded no excuse, but refused to give anything. We had expected a contribution of silver from Mrs. Govan, but the Yankees had stolen all she had. We had thought perhaps Mrs. McCulley would be more generous than her husband and called on her. She and Miss Pet were very much interested in the cause, but Miss Pet had nothing, and Mrs. McCulley must consult Mr. McCulley. As we were leaving, Sister said, 'Mrs. McCulley, I must tell you we have seen Mr. McCulley, and he refused to give anything-he was the first person who refused to contribute.' She seemed mortified and said, 'He was?' and told us to tell him she was willing to give anything he chose, if it were a hundred or a hundred and fifty dollars. Went on to Cousin Sue's and got dinner. She gave $10.00 in gold. Next went to Mr. Fort to report. Col. Goodrich was again* standing before his office door, and we asked Mr. Fort to call him over. We told him what we had told Capt. Chew and asked if he had seen him-he had not. Sister said, 'Col. Goodrich, what are you going to give?' He said he thought if he bought up all the gold-headed canes and notes, etc., he would be doing his part. Said we did not want to trouble ourselves with these hard old cases, but wanted to get everything a good-natured fellow like him had. We went next to Mrs. Minor's and received a liberal contribution there. Mrs. Minor and Mrs. Mickle each subscribing $40.00 in gold. Miss Diana will give freely too, I know, but I must see her mother first. Went to see Miss Reese Jones. She promised to contribute all her jewelry and whatever else she found she could when her mother came home. Next to Mrs. Mayer's.[19] Found them unable to assist the treasury there, Johnny to mount and equip and their means much straightened. Judge Trotter's was our next place. Judge Trotter is a true patriot. He told us to count on him for a large contribution. Said he would consult with his family tonight and call to see us tomorrow morning. I wish very much that he would contribute liberally, for Mr. Hoppy Thompson, Mr. Jim Simms,[20] Mr. Nat Williams[21] and several others say they will give as much as anyone else, and we would like someone to start generously. Miss Bettie Trotter joined our society. Kate Bonner and Ruth[22] came in just as we were leaving, and in an excited manner, asked if we had heard the dreadful news. 'No! What?' was the eager response. 'Why, Lee and his whole army are captured! But we all rejected the idea.[23] Coming home, met Mrs. Dancy, and she walked home with us. While we were talking at the gate, Ben Walthall came up on his way home. We asked him if there was such a report in town as the one we had heard at Judge Trotter's. He said there was, and it was undoubtedly true. I never sustained but one greater shock. If I had not held tightly by the gate, I think I should have fallen. He told us the information was contained, it was true, in a Yankee paper, but the correspondence between Lee and Grant was published, and no one could doubt its truth. Still, I would not credit it, and would see for myself, so Sister and I started for Mr. Fort's to see the paper. Miss Carrie and Stell and Betsy came in as we were going. Oh! If this awful calamity arouses the feeling in all our people, which they manifest, it may be a blessing in dis-

guise! 'Man's extremity is God's opportunity.' These three were among the most lukewarm the day we were talking about having a meeting to devise means of aiding our Country, but now they express the utmost devotion to our Cause, the strongest hope and belief in our ultimate success, and the most inflexible determination never to yield until all is lost. Promised to call at Mrs. Hull's on our return from Mr. Fort's and tell them all we heard. Found Mr. Fort sad, but not at all of the belief that this would end the conflict. We saw the paper and can no longer doubt the correctness of the statement it contained. Lee's army was doubtless worn out by laying in the trenches, battered and bruised by four days-and almost four nights-of fighting, reduced in numbers, unable to proceed rapidly with all the railroads out and without adequate transportation, over miserable roads, and pursued by Grant's immense army. God help us! Human hope seems well-nigh vain. Stopped at Mrs. Hull's. They cannot bring themselves to believe it. Cousin Sue came in. Said she had just found out she wasn't whipped. If that feeling may only become general!

"News of Lee's Surrender"

Olga Reed Pruitt captured the excitement of these moments when she wrote that probably the most important event that ever occurred at the Holly Springs railroad depot took place in April 1865, when the first news received by North Mississippi of Lee's surrender clattered over the Mississippi Central's wires. "One of Henderson's scouts brought the news from Memphis whereupon the operator sat down and hastily sent this message: 'Hell's to pay, Lee's surrendered.'"[24] Cora Watson, of course, did not know that on this day Lincoln would be assassinated in Washington, D. C.

Friday, April 14, 1865. *Several persons came in this morning, but I felt so oppressed and weighed down by the news of Lee's surrender that I could not bear to see anyone and went up to my room to be alone. In agony I asked how could I bear to leave the graves of all I loved, to tear myself away from all the old familiar scenes of my happy childhood and still happier married life, and break forever*

Helping Poor Soldiers' Families

the ties that bind me to home, life country, and kindred. But dreadful as it was to think of, I felt then-and feel now-that it is far preferable-yes, even death were bliss in comparison-to remain here. I took my Bible and sat down to read. Found comfort in the 54th Chapter of Isaiah. Sister came up after awhile. Darling Sister-it will be a comfort that we will be together-Mr. Paine came in the course of the evening. Still very much depressed. Thinks, and Sister and I agree with him, that Lee, as Commander-in-Chief of the Confederate armies, had no right to surrender himself with the army of Northern Virginia. The papers brought out by Mrs. Simms only serve to confirm the news-give accounts of the general jubilee throughout the Yankee states. Heavy rain this evening.

Sunday, April 16, 1865. Directly after church, I went upstairs to read and think. Sister soon came running up with a note from Miss Carrie which said Mr. House had just arrived from Memphis, bringing the news that the report of Lee's surrender was considered a 'hoax' by many high officers in Memphis, that it was believed that Lee had united his forces with Joe Johnston and defeated Sherman, capturing 30,000. I scarcely dare hope. It seems too much like the reception of the news of the fall of Vicksburg. I am sorry to see the people catching so readily at this news Mr. House brings. I hope fearfully, timidly. Mrs. Hull came over just before church to tell us about it. Said she never saw anything like the effect it produced on Mrs. Mickle. That she screamed, jumped up and down, laughed, wept and prayed, and ran up into Mrs. Brodie Crump's room and threw her arms around her exclaiming, 'It isn't so!' Mr. Crump got home from Memphis this evening, and he says it is true, and I'm afraid it must be, for by some papers of the 12th and 13th sent me by Mrs. Jones, I see nothing but confirmatory news. Even the names of the generals captured were given.

"Lincoln's Assassination and Plans for Teaching Go Forward"

Even in defeat, the Watson family's deep commitment to education showed through.

Tuesday, April 18, 1865. This morning eleven of the girls met at our house to arrange plans for the operations of our committees.

Got a list of the indigent families of soldiers, some thirty in number, and divided them in four, giving one of the divisions to each part of the committee of eight, two girls being put together. This is the Education committee, and the members are to wait on the families whose names they have, and offer to have the children instructed. After that is over with, they must get the names of girls willing to teach, and then some division of the pupils must be made. . . .This evening Reese Jones, Carrie and Susan came in to report their success in performing the duties of the Education Committee. They have eight scholars-perhaps ten. Say the poor women were so grateful to have their children taught. . . .Sister and I were just setting out on some visits when Mr. Paine came. He said it had been telegraphed that Lincoln and Seward are dead. The Yankee papers are in mourning. These colleagues in crime met their doom at the same time. Lincoln was assassinated in the Washington theatre, one of the accomplices turning off the gas while the other shot Lincoln in the darkness. Seward had his throat cut in his house. Mr. Paine says that it was the just judgment of God that these violent men should die violent deaths. Their souls go down stained with the blood of thousands of their own countrymen, and of thousands of our own noble Southern soldiers. Mr. Paine says it seems to be true that Gen. Lee surrendered himself and about 7,000 of his army. That his men would not surrender without him, and he was obliged to give himself with a small portion of the army, or lose the entire army and escape himself. He delayed the correspondence with Grant several days, all the time sending off his men to Johnston, and then sacrificed himself for his country. Noble patriot! Can anyone take thy place in the counsels of the nation![25]

Wednesday, April 19, 1865. *Coming home today met Sallie Hamner and Clemmie Clapp who are on the Education committee. They were on horseback and had been way out-two or three miles in the country to see poor families and offer to have the children taught. They were much elated with their success.*

Monday, April 24, 1865. *Sister had been busy all the morning drawing up a petition in the name of the Society to the citizens of Madison and Yalobusha Counties for aid, and this evening going around* on Society business. Tonight I am to copy the petition, and must leave my journal.

Tuesday, April 25, 1865. All this morning Willie Mayers and I were busy going around asking contributions for a box of goods we wish to send South and exchange for corn and meat. Visited all the houses on this street. . . . We were quite successful in obtaining promises of contributions. This evening, some contributions have come in, quite a liberal one from Mrs. Long and others.

"A Charity Box and May Day Coronation"

Besides the plan to teach the children, the women gathered supplies-bonnets trimmed in the latest style and eighty pounds of coffee, to send to the destitute further south. Cora's comments illustrate the manner in which John Wilkes Booth enjoyed temporary adulation as the South's avenger in the death of Abraham Lincoln.[26]

Monday, May 1, 1865. I have not had leisure to write in my journal since last Tuesday, so busy have I been with the affairs of the Society, and our success has fully repaid me for my exertions. Great interest was manifested by the majority of the people in the box. The girls trimmed the bonnets, which others contributed, in the latest style. Many pretty and valuable donations came in, and Friday Miss Stewart came down and marked the goods, which amounted to over $500.00 (greenbacks). Besides which we devoted the money collected as admittance fees to the purchase of coffee, which Mr. House kindly sold us at the Memphis price (45), and adding to it small contributions of coffee which had come in, we had a sack of coffee weighing eighty pounds. Sister and I were up until midnight packing and fastening up the boxes and sack, and Mr. Walker set off with them yesterday morning. . . . Today there was a coronation at the other end of town. Our children, and indeed, almost everyone in town attended. <u>Leonora H.</u> was queen! (As the Yankees dub their new-fledged war aristocrats 'shoddy' I think we may call ours 'blockade-running aristocrats.') She shone resplendent in a crown of gilt paper and artificial flowers. The dinner was abundant and nice. The girls down here are going to have a

May party next Saturday, and Belle is to be the queen. . . . The ladies are going to commence teaching tomorrow. Those who are willing to teach met here this evening to choose a principal to whom they will report monthly. They, of course, elected Sister. . . . Amelia McCarroll told me of the murder of Dr. Glover at Grenada recently by one of his Negroes. When he attempted to correct the Negro's wife, the man sprang up and cut his head open with an axe, killing him instantly. Mattie Shaw saw him raise the axe, and sprang before her father, and the axe slipped and cut her severely on the shoulder. It is such a horrible thing. . . . I have no definite idea of the condition of our affairs, but am afraid it is very bad. Last Wednesday we were much buoyed up by a dispatch from General Marcus Wright at Grenada to Captain Bonner here,[27] announcing an armistice, and followed by one from Captain Henderson, instructing him to call in his scouts. Rumors were rife of French intervention-a French fleet was actually reported to be at New Orleans-and many regarded the truce as a precursor of peace.[28] Thursday, however, blasted all such hopes. The armistice was agreed upon between Johnston and Sherman in order to effect an arrangement for peace between their respective countries. It seems not to have extended to this department, for the Yankees have never regarded it, but have made prisoners of several of our men, among them Captain Bonner, who went home expecting to enjoy the first quiet visit there he had had for four years. Now that I have seen the terms upon which the peace (?) would have been based I am delighted to know hostilities are renewed-a return to the Union, a bowing to Federal authority, the laying down of our arms, the acknowledgement that what we have been fighting for all along was wrong, the branding of our noble dead as traitors-no! Extermination were better than submission to such humiliating terms.[29] But it shows the cruel spirit of the North and their wicked intentions towards the South to know that they refused the terms Sherman proffered 'because they were too liberal to the Confederates, re-establishing slavery and abolishing confiscation,' and even talked about relieving Sherman of his command. I have spent the entire past week in a state of mind almost indescribable. Contending hopes and fears, alternate indignation and despair have agitated and filled me. Every few hours contradictory reports about Lee's army have reached us, but now the most sanguine have begun to realize the possibility of Lee's having surrendered, and I have given up all hope on the subject. A thousand wild rumors fill the air, and truth can be obtained from no quarter. Lincoln's assassination is confirmed, though Seward was, at last accounts, recovering. Andy Johnson, the renegade, the Tory, is the Yankee president. He will doubtless show little mercy towards the South if she is conquered, and if she continues to resist, will conduct the war on more barbarous principles than his predecessor. J. Wilkes Booth is universally considered to have killed Lincoln. Though I doubt the wisdom of the policy, I feel unbounded admiration for him. I regarded him with horror, as an assassin, until I read in the Chicago Times a letter written by Booth last November and signed in January, explaining his sentiments, and vindicating some act he seemed to contemplate performing. He was actuated by the noblest patriotism, the most perfect self-abnegation, the most exalted Christian feeling-he voluntarily relinquished all fortune, profession, fame, home, and friends; and espoused hardship, obscurity, danger, risked death itself, for the love he bore the cause of the South. His letter expresses his feelings forcibly and eloquently. Sister says it deserves to become classic. The Yankees canonize Lincoln, and are leaving no stone unturned to discover Booth's whereabouts. Oh, may the same kind Providence which preserved him in the theatre protect him now! After tea Capt. Dick Holland[30] came in and sat two or three hours. He does not at all believe that Lee's army has surrendered. Says no official intelligence of Lee's surrender has been received, and actually seemed to think those who did believe it, wanting in patriotism. But I told him those who cling to it, as if it were everything, showed less patriotism than those who could believe it gone and still hope and fight for the Confederacy. [31]

"Confederate Deserters Desecrate Presbyterian Church"

Bullet holes in the bricks-evidence of this incident-may still be seen around the front door of the Holly Springs Presbyterian Church. In 1995, when the church's heart-pine floors were refinished, two Civil War bullets were found embedded in the wood. Their trajectory seems to have been on a line from the gallery into the north aisle.[32]

Tuesday, May 2, 1865. *Sister and I walked down to Mrs. Craft's to try to hear some news. While we were sitting there, heard five or six pistol shots. Stell and I went to the door, and saw four or five soldiers-drunk-spurring their horses over the town cistern, riding furiously about the square, firing their pistols and swearing. All the gentlemen had retreated from the square and taken refuge around the corner of the Presbyterian church. I am sorry to see men wearing our uniform so disgracing themselves. These men were some of Fort's who refused to go South, and I suppose felt perfectly reckless since they had become deserters.*

Thursday, May 4, 1865. *Heard today Booth had been discovered in a barn near Bowling Green, Caroline County, Va. by the Yankees and killed, shot through the head. We have everything to depress us. . . .*

Sunday, May 7, 1865. *Capt. Fort's company was in town today. They went to Baldwin to join Col. McCullough, but found everything surrendered, and came back. Capt. Fort disbanded his men today, leaving it to their discretion how they will act now. For himself he wishes to cross over to Kirby Smith. Two of his men, Carey Newsome and Mr. Mackay, took dinner with us today. Carey was feeling dreadfully. Said he was ashamed to show his face to his mother and sisters, that he was almost 'plum crazy.' Poor fellows! I am so sorry for them. To think they have fought so gallantly and endured so much, and now have to give up.*

Monday, May 8, 1865. *Have heard no further news today. Everyone seems much depressed. We are expecting the paroled soldiers home. This evening saw two passing Missourians, just from prison-to find the cause lost. Walked down to Mrs. Craft's. Got a beautiful bouquet of roses.*

"Lida had her hair fixed in the most ridiculous Yankee fashion"

Cora Watson was most unforgiving of anything that appeared to indicate sympathy for or fraternity with the North, including her neighbor's new hairstyle. Meanwhile Senator Watson was on his way home. It was said that he had to pawn his watch to obtain money for the trip.

Tuesday, May 9, 1865. *Lida and Rosa came in to see us today. Lida had her hair fixed in the most ridiculous Yankee fashion and did not look pretty at all-Two soldiers, Mr. Davis (a paroled soldier from Lee's army) and Mr. Charles Thomas (formerly of Johnston's army) who is returning from a visit to Kentucky and is not yet paroled) came in about 11 o'clock and remained until evening with us. Mr. Davis looked so sad. He had two brothers killed in our army, and I can understand the feeling with which he lays down arms and goes home-whipped. Perrin Fant,[33] Bob McLean,[34] and Mr. Nunnally[35] got home from Lee's army today. Bob McLean saw Father at West Point, Ga., coming home. He said he was very sad. The cadets were disbanded the evening Richmond was given up, and we suppose Jimmie is with his relations and will come home as soon as possible. This evening quite a number of soldiers are in town from Forrest's and other commands, going home. I suppose Amp and Branscome will be coming on in a day or two. A month today since Lee surrendered.*[36]

IX. A Popular Merchant Slain

When completed in 1858, Christ Church, Holly Springs was acclaimed one of the region's most beautiful churches, and the parish enjoyed no small measure of success. Organs were rare in the pioneer west (which this part of the South still was) during the 1850s. Trains had just begun to bring luxuries others took for granted, and by no means did all churches even in the prosperous East have an organ. A few Presbyterians and others still eschewed musical instruments on theological grounds. But the labors of music teachers had begun to sway old resolves, and most churches lacking an organ, enjoyed the artistry of a violinist or 'cellist, until the day came when financial reserve gave way and an organ was installed.[1]

One Sunday in 1862, Christ Church's rector, the Rev'd J. T. Pickett, found himself confronted by Federal troops, who ordered him to refrain from reading the prayers required by his Church on behalf of the Confederate President, or be shot. Witnesses said that he ignored their commands and continued the service.[2] The soldiers withdrew, but the church was taken over for a stable. The altar became a feeding trough, and the pipe organ was dismantled. Helen Craft Anderson told how the soldiers went through the town blowing crude tunes upon the pipes. (The congregation eventually received $600 from the U. S. government for damage done by the occupation forces.)³

As soon as hostilities ended, members went to work raising money for a new instrument. Singers from all the churches banded together to perform an oratorio, which the town turned out to attend.

Meanwhile, Belle lets us know some of the local sentiment surrounding the death of President Lincoln and capture of his assassin, John Wilkes Booth. But closer to hand, a horrific incident perpetrated by renegade Southern troops aroused the town's ire.⁴ James Henry Nelson, who lived in the house now known as "Grey Gables," on E. College Ave., was a respected citizen who worked on the town square. Nelson had sheltered his neighbor J. W. Clapp, when the latter was pursued by a Union raiding party, and the Nelson household once suffered the loss of forty barrels of salt to Federal soldiers. This time, the offence was at the hands of Southerners, making it even more difficult to bear.⁵

Tuesday, May 9th 1865. *I have not written in my journal for a long time but I will again try to keep it up. We went in school yesterday and knew all of our lessons very well. We are going to have a cantata here for the Episcopal Church to try and get an organ⁶ for the church, and I have to sing in it. We went to practice yesterday because we have to practice every evening.⁷ While I was not writing in my book Lincoln was killed by Mr. Booth who has since been killed for it. Papa has been up here. He came Wednesday night and went away day before yesterday. The Yankees were in here Wednesday and Thursday and stayed all day both days. They were away Thursday evening and have not been in here since. Friday night the robbers came in here and took Mr. Nelson uptown and wanted to get in his store but he did not have the key. Mr. Winborn⁸ had the key and threw it down when he found out what they wanted. When they saw Mr. Nelson and Mr. Winborn talking to each other, they fired at Mr. Winborn but did not hit* him at first, but hit him in the shoulder the second time.⁹ They shot at Mr. Nelson and hit him right through the head after they had popped three caps on him. He died that night at four o'clock. . . .

"Cora Watson's Account of the Nelson Incident, May 6, 1865"

So stunning have been the events of the time that a space to be reckoned by years seems to intervene since I wrote last. Local and public calamities of the most horrible nature have followed each other so rapidly, the whole community seems bewildered, stunned. I feel, as I always do under the first shock of a great sorrow, a crushing sense of some terrible blow, without realizing its nature or extent. I have wept so many and such bitter tears that my eyes seem on fire and my brain benumbed.¹⁰. . .Late in the afternoon yesterday Mother and I walked out to the graveyard, and coming back, met Hal and some other boys who told us the Yankees were in town, and a moment after we heard they were Fort's men. We walked on and, just as we were turning Dr. Smith's corner, met two, who asked us if Mr. Nelson lived there. Mother told him, 'No, Mr. Nelson lived at the end of this street.' When they galloped madly off, I said to Mother, 'What desperate, reckless-looking men they are.' One, the one who spoke to us, had long, waving, glossy black hair reaching his shoulders, and a dark, Spanish face. He wore a black hat fastened up at the side with a star as large as the palm of my hand. I told Mother he had a bad face, I thought. We stopped at Mrs. Hull's gate, where all the ladies of the family were standing, and found that the soldiers or men in town were not of Fort's company, but were regarded with much suspicion by the people on account of their mysterious behavior and ruffianly [sic] appearance. Many of them were in Yankee clothes, and almost everybody at the gate said they knew they were a band of robbers and prophesied that the town would 'go up' that night. But I thought it was doubtless a guerilla company of our men, probably Quantrell's who were said to have passed through town four or five days before, and so felt not the least anxiety or fear. . . .A little while after, as we were in the sitting room talking, we heard three or four shots in town, and thought some of the soldiers were drunk and firing their pistols in the air. Eddie seemed to mistrust the men. He had seen them all, and said he expected they were firing at some of the citizens. But we all rebuked him for speaking so of our soldiers, said we could understand so well, and sympathize with, the feelings of brave Southern men now, driven to desperation by the loss of our Cause. Mother and I walked to the front door, and just then the command came down our street from town, and we near the gate. As they came on by, Mother said, 'Are you our men?' and one answered, 'We are Confederate soldiers.'. . .After passing the corner of the yard, one rode back and asked, 'Are you Union people or rebels?' Mother said, 'You will find nothing but rebels here.' He said, 'Ladies, we were in this town five or six days ago and we couldn't buy a thing with our money, couldn't get a chew of tobacco with it, and we have taken a few things we wanted,' and Mother said, 'I can't blame you,' and asked to what command they belonged. He answered 'Texas Rangers.' Then I said, 'They have fought so gallantly, I feel so much sympathy for them.' He started off then, and Mother asked him to come in and get supper, and he declined and rode away. . . .His manner was so respectful and his vindication of the behavior he represented them as [wording unclear]. Besides he spoke in a rather excited manner, and his voice trembled, and we said, 'Poor fellow! His only pay Confederate money, and his home way off in Texas, we cannot blame him!' We heard several shots soon after this, and while we were sitting at the supper table heard screams. We ran out, and were told the soldiers were behaving badly at Mr. Nelson's. We started down that way to see if we could find out anything about the disturbance, and were overtaken by Church,[11] who told us that Mr. Nelson had been shot in the head, and he was going for Dr. Dancy. We were horror-struck and came back home. . . .Saw Dr. Dancy returning from town, and Eddie ran out to enquire about Mr. Nelson. He was shot, Dr. Dancy said, for refusing to give up his store key. The wound was in the head, and Dr. Dancy said he was insensible and in a very bad condition. . . .They say the men went to Mrs. Nelson's after shooting her husband, killed the dog in the yard, and went into Mrs. Nelson's drawers and trunks, taking Mr. Nelson's and Tommie's clothes (I have since heard, not leaving enough to shroud Mr. Nelson) and Willie's watch. They made Mrs. Nelson sit down, and one put his pistol to her breast, and told her he would shoot her if she stirred, and another fired his pistol in the house to frighten her. She did not know Mr. Nelson was shot, but one of the men told her they had 'hurt the old man a little.' It was after they left that she gave the screams we heard and started down in town, thinking there was a command there, and that she could get protection. When Church told her about Mr. Nelson, she fainted and was carried home, has fainted several times since, and raves deliriously. Oh, how sorry I am for her, poor woman! While the horror of this black deed is still brooding over us comes in quick succession news (which leaves no longer a doubt of Lee's surrender) of the arrival of numbers of paroled soldiers from the Army of Northern Virginia in Meridian; of Johnston's surrender to Sherman; of Dick Taylor's surrender yesterday morning of his Western department to Canby, which surrender includes Gen. Forrest's and Gen. Maury's commands; and of the escape of President Davis,[12] Vice-President Stephens, Secretary Benjamin, and Generals Beauregard and Bragg across the Mississippi. And now the last faint hope of our Confederacy is dead, and for our future we have exile from our native land, our kindred, our friends, and the graves of our thrice-happy dead-or a more unendurable alternative, ceaseless humiliation, oppression, worse than slavery to a race whom we already hate and loathe. Jimmie Crump got up from Grenada today. Says there is not a soldier west of the Mississippi-all are prisoners. Says he expects to be at home for good in a week. Captain Mickle wrote his wife word that he would come home soon and go to work for her and the children. Major Strickland is going down tomorrow with Jimmie Crump. He ran away yesterday evening at the rumor of Yankees, but came back this morning-We have had a pleasant evening, though all felt the shadow which is resting over us.[13]

"Federal Occupation Forces Arrive"

Mississippi was occupied for years by troops sent to oversee Federal reconstruction of the state. Three companies were stationed at Holly Springs in 1865. In 1866 this force was reduced to 162, who occupied St. Thomas Hall, the military school for boys. Holly Springs was occupied until 1875-longer than any other city except Jackson. The soldiers' presence was bitterly resented by citizens.[14]

Wednesday, May 10, 1865. *Cousin Sue and Mason walked around after supper and spent the evening. Say the Yankees will be here tomorrow to occupy the town. Mrs. Cage came out from Memphis today bringing the news. I never was so displeased at the idea of seeing them. I am more rebellious than ever. I have been reading today some Yankee papers brought out of Memphis by Mrs. Craft, and their tone is in the last degree insulting to the South. General Ord,[15] commanding at Richmond, issues an order designating some obscure hotel in that city as a place of entertainment for paroled rebel officers and soldiers. Those occupying rooms at the Spottswood House are requested to vacate them immediately, and the proprietors are ordered to entertain no more 'rebel military men.' And the same Yankee officer offers passports and transportation to such of our paroled men as wish to go to Europe. I might think these ebullitions of mean spite from some low Yankee-a la 'Beast Butler'[16]-would be received with disapproval by the government, but from something from a higher source, I see they represent the spirit and policy of the administration. Secretary Stanton writes to ask Attorney-General Speed if paroled rebel men shall return to their homes in Washington, and other 'loyal localities,' and whether they shall wear their uniforms. Speed answers to the first, certainly not, that places once their homes in such localities are no longer so, and to the second he returns as decided a negative. 'It is just as bad to wear the traitor's garb as to carry the traitor's flag, and paroled men wearing it in loyal districts shall be regarded as guilty of a fresh act of hostility.' Magnanimous victors! 'Only wish to restore the Union!' When poor Booth was caught, his captors cut out his heart (after they had shot him in the head) and cut off his head and sent it to a museum. They wrapped his body in a blanket and buried it near a penitentiary, leveling the grave to prevent its recognition.*

Friday, May 12, 1865. *Mr. John C. Walker got up from the South today. Could, of course, make no disposition of our boxes, and they will be brought back. Disbanded soldiers are plundering all the Com-*

missaries and Quartermasters on this line of the R.R. What an unsettled, dreadful condition the country is in.

Saturday, May 13, 1865. *Well, we are under Yankee protection! Our protectors got in about 3 o'clock this afternoon, and have established themselves on the hill by Green Mill's taking Mrs. Cherry's for headquarters. Invited, they say, by the citizens to defend them from robbers and paroled soldiers. Miserable, cowardly, contemptible old wretches! To appeal to the Yankees for favors now, especially the favor (?) of their presence. This morning Miss Diana and Mrs. Minor were in. They are people who deserve liberty, and as they cannot have it here, pine, as we do, for the precious boon in a foreign land. We talked over Brazil and read all there was about the country and examined its situation, etc. in Cotton's atlas. Mother spoke more favorably of the project than I have yet heard her. She seems to have a strong disinclination to leave this country to go to one untried and unknown. Flattering herself into the belief that the Yankees will let us alone now that they have 'restored the Union.'*

"Yankees, Yankees Everywhere"

Hostilities were not nursed endlessly-at least not by all. Dr. Charles Bonner, who had directed the town's military hospital, was one who saw advantages in peace. On the Sunday after occupation troops arrived, he rode to the Federal camp and escorted the colonel and other officers to church. No doubt the gesture eased the way for his rector, who had probably not yet comfortably resolved the issue of reinstating the Prayer Book's intercessions for the President of the United States.[17]

Monday, May 14, 1865. *Yankees, Yankees everywhere-yet behaving, and going on no private property.[18] Dr. Bonner and Mr. Frost went out to the camp and escorted the Yankee colonel and another officer in to church. Episcopal and Methodist churches full of them, none in ours. This evening I went, no Yankees out on the streets or anywhere. Willie heard from his father. Commissariat robbed before he got there. Captain Hudson 'cleaned out at Carthage, by women', soldiers' wives.[19]*

"A Sad Homecoming"

J. W. C. Watson arrived home by a circuitous route, nearly a month after the Confederate Congress was sent packing by Richmond's fall. Penniless and despondent, he no longer displayed his characteristic air of authority. Still, Cora deferred to her father-in-law.

Tuesday, May 15, 1865. *Father got home tonight, much fatigued by his trip. I can scarcely gather from what he says what he thinks is best to be done by us now except 'to be resigned,' and wait for future events to decide our course of action.*

Saturday, May 20, 1865. *All the store-houses in town are rented by Yankee merchants, and in two weeks the town will teem with Yankee shop-keepers and their boys. Lowenstein intends putting in a branch of his store here. Levy and Rhine are coming back.[20] A Mr. Cameron has also engaged a store, and a Yankee Brigadier (of Negroes) was out this week making arrangements for the setting up of a friend of his in a drug store. I suppose that for the present we can do no better than endure. Father says that it would be next to impossible for him to leave the country. The Yankees have made a law preventing rebels from selling real estate, pronouncing all such sales null and void. Father could not dispose of his property, and we would not even have means to get to a foreign country on. Father says he will wait and see if we can live here. I am sure he will do right.[21]*

Sunday, May 21, 1865. *All went to church this morning. Seven Yankees at our church, two officers. It seems so strange to see our men in their gray suits[22] and the Yankees in blue, all sitting together so quietly. Mr. Paine preached a good sermon, teaching submission and resignation to the will of God in all afflictions of his providence. Let the Yankees know we were in distress.[23]*

Friday, May 26, 1865. *For two weeks I have given Sister some assistance in her school, hearing Willie and Belle read in Scottish history (Tales of a Grandfather) and spell for an hour, and hearing Helen and Eddie read Roman History for an hour.*

"Desolation on the LaGrange Road"

The LaGrange highway which made its way through Hudsonville and Lamar was once the site of many plantations. The road saw troop movements by Sherman and Grant, as well as Confederate forces, so that by war's end all but two or three of the plantations had been broken up, the fences destroyed, houses burned, and the land left fallow to erode. Cora Watson's account corroborates scenes portrayed by many observers:

Thursday, June 1, 1865 *[en route to Tennessee] Father was not well, and Cousin Charles drove me up today. The ride was not a pleasant one, if physical comfort be taken into consideration, though I enjoy the society of Cousin Charles and Cousin George. Cousin Charles showed me the scene of his capture, and gave me a full account of it. The Yankees have destroyed the houses so on the road[24] that we could get no water to drink, and ate dinner without any. Cousin Charles got me some dew-berries, which were as refreshing as water. Drove into Col. Worsham's to drink and water the horses. Two young ladies came out, and taking a broad hint from Cousin George, invited him in to wash his face. He came out again looking quite radiant, and told us that after his ablutions were over, the prettiest of the girls had combed his hair. I told him he must credit her patriotism with it.[25] It was evening, and as we were entering the town we met squad after squad of Yankees going down to the river to water their horses. Many of them Negroes. In town saw [President] Johnson's proclamation. All civil officers of our Confederate government, all officers in the army above the rank of colonel and in the navy above the rank of lieutenant, all persons educated at military schools by the U. S. government, all persons whose property exceeds $20,000, and <u>perhaps some other classes</u> which I have forgotten, are excluded from amnesty. Got to Uncle's about sundown.*

X. Miss Lizzie Expands Her Educational Efforts

After teaching for a year in her home, Elizabeth Watson was busy with educational plans in the summer of 1865. We gain a clue to her thinking from Cora Watson's diary, August 3, 1865, during her visit to Covington, Tenn.: "Mrs. Murdaugh and Mrs. Barrett got back yesterday from Holly Springs bringing me a letter from Sister containing astounding news of a 'Select School for Young Ladies' at the 'residence of J. W. C. Watson,' under Sis. Lizzie's superintendence." The idea for Elizabeth Watson's "Select School for Young Ladies" grew out of work she had done with neighborhood children in the fall of 1864 and the spring of 1865, whom she and Cora had taught in the rear parlor of her father's home. With the town's Female Institute in ruins, a different approach was needed. Elizabeth Watson was a pioneer, and the school she conceived would have a great impact. At first, the effort was conceived or at least justified as a way to raise money to send her brother to college, Judge Watson being unable to educate his son through his now-crippled law practice. As Cora confided to her journal, "I am very sorry the privacy of our home is to be invaded by four school-girl boarders, but I suppose it is necessary and must be submitted to. The object is a noble one-to send Jimmie to the University of Virginia. That only reconciles me to it."[1] Elizabeth Watson's school became a fixture of the community, and she was revered for her service. But before Belle describes her school days, she tells of a honeymoon on the rail and the series of weddings that followed.

"Miss Carrie and Mr. Jimmy Crump Went to Memphis Last Night on the Cars"

Until 1884, when the Kansas City, Memphis & Birmingham Railroad laid tracks through Holly Springs, train travel to Memphis was by way of the famous "Grand Junction," in Tennessee. The trip on the Mississippi Central Railroad, though faster than stagecoach, was still tedious, and schedules left much to be desired. Ten and a half hours were required to make the northbound trip, with long, dreary waiting at Grand Junction before changing to the Memphis & Charleston line, and high fares.[2] A European on his way from New Orleans to the East Coast, wrote in 1861 that "it was a relief to get out of the train for a few minutes" at Holly Springs, Miss., "where the passengers breakfasted at a dirty table on most execrable coffee, cornbread, rancid butter, and very dubious meat."[3]

Thursday, November 30th 1865. *I have been going to school ever since Sept. and have not had much time to write in my journal lately. There are three or four cases of smallpox in town now and Miss Lizzie has stopped teaching school for two weeks but will take up today. Miss Cora Watson has gone to Tenn. Eddie will go after her tomorrow. Miss Carrie Smith and Mr. Jimmie Crump got married last night.[4] Everything was so pretty. . . . There were eight waiters and one pair was Jennie Mickle and Brodie Hull. All of them had on white kid gloves. Papa is going to Canton tonight. I am writing for Wednesday though I dated it Thursday at the top. We did not have regular school today because Miss Cora wasn't here. She has nine classes, I believe, and Miss Lizzie could not hear them all. Miss Carrie and Mr. Jimmy Crump went to Memphis last night on the cars. They want to stay there until Monday. Several persons are going to give them parties. Next*

Thursday Miss Julia Little is going to be married. Next Tuesday Miss Mit Finley is going to be married, too, and the next Tuesday, a week after Miss Mit's marriage, Miss Mary Jane Dancy is going to be married. They say that Miss Amelia McCarroll is going to marry Mr. Williamson and Mr. Walthall, too, and we don't know which she will marry.[5]

Thursday, November 30th 1865. *I got up right early and went to studying as soon as I was dressed. Soon after breakfast I took my music lesson for half an hour. I then came back and wrote in my journal about yesterday. I then learned my geography, and said my grammar, and then said my geography. At twelve we had recess 'till half past twelve. As soon as recess was over we said our Mental Arithmetic 'till one. I then ciphered three quarters of an hour. As soon as school was over and I had eaten my dinner. . . .I then read some in "Swiss Family Robinson." I played some backgammon with Miss Corrinne Leggett.*[6] *Miss Clara Clayton staid all night with us last night and staid 'till dinner. I will study my lesson tonight.*

Friday, December 1st 1865. *I got up this morning and studied my lesson and then dressed Minnie and ate my breakfast. We went in school but there were not many here. I knew all of my lesson and came out of school very glad. I did not practice this evening because I went to sewing and forgot about it. I will study my lesson for Monday tonight.*

"Dr. Butler Came and Vaccinated Us"

Dr. Jasper F. Butler, who had come to Holly Springs from Arkansas, owned a pharmacy on the square where Tyson's Drug Store is now.[7] He was prominent in local social circles.[8]

Saturday, December 2nd 1865. *I got up soon this morning and, as I had no studying to do, I read some. After breakfast I went to* *sewing again and did not stop in a long time. Dr. Butler came this evening and vaccinated all of us. It hurt right bad at first but it stopped soon. Miss Cora got home and said that the reason that she [did not arrive] the day before was because Eddie wanted to stay and hunt.*

"A Court Said There Should Be No Public Meetings"

The U. S. authorities, treating Mississippi and other Southern states as occupied territories, instituted harsh measures, which saw the regular suspension of constitutional privileges, including the right to the free exercise of religion and the right of public assembly. The dictates of the military court upset the community so much that even Miss Lizzie gave up trying to hold classes.

Sunday, December 3rd 1865. *A court was held the other day saying that there should be no public meetings and stopped church and Sunday school. There was therefore no church and we all stayed at home. I read some in my Bible and several other books. This evening I learned the hymn that begins, "Look, ye saints, the sight is glorious," and then we all sang some.*

"Professor Tepe, French Confederate"

John Mickle remembered Professor F. A. Tepe as "an able teacher of music at Franklin Female College, a polished Frenchman and a fine musician."[9] He directed the production of *Belshazzar's Feast*, given before a capacity audience in the Methodist Church. His studio was the meeting hall for the Holly Springs Philharmonic Society. He proved his devotion to the Confederacy, volunteering for the "Home Guards," whose members represented many of the families that supported the town's academies and music organizations.[10]

Miss Lizzie Expands Her Educational Efforts

Monday, December 4th 1865. *It rained very much last night and is raining still. I don't believe that there will be many scholars today. As I have to dress Minnie every morning I did so this morning.*[11] *After breakfast when it was school time and we were ready to go in school, there [weren't] but two scholars in school, for Miss Corinne had stayed with Mrs. Minor*[12] *last night. We did not say all of our lessons. . . .Miss Lizzie thinks that everything is so irregular that she will turn out school. I did not take my music lesson today because I did not know that Mr. Tepe had come back.*

Tuesday, December 5th 1865. *Miss Lizzie turned out school this morning and none of the scholars knew it, but Miss Corinne and I. I was very anxious for tonight to come because Miss Mit Finley was going to be married to Mr. Thornwell Dunlap. This evening we heard that Miss Julia Little and Mr. Hugh McGehee were going to be married tonight too. We are going tonight with Mr. Watson.*

"A Church Wedding"

Weddings of this period were usually solemnized at home, and when vows were spoken in the church, the ceremony was utterly simple-often conducted before or after the Sunday service. However, a trend toward church weddings had begun, and Belle describes one of the earliest on record in Holly Springs. The town must have buzzed as two dear friends attended each other as maid and matron of honor at their nuptial occasions, both on the same evening. Weddings for servants were also common, though humbler occasions, as the events of the following day reveal.

Wednesday, December 6th 1865. *We went to the wedding last night. The church was trimmed mighty prettily and everything looked beautiful.*[13] *Miss Mit waited on Miss Julia at home and then went to the church and Miss Julia waited on her after she* was married. *Miss Clara Clayton and another scholar came today but there was no school. Miss Clara stayed all day with us and will stay all night too. She taught me how to play chess this evening.*

A Slave Wedding

John W. Blassingame wrote that, concerned about the impact of sexual immorality on both blacks and whites, Presbyterians, Methodists, Baptists, and Episcopalians "all devoted a great deal of attention to the wedding ceremony in the quarters." Although some masters would not permit slaves to have marriage ceremonies (so as to make separation of spouses easier when sold), others would have the white minister or black plantation preacher perform the wedding and then give a feast in their own parlors for the couple and their guests.[14]

Thursday, December 7th 1865. *Miss Clara wrote to her Ma yesterday to send for her as soon as possible and Miss Corinne will go home with her I expect when they come after her. Mrs. Hull has a servant that is going to be married tonight and Miss Susan and Miss Betsy has been making cakes for her.*[15]

"Judge Clayton Came for Miss Clara"

Alexander Mosby Clayton (1801-1889), close friend and political ally of Judge Watson's, was influential in public affairs. Born in Virginia, he read law at Lynchburg and was admitted to the bar in 1823. In 1836, President Jackson appointed him federal judge for the Arkansas Territory, and later he moved to Marshall County and practiced law in Holly Springs. In 1842, he was appointed to the Mississippi Supreme Court where he served eight years and established a reputation as a master of jurisprudence. He was a founder of the University of Mississippi, and was a trustee of the institution for much of his adult life. The university awarded him an honorary doctorate in 1859. After appointment as American consul to Havana (1853), he became active in the movements that led to the secession of the Southern states. With L. Q. C. Lamar, he drew up the ordinances of secession creating what some called the Republic of Mississippi in January 1861. Clayton lived at "Woodcote," a country estate a few miles from Lamar. It burned during the Civil War but was rebuilt. Clayton was devoted to his daughter, Clara, who later married Judge Watson's law partner, James T. Fant.[16]

Friday, December 8th 1865. Miss Clara came by for Miss Corinne to go up town with her, and while Miss Corinne was getting ready Cousin Laura Thomas was here. I went up town with them. Miss Clara bought a doll for her niece. When we got home Judge Clayton came for Miss Clara, and Miss Corinne went with her. Miss Cora read to us the rest of the evening.

"Miss Cora Has Been to Tennessee after Her Husband's Corpse"

Belle describes in a matter of fact way the sad journey that Cora Watson had made to bring her husband's remains back to Holly Springs. The Civil War was the first major conflict in which bodies were returned home on a large scale. Meanwhile, Belle goes on to describe her family's quiet celebration of Christmas.[17]

Monday, December 25th 1865. Nothing very particular has occurred since I wrote last with three or four exceptions. Since I wrote last Miss Cora has been to Tennessee after her husband's corpse.[18] She brought him home last Wednesday and he was buried Friday.[19] Friday was Dora's birthday. She, Dora Clark, was eight years old. I was invited to come and eat a cake with her and her sister. I went down at three o'clock and stayed all night with her. I haven't got anything to do these days and I am very lone-

some. *I forgot to say that Tuesday Papa gave [me] a book of queens of England to read by Christmas, which I thought I could do very easily but there were three volumes in one and I cannot read them all. I only read one, which I did very easily by Saturday night, not having read any Friday. We all hung up our stockings and got them very full of good things. We did not get any toys in our stockings but we got them full of candy, raisins, nuts, and all such things. Monday morning we got our presents. I got two bottles of cologne and a candy heart and fish. I also got a cologne bottle. Christmas day I went up to see Aunt Mollie and caught her Christmas gift. I took dinner with Mrs. Govan with Papa, and Mrs. Govan gave Minnie and me some candy and cake which we brought home.*[20]

"Christmas Was a Secular Occasion"

Allen Cabaniss has remarked that whereas the Puritans of New England "looked with suspicion upon Christmas as a 'popish' day...southerners generally encouraged a joyous celebration."[21] Just so, "gentleman farmers, in particular" (with whom the Stricklands and Watsons might be classed socially), "regarded the day more as a time of relaxation and social activity than as a religious holiday."[22] Exotic presents were not unknown, even in these times, and if Senator Watson could find something unusual to give his children, he was ready to do so. Bananas, brought from Central America to New Orleans and somehow smuggled through U. S. lines, filled the bill, even though they arrived from the Crescent City a few days late.

Tuesday, December 26th 1865. *I have not practiced this week, it being Christmas week. Mrs. Hull is going to have a party tomorrow.*[23]

Wednesday, December 27th 1865. *I did not write in my journal Christmas day.*[24] *Every day I read aloud in "Joseph II [?] and* his Court." There will not be any Sunday school this week, I don't think, because Mr. Paine didn't say there would be any.

Friday, December 29th 1865. *Jimmie Watson came up from Oxford last night. Mrs. Hull had her party last night. Papa went to his farm today and will come back this evening I suppose.*

Saturday, December 30th 1865. *Papa came back yesterday evening. He is going to Mrs. Leak's[25] this evening and will be back Monday morning. Soon after dinner Papa brought over a box from New Orleans full of things. He brought a branch of bananas.[26]*

"A Letter from Buddie"

A letter to Belle survives in her brother William Strickland Jr.'s handwriting. It describes a grand tournament held in Holly Springs. A newspaper account of the tournament exists, and it is printed in the endnote below.

Holly Springs, July 9, 1866.

My Dear Sister:

Papa received your letter yesterday dated the 6th talking about your and Kate's play-house and about Miss Mollie's asking you to have something that was not on the table. She used to do me that way, too. Last Tuesday night Mrs. Pugh Govan gave the grown people a party-it was given mostly to Miss Hallie Harrison from Columbus. Hannie Robinson was dead in love with her and carried her to the party. Mr. Hardin Perkins, Mrs. Dawson's son died last Saturday, morning at nine o'clock drunk. They took his remains to Memphis this morning. It is lonesome. I almost wish school was going on. A Mr. Lewis from North Carolina commenced his school here last Tuesday. The boys say he is mighty tight. It is raining right now. Miss Fannie Latimer that gave me that lock of hair is coming up to the Tournament[27] from Canton. The men have got up a good many seats out at the Tournament. Papa is up at the Courthouse now. We miss you very much. I saw Bettie McCarroll[28] this morning and told that I was going to write to you and asked did she have any message to send. She said [she] did not but to tell you that you must make haste and come home and sent her love to you. Minnie and Papa and all of us are well and Willie Govan too. Excuse my writing and don't let any body see it. All of us send our love. Give my love to Mrs. Coffman and all of the family.

                                        Your affectionate

                                        Brother.

XI. Elizabeth Watson and Fenelon Hall

Margaret Burr DesChamps has written that "Presbyterians seem to have taken greater interest in the education of women than did other denominations, although most of their schools were not established until the late antebellum period." This was certainly true in Holly Springs. The Watsons and others in the Presbyterian Church had been greatly interested in the Holly Springs Female Institute, and though it was not formally affiliated with the church, it could not have succeeded without Presbyterian patronage. But the town's most prestigious nineteenth century educational effort was a Presbyterian venture, and in these entries Belle describes its genesis.[1] In 1865 William Clark, assisted by Elizabeth Watson, had begun a girls' school in what is now the old Buchanan home on College Ave. It was called Fenelon Hall, in memory of François Fenelon, the celebrated French pedagogue. The next year Clark taught separately, and Watson began her "Select School for Young Ladies" in the rear parlors of her father's home. It continued the name Fenelon Hall.[2] As Belle's comments indicate, the school made a very modest beginning.

> *Monday, February 3rd 1868.* 1 have decided to commence my journal again and hope that I shall be able to continue it. Two years have passed since I last wrote in it and of course a great many things have transpired within that long time.[3] I have been

going to school regularly ever since to Miss Lizzie and Mr. Clark. Last ten months Miss Lizzie and Mr. Clark taught together and I went to them but Miss Lizzie did not teach the next session and Miss Lucilla Reed took her place. I went to school there last five months and commenced studying algebra, which is very interesting. I think Miss Lizzie commenced teaching yesterday again and I started to her on the third of February. I came to school and found only one scholar, Miss Fannie Phillips, and we selected our desk and are sitting together. We did not say any lessons but staid there and read until nearly one o'clock and then went home to dinner. I returned in the afternoon and ciphered in algebra until four o'clock and was dismissed. In the evening I read some before supper and also afterwards. Then I retired to sleep.

Tuesday, February 4th 1868. *I rose very early to learn my Familiar Science lesson and after breakfast came to school where I found Miss Lizzie but not Miss Fannie as it was snowing very hard indeed. I recited my Familiar Science lesson, which was about the flame of a candle. I was working my examples in arithmetic when Miss Fannie came in. I learned a Mental Arithmetic [lesson] with her at twelve o'clock, and then Miss Lizzie dismissed us for dinner. I did not go back in the afternoon because I thought Mr. Stanford was going to give me either a music or drawing lesson, but he did not come. Papa told me to carry him a note as soon as it ceased raining. Late in the evening I went to Professor Stanford's but nearly mired up in the mud. He was not at home so I came home. After supper Mama baked some cakes and after she finished I retired.*[4]

Wednesday, February 5th 1868. *I came to school this morning and no one was there and I was very sorry not to find Miss Fannie there. Miss Lizzie came in after a while and I recited my Familiar Science. The lesson was of metals and was very interesting. I then ciphered in algebra and while I was doing so Mr. Paine taught*

Miss Rosa and Lilla. So we have four scholars. Miss Cora is not very well so we will not read.[5] We have heard of another scholar and, I suppose, before long Miss Lizzie will have a nice little school.

"Algebra and Shakespeare Were Subjects Studied"

The organization of Fenelon Hall was typical of schools for young ladies in the nineteenth century. Belle and her classmates studied the Bible and practical subjects, such as "Familiar Science," but also Shakespeare, algebra, and French. Indeed, these subjects were introduced at a younger age than is customary today. Vocal and instrumental lessons were also available.

Thursday, February 6th 1868. Yesterday evening after I returned home I began looking at some puzzles and was employed in this manner until night. I found them very interesting indeed especially the geographical ones. This morning I recited my Familiar Science, the subject of which was metals and glass. The latter subject was the most interesting one of the two because it is the most uncommon. My algebra lesson was about extraction of square root. Miss Cora heard our reading lesson today and we commenced the play "As You Like It." I am very fond of Shakespeare indeed and was very glad when Miss Cora made us read in it.

Friday, February 7th 1868. Last evening I went in the parlor and staid a long time waiting for Mr. Stanford to come and give me my lessons for he said he was coming at three o'clock. But he did not come until nearly four, so I was a little disappointed, fearing that he would not come. He came, though, and gave me a French and music lesson. I like French very much so far but it has scarcely been long enough to judge yet a while. He gave me three or four pieces of music to learn and said that he would come again next Tuesday to continue my lessons. He would have come Saturday but he had some business in the country. He did not give me a drawing lesson for he did not have time. This morning I recited my Familiar Science lesson, which was a review. We finished the play in the reading class.

"Shopping on the Square"

During Reconstruction white women feared what they saw as brash behavior by black persons. But Belle was young, and was allowed to go "to town" to buy school supplies and other things. Meanwhile, without prompting from the adults in her life she went to Sunday school and was devoted to Mrs. Calkins, her teacher.

Monday, February 10th 1868. Friday evening I went up town and stayed up there nearly the whole evening.[6] It was very windy indeed so that it was not very pleasant shopping.[7] I learned my French lesson after supper and wrote the exercise also. Janette and her family came that morning and on Saturday she commenced cooking, and Aunt Harriet[8] went to find a place. Papa had the headache all the evening and Sunday too.[9] I went to Sunday school and Mrs. Calkins,[10] who is my teacher, was not there, as it looked very much like rain. Bettie and I came home before Sunday school was dismissed because we thought it was going to rain. We just did reach home before it rained very hard. Every Sunday night we always read in the Bible, and we are reading in Isaiah now. I like it very much and besides being a good way to spend our nights it is very improving. This morning I came to school in a hard but very pretty snowstorm. I did not want to come much because I did not think there would be many scholars. I recited my Familiar Science, which was about sugar. We read a part of "Hamlet" and then we wrote.

"Snow in Holly Springs"

It snows in Holly Springs once or twice a year. Then, as now, school was usually dismissed on these occasions.

Belle's Home
Cover painting by Herndon Davis, noted painter of early American homes.
Originally commissioned for the Memphis Commercial Appeal (April 13, 1941).

CIVIL WAR WOMEN

Chesley Thorne Smith with her doll, Belle, given to her in childhood by her "Aunt Belle" Strickland. (No photo of Belle Strickland is known to exist.) Photo from the collection of Chesley Thorne Smith.

CIVIL WAR WOMEN

Perle Strickland Badow stands between the unusual gateposts at the Strickland Place. Photo courtesy of Bart Ryan.

CIVIL WAR WOMEN

John William Clark Watson
Photo from Hines and Allied Families.

Catherine Davis Watson.
Photo courtesy of the Holly Springs
Presbyterian Church.

The J. W. C. Watson Place.
Photo from the collection of Chesley Thorne Smith.

CIVIL WAR WOMEN

Belle's Mother,
Martha Mildred Thomson Strickland.
Photo courtesy of Hubert H. McAlexander.

Belle's Aunt Mollie and Cousin,
Mary Fontana Thomson Hudson
and daughter Fonta.
Photo courtesy of Fonta Woodson O'Dell.

Baker-Hudson-McGuirk Cottage (now known as "Alicia"),
Home of Belle's aunt and uncle, Mary Fontana Thomson and John Lewis Hudson.
Photo by Robert Milton Winter.

CIVIL WAR WOMEN

The Thomson-Walker Place, home of Lewis and Sarah Merrill Thomson, neighbors of the Stricklands and Watsons, now known as "Herndon." Photo courtesy of the Holly Springs Garden Club.

Henry Craft, Judge Watson's junior law partner. Photo from the collection of Chesley Thorne Smith.

Hugh Craft, one of the town's early settlers, close friend of the Strickland and Watson families. Photo from the collection of Chesley Thorne Smith.

CIVIL WAR WOMEN

Presbyterian Manse, home of the Rev'd Henry H. Paine, friend and confidante of the Watson and Strickland families. Pen and ink drawing by William M. Wage.

Edward Minor Watson, "Eddie" in Cora's and Belle's diaries. Photo from Hines and Allied Families.

The minister's daughter and Belle's teacher, Mary Rowland Paine. Painting by Loulie Raymond Anderson

CIVIL WAR WOMEN

Belle's teacher, Professor William Clark.
Photo from Dunbar Rowland,
Mississippi, Heart of the South.

The Rev'd James
Thomas Pickett, D.D.
Photo courtesy of
Christ Episcopal Church.

William Albert Anderson.

Helen Craft Anderson.

CIVIL WAR WOMEN

Negro family in Marshall County in about 1880-a scene reminiscent of those described by Belle Strickland and Cora Watson. Photo by Lem Johnson from the collection of Chesley Thorne Smith.

CIVIL WAR WOMEN

View of the Hull Place, showing its proximity to the Watson home. Photo from the collection of Chesley Thorne Smith.

CIVIL WAR WOMEN

The Walthall-Freeman Home, home of Catherine Watson's friend, Sarah Walthall. Photo courtesy of Hubert H. McAlexander.

CIVIL WAR WOMEN

*Later view of the Gray Washington Smith home (now called "Linden Terrace").
Photo from the collection of Chesley Thorne Smith.*

*Coxe-Topp House
Photo from the collection of Chesley Thorne Smith.*

CIVIL WAR WOMEN

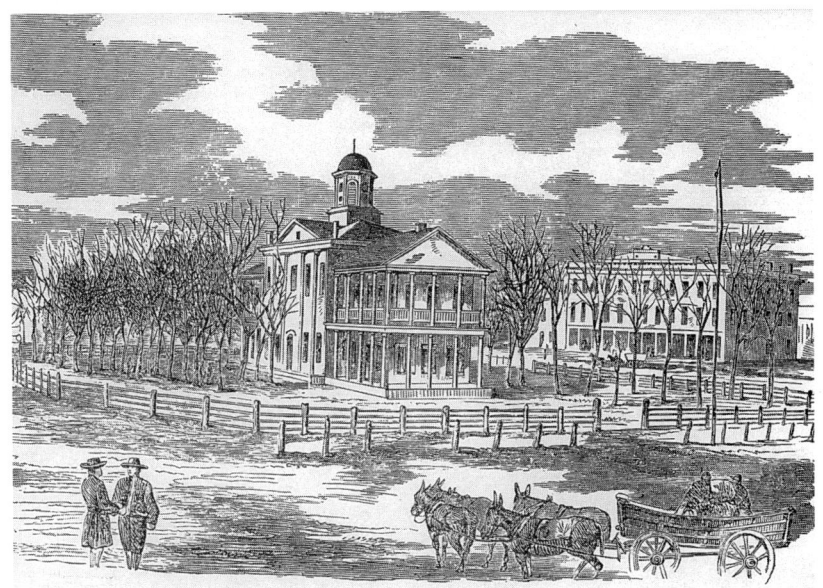

View of the Holly Springs Courthouse that burned in 1864, sketched in December 1862 by A. Simplott, for Harper's Weekly.

*The McWilliams-Jones-McCrosky Place.
Photo courtesy of Mrs. Janice Tyler Calame.*

CIVIL WAR WOMEN

The Holly Springs Foundry, where Belle went "for some tacks," sketched in December 1862 by A. Simplott, for Harper's Weekly.

The McCarroll Place, which stands next to the site of the Strickland house. Pen and ink drawing by Netty Fant Thompson.

CIVIL WAR WOMEN

*Marshall County workers picking cotton, recalling the harvesting and trading of the cotton mentioned in Belle's diary and related correspondence.
Photo from the collection of Chesley Thorne Smith.*

Youngsters play in front of the office that belonged to Col. A. W. Goodrich across the street from the Presbyterian Church. Photo from the collection of Chesley Thorne Smith.

CIVIL WAR WOMEN

*The Hugh Craft Place.
Photo from the collection of Chesley Thorne Smith.*

Later view of the store associated with the murder of James Henry Nelson by marauding ex-Confederates, as described by Belle and Cora in their diaries. Photo by Olga Reed Pruitt.

CIVIL WAR WOMEN

This building which still stands on the Holly Springs square once housed Dr. Butler's drug store. Photo by Olga Reed Pruitt.

The First Methodist Church of Holly Springs, trimmed for a wedding in 1886, such as the one Belle witnessed in 1865. Photo courtesy of Hubert H. McAlexander.

CIVIL WAR WOMEN

*The Holly Springs Baptist Church, erected in 1855.
Painting by Mrs. Tommy Tudor,
Photo courtesy of the Marshall County Museum.*

CIVIL WAR WOMEN

Mississippi Central Railroad Depot and shops in Holly Springs, sketched in December 1862 by A. Simplott, for Harper's Weekly.

CIVIL WAR WOMEN

Old St Joseph's Catholic Church.
Photo from the collection of Chesley Thorne Smith.

Elaborate decorations adorn Christ Church prepared for special service, in this photo taken in 1888. Photo courtesy of Hugh H. Rather.

CIVIL WAR WOMEN

In a scene reminiscent of the day Belle went to town just as a crowd assembled for the delivery of the mail, this photo of 1894 shows the town square with cotton piled high, many wagons, and the tower of Presbyterian Church in background. The two-story building just to the right of the church in the photo is the store where Mr. Nelson was murdered. Photo from the collection of Chesley Thorne Smith.

CIVIL WAR WOMEN

The Confederate monument in Hill Crest Cemetery has seen many decoration ceremonies, such as the ones Belle describes in her diary. Photo from the collection of Chesley Thorne Smith.

CIVIL WAR WOMEN

Scene of the Holly Springs square with an advertisement for a circus, such as the one to which Belle and Miss Lizzie looked forward. Photo courtesy of Hubert H. McAlexander.

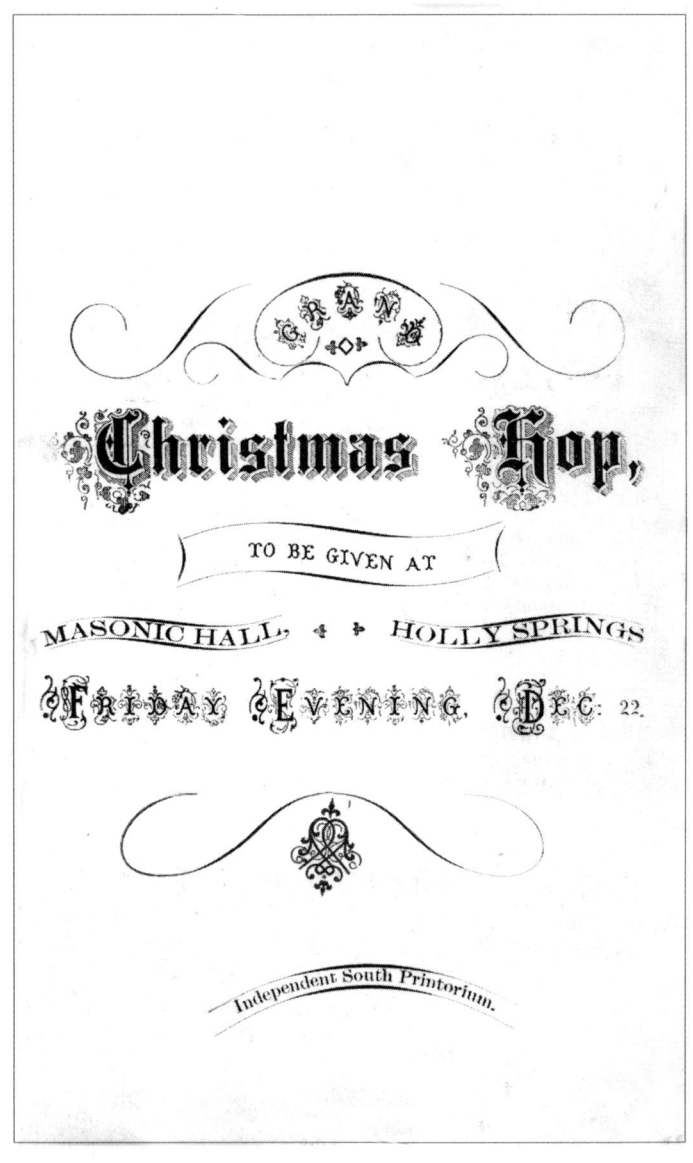

Invitation to a ball in the Masonic Hall, such as the masquerade Belle attended. Courtesy of Hubert H. McAlexander.

CIVIL WAR WOMEN

*The 1870 Masonic Hall decorated for a ball.
Photo from the collection of Chesley Thorne Smith.*

*Boling's mill in Spring Hollow, near the spot where the owner's young son was tragically killed in an accident Belle describes.
Photo courtesy of Hubert H. McAlexander.*

CIVIL WAR WOMEN

Student group at Maury Institute, with Elizabeth Davis Watson and her pupils. "Miss Lizzie" stands in the back row at the far left. Photo courtesy of Hubert H. McAlexander.

CIVIL WAR WOMEN

Sheep are driven past the Baptist Church, where Belle's father was a trustee. The 1870 Masonic Hall can be seen in the background (center), and also the I. C. Levy store at the far left. Photo by Lem Johnson from the collection of Chesley Thorne Smith.

Tuesday, February 11th 1868. *It was snowing very hard all day yesterday and I went home in the snow. It was the prettiest snowstorm I believe that I ever saw. It snowed most of the night, too, I think, and of course this morning the snow is very deep.*[11] *I came to school, though, and my feet were perfectly wet as I came across the street, where nobody had been walking, and the snow came over my shoe tops almost. There was not a single scholar here when I reached here and nobody came and so I had to recite my lessons by myself. There was not enough to read in "Hamlet," and I was afraid that my reading lesson would not be as interesting as usual but Miss Cora found a book of poetry which had some very pretty pieces in it, and I was as much pleased as I would have been reading in Shakespeare by myself. My mythology was quite hard and not very interesting as it was in the introduction. The subject of my Familiar Science was fermentation and wine.*

"Yesterday I Heard of the Death of a Negro who Froze to Death"

After emancipation, Marshall County blacks gradually acquired land and began to farm and raise livestock. The way was not easy, and Belle shows a sensitivity that was sometimes not felt by others for the plight of blacks who suffered.

Wednesday, February 12th 1868. *Last evening Mr. Stanford came and heard my lessons. He staid until quite late and said he was coming again tomorrow. I recited my Familiar Science by myself, the subject of which was bread. I have just finished ciphering and it is time to read. Miss Cora came in and we read in "Hamlet." We finished it and will begin the next play tomorrow. Miss Rosa Paine took the part of Hamlet, and read it very well indeed. Yesterday morning I heard of the death of a Negro who was frozen the night before or Monday night. He went out after some cows and froze to death. His wife went out after him in that* deep snow but could not find him as he was lying in a ditch. She said she heard someone call but did not know that it was him. I suppose that it was him calling in his last moments for her; it is awful to think of.[12] His name was Dick Hampton, and his funeral is to be preached this evening.[13]

"Mama and Papa Went to Memphis Yesterday Evening"

It was part of Holly Springs etiquette to accompany travelers as far as Memphis when they left on extended journeys, and for many years after this writing, ladies would check into a day room at a Memphis hotel to refresh themselves for further shopping or travel.[14]

Thursday, February 13th 1868. Mama and Papa went to Memphis yesterday evening and I hope they will have a pleasant trip. Minnie and I came over to stay with Mrs. Watson and intend staying here until they return. This morning Miss Fannie Phillips came in for the first time this week. Lillie Moore came just now so we have another scholar at last. Our mythology lesson was about the temples erected by the ancients to their deities. We read this morning "Much Ado About Nothing" and I took the part of Beatrice and Miss Rosa the part of Benedict.

"Outdoor Excitement on Valentine's Day"

When Bettie McCarroll came to take a music lesson, the family dog gave chase. The neighbor girl, being unused to dogs, ran, and was much afraid. The excitable "Rip" had other adventures, as Belle's comments reveal, was later bested by some other creature.

Friday, February 14th 1868. Last evening Mr. Stanford came about four o'clock but I was so much excited that I could scarcely play at all. Bettie McCarroll came over to take her vocal lesson, when Rip saw her and ran after her. She ran from him 'till she got to the wall and could go no further, and the dog was trying to get to her throat, but she kept him off until we succeeded in governing him, and then she began crying. But she was not hurt at all; only her dress was torn off of the waist and into half a dozen strips. I was very much frightened; indeed, all of us were. I was so much excited, therefore, that Mr. Stanford said it was almost useless to attempt hearing my music much. Today is Valentine's Day but I had almost forgotten it, and I reckon that scarcely anyone will remember it. Lillie read with us in "Macbeth." We did not quite finish it but nearly, we will finish it Monday. I liked it very much especially the scene where Macbeth saw the Ghost of Banquo.

Monday, February 16th 1868. 1 was very sick Friday evening, and retired quite early. Ruth Bonner staid all night and they played until twelve o'clock but I was so sick that I could not join with them. I was not very well all day Saturday and did not go home until nearly night. Cousin Boothe was there and spent the night but I didn't see him long. I was too unwell to go out Sunday until nearly dark when, as I was expecting Papa and Mama, I went over home. They came and Minnie and I returned home. This morning Miss Mittie Manning came to school and commenced reciting lessons. We finished "Macbeth" and read "As You Like It" again.

Tuesday, February 17th 1868. Yesterday evening I was not very well and retired quite early. This morning the subject of my Familiar Science was "Animal Heat" and was quite interesting. This book teaches of all things right around us; as fire and bread and such things. We finished the play we were reading and commenced "Othello." This was Mythology day and the subject of our lesson was "Sacrifices."

Wednesday, February 18th 1868. *Mr. Stanford came yesterday and Bettie came also to take her vocal lesson. He gave us the song called "Nora O'Neal" and it is very pretty. He brought his paints and pencils and some pictures. This morning the day overhead was quite different from yesterday, being cloudy and damp. I came to school, though, and there was no one here but Lillie. I ciphered an hour and a half in algebra and then we finished "Othello." Miss Cora had been out all day trying to collect something for the orphans at Lauderdale who have nothing either to eat or wear, and the persons who have the care of them say that unless some aid is sent to them they would be obliged to turn them out in the world. I feel so sorry for those poor children who have nothing to depend upon and know not how they can ever get anything. I hope we can always be able to do something for the children of our brave soldiers who fell in the defense of their country; but it will be very hard to do anything for them if this state of things continues. For we can hardly support ourselves.*

Thursday, February 19th 1868. *Yesterday evening I went over to Mrs. McCarroll's to practice and Bettie and I learned two songs "Nora O'Neal" and "Annie Don't You Know?" This morning school was taken up when I got here and I said my lesson right away the subject of which was "Food." My lesson in mythology was quite hard and was also long. We read some in "The Tempest." Mr. Stanford is coming this evening and so I expect to have a pleasant time.*

Friday, February 20th 1868. *Bettie did not come yesterday evening to take her vocal lesson and Mr. Stanford and I were alone. He is coming this evening to give me a French lesson and he is going to try and come every day. This morning school was taken up and I said my lesson immediately. We finished "The Tempest" in reading and read some in "Romeo and Juliet." This is a very sentimental piece and is also tragic. We are going to read* in English Literature three times a week and will commence next week.

"Attending the Baptist Church"

Following a common custom, Belle attended Sunday school in one congregation and divine service in another. Belle was devoted to her Baptist minister, the Rev'd E. D. Miller. A native of Ohio, with forebears who had been Baptist preachers, Elkanah D. Miller represented a new generation of Baptist ministers, in that he was quite well educated. He was a graduate of Georgetown College (1854), coming to Marshall County, three years later, where he married Margaret Ford, a Virginian who was visiting her brother at Ford's Pond (now Spring Lake-the center of Wall Doxey Park, a few miles south of Holly Springs). Before the war, Miller farmed and was pastor of the Holly Springs Baptist Church. During Reconstruction, he preached without salary, taught school and was the county's first superintendent of public education. He served the little congregation which worshiped in a pretty clapboard building on S. Market St., for thirty years, retiring in 1888.

Monday, February 23rd 1868. Friday evening I finished drawing my picture, and then went out to take Mama's place in planting roses, and was employed in this way until night. Saturday morning I wrote my composition and this took up a great deal of my time. I dislike to write compositions very much indeed and especially on such subjects as "Animal Heat," or anything of the kind. I then watered the flowers and while I was there Rosa and Dora Clark came to see me and spent the day. Sunday morning I went to Sunday school and found Mrs. Calkins very glad to see me, I having been sick for several Sundays. I went to church to hear Mr. Miller[15] and he went home to dinner with us. We read after supper and finished Isaiah. This morning I arose and it was very cloudy, and damp and has been looking all day like it was going to rain. We finished "Romeo and Juliet" and are going to-

morrow to read "The Merchant of Venice." The subject of my Familiar Science lesson was "Sleep" and "Acids."

Tuesday, February 22nd 1868. Yesterday I helped mama put down a carpet and we didn't finish until dark. This morning I came to school notwithstanding the clouds floating overhead. The subject of my Familiar Science lesson was "Oils" and a little part of it was of "Poisons," and this was quite interesting. We finished "The Merchant of Venice" today and I took the part of Antonio ...

Wednesday, February 23rd 1868. Mr. Stanford came yesterday evening and staid a very short time. It was raining very hard, but he came in the rain. It was not raining this morning, but it was cloudy and very muddy indeed. "Meteorology" was the subject of my Familiar Science lesson this morning and I enjoyed it very much, but I will have to say a great more such lessons in it. We commenced "King Lear," but did not finish it.

Thursday, February 24th 1868. Mr. Stanford came to hear my French lesson but did not stay any time, scarcely. I tried to paint my picture but did not succeed very well, as I never painted any in my life. Papa and mama are going to Mrs. Leak's tomorrow, and I am going to stay at Mrs. Watson's and will have a pleasant time. The subject of my Familiar Science lesson was the "Barometer," and it was quite hard to memorize and understand. The Furies was the chief subject of my mythology lesson.

Friday, February 25th 1868. Mr. Stanford did not come yesterday evening until nearly five o'clock and then had very little time to hear my lessons. He came this morning to tell me goodbye as he is going to Grenada very soon, and so he will not give me any more lessons. He staid a very short time here, and scarcely gave us time to decide about his teaching or his character. It is nearly *time for papa and mama to start, and I will have to hurry home. Last night I sat up quite late talking to mama and she was quite busy herself, although she was sick. I had a review lesson in Familiar Science this morning and it was very hard indeed. "Meteorology" was the head under which it came and I don't think that I will ever study the large book called by that name if I can help it. We are going to say a lesson in English Literature Monday and "William Shakespeare" is the author we have for our lesson.*

"Dr. Gholson Came to See Me Twice Sunday and Once Monday"

Samuel Creed Gholson, born in Farmville, Va. in 1828, moved to Holly Springs in 1846. A graduate of the Medical College of Virginia, he married Miss Hannah Caruthers, of Holly Springs, and to them were born eight children. Mary Caruthers was a devoted housekeeper, justly famous for her bountiful repasts.[16] Belle's frustration in hearing her minister preach was not due to Mr. Miller's carelessness, but due to the fact that pastors of this era often kept appointments at several churches. (Holly Springs ministers, for example, usually cared for the nearby country congregations of their respective denominations.) Travel by horse or train could render the minister subject to a hundred kinds of delay; hence, missed services were common.[17]

Monday, March 9th 1868. *I staid all night at Mrs. Watson's and sat up 'till after twelve o'clock, and when I retired my throat felt a little sore. Next morning when I arose my throat was right sore but I paid no attention to it. After breakfast Lillie Moore and I went to see Miss Helen Jones, and after I went to Mrs. Watson's I commenced using something for my throat. Sunday morning I had to stay in bed and Dr. Gholson came to see me twice Sunday and once Monday. I staid in bed all the week and didn't get up until Thursday evening. Friday evening I went over home and* came back to Mrs. Watson's and staid all night another Friday, not having been in school at all. Ruth Bonner and Nettie Wooten[18] spent the night with Lillie and, as it rained hard all Saturday, they staid until Sunday morning. I was expecting papa and mama that evening but nobody came to tell me and Mrs. Watson wouldn't let me go over home, and so I gave them up. I was sitting in the window very late when I saw papa coming up the walk. He came and took me home and I did not find it very muddy. Papa consented for me to go to Sunday school notwithstanding I had been sick. I went to the Baptist Church, but Mr. Miller didn't come. It was too late to go anywhere else, so I went home. I spent the evening learning my Sunday school lesson. I came to school this morning and said my Familiar Science, but on account of not knowing one little question can't get an extra mark. I said a lesson on English Literature this morning for the first time and the subject was "Sir Walter Raleigh."

Tuesday, March 10th 1868. This morning I did not come to school until nearly eleven but I have to come in the evening to cipher. I took my music from Miss Harrell and like her very much indeed. She gave me "Shamus O'Brien" and "The Lancers" for my next lesson, and it will be a right hard one. My mythology lesson was about "Io" and "Inachus," and it was very hard. It told about Io being transformed into a cow and wandering over the whole earth and how at length she found rest on the bank of the Nile and was worshiped as a goddess. I will have to say my Familiar Science lesson this evening after I finish ciphering.

"The Philomathesian Society"

In 1866, Elizabeth and Cora Watson organized the Philomathesian Society, the first literary club in town to include women among its members. Its primary purpose was to encourage young ladies who had studied under Elizabeth Watson to continue their work, but men also were part of "the Philo." Some prestige accrued to the organization by having a name (denoting lovers of knowledge) suggested by L. Q. C. Lamar. Major Strickland was president, and members were Major and Mrs. Addison Craft, the Rev'd J. T. Pickett, James T. Fant, Howard and Kinloch Falconer, Mrs. Andrew R. Govan, Miss Bettie Govan, Mrs. Rosa B. Tyler, Mrs. Kate Freeman and her daughter Miss Cary Freeman,[19] Mr. and Mrs. William Clark, Dr. F. B. Shuford, Mr. and Mrs. Heber Craft, Helen Craft, Henry M. Paine, Kate Bonner, and Miss Mary R. Paine. Hubert McAlexander wrote that

> these families formed a definite circle, one that cohered even more strongly because of the bond of wartime suffering and post-war confusion. The members of this group mutually sustained each other, and in their insistence on preserving an intellectual and cultural life amid a land in ruins, they probably succeeded in creating a far more stimulating environment than the one that had existed before the war.[20]

Wednesday, March 11th 1868. *I came to school yesterday evening and ciphered an hour and a half and afterwards recited my Familiar Science. I went home after school, and after practicing some, I went up town. I bought a copybook and found that Miss Harrell had selected a piece of music for me and I got it also. The Philo was going to meet at our house, but I was too sleepy and tired to sit up and so I retired. I don't believe many came though, and there was no meeting.[21] This morning it was cloudy and looked very much like rain. I learned my English Literature and Familiar Science and came to school rather before the time for fear of getting wet. The subjects of my English Literature were "Elizabeth Carey" and "James Daniel"; neither of them were hard...*

Thursday, March 12th 1868. *Miss Harrell made me sing out of a book called "Cooke's Vocalist" and made me sing "alto" in a chorus book. This morning it was raining very hard but when I* *came to school it was not raining scarcely at all. My Mythology was about "Styx," the river of Hell, round which it flows nine times and "Hecate," who was the goddess of magic, and who presided over the fate of men. My Familiar Science, which comes in the evening, had for its subject, "Periodical Winds," which blow over the equator and the different seas. There were not many scholars, in fact, only two besides myself, so we did not read in Shakespeare, but Miss Cora had another book and made us read in it.*

"Buddie is Going to the Plantation next Week"

Buddie was appointed to see the Strickland farm near Hudsonville. Meanwhile Belle saw to his needs, as Emma Finley had for her brother on her family's plantation near Holly Springs a decade before. As Emma told her diary, "I [am] making my big brother a shirt [and] trust I shall not lose the art before it is necessary to make another." Emma's father had died at an early day, and the sons of Woodland had to go to work while still very young men. Emma spoke proudly of her brother George's developing competence as a planter:

> I must not omit the important fact that we're under a <u>new administration</u> and that of no other than Mr. Geo. Finley. Our overseer wishing to pay his mother a visit got leave of absence last Friday and our brother had to take his place. It has been very hard work for the Honorable gentleman to rise early enough- he in fact being about the last in the house to get up- until this morning when we were waked by- daylight- I believe & breakfasted by sunrise! Some hopes of him yet.[22]

Friday, March 13th 1868. *Yesterday evening after I went home I went to sewing for Buddie, who is going to the plantation next week, and had to have some things. This morning I had to take a music lesson at nine o'clock. I came to school, and as Miss Mary was not there I went out to the music room and played over my* pieces. *I wrote a piece of poetry to be copied again at the end of the lesson, to see how much I will improve. The subject of the English Literature was "Fletcher" and "Bacon." Not much is known of the former's life, but the lesson told of the rise of Bacon and his fall and disgrace. He disgraced himself by receiving bribes from those whose cases he had to decide.*

"Belle Joins a Singing School"

Singing schools were popular in nineteenth century America, with divided opinion as to their effectiveness. Traveling music masters itinerated throughout the country, and their work was said to bring culture to young singers, as well as to build up a supply of musicians for church choirs. The argument was most strident among Presbyterians, who debated all aspects of church music. *The Presbyterial Critic* described the situation as follows:

> Our churches formerly insisted on having their music led by a precentor. . .Under this leading, the people neglected to cultivate music, and it degenerated until it became intolerable. A reaction. . .followed. A few persons in each church would be found, who with strong natural tastes for music, desired to cultivate the art. Music teaching then became a profitable business, as also the manufacture of church music books. The few in each church who cultivated music, were deputed by the congregation to lead the singing, which they did under the guidance of their hired teachers, using the newly manufactured tune books and tunes. These choirs, aiming to please themselves in respect to the character of the music sung, the people were generally unable to unite with them, however imperfectly, until at last the semblance of congregational singing disappeared in a great proportion in our churches. And, at the present time, what do we see as the fruits of this process?. . .The congregation praises God through a delegated committee."[23]

Monday, March 16th 1868. *Saturday I sewed nearly all day, and forgot that I had promised to go to see Mrs. Calkins. I went to Sunday school and also to the Presbyterian Church with Minnie,* *papa and mama both being unwell. I had an easy Sunday school lesson to study for next Sunday, and so I went to Singing school. ..."Donne" and "Drayton" were the subjects of my English Literature. "Donne" was born in London and became an eminent preacher. He wrote some poetry, but he is chiefly liked for his prose, which consists chiefly of sermons.*

"It Rained Very Hard about School Time"

Because people walked, traveled on horseback, in buggies or carriages over unpaved roads, rain could cause the cancellation of events. Buddie's plans for outdoor activities having been ruined by the storm, he accompanied Belle to school.

Tuesday, March 17th 1868. *Yesterday at dinner it rained very hard about school time, and so Buddie came with me to school. When I got here, I did not find any scholars, but some came after awhile. It rained very hard indeed all the evening and last night there was a very hard thunderstorm, which lasted at least an hour.*[24] *It was quite damp and cloudy this morning but not raining when I came to school, sooner than usual, to take my music lesson. We recited mythology today, which was a review of every source we had been over. Pickett is going to Trenton today, and Buddie is going to the plantation soon, and our family will be quite small. . . .*

Wednesday, March 18th 1868. *Buddie went to the plantation this morning, and now our family is quite small. Miss Harrell gave Lillie and I a singing duet called "Listen to the Convent Bells." I have to sing alto, and as I never tried it before, it is quite hard. I learned about "Jonson" and "Herbert" in my literature lesson, and memorized a quotation from a piece of Herbert's called "Sundays."*

Thursday, March 19th 1868. *Yesterday evening, Miss Mary Harrell gave us a vocal lesson, and made me sing soprano in a new chorus. This morning we had a [soon?] breakfast, as papa had to go up town and I had more time to practice. After practicing an hour and a half I learned my lessons. The main subject of the mythology was "Prometheus," who first was the maker of man. We had a review also, and altogether it was quite a hard lesson. We have to take another vocal lesson this evening.*

"Miss Lizzie's Clock Being Faster than Ours"

Digital timepieces not having been invented, all depended upon careful winding of clocks to ensure accuracy. Standard time was not instituted in America until 1883 (at the behest of the railroads), so that people depended upon "sun time," with all manner of local variations. Thus, disagreements were legion about the correct interpretation of the clock.

Friday, March 20th 1868. *Yesterday I hurried to school but was five minutes too late, Miss Lizzie's clock being faster than ours. We had a very pleasant time last evening the little time that we staid. We were singing and Lillie Moore told Miss Mary that a storm was coming up and so she let us go. It rained very little though, and if we had stayed and finished singing we would not have gotten wet, I don't think. I love Miss Mary so much! She is so sweet, and besides that she is very smart indeed. She gave me another music lesson this morning and gave me. . .the piece, "What are the Wild Waves Saying?" (instead Lillie and I have taken a duet together which we will sing at the musical soiree the last Saturday in this month). Miss Mary is going to have one at end of every month at Mrs. Mason's, but there will be no one there but the girls. I have to write a composition on "The Merchant of Venice" which will be quite interesting as well as easy. We are expecting Buddie home tomorrow and we will be right glad to* have him with us again. Though he has not been away but a short time, yet we miss him very much.

"There Was No One to go after Eggs but Myself"

Women preferred to send others to bring home the goods. But those lacking a man had to face the traffic themselves. Belle may have collected the order, but "Papa" paid the bill!

Monday, March 23rd 1868. *Friday evening Rosa and Dora Clark came to see me, and mama let us stay all night with them. Buddie being gone, there was no one to go after eggs but myself, and so mama sent me uptown after them, and papa bought eight dozen, and they nearly weighted me down. Saturday, it took me all the morning to write my composition and in the evening Buddie came and I didn't do much of anything until he left. . . .I went over to Mrs. McCarroll's and staid the rest of the evening. Sunday morning I went to Sunday school and went also to the Baptist Church. In the evening. . .I went to Singing school. Buddie went back to the country that evening and we are quite lonely again. . . .Miss Nettie Wooten came to school today and is going to board at Mrs. Watson's. We had a review lesson in English literature this morning, besides an advance lesson.*

Tuesday, March 24th 1868. *Yesterday evening, I wrote a letter which took up nearly the whole time. This morning I came to school at nine o'clock as I had to take a music lesson. Miss Mary was there waiting for me, but I just was in time. We finished reading "Henry VIII" and commenced "Hamlet," and are going to read the book again. The subject of my Familiar Science lesson is "Dew," and is interesting although it is hard. I expect to go to see Mrs. Calkins this evening, and am anticipating quite a nice time. I went to see her once before, and was so highly entertained that I staid until nearly dark. I have been promising to go to see her all the winter, but every time that I appointed to go, some-*

thing would happen, and I have never been yet. But I hope nothing will happen this evening.

Wednesday, March 25th 1868. *Yesterday evening I spent a <u>very</u> nice time with Mrs. Calkins and was really sorry when the sun went down. She seemed very much pleased at my visit and invited me to come again, very cordially. I don't think I will put off my next visit so long, for every time I see her, I love her more and more if possible. Mr. P. Myers took tea with us last night, but as he is a lawyer he couldn't stay long. The subjects of my English Literature lesson this morning were "Drummond" and "Crashaw." I knew that lesson and I know my Familiar Science this evening I will get an extra mark. Miss Rosa came in time for school for the first time this session. We all had to speak of it, as it was so remarkable. We have to take a vocal lesson this evening, and I hope we have a nice time.*

Thursday, March 26th 1868. *Miss Mary Harrell made me sing alto on another chorus yesterday evening, but I do not find it near so hard now, as at first. . .Saturn was the subject of our mythology lesson today, and we had another review. We can't read but a half hour in Shakespeare now, as Miss Lizzie is going to commence a Mental Arithmetic class soon. Batie Athey came to see Minnie yesterday evening, and I gave him some flowers, and he thought there were more flowers in our yard than he had seen in a long time. Mr. Frank Leak came yesterday evening and is going to stay with us a day or two.*

XII. President Johnson Impeached

A child's diary would not be expected to contain a running commentary on national events (Belle, for example, does not mention Lee's surrender), but so much talk surrounded the impeachment of President Andrew Johnson that even a thirteen year-old would be aware of the controversy. Belle knew about the conundrum in Washington over whether to put Confederate president Jefferson Davis on trial for treason. Davis, whose son-in-law was born in the city, was a friend of Major Strickland and had stayed at the Strickland home.[1]

> *Friday, March 27th 1868. I have a dreadful cold, and I am afraid I can't sing tomorrow. . . .Miss Mary Harrell has made out a program for it, and probably it will pass off very well. Mr. Carter is going to lecture tonight, and as his first one was quite interesting, I reckon this one will prove the same. His other subject was "New Zealand," but I believe he is going to take the "Holy Land" for his subject tonight. The Senate of the "<u>United States</u>" is now trying President Johnson for breaking the Constitution. I don't suppose that "Mr. Davis" will be tried as long as they can possibly put it off. The subjects of my lesson in English Literature were "Fletcher" and "Halington," but they are scarcely remembered and are not interesting characters as far as I know.*

"Mr. Carter Told of His Trip to Jerusalem"

Even though Holly Springs was garrisoned by troops of an occupying army, members of the privileged class devoted an amazing amount of energy to activities of cultural enrichment and uplift. While some gave themselves to parties in honor of the occupation forces, the more serious attended lectures by traveling authorities. In the wake of Napoleon's conquests, interest in the Mid East was high, and because of the sympathy Southerners had perceived from Great Britain during the Civil War, all were eager to hear anything an 'Englishman' had to say. Even though Holly Springs' impressive three-story Masonic Hall on the square, where such lectures would have been given had been blown up in Van Dorn's raid, alternate locations were available, and the townspeople assembled to hear visitors whose interesting knowledge would help them pierce the Reconstruction gloom.

Monday, March 30th 1868. I went to the lecture Friday night, and was very much interested. Mr. Carter told of his trip to Jerusalem and of his walking in the footsteps of our Savior. Saturday morning I went up town with mama and stayed until nearly dinnertime. In the evening I went up to Mrs. Mason's and found a good many of the girls there. I was very much frightened the whole time as none of the pupils knew when they had to play. The soiree passed off very well, I believe. I went to walk with Bettie McCarroll, but did not go far. Mr. Everett came that evening and brought several persons with him. He is an Englishman who is traveling around in the South and making speeches wherever he goes. He spoke Saturday night, and so did several other gentlemen, and we stayed 'till nearly twelve. He left for Jackson yesterday evening, and is going to speak at Oxford today. Papa is going to Jackson this evening, and we will be quite lonesome without him.

"I Went All Over Town Trying to Match Some Calico"

Women shied away from the square because most stores also sold whiskey by the glass, and even though they advertised large inventories, shoppers like Belle found only a small range of goods from which to choose. Items were kept behind counters, and customers had to ask clerks to display each one. As John Mickle described the east side of the square, it was "the heart of the town in business, politics, gossip, pleasure, and had more than its share of fist fights." He wrote, "There were few cash sales during the summer, most people in town and county having yearly charge accounts. Saturday was the great shopping day for out of town customers, white and black, from spring until fall, and stores were crowded. But on other weekdays there was little doing, and bosses and clerks would play checkers just off the curb."[2] Meanwhile, Major Strickland went to Jackson on the train.[3] The Strickland home was at the eastern edge of a plateau on which the town stood, and a half-mile valley separated the town from the ridge on which the railroad tracks passed from North to South. On a clear day, one can see and hear the movement of trains from the site of the Strickland Place.[4]

Tuesday, March 31st 1868. Yesterday evening I went all over town trying to match some calico, but didn't succeed.[5] When I reached home papa was getting ready to go to Jackson and I did not have much time to see him. We stood at the gate and watched him until he got nearly to the depot,[6] and then a wagon prevented our seeing him. This morning I looked at the clock, and it was nearly eight, but I made a mistake and thought it was nine, and so I came to take my music lesson. I soon found out my mistake, but I did not go home. Therefore as I had nothing to do until nine, I went out in the music room and practiced an hour. We read in "Hamlet" today, and have nearly finished the play. I have the part of Hamlet, and therefore have to read more than almost any one else. We have read through the book once, but [as] it will not be amiss to read Shakespeare as often as possible, we are going to read it again. "Hamlet" is the first play, as arranged in our book that we are reading.

"Several Gentlemen of the Town Went Down with Mr. Everett and His Company"

Everett, the British lecturer had excited so much attention that Major Strickland and others went to hear his lectures in Oxford and Jackson. Meanwhile, the ladies stayed home.

Wednesday, April 1st 1868. Today is the first day of April, or "April Fool" day, and I would like to fool my journal and not write at all. We are expecting papa home this evening, but as we cannot put any confidence in this day, he may fool us and not come. Several of the gentlemen of [the] town went down with Mr. Everett and his company. I have to take a vocal lesson this evening, and though I love to sing very much, yet this time I should like to stay at home and see papa. He is coming nearly [at] the time I go to school in the evening, and I won't be able to stay with him much. We had "Fuller" for our lesson in English Literature, and his writings are very quaint indeed. We turn on to the back of the book and read after we finish reading the writings of the author we have for our lesson. The reason that we do this is that we did not commence at the beginning and will not have time, I don't think, to finish it this season, so it doesn't make any difference. I want to see papa very much although he has been away such a short time. We were quite lonesome without him.

"The Negroes Had a Large Tableau Last Night"

Black minstrels were an immediate outgrowth of emancipation. The entertainment raised money for their churches and schools, but as a scholar of African American studies remarked, it is something of a paradox that the South's popular desire for a cultural tradition to set it apart from the perceived imperfections of the industrial North and imperial Europe-should induce the region's whites to turn to its blacks for their music, dance, and humor. In pre-war days, parts in these shows were taken by Caucasians who blackened their faces to accentuate popular caricatures of slaves as happy-go-lucky "dancing darkies."[7] Ironically, portrayal of blacks through comic routines created sympathy for the abolitionist cause. But the performances also laid the groundwork for better appreciation of Afro-American music and humor. After the Civil War, Negro entertainers joined the ranks of minstrelsy, and even though they conformed to stereotypes and served at the behest of white stage managers who siphoned off the profits, minstrel shows offered one of the first ways that blacks could escape traditional channels into which their labor was directed. These performances were popular in Holly Springs until after World War II.[8]

Thursday, April 2nd 1868. Yesterday evening I went to take a vocal lesson, a song, but did not sing much as Miss Mary was teaching the larger girls a song. Papa came at half after one, and when I got home I found Buddie there too. It was raining this morning, but I came to school through it. I found some of the pupils absent. The subject of my mythology lesson was "Jupiter," and it was not interesting at all, and therefore quite hard. The Negroes had a large tableau last night,[9] and I heard that it went off very well. They had a large supper and charged fifty cents to eat. As there were so few at school today, we could not read in Shakespeare, but Miss Cora let us read in "Gleanings from the Poets." We read "The Prisoner of Chillon," which is very interesting indeed. I think it is one of the prettiest pieces in the book.

"Belle Anticipates a Recital"

Generations of children have dreaded recitals, considered necessary by music teachers to demonstrate the ability to learn and perform a piece of music with proficiency.

Friday, April 3rd 1868. After school yesterday evening I stayed after I finished my lesson in Familiar Science and worked a sum. I sewed until right late, as it was raining, and I couldn't go out. This morning I was at school before Miss Harrell came, and I practiced a little while. She wanted to look over my music, and so I went home after it. Miss Lizzie gave me a set of papers to draw maps on, and I was going to draw some the time that I went home, but when I got back it was too late. I then learned my Familiar Science, which is a review, and my English Literature. The subjects were "Herrick" and "Mrs. Philips" of the literature lesson. We asked Miss Fannie Phillips if the last subject was any relation of hers, but she says that if she was, she never had heard it. Today is Friday, so we won't have to come to school tomorrow, but we have a composition to write. Miss Lizzie has not given our subjects; but I either hope she will forget it altogether, or give me an easy one. Miss Harrell says she is going to give a large concert at the end of the session, and I am so sorry for I am always so frightened, that I fail entirely.

"I Wanted to Go to the Catholic Church"

Belle was ecumenical before the word came into vogue. Holly Springs' Catholic Church, dedicated to St. Joseph, father of the Lord Jesus, was the first Roman Catholic congregation in North Mississippi. The first members were Irish workers who came to build the Mississippi Central Railroad. In 1857, when Christ Church laid plans for a new building, the nascent Catholic parish bought the lovely clapboard chapel where Christ Church's had worshiped since 1840[10] and moved it to its present site on E. College Ave.

Monday, April 6th 1868. Friday evening when I went home I found two or three babies there, and then I was in my glory for I love them better than anything almost. After awhile Alice Rutland and Dora Clark came for me to spend the night with them. Amanda Malone and Rosa had gone to Mrs. Martin's with Anna and

Amelia. I had a very pleasant time, but did not stay up very long. In the morning I went home as I had a composition to write on "Habits We Should Cultivate." Miss Lizzie did not forget it as I had hoped. I sewed then 'till dinner, and then copied it. In the evening I went uptown and had my hair cut. Sunday morning I went to Sunday school and knew my lesson, I believe, quite well. We are going to have a May celebration, just the School, on the first day of May. I hope we will have a very pleasant time, as I expect it will be a very fine day. I wanted to go to the Catholic Church,[11] but after Sunday school it was too late, so I went to the Presbyterian. After learning my lesson for next Sunday, I went to Singing school. Mr. Henry Anderson[12] was there and spoke to us very kindly about the improvement we had made. I was in hopes that he had come to stay, but he says he only came on a visit.

"Two Belles, a Wedding, and Good Friday in Christ Church"

Good Friday and Easter were hardly observed by the Puritan-influenced churches outside the Roman Catholic and Episcopal communions. For example, Emma Finley told her diary about her family's celebrations of Christmas and Easter, but left the pages blank as to what, if anything, was said on these occasions from the pulpit of her Presbyterian church. Eschewing sanctification of any but "the Lord's Day," it was not until the 1940s that Good Friday was observed with services in the Protestant churches of Holly Springs, except in the one mentioned above, which had a service prescribed for the occasion in its Book of Common Prayer. Meanwhile, the family was preparing to celebrate another slave wedding, and the Strickland servants, presumably members of some communion other than the Episcopalian, did not feel bound by that Church's traditional proscription of marriages during Lent.

Tuesday, April 7th 1868. *Yesterday when I went home it was raining very hard, and I was a little wet. It rained all the evening, and most of the night, I believe. Cousin Boothe Baskerville came to see us Sunday evening, and has not left yet. I suppose he will go today. I have half an hour to write in my journal today for it was raining so that I could not go uptown after a copybook, and papa is in the courthouse all the time, and he couldn't get it for me. We finished reading "Hamlet" today, and just read the first scene in "Much Ado About Nothing," taking the characters as we came to them, so I don't know what one I am going to have. A Negro girl that we have hired is going to get married Thursday, and she pretends to be very much frightened. Her name is Belle, and a few mistakes have been made by there being two Belles on the place. Papa says he wants me to commence French, and I like it so much that it will please me very much. I took a music lesson this morning, and Miss Mary gave me "Her Bright Smile Haunts Me Still" to play at the soiree at the end of the month. She says she can't give me a lesson Friday, for it is "Good Friday" in the Episcopal Church, and she will have to go to service, so I will have to take my lesson Saturday morning. Miss Harrell is not going to let us have our music in the last Saturday in the month as that is the day for decking the soldiers' graves, and she says she doesn't want to deprive anyone of that pleasure. We will, therefore, have to have it the first Saturday in May. I have to take a vocal lesson tomorrow evening, and I am very glad, for I like to sing so much. She is going to give us little ones a piece by ourselves next time. I have to cipher in arithmetic this evening, and I hope I will do better than I generally do in algebra.*

"I Happened to Go In Just as the Mail was Opened"

One of the unspoken blessings of the war's end was resumption of regular mail delivery. In Holly Springs, as in all rural communities, arrival of the daily post was a major event. Preachers condemned Sunday mail trains. There were no post office buildings yet-mail was handed out over the counter of local stores that were willing to have the postal contract. Thus, at the hour when the mail arrived, a minor social event occurred in each of America's cities and towns-all came together to see what was the latest "news."[13]

> **Wednesday, April 8th 1868.** *I went to town yesterday after a copybook, and I happened to go in just as the mail was opened, and it was very much crowded. I went to Mrs. Craft's after a French Grammar, and when I got home it was right late. A gentleman by the name of Mullaly lectured last night. He is the editor of "The Metropolitan Record," and I heard that he made a very good speech, but I did not go. Mr. Frank Leak came in town yesterday, but went home this morning. I wrote to Miss Ella, but he was in such a hurry, that I didn't have much time. It was a very pretty day this morning, but I believe it is clouding up again. I am so tired of rain and cold! I wish it would clear off and get warm. We had a new scholar this morning, Katie McGuirk. She is a little girl, and will be in Katie Wallace's classes.*[14] *I knew my lesson in literature today, and now if I just know my Familiar Science this evening, I will get an extra mark. Saturday we don't have to write a composition, but we have to copy one.*

"I Almost Wish Miss Lizzie was an Episcopalian"

Blacks suffered as much or more than whites under the inefficiency of Reconstruction governments in the Southern states. Unable to obtain a marriage license at the Holly Springs courthouse (still in temporary facilities due to the burning of the building in 1864), Belle, Jane Strickland's servant, and her fiancé rode the train to Oxford, where they hoped to get a license and carry out plans for their Maundy Thursday nuptials. Meanwhile Mrs. Clark announced that her classes would be dismissed for Good Friday services in Christ Church. In Holly Springs, only Episcopalians and

Roman Catholics held Easter services, and Belle laid plans to visit the town's two liturgical congregations on Easter Day-revealing as a reason for her interest that "the ladies always decorate the churches very prettily, and I want to go very much."

> ***Thursday, April 9th 1868.*** *I took a vocal lesson yesterday evening, and Miss Harrell gave the second class a song, and put me on the alto. I went home, and some company came soon after. Belle, the Negro girl, can't marry today as she intended, because she can't get the license or something of the kind. So they are going to Oxford on the five o'clock train, and be married there tonight. She was very much disappointed, I think, at the idea of not marrying at the appointed time. Mr. Mullaly spoke again last night, but I don't believe he made an impression on the people, the same as the night before. Tomorrow is "Good Friday," and Mrs. Clark is going to give holy day, and I almost wish Miss Lizzie was an Episcopalian,[15] for then we would be free, too. But there is no use wishing, for tomorrow will have to be the same to us as any other day. Sunday is Easter, and I am going to the Catholic Church in the morning, and maybe to the Episcopal in the evening.[16] I have never been to the Catholic Church at all, and have never been to the other on Easter. The ladies always decorate the churches very prettily, and I want to go very much.[17]*

"Mr. Clark and Miss Amelia Came to See Us Yesterday Evening"

Making and receiving visits was part of social life in Holly Springs and all American communities in the nineteenth century. An elaborate etiquette surrounded such occasions, including standards of dress, proper subjects for conversation, and the presentation of engraved calling cards at the door. As Emma Finley noted for her diary in 1859, "We spent the week beginning Mar. 6 in [Holly Springs] with Aunt Mary. Amused ourselves shopping visiting, & receiving visitors. Altogether spent a very pleasant time."[18] Those who received calls were obligated to return them within a few days. The fact that Major and Mrs. Strickland were ill was not allowed hinder hospitable reception of their guests. The Clarks no doubt came and went without being the wiser as to the illnesses from which their hosts suffered.

> *Friday, April 10th 1868. Mr. Clark and Miss Amelia came to see us yesterday evening and staid a short time. Papa was very sick all day yesterday, and we thought he was going to have bilious fever, and it frightened me very much. Mama had a headache, too, but she said she did not want to get sick while papa had a headache, and so she didn't say anything about it. Papa went to the courthouse, though, this morning, but he is not much better. I went over to Mrs. McCarroll's last evening and stayed 'till almost night. I went up to town today, and found that Mr. Frank came home from New Orleans yesterday. Miss Lizzie is going to hear the whole school a lesson in Geography this afternoon instead of Mental Arithmetic. I commenced Mental Arithmetic yesterday and am going to begin French Monday. I liked French very much the little that I studied it under Mr. Stanford, but the book that I am going to study now is a good deal harder, and I don't know whether I will like it or not.*

"I Was Highly Delighted at the Performance"

Belle was pleased with what she saw and heard at the Catholic and Episcopal churches. Like many in her generation, she was unaccustomed to a liturgical service, and the solemn occasions made their dramatic impression. Indeed, just forty years before, the Rev'd Colly A. Foster wrote to Bishop Leonidas Polk that the organization of an Episcopal Church in Holly Springs had excited interest because the church used a prayer book in its services. Foster told the bishop that extra benches had to be procured for the courthouse, where the initial services were conducted. He said: "The

Episcopal Church is in every person's mouth as the common topic of conversation."[19]

> *Monday, April 13th 1868.* Last Friday evening I went after Alice Rutland to spend the night with me, but she had company, Miss Annie Lewis and Bettie McCarroll. We all went to walk and Dora had a spell at Mrs. Topp's gate,[20] and we had to take her in there. Then we had to wait 'till she woke, and she slept a long time. Alice stayed with me, and we had a very pleasant time. Saturday morning I went to Mrs. Mason's to take a music lesson. In the evening, mama, papa, and I went to Mr. Frank's store,[21] and stayed 'till nearly night. Sunday I went to the Catholic Church with Mary,[22] and was highly delighted at the performance. It was Easter and the Church was trimmed very prettily indeed.[23] There were a great many people there from other Churches, and some of them couldn't get seats. Last night I went to the Episcopal Church, and while I was there, a very hard storm came up, but we did not get wet going home.

"Mr. Neilson Fixed our Piano"

Pianos required tuners, and Holly Springs reveled in its music. As soon as peace was restored, the local Philharmonic Society raised money for a fine Knabe piano and presented Schiller's *Song of the Bell* in the unfinished Presbyterian Church.[24]

> *Tuesday, April 14th 1868.* Mr. Owen came yesterday, and mama and I went up to town with him, to get some things for Miss Donna and Olena. We went all around town, and when we finished shopping and went home, it was nearly dark. The gentlemen had a shouting match yesterday for a pipe, and Mr. Fant won the prize. He brought it down home today for us to see, and it was the prettiest pipe I ever saw, almost. It had some carving on it which was exquisite, and very delicate. It represented a dog and a bird, with a stump in the rear. It cost fifty dollars, as it had

an amber stem. Last May a man by the name of Mr. Neilson fixed our piano, and this morning his brother came to examine it. He said Mr. Stanford had done a great deal of damage to the pianos in town, which, of course, gave him some work to do. Mr. Owen went home this morning, I believe, but I didn't write by him.

"Papa Has Had His Lot Fixed"

Victorians made a fetish of their mourning customs, and lavished more attention on cemetery properties than is customary today. Elaborate tombstones and landscaping were employed. Indeed, as Gaines M. Foster notes, Southerners manifested such tremendous pride in their "cities of the dead" that one Northerner reported that the first question you are asked on entering a southern city is: "Have you been to the cemetery?"[25] The older part of the Holly Springs cemetery was deeded by R. H. Byrne, February 23, 1845, but at least four markers may be seen dating to 1838."[26] The oldest part of the cemetery fronts S. Center St.-the old road south, and as the town grew additional sections were added until now the cemetery, a park-like setting-since 1905 called Hill Crest-embraces thirty-five acres. In the years after the Civil War elaborate tombstones and elegant iron fences were erected, and Holly Springs boasted its own skilled artisan in marble, Adam Preher, whose monuments are now recognized as fine sculpture in their own right.[27]

__Wednesday, April 15th 1868.__ Yesterday evening Bettie McCarroll and I went up to town, and then to the graveyard. Papa has had his lot fixed, and it is as pretty as any there at all.[28] Sunday night, Rip, our dog, was badly hurt in some manner, and can hardly walk, but I think he will recover. I forgot my music yesterday and left it at school, and I had to practice my pieces without the instruction book. Papa said last night that he didn't want me to sing alto any more, because he thought it was ruining my voice. That suits me exactly, for I can't bear to sing it. We will have to take a music, or rather a vocal lesson this evening, and I will have to tell her then. We said a very good lesson in English Literature today, and read extracts from the works of Milton. The quotation that I learned was, "Hesperus, that led The starry host, rode brightest; 'till the moon, Rising in clouded majesty, at length Apparent queen unveil'd her peerless light, And o'er the dark her silver mantle threw." There were some beautiful passages in our lesson, and I would like to learn them all, but that, I reckon, is impossible. Lillie Moore has been sick for a good while, but she is about well now, I believe.

Thursday, April 16th 1868. While we were taking our vocal lesson last evening, a storm came up, and we had to go home. Emma Myers stopped with me to keep from getting wet, and it rained so hard that she couldn't go home, so she had to stay with me. We studied a little while, and then retired, but we stayed awake and talked for a long, long time. She went to school this morning, just before I came, and, said she enjoyed herself very much. Miss Lizzie changed the time for taking up school in the evening to half past two, and dismissing at four. She said, too, that everyone who got nine in all their lessons could get an extra mark, for it was very hard to say every lesson perfectly and receive ten in all of them. If I keep on today as I have begun, I will get one this evening, I believe. I had more marks than any one else, but we are going to commence fresh, and not count those that we have received before. We finished reading today, "Much Ado About Nothing," and commenced "Macbeth." The former play I like very much, especially the character of Dogberry. I had the part of Benedick, which was another important character. Maybe I will go home with Miss Fannie Phillips this evening.

"Lingering at the Front Gate"

Almost every yard was fenced in those days-the better to keep roaming cattle and wandering chickens at bay, and those who craved excitement, or at least hoped to see somebody, loitered at their gates. It was a favorite pastime of children and busybodies, and like almost all pleasurable activities of the time, was frowned upon by the prim.

> ***Friday, April 17th 1868.*** *It looked so much like rain yesterday evening that I could not go home with Miss Fannie, but it did not rain at all. I went up town, and when I came home, spent the rest of my time at the front gate.*[29] *I had a hard French lesson, and I studied a long time on it. It is not very interesting yet, for I am just learning the pronunciation of the words. I will, though, be at the more interesting part in a few days. Eliza Cummings is in town, and will stay some days I suppose. She is looking as pretty as usual, and is so sweet. I told Mr. Fant, who is one of her greatest admirers, that she had come, but he was before me. Miss Mary Harrell is going to give me a new piece Tuesday, and I am glad of it, for I am tired of the piece that I have just finished, for I have been taking it ever since she began teaching me. We had "Sir Matthew Hale" for our subject in English Literature today.*

"A Visit to the Methodist Church"

Thirteen-year-old Belle was not old enough to attend the balls for which Holly Springs was famous.[30] Meanwhile, worshiped with the local Methodists. The Methodist Church, erected in 1849, was on the same street as the Strickland Place. After the courthouse burned, the county used the Methodist Sunday school hall on the lower floor as a courtroom until 1867, when the police board and Masonic Lodge bought a house jointly, which was used as a court and lodge-room until the new courthouse was erected three years later. Judge Watson and others were appointed in 1865 to go to

Washington to apply for government aid to rebuild the courthouse.[31] They were unsuccessful.[32]

> ***Monday, April 20th 1868.*** *Friday, I spent the pleasantest evening that I have spent in a good while, as I went home with Miss Fannie. She was going to the party that night, and she wanted me to go, too, but papa said he couldn't let me go during school time. I stayed 'till right late, and then went by papa's office[33] after him. Saturday I was busy all the morning, and so did not have time to write or study. I came over to school after some music, and as I owed them all a visit, I was persuaded to stay a little while. The first thing I did after dinner was to write my composition, the subject of which was "Milton." It was quite an easy subject, but took some time to read about him. I went over to Mrs. McCarroll's late in the evening to swing, and while Bettie and I both were swinging, the swing broke, but neither one of us were hurt. I went to walk, but did not stay long. Sunday morning, I learned my lesson, and after breakfast went to Sunday school. There was no church at the Presbyterian,[34] so I went to the Methodist. I went to Singing school, and Mr. Henry Anderson led us.*

XIII. Decorating the Soldiers' Graves

The custom of decorating Civil War soldiers' graves probably began as individuals placed flowers at the tombs of loved ones lost in the war, and while several communities claim to have begun Confederate Memorial Day, many believe it to have originated in Columbus, Miss.,[1] April 26, 1866, at the town's Friendship Cemetery.[2] The ritual was always held in the spring, with dates generally later in the upper South, in order that an ample supply of flowers would be available.[3] Ceremonies such as the one Belle describes took place all across the country, for both Confederate and Union dead, but as Charles Reagan Wilson has noted, "Every time a Confederate veteran died, every time flowers were placed on graves on Southern Memorial Day, Southerners relived and confronted the death of the Confederacy."[4] Belle's new composition was the piece by Wollenhaupt which the famous musician had dedicated to Maria Mason, and which Mrs. Mason had recognized when a soldier entered her house uninvited after Van Dorn's raid and played her Steinway piano.

Tuesday, April 21st 1868. I went up to town yesterday evening after some music, but Miss Mary had not selected it.[5] I went to the graveyard with Emma Boling,[6] and we started to the soldiers' graves, but Bettie McCarroll and Tillie Paine wanted to come home, and we came too. Emma walked home with me, and then I went with her a little way. Papa went to Oxford on the five o'clock train yesterday, and will be back probably Wednesday. Miss Mary gave me a new piece called "Whispering Wind," which is quite hard, and is fifteen pages long. I have finished, "What Are the Wild Waves Saying?", but as I am going to play it at the soiree, I will have to continue practicing it. We read in Shakespeare this morning, and we have to say a spelling lesson, too, later by. We are reading the play, "Macbeth," and I have the part of the 2nd Witch, and also of Banquo. I knew my French lesson today and also my mythology, and now if I just know my Familiar Science, I will get an extra mark this evening. I hope I will, for I want to get the prize at the end of the session.

"A Very Long Sermon"

While brevity of preaching is characteristic only of twentieth century sermons in the liberal churches of Europe and North America, all ministers preached longer in times past, when it seems there were fewer distractions and more regard for the work of the pulpit. Records from this period contain few complaints about the length of sermons; rather, ministers were sometimes dismissed because their messages were too brief. Sermons were news events, as newspapers of the era reveal, and as Walter Brownlow Posey remarks, "Having spent all week writing down every word of a sermon, the preacher had no aim to be hurried in the delivery of his discourse." Moreover, those who heard the minister had taken trouble to attend and expected sufficient homiletic effort for their sacrifice. By Posey's account:

> Presbyterians of the period often spoke for two hours or more. The Rev'd Gideon Blackburn, of Nashville, Tenn. once preached to a crowd of fifteen hundred in a graveyard for two hours while a constant rain fell. About 1820, Governor Carroll of Tennessee listen to Blackburn preach a sermon which lasted three and a half hours. The governor asked a companion how he stood a sermon of such

length, and the companion replied that he could have listened until midnight![7]

Robert B. Alexander, a member of the Holly Springs Methodist Church, recorded that he "heard Rev. Joseph Brooks preach two hours."[8] Holly Springs of this era was beginning to cultivate a taste for briefer sermons. Belle's comments indicate that even if her spirit was willing, her flesh grew weary under the discipline of a long discourse by the Rev'd Samuel Irwin Reid, a respected Holly Springs minister and schoolmaster.[9]

> **Wednesday, April 22nd 1868.** *I went to see Bettie McCarroll last evening and stayed 'till nearly night. I went to hear Dr. Reid preach probably his last sermon in Mississippi, as he is going to Illinois.*[10] *He preached until ten o'clock, and I became very sleepy, and so did some others that were there. When we were coming out, we saw papa at the door, and were much surprised, as we were not expecting him until today. He would have come at one yesterday, if there had not been a break in the road. We said a lesson in English Literature, but I could not read well at all, on account of having a violent headache. I have these very frequently whenever I go out in the sun, and as I went up town for mama this morning, I have to pay right dearly for my trip. There was quite a crowd collected in the square, on account of a coon fighting with several dogs. I believe I know my French this morning, and also my Literature; therefore, if I only know my Familiar Science, I will receive an extra mark.*

"There is Going to be a Circus Tomorrow"

A visit from a traveling show was a major event in Southern towns of the 1800s. Colorfully decorated wagons drove though the streets drawing children out of their homes into a happy procession anticipating fun at the show grounds. The most popular circuses were John Robinson's Circus and Menagerie, W. C. Coup's

Monster Shows, and the Grand New Orleans Menagerie and Circus. The basic pattern was established by the 1850s-a parade to draw crowds, exhibitions under canvas tents, trained animals, clowns, acrobats and aerialists, jugglers, ventriloquists, and freak shows. Circus owners adapted to Southern morals by advertising their shows as classical and biblical-featuring chariot races and religious tableaus. Gamblers, hustlers, and pickpockets followed and always seemed to encourage drinking and fighting, so that preachers criticized circuses.[11] Still, as Charles Reagan Wilson notes, "The appeal of the circus was universal, but the poor and the children were its most fervent enthusiasts."[12] A story is told in Holly Springs that the lot on which the present Christ Church rectory stands, was acquired about 1887 due to its use as a circus-grounds. By one account, an elephant inserted its trunk through an open window into the church during a service, prompting the vestry to purchase the land and remove the circus from its proximity to God's house.[13]

Thursday, April 23rd 1868. I went to Mr. Clark's schoolroom to take my vocal lesson, and found that it was not time for me to take my piece. Last night papa gave me a book called "Jepthah's Daughter," and I read it through today. I was very much pleased with it indeed. It is a drama with five acts. My mythology lesson was about "Hades," and was easy because it was interesting. The only hard part was about the "Istonian Games," and the pronunciation of some names in the description of the home of Plato. We read a good deal in "Macbeth" today, and Tuesday we will finish it and commence another play. There is going to be a circus tomorrow, and Buddie came in today to go if papa will let him. I did not write in my copybook this morning, but copied my French exercises. I believe I will get on very well in French because I like the language, and love to study it. I will not have much to do Saturday, as I have to copy my composition of last week. It will not take me long to do that, though, because it was a short one.

Decorating the Soldiers' Graves

"I Fixed a Dress and Did Several Other Things Beside"

In Belle's era, women were expected to do their own sewing, for even if cooks and maids were employed, sewing was seen as a genteel art, worthy of even the most pampered ladies. No doubt Belle's stitchery was in keeping with preparations for Miss Mary Harrell's musical soiree.

Friday, April 24th 1868. *I was very smart yesterday evening after school, for I fixed a dress and did several other things beside. I studied harder last night than I have this session, at night. This morning I arose [a] good deal earlier than usual, for I commenced practicing at six, and generally it is nearly seven when I begin. Mr. Anderson came in and told us goodbye, for he is going home today. I am very sorry he is going, for I would like to have him for a citizen very much, and that is the general feeling, I believe. Tomorrow is the day set apart for decking the soldiers' graves, but I have not heard much about it. I always go, and suppose I will go tomorrow, too, but I am not certain. I believe there is a circus coming here today which will show tonight, but I have not heard whether it will come or not, today. Miss Fannie Phillips went home this morning, and will, I suppose, be back this evening. I took a music lesson today, and Miss Mary says she is going to have a soiree next Saturday, and we have not but a week to prepare for it. She is going to have some people there and I just know I will be frightened to death, almost. I have not heard papa say whether he was going or not, but I hope he won't. I asked Miss Lizzie just now if she was going to the circus, and she said, "Of course, she always went."*[14] *Today week is the first day of May, and is the time for the Sunday school celebration. We have to say a geography lesson this morning and I am sorry, for I have not had much time to study it. I think maybe I will get through with it, though, for it is easy. The time is out now, and I have written twenty minutes, and have written in my journal [a] little over a page.*

"Decoration Day"

"There's glory in gloom," wrote Father Abram Ryan (1838-1886), and, the solemnity of Holly Springs' Confederate Memorial Day made a great impression on Belle. She made wreaths for the honored dead, but the exertion and emotion of the day put the young girl into an uncharacteristically introspective mood. It was, perhaps, her first mature encounter with the mystery and seriousness of death.

> *Monday, April 27th 1868. It rained very hard indeed Friday night, the hardest thunderstorm that there has been in ten or twelve years. Saturday was the day appointed to decorate the soldiers' graves, and after copying my composition I went to work. I made several wreaths, and in the evening went over to Mr. Smith's after some flowers. I got as many as I wanted, and received a very cordial invitation to come after flowers whenever I wanted any. At four o'clock I went to the graveyard, and disposed of my flowers very quickly. When I got up on the hill, and saw the flowers reflected in the setting sun, the place looked perfectly radiant.[15] I hardly ever saw anything so beautiful. After reaching home, I found Cousin Boothe there, and he made me go back with him. When I got home again, I was so tired, I could hardly stand. I wonder if any of those who were there Saturday will ever be there again when the 26th of April comes to deck the Brave of our country with flowers. It is very doubtful indeed. Probably some of my loved ones will have been called away when time comes round to that time again. It is very sad to think of, and therefore we should strive to be prepared when the Angel of Death calls us from this earth. This morning I wrote to Dell Bowles.*

"April Showers"

Belle looked forward to May Day celebrations at her school. The holiday was very popular in Britain, but having been frowned upon by the Puritans it received less notice in America. Thus, as Belle and her friends celebrated the day, it had something of a moralistic cast, as did almost any occasion in nineteenth century Holly Springs.

> *Tuesday, April 28th 1868. I studied very hard after supper last night, and did not have many mistakes in my exercises. It was very stormy all the evening, but it stopped thundering before I retired. Towards morning it began raining, and has been showering ever since. I hope it will stop, so it will be dry by Friday, for I am afraid it will break up the celebration, which would be a great pity. Papa had the headache this morning, so I could not practice very well. I did not much expect Miss Mary today, but she came through all of the mud and rain. She said she was going to give me a pretty song next month for papa said that I shouldn't take but one a month. We had a very small reading class today, for several of the girls were absent on account of the rain, I suppose. But the sun shines out occasionally very brightly. When I came this morning, I didn't think any one else would come, and probably Miss Lizzie would teach right on, and get through by dinner, but Tillie Paine came after awhile. I said a very good mythology lesson, although I had to recite it by myself. The subject was "Demeter," and of course very interesting indeed. I am trying to get the prize for extra marks, and for that reason study harder than I otherwise would, probably. The prize in view stimulates the scholars a great deal, I think, and makes them careful about their deportment.*

"Just Beyond the Hill Crest, Lie the Plains of Peace"

Belle's description of a rainbow at the hilltop in the Holly Springs graveyard recalls circumstances surrounding an event that later gave the cemetery its name. By John Mickle's recollection, it was Helen Craft Anderson who suggested the name Hill Crest:

It was eight o'clock in the evening, July 24, 1905, and a group of friends were awaiting the funeral cortege of Hindman Doxey, uncle of Wall and Hindman Doxey, which had been delayed to await the coming of a brother on the evening train. The group stood on the crest of a hill, and as the moonlight flooded the valley and the hills beyond, Mrs. Anderson's mind recalled a line of poetry:

> 'Just beyond the hill crest,
> Lie the plains of peace.'

Mickle wrote that "All who lived in that era remembered how the horses which drew the funeral coaches were taught to walk at a slow step, out of respect for the dead, and how the bells of the churches would toll for the funeral procession.[16]

Wednesday, April 29th 1868. Miss Lizzie told me some incidents that occurred at the graveyard Saturday morning, which would be worthy of recording. In the morning the ladies that were there saw a widow with several children, each with a bouquet in their hands, going to decorate their husband and father's grave. When I went there the other evening I saw a grave dressed very prettily. Miss Lizzie said that a gentleman did it, for it was his brother buried there. He decorated it himself. While we were there Saturday, there was a most beautiful rainbow, right over the hill where the soldiers were buried. This was very appropriate I thought, coming while we were there thinking of our dead. I went to the Methodist Church last night to sing the pieces for the celebration, which is Friday. This morning was as pretty a day as I ever saw, the grass sparkled with dew and the leaves looked exquisite. Papa is well today and is busy at his office.

"Mr. Paine Attacked"

All were shocked that the Rev'd Henry Paine had been attacked and injured. Nothing so vividly illustrates the unsettled conditions of Holly Springs during this time so commonly and inaccurately termed "Reconstruction." It was for such reasons that otherwise law-abiding citizens found themselves acting in a vigilante manner to bring order to their neighborhoods. Meanwhile, Belle enjoyed her May Day, which was festooned with singing, prayer, and a speech by her father's law partner, James Fant. She also attended a masquerade ball-but because she was too young to date, went as a "spectator."[17] Meanwhile, Belle was relieved that most of the adults stayed away from the children's musical recital.

Monday, May 4th 1868. Friday is past at last. I went to the celebration and enjoyed myself very much. We had singing, prayer, and speaking. Mr. Fant's speech was splendid. Mr. Paine was going to speak in the evening, but the night before he was attacked by some one, and was unable to leave his room, but he has recovered, I believe. We stayed at the grounds and played 'till nearly dark. I would like to tell something else about the day, but I have not time. I went to the masquerade Thursday night as a spectator, and enjoyed myself very much.[18] *I found out who every one of the persons was, nearly, before I went home. Miss Mary Harrell had her soiree Saturday evening and had invited several persons, but they paid us a great compliment by staying away. Miss Lucilla Read was the only auditor. It rained a little yesterday, but I went to Singing school. There was a right hard thunderstorm in the morning, but it abated in time for us to go to Sunday school and church.*

"Presbyterians and Women's Education"

Belle seems to have aspired to a more academically challenging course of study than was usually attempted by Southern girls. But she had come under the influence of the Watson family, and true to their spiritual heritage, the Watsons believed in a good education for young ladies. Indeed, unlike some other groups, Presbyterians stressed education for girls as well as boys. William B. Sprague, a well-known Presbyterian, suggested that his church ought to provide higher education as "reparations to women who had been wronged by denial of such opportunity." A century before, most Americans were content if their daughters learned to read the Bible, repeat the catechism, and write a legible hand, but as early as the 1830s, most had agreed that women should be given more than rudiments of learning. It was Presbyterians who led in this work, and by the time of the Civil War, they had founded twenty-one women's academies in the South.[19] The Holly Springs Female Institute-established in January 1836 five months before lots were sold in the town-was not officially sponsored by any church, but Presbyterians formed the largest group among its supporters. A. M. Clayton later said of the Female Institute, that: "its educational advantages, were from the earliest day, of a high order" and helped establish Holly Springs as a center of learning.[20] Young ladies received the degree of M.P.L., presumably "Mistress of Polite Literature." The Female Institute never reopened after the war-hence, Elizabeth Watson's school for local children in her home.[21]

Tuesday, May 5th 1868. Last evening I read some in "Miss Landon's Works," and indeed I had a very pleasant time. I didn't have to study much last night, but I sat up as long as usual. I practiced hard this morning because I have a very hard and difficult piece. To be able to learn it, I will have to practice very much and very carefully. The name of it is "The Whispering Wind," and it is fifteen pages long. By the next time that I take a lesson, Miss Mary will have me a new song to take, and I will be highly delighted. Papa bought me a new instruction book by "Bertini." The reason Miss Harrell wanted it was to strengthen my fingers, and she says that it is a very excellent book. I believe I know my Mythology today, and also my French; now if I only know my Familiar Science, I will be very glad. I am going to try to know it for it is the last lesson, and I ought to have a perfect recitation. Papa says I needn't to take up anything in its place until next session, and then study Philosophy. I would like to study Rhetoric also.

"Pilgrim's Progress"

Next to the Bible and the Shorter Catechism, Bunyan's *Pilgrim's Progress* was the most honored piece of literature in a nineteenth century Protestant household. The compliments amassed on behalf of this devotional classic were legion. It is seldom read today.

> **Wednesday, May 6th 1868.** *Miss Annie Lewis went home with me yesterday evening and stayed a long time. I went to Mrs. McCarroll's with her, and enjoyed myself swinging. It rained right hard this morning, and was very muddy, and cloudy too. After saying my French lesson I went home to practice but it was thundering so that I thought it was going to rain, so I brought my music and practiced at school. Lillie came out there to practice at ten, and as I had nothing to do in the school now, I stayed there with her. It rained very hard indeed, but now the sun is shining out, and makes the ground look quite different from the sky. We had "John Bunyan" for our subject in English Literature, and his character is very interesting. He is the author of the celebrated book "Pilgrim's Progress," and I suppose all of us have read it. I read the book long years ago. It is supposed to have been published more than any other book except the Bible, which is [the] Book of all Books.*

"Mr. Paine's Bookstore"

In 1866, J. B. Lippencott of Philadelphia, Pa., built a store in Holly Springs, with Heber Craft, serving as contractor. The two-story structure still stands two doors north of the church,[22] and perhaps Henry Martyn Paine, son of the Presbyterian minister, associated himself with this enterprise, or operated a store in another location.

Thursday, May 7th 1868. I went down to Mr. Clark's school room yesterday evening through all of the mud, and when I arrived at my destination, I found that Miss Mary had put off the vocal lesson until this evening. Lillie Moore went home with me, and we stood at the gate for along time. I read some, but not much, for I went up town. I went to Mr. Paine's bookstore and looked for some songs. But all that he has are not pretty at all. Last night I sat up writing my exercises 'till every one else had retired, and after writing a long time, I began to get frightened, and so retired. I have a very strong imagination, and it causes me to be afraid very often. It was a pretty day this morning, although it was a little cool. Papa awoke with one of his severe headaches, and he was still suffering when I went home at nine o'clock. Mama sent me to Mr. Frank's store, but I did not stay long. There is a Yankee in the next room now, talking very loud, and I would not be surprised if he was drunk. The time is out, and I am glad, for my subjects are out also.

"I Took Some Time Reading My Journal"

Belle reflects on her journal-keeping, which now has extended over parts of four years, and there seems to be the first germ of recognition that the exercise has been a valuable one.

Friday, May 8th 1868. I took my vocal lesson yesterday evening, but it did not last as long as usual. When I got home I could not make any noise (as I usually do) because Papa was still suffering very much. At the supper table I remembered that I had left my French book at school, as I practiced an hour last night, and came over here and learned my lesson. I have not written as much as the others, for I took some of my time reading in the first part of my journal. When I used to keep it, Miss Lizzie told me that when

I [grew] large, I would like to read what happened then. But I told her that I never would love to read it. But even now I like to read what happened in my younger days. I got two new pieces this morning. One of them is the "Lament of the Alpine Shepherd Boy," and the other is "Music of the Rain." Both of them are songs and are very pretty. Miss Mary carried them back to the store and I will have to get them before Tuesday. She gave me the song, "'Tis But A Little Faded Flower."

"Jimmie Let Us Shoot His Pistol"

Firearms were more accepted in the rough and tumble world of 1868. James Henry Watson, no doubt impressed his little friends with his sidearm, and the girls were only too eager to demonstrate their prowess.

Monday, May 11th 1868. *Friday evening I stayed at Mrs. Watson's after school to spend the night. Lillie and I walked to the bridge, and when we came back Jimmie let us shoot his pistol.*[23] *We shot until nearly supper.*[24] *We went into the music room, and enjoyed ourselves very much. We played blindfolds, and had a gay time. I slept with Miss Annie, and we talked 'till after eleven o'clock. In the morning, I went to the bookstore after some music, and then went home. I gathered strawberries until dinner, and in the evening copied my composition and was sewing when some girls came in. They stayed until very late. Sunday morning it was a beautiful day though a little chilly in the morning. We went to Sunday school, and Mrs. Calkins said that she was going north Tuesday, and that I must come to see her this evening. I am very sorry, and don't know what we can do without her. She said probably she would get Mrs. Addison Craft*[25] *to take our class, but she was not certain. I went to the Baptist Church and in the evening went to Mrs. McCarroll's to see Mrs. Miller*[26] *who came in with Mr. Miller. She asked me to go home with her, but as I am going* to school, papa wouldn't let me go. This morning I came to school, and then went down to Mrs. Anderson's after some patterns.

Tuesday, May 12th 1868. *It stopped raining when I left home, and so I went after Bettie, and we went to see Mrs. Calkins, and we enjoyed ourselves very much. Mrs. Calkins is so very pleasant and entertaining that we felt right sorry when we had to leave. She did not sing for us, because she had such a cold. I regret so much that she is going, but I am very glad that she is not going to live [in the North]. She said that Miss Stella Craft[27] was to take our class. She will be a very good teacher, and probably will play for us in Sunday school. There are no girls here today, but Nettie Wooten, and two others besides myself. Lillie Moore and Miss Annie Lewis are both sick. It was raining so hard this morning that the rest did not come. It is raining hard now, and I want Miss Lizzie to let me cipher now, and not come back this evening, but I don't think she has quite decided what to do. Mrs. Calkins said probably she would go today, but I don't suppose she went as it is such a bad day.*

"Mrs. Watson has Someone Sick All the Time, Nearly"

A near-epidemic of sickness among Belle's classmates seemed to accompany each change of season. But fortunately it was not the sickness that was dreaded more than any other-yellow fever, or one of the other malarial fevers which, until the discovery of their cause, made life in Mississippi so uncertain and unpleasant.

Wednesday, May 13th 1868. *It rained hard yesterday morning, and so Miss Lizzie let us cipher, and get through in the morning before dinner. It rained all the evening, and I employed myself sewing in the house. Just before supper I was taken with a very severe headache, and ate no supper. I studied very little, and when I arose this morning, I was still sick. I practiced, though, and* learned my French lesson. After breakfast I came to school, and found two scholars here. Miss Annie Lewis was sick and I went up to see her. Afterwards I went in the sitting-room, and was looking over some magazines when the school bell rang. Miss Fannie Phillips was sick today and did not come to school. Miss Mittie Manning was taken sick and went home. I scarcely saw so much sickness. Mrs. Watson has someone sick all the time, nearly. We had two very prominent characters in our English Literature this morning, "Richard Baxter," and "John Tillotson." Miss Mary Harrell is going to make us play scales at the concert, and give an honorary card to those who excel. One for those who have a "Bertini" exercise book, and another for those who have a "Richardson" book. I commenced corresponding with Mollie Hughes again today, and I hope we will keep it up. We used to correspond some time ago, but something stopped it, and I never started again, until this morning. We have had very rainy weather for the past month, and this is the coldest weather we have had in a long time for May.

XIV. A Difficult Era in a Proud Community

The years of Mississippi's reconstruction were perhaps more trying than the war itself. The Civil War had not meant defeat but freedom for a majority of the people who lived in Marshall County. But now, African Americans with tragically limited education were being placed in positions of great responsibility. Freed slaves filled the ranks of the U. S. occupation troops, increasing resentment among whites in the community. J. W. C. Watson exercised a powerful role in the state's reconstruction affairs, bringing a moderating voice to radical policies put forth both by northern Republicans and bitter Southern Democrats. He took part in the Mississippi Reconstruction Convention of 1865 and was nominated to chair the 1867 Mississippi Constitutional Convention, where he argued that education of freed slaves was necessary. At the beginning of Grant's term as president, Watson led a delegation to Washington pleading for more liberal treatment of their state. Yet, Federal troops were stationed in Holly Springs and remained until 1875.[1] White people felt harassed by the authorities, and occasionally unfortunate incidents resulted. The Ku Klux Klan functioned in the county, but the Stricklands, the Watsons, and their friends furnished it no leadership.[2] Tensions ran high, but never to the point that lives were lost. In spite of all, Miss Lizzie strove to see that the pupils in her school maintained a "ladylike" serenity-as it were, "above the fray."

Thursday, May 14th 1868. *I went down to Mr. Clark's yesterday evening, to take my vocal lesson. Miss Mary taught us a new chorus, "Trip Away," and it is quite pretty. Mr. Carter took supper at our house, but left afterwards. He told us that some Yankees had come down to Col. Bowles' to arrest Willie and several other little boys, for frightening, in play, some Negroes. They had Lieut. Newton and the "Negro Bureau" at their heads, both of which men are little more than brutes. Papa says that he would not be surprised if they brought the boys here, under arrest. Miss Lizzie told us just now to record in our journals something that we have learned in our lessons every day. I haven't said but two lessons today, and the chief thing I learned was of Diana. She was considered by some of the ancients to be the same as Isis, for both of those goddesses have the moon for their archetype. Diana was the goddess of chase and hunting, and was the most chaste of all the deities.*

Friday, May 15th 1868. *Mama sent me up to town last evening, and when I returned, I amused and employed myself gathering cherries. I read some in "Miss Landon's Works" just before dark. This morning I commenced practicing at half after six, and had nearly finished when Mr. Fant came to his breakfast. I learned today that "Richard Baxter" was a very distinguished divine, and that he was a non-conformist. He was arrested for writing his "Commentaries on the New Testament," something against Episcopacy. Nettie Wooten told me that the Yankees who went down to Col. Bowles' had returned, and that they had them confined in the guardhouse. Eddie Watson went up to see them, and he said that Willie Bowles was not there, but he saw someone else that he knew. Nettie told me this, but she might have been mistaken. When papa comes to dinner, I will inquire further, and write it tomorrow. Miss Lizzie has not given our subjects for compositions, but there is no possibility of her forgetting about it. We are expecting*

Cousin Will Strickland today on the one o'clock train. We looked for him yesterday, but he did not come.

"Memorizing the Catechism"

In the churches, the young were carefully nurtured toward the day when they should make a profession of faith. In Calvinist households instruction in the Westminster Shorter Catechism was essential to this preparation. By this time other Sunday school materials supplemented catechetical drill, but it would be another half century and more before the catechism was laid aside.[3] Memorization of the catechism inspired denominational loyalty, and created a theologically literate body of hearers for sermons that were more complex and doctrinally principled than today. Some scholars believe that Sunday schools prepared the way for public schools in American culture-a development which local leaders such as the Watsons supported. W. A. Anderson, first principal of the Holly Springs Public School, was superintendent of the Presbyterian Sunday school for thirty years.

Monday, May 18th 1868. I woke up Friday night very sick indeed, and when papa came to me I was nearly dead as I thought. He was very much frightened, and said that if it was cholera times, I would have died. I was not well at all Saturday, but wrote my composition, the subject of which, was "A Walk." Saturday night I was too unwell to write my French exercise, and so retired. Sunday morning I went to Sunday school, and as Mrs. Calkins had gone, I found Miss Stella Craft installed as our teacher. I will like her very much, but she is very strict, and will, I hope, make Bettie and Lillie help me answer the questions in "The Shorter Catechism." She conducted the Singing school in the evening, and we got on admirably. Papa went to Panola yesterday evening on the five o'clock train. He expects to return Friday night. In the English Literature, I learned about "Sir William Temple." He was born in London, and educated at Cambridge. He wrote a book, which caused one of the most celebrated controversies in England, entitled "Essay on Ancient and Modern Learning." Miss Mary McCarroll came over with her work today, and was at home when I left. Sunday was the anniversary of our May celebration.

"Sending a Letter to Fannie Leak by Col. Falconer"

The postal service was again delivering mail, but local people still preferred to send letters in the care of friends. This method was cheaper and considered more reliable. Howard Falconer, a friend of the Stricklands, was a witty young attorney who took part in the local dramatic club and appeared in several of its productions. The son of Thomas Falconer, brother of Mississippi secretary of state Kinloch Falconer, and a Civil War veteran, Howard worked in the local newspaper business. He was part owner with A. M. West and T. J. Malone of a firm that manufactured wagons and buggies. Howard Falconer died in the yellow fever of 1878.[4]

Tuesday, May 19th 1868. *Mama sent me to town, and I went to every store, and did not succeed in getting what I wanted. Last night I wrote my French exercises and stayed up a good deal later than usual. I could not practice this morning, for I hurt my hand very badly, cutting some cheese last night. I did not think that I could take my music lesson, but my finger was not too stiff when the time came. . . .It is a beautiful song and accompaniment. I do not generally go home music lesson days, but as I had nothing to do I went home, and stayed an hour. I learned today how Diana is represented. She is represented as drawn in a chariot by stags, or her nymphs, or with a crescent on her head and a quiver on her shoulder. This latter is the way she may be known in the "Council of the Gods." In the reading class we are reading the play "As You Like It," and I have the part of "Celia." It is a very interesting play indeed, and is a comedy. Mr. Howard Falconer came to see us yesterday evening, and said he thought of going to Mrs.*

Leak's Thursday. If he does, probably I will write to Fannie by him.

"We Think Probably Papa Will Come Today"

When men traveled in this era, the women usually stayed behind. Trains were slow, hotels primitive, and social life on the road generally unsuitable for feminine sensibilities.

> **Wednesday, May 20th 1868.** Miss Fannie Phillips did not come to school today for some reason, and I brought her a beautiful cluster of double roses, though they are withering now. Miss Mattie Manning is absent also, from sickness. Today in the "Life of Dryden" in English Literature, I learned that he was one of the distinguished persons who are buried in "Westminster Abbey." He is generally recorded as ranking with the first poets, though he [was] not so considered by that author. I went all around town yesterday evening twice, and last night I was right tired. This morning I finished practicing before Mr. Fant came in the parlor. I studied my French lesson then 'till breakfast was ready. I got a ten in English Literature, and if I succeed in my other lessons as well, I will be as happy as such things can make me. We think probably papa will come today, though he said he was coming Friday. And think mama will be a little disappointed if he does not. She is going to look for him. Today is vocal lesson day, and we can take a long lesson, for it is not cloudy, as usual. Miss Lizzie told me to let her read over my French lesson for tomorrow, and my exercise for this morning.

"President Johnson Was Acquitted"

Belle makes brief reference to the impeachment of Andrew Johnson before the U. S. Senate. The president, who survived in office by a single vote, was rendered impotent and the country was governed by those to whom white Southerners referred as "Radical" Republicans. Some in Holly Springs affiliated with the Republican party in this period.

> ***Thursday, May 21st 1868.*** *I finished a piece in "Miss Landon's Works" last evening, and then as mama had the headache, I stayed out in the yard most of the time 'till supper. I sat up quite late writing my French exercises, and was the last one to retire, with the exception of Mr. Fant. I practiced an hour before breakfast, and then came almost immediately to school. I read a piece in a magazine called "The Unclaimed Portrait," which is a beautiful piece. I learned today that "Minerva," who sprang from the head of "Almighty Jove," was the "Goddess of Wisdom," and one of her chief delights was warlike pursuits. It is very cloudy today, and has been raining some. We heard a short time since, that President Johnson was acquitted, and I heard one gentleman say, "Bully for Johnson," a very illiterate expression, but the only one to express his joy. Miss Lizzie made a new rule or two, which were that we must not speak to her without raising our hands and must not say any impatient word or words during the day. She requires us to have our books arranged when school is dismissed, and if we have not broken any of these during the day she gives us an extra mark, without reference to our lessons.*

"The Negroes Have a May Day Celebration Today"

May Day was marked by both races, but in separate observances, of course. Despite the strict segregation that was enforced in public society, black and white children did play together, and whites were not above playing tricks on Negroes-tricks that seem to be almost the childhood equivalent of the measures then being perpetrated by the Ku Klux Klan. The incident Belle describes was approved by Mrs. Strickland.

> ***Friday, May 22nd 1868.*** *I read yesterday evening until five*

o'clock when I went to the gate to see if papa came, but I was disappointed again. Last night I wrote my exercise and then we had some fun. A little Negro boy named Eli wanted to stay with Janett's[5] child, Alfred. Mama let him that time stay, but for fear that he would [want] to do so again, she sent Buddie out to frighten them. He opened the door, and knocked on the window, but as we heard no one moving we thought they were asleep. This morning we asked Eli if they heard anything, and he said they were very much frightened, and that he was not going to sleep out there any more. Janett had gone to church, and when she came back they were very much frightened indeed. (What I learned today was a brief outline of "The Miracle of Changing the Water into Wine." Something to be remembered for its beauty. Miss Cora said she had forgotten when she read it, but she thought it was in some paper. Some person offered a reward to anyone who would give the best paraphrase of it. A student brought his which was, "The conscious water saw its God and blushed." The most beautiful thing of the kind, I believe, I ever read. He of course received the prize. It is a great pity that we do not know the parties.) The Negroes have a May Day celebration today, and they marched all around town with the Yankee flag, and [a] standard bearing the inscription: "The First Colored School of Holly Springs." Most of the girls went to see them, but I would not look at the things for anything.[6]

Monday, May 25th 1868. When I came back to school Friday evening, Mr. Fant gave me his knife, and I was trying to cut something, and succeeded very well, for the knife slipped, and cut my finger very badly indeed. I haven't been able to practice since, and it pains me very much yet. Papa came Friday at one o'clock, and that expression, "It never rains but it pours," was appropriate, for Mrs. Leak came afterwards, and then Cousin Boothe, then Mr. Morgan, and we had a house full. Saturday Rosa Clark came for me to spend the day with her, to eat a birthday dinner. Her birthday was Thursday, but she had her dinner Saturday. She was twelve years old. Sunday morning I went to Sunday school and to the Methodist Church with Mrs. Leak. I did not go to Singing school, for papa wants me to stop going. This morning my finger was still too sore to practice, and I gathered Mrs. Leak some strawberries. I learned my French lesson, and when I came to school Miss Fannie Phillips told me all about the Ball they had Friday night. It was a masquerade, and she went. She had a delightful time, I believe. I learned today that "Bunyan" was confined twelve years, and during that time, wrote his celebrated work "The Pilgrim's Progress," and that it had been published more than any book except the Bible.

"To Hear Cousin Boothe Baskerville Preach"

Belle's cousin, the Rev'd Boothe Baskerville, was a Methodist preacher of note. Citizens of Holly Springs loved nothing more than to go and hear good preaching. Auditors were all the more attentive when they could claim kinship to a pulpit orator.

Tuesday, May 26th 1868. *I sewed some last evening for mama, and then Rosa Clark came for me to go to walk with her. I did not want to go but went to the gate with her, and saw papa going home with Mr. Ross. He let us go with him, and Mr. Ross gave him a beautiful bouquet, and I had to carry it for him. We stayed 'till quite late, and when I got home, I got ready for church. Cousin Boothe Baskerville was going to preach, and I was very anxious to hear him. Mr. Fant went with Mrs. Leak and I, and we were not too late. He preached a splendid sermon, and a very short one.*[7] *I wrote an exercise this morning before school. I learned seven pages in mythology today, but I can't think of anything to record. She was the protecting deity of Ulysses and his son. She is the goddess of war, and of the arts, the superintendent of the building of the ship Argo, and also the wooden horse by which Troy was conquered. She embroidered her own, and Juno's robe, which* were exquisitely wrought. She is said to have taught mortals the art, who[m] she favored. When Mrs. Leak goes home, Miss Ella is coming to see us. I will be highly delighted, for I love her so much.

Wednesday, May 27th 1868. *I read nearly all the evening after school yesterday, and I, of course, enjoyed myself hugely. Cousin Boothe preached again last night, and we went the second time, with the addition of papa's and mamma's company. He of course preached a splendid sermon, and we were highly delighted at his success. I practiced this morning as my finger has improved, and studied my French lesson. I learned today that "Thomas Parnell" was a very fickle character. He was at first a Tory, but seeing that the other was in the popular side, he became a Whig. He wrote a very celebrated piece called "The Hermit." It was too long to write in full, so they printed a sketch of it at the bottom of the page. As it is very interesting I would like to see the whole piece. Mrs. Leak says that someone is coming after her Monday-next, and Miss Ella is coming also to see us and spend two or three weeks with Mama. Today is the time for vocal lesson, and I am very glad, for I like to sing, but some of the scholars dislike the lessons a good deal. This morning papa had a headache, but probably as he has so much work to do today, he will get well by night or dinner.[8] I always hate for him to have the headache, because everything has to be so quiet, and I am so noisy that it is difficult for me to be silent. Of course, that reason is not the principal one, for I sympathize with him very deeply. I have the headache every day, and am suffering very much now.*

Thursday, May 28th 1868. *I read a little while yesterday evening, and then wrote some in my French exercise book. Mr. Frank Leak came at dinnertime yesterday, and left this morning. He was not well at all when he left. I played with Robbie and Minnie a long time before I came to school. I have finished in my copybook, and therefore had twenty minutes to write in my journal today. In my* *mythology this morning, I learned about "Vulcan" and "Minerva." The "Parthenon," the latter's chief temple, was at Athens, on the Acropolis hill. It was once the most elegant of the temples of the superstitious heathen, but now it has been so much destroyed, that the shape can hardly be distinguished. Miss Lizzie said that the writings of a person who traveled there and saw it in 1676, nearly two hundred years ago, said, then, all of this building was standing except the roof. But soon afterwards the city was besieged by the Turks, who threw a shell in the temple and exploded some powder that was secreted there. The place was nearly entirely destroyed, but sufficient remains to convince us of the ancients' skill in architecture. Miss Lizzie told us of it today, and how much I would like to go there, and see these things myself.*[9] *It would be the greatest wish that I have satisfied if I could only travel to Italy and France. Miss Mary Harrell taught us the song or chorus that we are to sing [-] the last piece at the concert [-] yesterday evening in the vocal class. She said for me to sing a duet with Alice Rutland at the end of June, but Alice will not sing alto, and papa won't let me sing it, and so I don't suppose I can sing with her. Monday next is Minnie's birthday, but she is I believe, going to postpone her party 'till Ada Leak comes. She is not very well today, but is better than she was yesterday.*

"One Month From Now School Will Be Out"

Like all children, Belle longed for summer vacation. School terms were shorter than now, but primarily because they began later in the fall.

Friday, May 29th 1868. *Today is the last Friday in May, and one month from now school will be out. I will commence, as soon as June comes, to count every day. Miss Mary Harrell said I might play and sing "The Lament of the Alpine Shepherd Boy" at the concert, and I greatly prefer singing it to a duet with anyone. It is a beautiful piece, and the words are as pretty as I have heard in a* long time. I learned today of "William Penn," who founded the city of "Philadelphia," which means "Brotherly Love." He carried his family to America to live, but they were not satisfied with the crude habits of the people, and prevailed upon him to return to England where he died, after various troubles. I forgot my copybook yesterday evening, and so wrote in my French lesson book this morning. . . .A year ago today, I went out to see Miss Fannie Phillips and enjoyed myself very much. I made a mistake-it was on Friday, but will not be a year exactly 'till Sunday. I came back the next day to Minnie's birthday party. I am, I believe, going to write some on my composition tonight so I will have more time tomorrow. Maybe I will go to church.*

"None of Us Went to Church Friday Night"

Friday services were to prepare for celebrations of the Holy Communion. As Mary Virginia Grigsby Foley, whose father was pastor of the Holly Springs Presbyterian Church 1897-1904, recalled: "On Wednesday nights we attended prayer meeting, and once a month on Friday nights before Communion Service the following Sunday we attended Preparatory Service. A tight schedule for all, but not disagreeable when you are accustomed to it."[10]

Monday, June 1st 1868. *None of us went to church Friday night, because Minnie was a good deal worse. She did not improve much Saturday, nor Sunday, but as today is her birthday, she got up and dressed. I went up town Saturday evening and bought her a beautiful doll for her present. I went to Sunday school and the Presbyterian Church yesterday, but have stopped going to Singing school because papa did not like me to go. Papa went to Oxford yesterday at five o'clock, but will be home Wednesday. I had the headache last night, and this morning too, so did not practice. I have written nearly all of my composition, but I can't think of anything else. "Joseph Addison" was the subject of our English Literature this morning, and we had a long lesson, for there was a* good deal said of him. He married the "Countess of Warwick," but she was probably the cause of his dying so soon, because she was capable of appreciating his noble genius. His death-bed scene was very affecting. His son-in-law was very dissipated, but quite amiable. He was sent for by Addison. Lord Warwick came, and told him that he hoped that he had something to say to him, and that everything he said, would be kept sacred. Addison could scarcely speak, but rising up he said, "See with what peace a Christian can die," and expired. . . .

Tuesday, June 2nd 1868. Last night Mrs. Leak took tea at Mrs. McCarroll's, and after supper Miss Mary and Mrs. John Leak came home with her. Mr. Falconer with Miss Travis and his sister Miss Sophronia came to see Mrs. Leak. The latter, Miss Sophronia, is to be married tomorrow night. Today I learned that Venus loved Adonis, and that a boar killed him. She was quite disconsolate at first, but afterwards she put nectar on the spot, and caused the flower Anemone to spring up there, which from its frailty represented how Adonis had been cut down in the flower of his youth.

"Visiting the Dentist"

Dentistry was not an advanced profession in 1868, but such as it was, only the well off could afford a dentist's care. A decade earlier Emma Finley wrote of her sister that: "Ginnie went in to have her teeth fixed." A few days later, Emma recorded: "Wed. morning had my teeth plugged- & a siege I had of it too."[11] Dr. S. P. Cutler was the local dentist and taught chemistry and geology in Franklin Female College.[12]

Wednesday, June 3rd 1868. Miss Lizzie dismissed school sooner than usual last evening because it was going to rain very hard. It did rain some, but during the night there was a very hard storm indeed. The wind blew, and it thundered and lightened. This morning I came to school, but was a little too late by <u>Miss Lizzie's clock.</u> When I returned home I found papa there before me. I learned today of a beautiful ode by "Esther Vanhomigeh" who was "Vanessa" whom "Swift" pretended to love for a long time. Today is vocal evening, and I suppose Miss Mary will tell us something about the concert. It (the concert) is so near that I am afraid we will not be prepared for it. Buddie has not been to the country to stay for a good while, but as papa does not have to leave home very soon, he will have to go. Mrs. Leak started home yesterday evening just before the rain, and as she had seven teeth extracted in the morning, we are very much afraid that she is sick. I intended copying a piece of poetry in the back of my book, but Lillie Moore has the book.

Thursday, June 4th 1868. I took a vocal lesson yesterday evening, and Miss Mary taught us a chorus to sing at the concert, and will teach us another next Wednesday. I went home and copied them. One of them was called "The Parting Song," and the other "Summer is Coming." I gathered raspberries 'till late and after tea wrote my exercises. I slept upstairs with Miss Ella, and did not wake soon enough this morning to practice. When I went home I practiced and made up for it, though. Today, "Hermes" and "Mercury" was the subject of our mythology lesson. We learned of his inventing the lute, out of a tortoise shell, and of his stealing fifty oxen belonging to Apollo. He made shoes for them, to hide their tracks, and he sacrificed two oxen to himself. When Apollo called him to account for his conduct, he pretended to be very much surprised that a boy like him just a day old could drive and steal oxen from a mountain. Apollo gave him a wand to settle all differences. He saw two snakes one day fighting, and he struck the ground between them, and they wrapped themselves around his staff, and ever since his staff is represented with snakes around it.

"The Temperance Movement Comes to Holly Springs"

There can be no doubt that some drank too much in this era. Heavy drinking had become more prevalent following the American Revolution, and the same seems to have been true during and after the Civil War. In 1792, secretary of the treasury Alexander Hamilton reported that the annual consumption of spirits was two-and-a-half gallons per person. By 1810, this amount had increased to four-and-a-quarter gallons. The figure peaked in 1823 when the *Boston Recorder* estimated that each American drank an annual average of seven and a half gallons. In the early days of the republic, all who lived on the frontier were regarded as "intemperate."[13] "The conditions in those days," as historian Roger Burlingame has noted,

> when, in the West, whiskey supplanted rum as the prevailing beverage, when it was homemade, untaxed, and essential to every celebration-civil, military, and religious-were so entirely without restraint that, in the light of modern researches into alcoholism, the survival of our rugged ancestors and the evidence of their immense achievements are astonishing indeed.[14]

It was not Puritanism, but the easy availability and abundance of fortified liquors after 1800 that caused many church members to begin to advocate total abstinence from intoxicants of all kinds. Temperance societies first formed outside the churches, but churches supported their efforts. Col. Peter Lucas was an early Holly Springs speechmaker for this cause, assisted by his son-in-law, J. W. Clapp. Clapp gave a stirring address on the subject at the Holly Springs Methodist Church, March 8, 1842, which was published. On Christmas Day 1847, he spoke again when the Sons of Temperance met in the Presbyterian Church as the ladies of the city honored their organization with the presentation of a Bible.[15] While most church members acknowledged that drinking, in itself, could not be condemned on the basis of scripture, the increased use and apparent abuse of alcohol after the Civil War led temperance societies to redouble their efforts. These argued that total abstinence was the only effectual remedy. Maine adopted the first statewide prohibition law in 1851, and many states followed suit. J. W. C. Watson devoted much effort toward enacting a prohibition law for Mississippi and to the prosecution of individuals in his congregation who drank.

Women were particularly interested in the temperance,[16] for they stood to gain most if it were practiced, or to suffer the most perilous loss and abuse if their fathers and husbands were drunk-hence, Belle's interest in Mr. Freeman's invitation to her brother.

Friday, June 5th 1868. Yesterday was Mrs. Barrett's reception day, but mama didn't call on her, for she was sick. Miss Ella and Miss Sally McCarroll called late in the evening. Russell Freeman came after Buddie last night to go to a temperance society, I believe, or something of the sort.[17] He stayed out on the porch a few minutes discussing with papa whether Buddie should go or not. Papa at last consented, and they went off together. I told Miss Fannie yesterday, maybe I would stay with her tonight, but as I have not asked mama, I am not certain yet. "Rachel Russell" and "George Lowell" were the subjects of our lesson today, but I am at a loss what to say of them. I will try to say something. The former's husband was executed for treason, and during the trial she was his amanuensis. She lived forty years afterwards, and during her life, wrote many letters which were full of truth, and nature, things which come from the heart alone. When I went home this morning Mama and Miss Ella had gone up to town. Minnie was there alone, sewing for her dolls, or rather making a needle case. I received a letter from Mollie Hughes last night, and it was as sweet as could be, the kind she always writes.

"I Went to the Episcopal Church to See Mrs. Clark's Baby Baptized"

Baptisms in this era were often private. In olden times, the child was taken to the church almost immediately after birth by godparents. But by the nineteenth century, it was thought that the parents should be present, and new mothers-having recently been through the ordeal of birth, wished for modesty's sake to have the sacrament administered in a more intimate setting-either a family gathering at home, or in a special service at the church on Sunday afternoon.

> *Monday, June 8th 1868.* Friday evening Mal Williamson[18] came for me, and after a good deal [of] entreating, papa consented for me to spend the night with her. Rosa Clark also stayed, and we had a right nice time. I didn't do much of anything all day Saturday, as we did not have any composition to write, for Miss Lizzie excused us. Sunday I went to the Methodist Church with Miss Ella. In the evening I went to the Episcopal Church to see Mrs. Clark's baby baptized. It did not cry at all, but when the minister, Mr. Pettis,[19] took her she pulled his whiskers, and scarcely anyone could keep from laughing. This morning is a very pretty day, but not as warm as usual. I learned today of "Richard Steele," who was born in Dublin and educated at Oxford. He at first wrote for the stage, but afterward published a periodical, called in honor of the fair sex, "The Tattler." He wrote under the assumed name of "Mr. Isaac Bickerstaff," a name under which "Swift" also wrote for a time. Miss Cora says probably she will go to Oxford to the Commencement on the twenty second, and she will excuse us from our lessons from that time. When Miss Cora goes to the Commencement, some one is going to take her place: I heard afterwards.

"A Political Meeting and Tragedy at the Distillery"

Political campaigns were bitter during Reconstruction, and Belle gives a full account of one of the worst incidents. Meanwhile, tragedy befell a family of Belle's acquaintance. Following the Civil War, Spires Boling, the local builder whose talent played its part in the building of almost every home and church in Holly Springs during the 1850s and '60s, operated a distillery[20] in Spring Hollow,[21] behind the large home he had built for himself, where Randolph St. meets the Salem Rd. Many opposed the distillery, as well as the saloons it supplied. But misfortune occurred when Boling's son fell into a vat of boiling water. The child died two days later.[22]

> ***Thursday, June 9th 1868.*** *Yesterday some Radicals came here to speak to the Negroes, and were speaking all day. They talked very badly and several persons resented it. In the evening "Gill"[23] arose and began speaking, and he was so insulting that some of the gentlemen could stand it no longer. Mr. George Myers[24] rushed forward, and ascended the platform, and succeeded in precipitating one of the Radicals to the ground, which broke his leg. He crept under the platform and cried out several times, "Don't let them get me," all the time clinging to some rocks near him. Col. Myers was prevented from going forward by several persons, and meanwhile Capt. Powers had brought his men and drawn them out on the north part of the square. When the Negroes saw them coming they said, "Now we'll have our rights," thinking that they were to be protected. Maj. Powers ascended the platform, told Mr. Gill to hush, ordered the meeting to be broken up, then went back to his men, amid the shouts of our people, for "Three cheers for Powers." Nearly everyone was greatly excited to death. Gill carried the Negroes to his house, and I believe had more speaking there last night. Col. Myers was fined, but not allowed by his friends to pay the fine. Mr. Jimmie Fant says he never saw anyone as cowed as Gill was, and Mrs. Gill,[25] who was sitting on the*

stand literally rolled off. I have taken up so much time describing the fray, that I have no time for anything else.[26] *I learned today of "Mercury," who was represented with winged sandals and cap. Mr. Boling's little son fell into a tub of boiling water and is nearly if not quite dead. I have not heard anything of him today, but I hope he is better. He was scalded from his feet to his breast.*

Wednesday, June 10th 1868. *Mr. Boling's little son died yesterday at eleven o'clock, and will be buried at three this afternoon. I heard afterwards that he fell into a pit or something of the sort, for his father keeps a distillery. I think that ought to be a warning to him to stop keeping one. Miss Mary Harrell is not going to have a party, but we don't know yet what she will have. "Daniel Defoe" was the subject of my lesson today. He was born in London, and wrote the celebrated book, "Robinson Crusoe." That is a book that I never read. I don't know why but if I take it up I can't read any time before I get tired. Today is the time to take vocal lessons (Thursday). I heard today that someone was to take Miss Cora's place.*

Thursday, June 11th 1868. *The funeral service was preached yesterday evening, and I was very anxious to go, but I could not. All of the other schools were dismissed, and Mr. Clark's went in a procession. Mr. Anderson dismissed his because the little boy went to school to him. We did not take a vocal lesson last evening, for some reason, I do not know what. Miss Mary sent us word to come this evening. Last night I studied a good deal harder than usual, and today I knew my French very well. I learned in Mythology just nothing at all, but I will try and think of something to put. The subject was "Penates" and "Genius." That is all I know. Miss Lizzie says a Mr. Reed was stabbed at the distillery yesterday by one of the workmen, whom he had accused of stealing, I believe. The man was not dangerously wounded, though the wound was very serious. I have not heard anything else, though*

I think there are a good many things occurring during this week, and therefore it might be called a momentous one. The time is now out, and I am glad.

Friday, June 12th 1868. *Two weeks from today, and school will be dismissed. The only [thing] I dread, though, is the concert. I reckon Miss Lizzie will have to give us holiday, for Miss Mary said today that she wanted to have a rehearsal that morning. I am going to sing "Lament of the Alpine Shepherd Boy," and play "Come where My Love Lies Dreaming," with variations. We played and sung our pieces last evening. At least all of them except myself, for I have not learned mine yet. Some of the pieces are beautiful. Bettie McCarroll is going to play, "Falling Leaves," a piece which is very hard, but the difficulties are compensated for by the beauties. I wrote my exercise last night, and consequently sat up quite late. This morning "Gay" and "Arbuthnot" were the subjects of my lesson. The former was an apprentice, but on account of his fondness for poetry and literature, he became a poet. He wrote a piece called "The Beggar's Opera," which he sold to "Mr. Rich," proprietor of a theatre, and people, on account of its popularity, said that it made <u>Gay rich</u>, and <u>Rich gay</u>.*

"Mr. Tucker was Found Dead by the Roadside"

Murder and mayhem seemed to abound on the streets of Holly Springs in these days, contributing to the uncertainty felt by all-both black and white. Meanwhile, Belle's thoughts centered upon the upcoming recital in which she was to take part, and, following that, summer vacation!

Monday, June 15th 1868. *Friday night, I went with Mr. Fant to a "dramatic reading" and was highly interested, for the selections were mostly poetical, humorous and sad. He read a beautiful piece of poetry, "The Drummer's Bride," the story of which was, that the Drummer was killed in the war, and his bride be-*

came a lunatic; he was (the man) a splendid speaker and read with so much expression. I went with Miss Stella Saturday, to have her picture taken, and then went to see Miss Fannie with her, Saturday morning, and a gentleman, <u>Mr. Tucker</u>, came in papa's office, and was talking very gaily and was, or seemed to be very happy. Late that evening he was found being dead by the roadside about eight miles from town. He had been shot by another man, who papa says is a rascal. He seems to have been surprised. He had <u>thirteen</u> (13) living children, and now they have no one to support them. Sunday we could not say our lesson for they had to talk about the distribution of the books, and during the time, Mr. Lane[27] became mad for some reason or other, and left. I don't think the man who killed Mr. Tucker has been heard from since. Mr. Jones met him soon after he had committed this terrible crime, and the scoundrel told him that he had just killed a man back there, and had left him in the road, weltering in his blood. He was shot with a shotgun, and killed instantly.[28]

Tuesday, June 16th 1868. *Miss Mary Harrell sent for me, and I went to Mr. Clark's school room to learn the alto of the chorus of the song, "My Willie's Over the Dark Blue Sea," a piece which is quite pretty, but as old as the hills. In the evening it looked very much like rain, and we hoped very much that it would. Towards night it began to thunder and lighten, and the sky looked as dark as it generally does when it rains. The lightning was the prettiest I ever saw, and it was zigzag. I retired fully believing that we would have a good rain, for we need it so much. I arose this morning and found that it just rained a very little shower. Miss Mary said today that we had to meet at Mr. Clark's the last day of school (Friday week) and have a rehearsal, and afterwards we had to decorate the school room. So I will not have to go to school at all that day. She wants me to play my piece tomorrow evening, and I have to practice very hard to learn it. She played it for me, and it is a beautiful instrumental piece of music. It is very oppressive* today, but I don't think it is as <u>warm</u> as yesterday was. Lillie Moore, Miss Annie Lewis, and Tillie Paine are all sick today. Tillie was taken sick in the reading class, and is upstairs now. I learned today of the "Penates" and "Lare," who are domestic deities, and are worshiped in every house, and every meal was the same as a sacrifice to them.

Wednesday, June 17th 1868. Last evening I practiced my piece,"Come Where My Love Lies Dreaming," for Miss Mary says I will have to play it this afternoon. I have practiced it very hard, but don't think I know it perfectly yet. I went downtown with Miss Ella, and came back right soon. I think I know my French lesson better than usual, this morning. The subjects of my English Literature were "Thomas Tickell," "Richard Bentley," and "William Somerville." The former was the bosom friend of Addison, and after the latter's death (Addison's) wrote an Elegy in the first part of his works. Miss Mary McCarroll came over to see us this morning, and I left her there when I came to school. We read today "The Battle of Lake Regilus," and I think it is perfectly beautiful. The description of the battle is perfect, that is, so far as I know about battles. One week from tomorrow and I will have vacation! Miss Mary is going to have a rehearsal this evening instead of the vocal lesson. When I go home to dinner, I think now that I will practice, and be able to play my piece in some manner today. When Miss Mary plays it, it is a beautiful piece, and will be very much appreciated by the audience, <u>if well played.</u> O! I hope I can succeed, and as my teacher says, "Get up a reputation for myself among the people." I think it is very probable that some of us will fail, for judging others by myself, it is enough to frighten one's life out of them.

"Oh! That I had the Wings of a Dove"

In the aftermath of her recital, a fit of melancholy set upon

Belle. But despite a rehearsal of theology, the dark mood passed, especially after her music teacher offered a complimentary evaluation of her performance.

> ***Thursday, June 18th 1868.*** *"Oh! That I had the wings of a dove, that I might fly away and be at rest."*[29] *I feel today as if I would be willing to die, and not live another hour. I have the headache and that keeps me from taking an interest in anything-not even my lessons. Today week, school will be out with me, and if I can go to Mrs. Leak's, maybe my health will improve. But I must not complain for my suffering is nothing to what my Savior suffered to redeem me. "Rise, poor heart, but do not break!" It is His will that I should suffer and I try, with God's help, to say "Thy will be done!" I played my piece tolerably well yesterday, and after I went home, I watered the flowers. I sat up later than usual, and <u>then</u> Miss Lizzie told me to write my exercise over. But I will try to do my duty. There were various subjects in my mythology lesson, so many that I hardly know how to say anything of them. It was about "Juno" and the other goddesses of the "Council of Jupiter." Next week we have two lessons to recite, and we will have to study right hard. Willie Bowles came yesterday, and will stay a week or two, I suppose. He looks very well, but I have not seen him very well. I want to ask him of Dell, but have not had an opportunity yet.*

> ***Friday, June 19th 1868.*** *Yesterday Nettie Wooten came to see me, and wanted me to go to walk with her, and we walked to Mr. House's. When we were returning we saw Maj. Ewen and Miss Kennedy riding as usual. Miss Cora said that she was going to Oxford tomorrow, and I would not be surprised if Miss Mary [Paine] heard our lessons until her return. I don't think I would like it much, although she would hear but one of my lessons. "Dean Swift" was the subject of our lesson today. He wrote predictions concerning a Mr. Patridge, who was an almanac-maker, and pre-*

dicted one year what would happen the next. Swift said that he would die a certain day and hour, and everyone believed that he would, and that he died at the appointed time. This morning Miss Mary gave me a music lesson, and said as one of my lessons would come on Friday next, and that [as] she would not or could not give it to me, she would come Tuesday and Thursday next week. She said I played my piece very well the other evening.

"Miss Mary Paine Heard our Lessons"

Miss Mary Rowland Paine (1839-1921), daughter of the Rev'd Henry H. and Mrs. Elizabeth Baxter Paine, embarked early on a teaching career that was to last a lifetime in Holly Springs. After her mother's death in 1870, she kept house for her widowed father who moved to Texas in 1872, after surrendering his ministry of many years under a cloud of charges by the presbytery. Mary remained in Holly Springs, where she taught in Miss Lizzie Watson's school and later as art teacher at North Mississippi Presbyterian College. She made her home with the Eagleton Smiths and later the Addison Crafts. Both church and community held Mary Paine in high regard, and she is remembered as one of Mississippi's early female portrait painters. In the meantime, as this portion of Belle's diary draws to a close, Miss Lizzie-true to her reputation as a Calvinist educator of the old school-held to her standards. Classes would not be dismissed for any "frivolous" purpose.[30]

Monday, June 22nd 1868. *Friday evening Miss Emma Gibbons spent the night with Miss Ella. Mr. Howard Falconer came by and Miss Ella went home with he and Miss Travis. I sewed nearly all day, and in the evening wrote my composition, but did not copy it until this morning. Miss Cora went to Oxford Saturday, and Miss Mary Paine heard our lessons. I don't like the way she asks the questions, but the reason is she [doesn't] know how Miss [Lizzie] does it. Late Saturday night, not very long before supper,*

Mr. Falconer came back and brought Ada with him. I went to Sunday school, and papa and mama and all of us went to the Presbyterian Church. I did not go to Singing school, but learned my Sunday school lesson. Miss Lizzie is going to make us copy the piece of poetry tomorrow to see who has improved the most. Mr. Clark has changed his plans, and is going to dismiss school tomorrow, and have the concert Wednesday. I believe he is going to Vermont Thursday. We will have to go to school Thursday and Friday, but I don't know how we can do it, for we will not feel much like studying those two days. Now I will have holiday, I reckon, Wednesday instead of Friday. I wish Miss Lizzie would dismiss us tomorrow, but there is no use in wishing, for there is no possibility of her doing it.

Epilogue

William Baskerville Hamilton has written that "the history of...Holly Springs might be said to be the history of her educational endeavors." Presbyterians began with a school for the native Chickasaw at Martyn Station, a mission about five miles west of Holly Springs in 1825, a decade before the territory was opened to white settlement.[1] They also encouraged the first school for whites in the Chickasaw cession. This was the Holly Springs Female Institute, organized in 1836. A teacher was employed, and she oversaw the raising of "a modest but comfortable structure of hewn logs with clapboard roof, overhung by friendly oaks," on a lot at the western edge of the village fronting on the Hernando Road. Soon after, a music room was added. Samuel Hurd, first minister of the local Presbyterian Church, served on the board of the Female Institute and taught there until the 1840s.[2]

As Reconstruction drew to a close, Elizabeth Watson's school for girls, Fenelon Hall prospered, even as in 1879 the town opened its first public school for whites. In 1882, during the presidency of Chester A. Arthur, Lizzie Watson, broadened her efforts, established a boarding school and named it Maury Institute in honor the famous Civil War naval commander.[3] The school provided the first kindergarten in Holly Springs. Desiring to make her school "the Vassar of the South,"[4] Watson built a large building behind her father's home, in which students boarded. The girls named their dormitory "Rocky Mountain," and it became a center of social interest for local boys. For a decade, Watson operated the school with success. Commencements were held in the Masonic Hall on the square.[5] The first graduate of Maury Institute was Irene Walter, later Mrs. Oscar Johnson, of Holly Springs and St. Louis. Miss Elizabeth Stuart, sister of Confederate general J. E. B. Stuart, taught for a time in Holly Springs, probably at Maury Institute. In 1888, the school was endorsed by the North Mississippi Presbytery of the Presbyterian Church, U. S.[6]

In 1891, deafness forced Elizabeth Watson's retirement. Maury Institute[7] was purchased by a local stock company and its name changed to North Mississippi Presbyterian College. Following a trend of the late nineteenth century, whereby many private educational institutions came under ecclesiastical control, the college was operated under joint auspices of a local board and the Synod of Memphis of the Presbyterian Church, U. S. In 1903, after synodical lines were withdrawn, the school was placed under the jurisdiction of the Synod of Mississippi and renamed Mississippi Synodical College. It was operated as a two-year liberal arts college for women, with a preparatory department embracing the lower grades. As enrollment expanded, buildings were added, so that the campus eventually covered parts of three blocks.[8] The school was known for high academic standards and was the first two-year college in the state to receive full accreditation (1916).[9] In 1939, as a result of the Great Depression, Mississippi Synodical merged with Belhaven College, another Presbyterian institution, and moved to Jackson, Miss., through which its influence continues to the present.[10]

In 1882, Belle Strickland married Charles Lee Bates (1849-1926), a distinguished attorney and newspaper editor,[11] whose lecture on admiralty law was an annual feature of the University of Mississippi Law School.[12] Belle died February 17, 1936, and her funeral was held at the Holly Springs Baptist Church, where she

Epilogue

had been a lifelong member. She was buried beside Judge Bates in Hill Crest Cemetery.[13]

After the war, Cora Watson married Major S. E. Carey and moved to New Orleans. An accomplished writer, she contributed a regular column for the New Orleans *Times-Democrat*. She died December 9, 1911, and her body rests in Hill Crest Cemetery.

"A Wedding at the Strickland Place"

Belle's half-sister Perle lived in the old Strickland Place. On October 2, 1926 the local newspaper carried this account of her wedding at the family home to Mr. Gerard Badow. Almost everyone in town attended. She was nearly sixty years old. The account gives a memorable description of the house, its history, furnishings, and ambiance.

"Miss Perle Strickland Becomes Bride of Gerard Badow"
by Mrs. Lucius Dancy[14]

The crowning event of a week of pre-nuptial festivities, the beautiful and impressive ceremony which united the lives of Miss Perle Strickland and Gerard Badow, took place Tuesday night at nine o'clock.

Picturesque, historic, old Strickland Place opened its heart and renewed its youth, to do honor to its latest bride, who had spent her life within its ancestral walls. The eager, loving hands of artistic friends had converted the place into a veritable sylvan bower and amid clustering evergreens and shaded lights one could almost vision the days when Stickland Place had been the gathering place for the stately men and fair women of the old South.

At the rear of the reception hall and opening into it, the dining room had been transformed into the semblance of a chapel, festooned and banked with dark, impressive pine, glossy evergreens and trailing vines. The altar was arranged facing the entry from the hall. It was white-draped and candle-lighted and adorned with a profusion of white carnations.

The hall was a masterpiece of elaborate decoration, the ceiling being literally covered by a canopy of glossy green, the stair railing massed and wreathed with vines and the chandelier shedding a soft glow from amid a mass of bridal tulle and evergreen.

On the left, as one entered was the living room where were displayed a wonderful array of gifts, magnificent in number and variety, mutely testifying to the popularity of the pair and the love and esteem in which they are held by a host of friends. Here glittering silver vied with brilliant cut glass but from the most ornate to the simplest token all found equal place in the heart of the bride.

The marriage of Miss Strickland and Mr. Badow united two prominent and aristocratic families, in this country and in Europe. The bride's family have been well and favorably known, not only in Mississippi, but throughout the South. The Stricklands have always stood for the best and highest ideals. Major Strickland, the bride's father was, in his lifetime, a lawyer of note and for many years one of Holly Springs' foremost citizens, while her lovely mother was representative of the old regime in the South.

The family of Mr. Badow have formed part of the ancient patrician element of a civilization far older than our own and as individuals they have ably carried on the traditions of their ancestors, but marriage is eminently an institution for individuals rather than families and in this beautiful union two interesting and unique personalities have met.

The bride, a charming and intellectual woman, one who has given her life in loving and unselfish service for others, ever counting the claims of friendship first, possesses to the fullest measure the artistic temperament and gift for self expression which should have carried her far in dramatic art, had not love for home and dear ones dominated her to the exclusion of ambition.

The bridegroom combines the best elements of the old world, in which he was born and the new, which he claims by adoption. He possesses the courtly bearing and distinguished appearance of his ancestors with the sterling business qualities and thorough up-to-dateness of our own United States. He adds to these things a quality of artistry which finds expression in his unusual ability as a composer and musician. Mr. Badow is a trusted representative of the Collins Agency for which he has traveled for years and whose representatives stand high in all banking circles.

The Marriage Ceremony

But to return to the great event of the marriage ceremony. On entering the reception hall, the guests were greeted by the ushers, Messrs. Francisco[15] and Doxey,[16] who showed the guests to their respective cloak rooms, after which the company scattered through the rooms to look at the array of gifts and admire the fairy-like scene. A profusion of growing plants seemed to reach up to the green canopy overhead. Everywhere were floating streamers of snowy tulle and over all the shaded candle light.

An air of suppressed anticipation dominated the large gathering of friends, many of whom were from a distance and from widely scattered points. More than a hundred of her own townsfolk had responded to the bride's oft asserted invitation to all her friends. Had all responded, even the spacious grounds of Strickland Place would not have been able to accommodate them.

Presently the hush of expectancy was broken by the strains of sweetest harmony, wooed from the piano by our gifted musician, Mrs. E. D. Smith. An appropriate program of wedding music followed, brought to a climax in a song, by Miss Mattie Hopson, of M. S. College, "The World is Waiting for the Sunrise." As the clear, girlish voice filled the place, every heart was quickened. The last silvery notes had hardly died away when they were replaced by the thrilling chords of Mendelssohn's Wedding March. Two beautiful little boys seemed to appear by magic and bore the ends of long streamers of tulle, caught at intervals by sprays of ivy. The other ends of the streamers were attached to the newel-posts of the stairs and as the children, Henry Fort Gholson and John Edward Rather, advanced to either side of the altar, they formed an aisle for the use of the bridal party.

The minister, Dr. Geo. L. Bitzer,[17] was awaiting the party at the altar and the bridegroom and his best man, Dr. George Brown of Water Valley, had quietly taken their places at his left. The first to appear was Mrs. Jacob Strickland, lovely sister-in-law of the bride, who acted as maid of honor, and as she drifted toward the altar the bride was seen descending the stairway, immediately preceding her two brothers, Frank and Jacob, who were to escort her to the altar. As she stood poised on the stairway she formed a picture which will long remain in the minds of those who saw it. Enveloped in her snowy wedding garments she was indeed a vision of loveliness.

As the altar was reached the Strickland brothers stepped aside and the bridegroom came forward to stand beside the lovely woman, soon to be his. The impressive Episcopal ceremony was read, with much feeling and appreciation by the officiating clergyman while the soft strains of "The Venetian Love Song" and "Oh, Wonderful One," filled the air. The bride's two brothers jointly responded to the question, "Who giveth this woman?"

At the close of the ceremony, loud and clear rang the notes of the recessional, "Lohengrin's Wedding March," and loving friends gathered close to press the hand of the proud and happy bridegroom and to shower even more tender greetings on the blushing bride. Then followed a delightfully informal hour of friendly mingling.

The newly married pair, the center of a happy group, pledged each other from a tiny silver loving cup, brought from the old country, while others of the large assembly sought the brimming punch bowl which was presided over by a bevy of dainty maidens, Misses Myers, Thompson and Mullins. Meantime salted nuts and delicious confections were passed among the waiting guests.

The costumes of the bridal party were of unusual beauty and richness, that of the bride being a sleeveless, semi-decollate model of ivory satin crepe draped with priceless old rose point lace and crowned with a floating veil that caught to her dark, wavy hair with sprays of lilies of the valley. Her arm bouquet was of Bride roses, lilies of the valley and ferns with streamers of satin ribbon.

Mrs. Jacob Strickland of Louisville, Ky., serving as maid of honor, was gowned in white crepe, heavily beaded in crystal and carried a bouquet of shell pink butterfly roses and violets.

Mrs. Smith, presiding at the piano, wore an elaborately beaded georgette gown of softest blue, and Miss Hopson, who sang, was the picture of girlish sweetness in white taffeta and lace embellished with rhinestones.

Mrs. Brown, wife of the best man, wore a charming model of pink chiffon with trimming of silken blossoms.

As the evening wore on the guests slowly dispersed, being denied a parting glimpse of the brown in her chic going-away gown, a brown fur-trimmed ensemble of silk and wool with hat and accessories in harmony.

The happy couple were determined to veil with mystery their immediate going-away plans, although those in authority say that there is to be a trip to New York via Philadelphia, and that they will sail for Europe on December 8, where they will make an extended visit to the bridegroom's widowed mother in Dresden, Germany, and will, of course, make various tours to points of interest. They expect to return in the late winter or early spring.[18]

"County Museum Idea Born at Strickland Place"

According to the Holly Springs *South Reporter*, the idea for a county museum was originated by members of the town's Thursday Club, in conjunction with a display of artifacts organized by the club in 1930 at the Strickland Place. The article is reprinted as follows:

> Historic Strickland Place was the scene recently of a display of many treasured heirlooms belonging to various members of the Thursday Club. Coral brooches and ear-rings, jewelry made of braided hair mounted in gold, graceful table silver, a rare Cathedral castor, Spanish lace, tortoise shell fans, quaint hair combs, historic documents, a meerschaum and amber pipe once belonging to Napoleon, several unique table pieces of pewter, picture books that were a joy to children many years ago, exquisite needle work and imperishable

"real Val" lace in baby dresses and caps, counterpanes of unbelievable weaving, daguerreotypes and miniatures made up a collection that brought back the "tender grace of a bygone day" and gave keen pleasure to all who were privileged to see it.

Two Peale miniatures dating back to Colonial days, one of Joseph Mattison, the other of Dr. Cary Wilkerson, an ancestor of Miss Clark's, were particularly beautiful, as was also a miniature done in hair showing the grandmother, "six greats back," of Mrs. James Driver (Bessie Craft), one of the Kentucky Breckenridges, weeping over the tomb of her husband.

The exhibit was brought together principally by the Misses Craft, Miss Helen Fant, Miss Kate Freeman Clark, Mrs. Frank Mattison, Mrs. Nettie Fant Thompson and Mrs. Gerard Badow. Hope was expressed that at some not-far-distant day adequate provision may be arranged for permanent museum display of the cherished possessions and of many others from the rich store of Marshall County.

Mrs. James B. Warren telling of pewter, Mrs. R. F. Cooper reviewing the Browning heirlooms in the collection of one of his descendants now living in Arkansas and Mrs. Allin Keen of Potts Camp, with Mrs. Faye Peel as her accompanist, singing a group of charming songs made up the program which preceded the "antique" display. An impromptu feature was the description of her visit to Bok's Singing Tower and bird sanctuary, given by Mrs. Ethridge who has just returned from a trip to Florida.[19]

Beginning in 1936, Strickland Place was featured on Holly Springs Garden Club pilgrimages.[20] When Perle Strickland Badow passed away in 1948, the house was bought by the Catholic Church and became St. Joseph's School. When the school outgrew these quarters, plans were announced to tear down the house, and the Marshall County Historical Society rallied to dismantle and move it to Spring Hollow, site of the town's founding. The plan never came to fruition, and in the mid-1960s, one of Holly Springs' most historic mansions was demolished to make way for the new St Joseph's Church.[21]

Endnotes

FOREWORD

¹ William M. Strickland Jr., whose home was called "Mimosa Lodge." Holly Springs *South Reporter* (Dec. 17, 1931, Mar. 17, 1932). [Hereafter abbreviated SR.]

² In 1983, after the death of Charles Dean, the Belle Strickland diary was presented by his aunt, Miss Mary Sue Burns, to the Marshall County Historical Museum, where it is preserved. Transcription follows the original as closely as possible, with a few minor omissions, as well as small changes in punctuation and spelling made for clarity.

³ Mildred Strickland's grave is in the Strickland plot in Hill Crest Cemetery, Holly Springs. The marriage ended tragically. Mildred's wartime letters give an interesting account of events during the war. They reveal a woman desperate to be reunited with her spouse. William Strickland volunteered for the army in 1861 and stayed away throughout the long course of the war. When he was finally transferred near enough to Holly Springs for Mildred to visit at his post in Grenada, in May 1863, they quarreled, and she wrote May 4, 1863, that she "regretted exceedingly that you were not satisfied with my company." She died of typhoid fever a month later at Grenada, presumably on another visit to her husband. Strickland letters. William Stebbins collection.

⁴ Elizabeth Davis Watson (1832-1912), gave her life to teaching in Holly Springs. She was a tireless worker in the Presbyterian Church.

⁵ Jane Leak had been a friend of Major Strickland's first wife, Mildred, who had entertained Jane at the Strickland Place shortly before she died. The Leak plantation lay in what is now Benton County, which was created out of Tippah and Marshall Counties in 1870. Jane Strickland died October 6, 1917 and is buried in the Strickland plot in Hill Crest Cemetery.

INTRODUCTION

¹ Cary Johnson, "Life Within the Confederate Lines, as Depicted in the War-Time

Journal of a Mississippi Girl," (M.A. thesis, La. State Univ., 1929). The original journal, 176 pages long, with entries over a period from August 13, 1864 to September 1, 1865, cannot be located by this researcher, but Johnson states that all references in her grandmother's diary which bear upon the Civil War or the life of the Southern people during that time are excerpted in the thesis.

[2] The house was built by Judge Frederick W. Huling in 1838 and sold in 1845 to Major Strickland's father-in-law, Dr. James Madison Thomson. Hubert H. McAlexander to R. M. Winter, Oct. 27, 2000. During remodeling of the house in 1928, workers found on a sill the date 1838. John M. Mickle, "Dramatic Club Here in Early Seventies," SR (Dec. 10, 1931): 2; "Many Other Places of Historical Note," SR (Nov. 20, 1930): 1; Interview with Mrs. Perle Strickland Badow, W.P.A. *Marshall County Survey of Old Homes*: 112-17; Mary Carol Miller, *Marshall County, From the Collection of Chesley Thorne Smith* (Dover, N. H.: Arcadia Publishing, 1998): 33, 100

[3] A pistol that belonged to Major Strickland may be seen in the Marshall County Historical Museum.

[4] Pruitt gives the date as 1828. A discrepancy exists which is easily resolved. The date 1828 became fixed in the public mind due to a newspaper misprint. Whites did not come to the area until 1835, and thus 1838 is the correct year.

[5] Olga Reed Pruitt, *It Happened Here: True Stories of Holly Springs* (Holly Springs: SR 1950): 51.

[6] Ibid., 50.

[7] *Diary of Henry Craft* (Mar. 6, 1849). Southern Historical Collection, Univ. of N. C., Chapel Hill.

[8] John M. Mickle, quotes from this account of the departure of soldiers, including Strickland's company, in the Holly Springs *Southern Herald* (Apr. 5, 1861): "Thursday, the 28th day of March, 1861, was a day long to be remembered in Holly Springs. It was the day appointed for the Volunteers from Marshall County, who had nobly responded to the call made upon Mississippi, by President Davis, for 1500 troops to go to Pensacola, to set out for the scene of action. The three companies who had been accepted for that service were Jeff Davis Rifles, Capt. Sam Benton; the Home Guards, Capt. Thos. W. Harris; and the Quitman Rifle Guards, Capt. Robert McGowan Jr.; the first two were from Holly Springs and the last named from Waterford. Three more brave and gallant companies, or companies made up of better material, social, moral and intellectual, were never mustered into service, in any age, or in any country. The farmer and the mechanic, the teacher and the pupil, the laborer and the artist, the merchant and the lawyer, the type and the editor, were all represented by some of their very best material. Some of the leading minds of the State, and men of the first class in all the departments of life, were there, to represent Mississippi in the camp, and, if need be on the battlefield. The slave-holder and the non-slaveholder stood side by side in those gallant ranks, and they go to teach the fanatic and deluded Yankee that they have a common interest in the maintenance of our glorious cause; the one fighting in defense of the social and moral position of himself and family, and the other in defense of his property and equal rights. But we

are digressing. It had been previously announced that these troops were to leave the depot of the Mississippi Central railroad at 8 o'clock on the morning of the 28th *ult.*, and at an early hour that morning a very large crowd of the citizens of the county were assembled there, to give the volunteers the parting hand and the parting blessing. An important feature of the occasion was the presentation of a beautiful flag to the Jeff Davis Rifles, by the young ladies of the Holly Springs Female Institute, of which Prof. Hackelton is principal. The flag was presented by Miss Jennie Edmonson, who represented the young ladies. She was most tastefully dressed, having on a jacket of gray, trimmed with black, with cap of similar material, to correspond with the uniform of the Rifle. Her address was replete with beauty, both in the matter and manner of it. Her graceful figure; her handsome features; her clear, distinct and musical enunciation; and yet more, the earnest feeling with which she spoke, all tended greatly to heighten the effect of the burning words and elegant diction of the address itself. The heart would have been hard and the eye cold indeed, that could have withheld the homage of a tear to the triumph of woman's eloquence, which she pledged to the parting soldiers the prayers of her own sex and the blessings of the people, and invoked in their behalf, in anxious and trembling tones, the benediction of Almighty God. That flag was received by Capt. Benton, as the gallant representative of his gallant company. Mr. Benton's reputation as a public speaker is too well established to need any encomium from us. His remarks were brief, appropriate and to the point-the promptings of a patriotism as profound as the speaker is known to be generous and brave. But the heart of the soldier was too full for any display of words. In plain and feeling language he thanked the young ladies for this token of their regard and confidence, and of their devotion to the cause of independence, and gave them a soldier's word that THAT FLAG, though perchance stained with blood, should never be stained with dishonor. Soon after this interesting ceremony the sound of the whistle indicated that the hour of departure had arrived. Then came the warm pressure of the hand, the silent tear, and, in broken accents from many a patriotic mother, the earnest words-'God bless you, my son; do your duty!' Then the conductor's quick, sharp cry of 'all aboard,' the tap of the engine bell, the whistle again, the quick and the still quicker panting of the iron horse, the rumbling of wheels, and the gallant Volunteers of Marshall were gone-flying upon the wings of steam to answer their country's call. How heavily was the train freighted with the hopes of a people, and the prayers and blessings of 'loved ones at home.'" "Roster of the Holly Springs Volunteers of 1861," SR (Nov. 20, 1930).

⁹ Mildred Strickland had written to her husband, April 4, 1861: "It seems as though all of our men are crazy for office. Why are they not willing to serve their country as privates if they are prompted by the right motives?" Strickland and his comrades did not see much action in the war. Mickle wrote that "the Jeff Davis Rifles, which with the Home Guards and Quitman Rifles were sent to Pensacola, Fla., where apparently the Confederate military authorities forgot them for a year." Some "considered themselves out of luck, with all of the fighting and glory to be had in Virginia, and some of the more restive slipped off up there and re-enlisted." Strickland found his way to Grenada, Miss., where he manned defenses around

the Mississippi Central rail line which passed south from Grand Junction, Tenn. and Holly Springs through that city toward New Orleans. SR (Dec. 10, 1931).

[10] St. Thomas Hall, founded 1844 on the north side of Salem Rd., just over the Salem Bridge. It burned during the Civil War. The school was revived in 1891 in the Pointer mansion on the west side of Salem bridge next to the Bonner House, on what is now the oil mill lot. It burned in 1898 and never reopened. Mary Carol Miller, *Lost Mansions of Mississippi* (Jackson: Univ. Press of Miss., 1996): 73; Hodding Carter Jr., "A Proud Struggle for Grace: Holly Springs, Miss.," in *A Vanishing America: The Life and Times of the Small Town* (New York: Holt, Rinehart & Winston, 1964): 64.

[11] Holly Springs Gazette (Sept. 28, 1849); SR (Nov. 27, 1930); *Goodspeed's Biographical and Historical Memoirs of Mississippi*, 2 vols. (Chicago: Goodspeed, 1891), 2:861; William Baskerville Hamilton, *Holly Springs, Miss. to the Year 1878* (Holly Springs: Marshall County Historical Society, 1984): 4, 25, 103, 120, 133, 145, 146; Interview with Mrs. Perle Strickland Badow, W.P.A. *Marshall County Survey of Old Homes*: 113-14.

[12] John Mickle recalled that before the Civil War, Strickland was a member of a Holly Springs Dramatic Club called the Thespians, along with James L. Autry, Henry, Addison, and Heber Craft, James T. Fant, Howard Falconer, H. W. Walter, and Richard L. (Dick) Watson. Mickle wrote that the club "flourished in the fifties and was composed of men only, as it was considered highly improper for ladies to appear on the stage." SR (Dec. 10, 1931).

I. BELLE BEGINS A JOURNAL

[1] Belle's little sister, born in 1859.

[2] Edward Minor Watson, younger son of J. W. C. and Catherine Davis Watson.

[3] Sarah (Mrs. John Davidson) Martin, who lived on the southwest side of town. Col. Martin was a founder of Oxford, Miss., said to have owned the site where the University of Mississippi was built. Hubert H. McAlexander, *A Southern Tapestry: Marshall County, Miss., 1835-2000* (Virginia Beach: Donning, 2000): 27.

[4] According to the Holly Springs *Southern Banner* (Jun. 25, 1841), Daniel B. Molloy was a local merchant. He invested in railroad projects and was a trustee of the University of Holly Springs. He moved to Memphis, but maintained old ties. Holly Springs *Guard* (Feb. 7, 1843) Holly Springs *Gazette* (Nov. 8, 1850); Hamilton, 24, 29, 46, 56, 60, 72.

[5] Son of Sheriff and Mrs. John R. McCarroll, next door neighbors of the Stricklands.

[6] Meridian was temporary capital of Mississippi in June and July 1864, as the governor and legislature fled General Sherman's incendiary acts at Jackson. Dunbar Rowland, ed., *History of Mississippi: The Heart of the South*, 4 vols. (Chicago-Jackson: S. J. Clarke, 1925), 1:804.

[7] A friend of Cora Watson's, from Somerville, Tenn.

[8] Pruitt, 47.

[9] "Craft-Daniel Place A Monument of Skill," SR (Dec. 20, 1930). A recent Civil War historian gives a listing of forty-seven fights and skirmishes. See Ken Parks, *The Civil War in Mississippi, 1861-1865*. The list was published in the SR (Apr. 28, 1983). Excellent sketches of

Holly Springs in the Civil War may be found in Hubert H. McAlexander, *The Prodigal Daughter: A Biography of Sherwood Bonner* (Baton Rouge: La. State Univ. Press, 1981): Chapter 1, and *Southern Tapestry*, Chapter 4.

[10] Running out of town at every report of Yankees must have been wearisome. As early as June 1, 1862, Mildred Strickland had written to her husband that "the news was received here last night that the Federals were at Grand Junction. Expect them to be here soon. All the prominent men will have to leave."

[11] Daughter of Sheriff and Mrs. McCarroll.

[12] Chills in summer were caused by malaria. In this era before effective treatment had begun, malaria was a disease which often became chronic, whose lingering effects had to be endured. Like yellow fever, it was spread by mosquitoes, though this fact was not yet known. Emma Finley, a Holly Springs woman who kept a diary, told how her younger sister Augusta and brother George J. Finley were brought low again and again by malaria: "Gus had a chill today & her absence will mar our pleasure somewhat....Gus took her quinine pills- for 'twas her chill day....George came home; he having had a chill was quite sick & did not get back till late in the evening." These similar notations occur in Emma's diary for dates in April and May of 1859: "Gusta- poor child- had been at home all this time nursing the chills,- had one Monday, tho' did not know it until Wed. when Mrs. Thomson- Mrs. Walker- and Reese Jones were here & was constrained to go to bed with another. Had not had a return but she looks badly and patronized iron & bitters....Gusta has had a return of chills and was in bed until eleven this morning- hope that they are broken up." Malaria, by no means uncommon, was regarded as serious, but much less so than the dreaded yellow fever, which at this time had not yet made its appearance in Holly Springs. *Diary of Emma Finley*, Aug. 25, Aug. 27, Sept. 5, 1858, April, May 1859, Cited in R. Milton Winter, *Our Pen Is Time: The Diary of Emma Finley* (Lafayette, Calif.: Thomas-Berryhill Press, 1999): 13, 15, 22, 76-77, 79.

II. HIDING FROM THE YANKEES

[1] Local citizens feared Federal search parties. Mildred Strickland wrote Major Strickland Mar. 26, 1863, that: "I get so excited when I hear they are coming. I dread them so much. They caught George Powell last week and he got away from them. They are coming after him-of course they will catch him."

[2] The Clapp Place, built in 1858, has long been regarded as one of Holly Springs' most elegant homes. After the Clapps moved to Memphis, it was briefly owned by James Jarrell House, the blockade runner. Later, the home was purchased General A. M. West, president of the Mississippi Central Railroad; Mrs. N. D. Deupree, "Some Historic Homes of Mississippi," *Publications of the Mississippi Historical Society* 7 (1903): 340-42; Mary Wallace Crocker, *Historic Architecture in Mississippi* (Jackson: Univ. Press of Miss., 1973): 162-63; Stanley Schuler, *Mississippi Valley Architecture: Houses of the Lower Mississippi Valley* (Exton, Pa.: Schiffer, 1984): 94-97; Helen Kerr Kempe, *The Pelican Guide to Old Homes of Mississippi, Vol. 2: Columbus and the North* (Gretna, La.: Pelican, 1984): 93; Jack Baum, "Holly Springs: The Architecture of a Small

Town" (prv. pub., Univ. of Tenn. architectural studies project, 1978): 50; Miller-Smith, *Marshall County*, 32. The Clapp Place, at 330 E. Salem Ave., is today's "Oakleigh," home of the late Chancellor and Mrs. L. Glenn Fant Jr., and recently purchased by Dr. Ben L. Martin and the Rev'd Mrs. Barbara Jamestone.

[3] James Henry Nelson lived in the house on E. College Ave. and now known as "Grey Gables," presently the home of Dr. J. A. Hale.

[4] *Memoranda of the Travels of J. W. Clapp*, 58-61. John D. Williams Library, University of Mississippi; SR (Jul. 24, 1930): 4; Memphis *Commercial Appeal* (Feb. 22, 1942); Seventy-eight years later, a pistol holder, saddle bags, and cartridge cases stamped "C. S. Arsenal," belonging to Judge Clapp were found at the entrance to the iron capitals in the attic walls of his former home. SR (Feb. 27, 1941): 1.

[5] Lewis Thomson, one of the town's prominent citizens, who with his wife Sarah Merrill Thomson, lived in a large house (now known as "Herndon"), at 255 E. Falconer Ave., near the Strickland and Watson Places. During the 1850s, the elder Thomsons lived in the house at the corner of today's Walthall St. and Falconer Ave., known since 1925 as the Doxey Cottage. It was originally a log cabin of not more than two rooms and was probably built in 1837 by German Baker, a Methodist minister and teacher. It was later covered with clapboard and given the refinement of a Greek Revival doorway. In 1853, while living at this location, the Thomsons built a larger brick house in modified Federal style next door in the center of the block. This house was home to the Thomsons as well as their daughter Janette and son-in-law John C. Walker, mentioned elsewhere in these pages. An addition was made to the house, probably at the time the family was enlarged. The Thomsons and Walkers held a high social position in Holly Springs. Many considered the furnishings of the house the finest in the city, and it was also noted for its beautiful garden on the northwest corner of the block. Hubert H. McAlexander, "A History of the Thomson-Walker House"; Robert Milton Winter, *Shadow of a Mighty Rock: A Social and Cultural History of Presbyterianism in Marshall County, Miss.* (Franklin, Tenn.: Providence House, 1997): 261; Mary Wallace Crocker, 159; Kempe, 86-87; Sigrid A. Conway and Bob Moulder, *Shrines to Yesterday: A Photographic Study of Antebellum Homes in Mississippi* (n.p., 1968): 27; Baum, 39.

[6] The Presbyterian minister.

[7] Mary Fontana Thomson (Mrs. John Lewis) Hudson, sister of Belle's mother, Mildred Thomson Strickland. Mary Fontana Hudson owned the house at 240 W. Chulahoma Ave., now called "Alicia," where Miss May Alice Booker presently resides, spoken of in these pages as the Baker-Hudson-McGuirk Cottage. The Hudsons also had a plantation near Hudsonville.

[8] On October 7, Emma also attended the consecration services conducted by the diocesan bishop, the Rt. Rev'd William Mercer Green, D.D., who preached from the story of Christ's cleansing of the temple: "Take these things hence, make not my Father's house an house of merchandise..." [St. John 2:16], urging the congregation away from all thoughts of 'worldly pleasure, earthly possessions, greetings of friends, congratulations and the like for such,' said the bishop, 'did not belong to the Tabernacle of the Most High.'" *Our Pen Is Time*, 31-32.

Endnotes

[9] Cited in *Southern Tapestry*, 48. John Mickle wrote of his church that "it is indeed a beautiful church-with its sweep of memorial windows, brass chandeliers, to the chancel and sanctuary, and the memorial window-'Christ in the Garden'-over the altar..." He believed that to see the interior at its best, it should be visited late in the afternoon "when the mellow rays of the setting sun filter through the windows in soft tones, filling the building with subdued but wonderful color." He wrote that "a holy calm seems to brood over the church and the impulse is strong to kneel in silent prayer. SR (Dec. 10, 1931): 12. See Elizabeth Claire Welch, "Ecclesiology: Its Influence on the Gothic Revival Episcopal Church in Antebellum Mississippi" (unpub. M.A. thesis, Univ. of Va., 1981): 37; Mary Wallace Crocker, 155.

[10] The Watsons, with whom Belle boarded, were a church-going family. According to her biographer, "practically every Sunday Mrs. Cora Watson's diary contained the simple words 'All went to Church to-day,'" with oftimes a comment on the sermon, or a bit of war news after the service." Johnson, 3.

[11] Old prints show a wrought iron fence surrounding Christ Church.

12 Hubert McAlexander pictures Watson and his family as "a Presbyterian household known for both rectitude and cultivation," *Prodigal Daughter,* 18. Emma Finley noted in her journal that "Sunday we went to hear the sermon that Messrs. Goodrich, Harris, Watson, Waite, and Finley requested Mr. Paine to repeat- 'Nature and Duration of Punishment'..." Watson, in a vein uncharacteristic of the historical Puritans, was an early and vigorous crusader for complete abstinence from the use of liquor. He brought a memorial to the North Mississippi Presbytery, Oct. 3, 1884, urging all ministers to preach against the evils of alcohol. See "The Strictest Presbyterian," *Shadow of a Mighty Rock*, 297.

[13] Helen Craft Anderson, "Commencement Address," Mississippi Synodical College (May 1930). The Watson Place stood at the northwest corner of College and Maury Sts. Like their friends the Hugh Crafts across town, the Watsons built a two-story frame house in the 1850s, surrounded by columns on the model of a Greek temple, as was the architectural fashion of the day. The Craft and Watson houses, while impressive, were the first of their type to be erected in Holly Springs, and were quite modest when compared to the famous Windsor mansion near Port Gibson (1859), which brought the genre of the colonnaded house to its acme in Mississippi. The Watson home was later used as a dormitory for North Mississippi Presbyterian College. It was torn down about 1945 to make way for the town's first hospital. The site is now occupied by offices of the Marshall County Department of Human Services. Miller, 71.

[14] *Memoirs of Mississippi*, 2:996-998. *Mississippi, Heart of the South,* 1:837. William Taylor Watson was killed April 10, 1863, and John Staige Davis Watson died May 28, 1864.

[15] Vicksburg *Times* (Mar. 20, 1869). William C. Harris, "The Reconstruction of the Commonwealth, 1865-1870," in *A History of Mississippi*, Richard Aubrey McLemore, ed., 2 vols. (Jackson: Univ. and Coll. Press of Miss., 1973), 1:568. *Memoirs of Mississippi*, 2:996; Hamilton, 120-22; Dunbar Rowland, *Jefferson Davis, Constitutionalist*, 6:512. R. H. Henry, *Editors I have Known Since the Civil War* (1922): 216. According to John M. Mickle, Watson, who for some

years in association with Mickle's father, Maj. Belton Mickle, edited the Holly Springs *Independent South*, a predecessor of the present *South Reporter*, once exerted himself against traveling theatrical companies of the burlesque type. The younger Mickle recorded that "sentiment in regard to theaters has changed greatly since those days, especially as to risqué performances, though such displays as they gave would be considered 'dump' now. Immediately on arriving advance agents would give the covert warning 'don't bring your wives or sweethearts,' with the intended result. To such an advance agent Judge Watson, who was a conscientious man, replied, shoving the agent's folder aside, 'I will write something about your show'-and he did, a double-leaded editorial, denouncing the show and calling on good citizens to place their seal of disapproval upon it by staying away. The morning of the show the owner called and asked for his bill. My father replied that as they had carried no ad there was no bill. 'But this notice was the best ad you could have given me,' the agent rejoined, 'and I am willing to pay handsomely for it; the house was sold out before we got here!'" SR (Dec. 15, 1932).

[16] William Strickland prepared a memorial to Judge Watson for the Mississippi Bar Association, *Proceedings of the Mississippi Bar Association* (Jan. 6, 1891). See also "J.W.C.Watson," in Dunbar Rowland, ed., *Mississippi, Comprising Sketches of Counties, Towns, Events, Institutions, and Persons, Arranged in Cyclopedic Form*, 3 vols. (Atlanta: Southern Historical Publishing Association, 1907), 2:941-942; "John William Clark Watson," in Benjamin McFarland Hines, *Hines and Allied Families* (Fairfield, Conn.: prv. pub., 1980): 67-69; "John William Clark Watson," *Biographical Dictionary of the Confederacy*, ed. by Jon L. Wakelyn (Westport, Conn.: Greenwood Press, 1977): 430-431; "John William Clark Watson," *Dictionary of American Biography*, ed. by Dumas Malone (New York: Charles Scribner's Sons, 1936).

[17] Capt. William Clark, a graduate of Amherst College in Massachusetts, was well-known in the Holly Springs educational community. His name appears in an advertisement for St. Thomas Hall in 1859. During the war he was an officer in the Confederate army. He married Miss Mary Barton in 1855. By John Mickle's account: "Shortly after the War of the Sixties, Capt. William Clark opened Fenelon Hall, a school for young ladies, on College Ave. One of the houses is Mrs. Rosa Tyler's home, the other Con Bonds'. Later he acquired old historic Franklin College, which stood on the site of the H. Myers home and which he conducted until his death in 1878. Mrs. Clark and her sister Mrs. Rosa Goodloe took up the work after his death. It was sold in 1890 and the name changed to Malone College." SR (Dec. 10, 1931): 18. The Clarks owned the Buchanan home, just east of Old St. Joseph's Church. *Southern Tapestry*, 69.

[18] Paine, who came to Holly Springs from Lexington, Va., was regarded as a fine preacher. A confidant of such Presbyterians as the Watsons, Crafts, Clapps, and Finleys, Paine and his wife moved among the leading families of Holly Springs. He was a graduate of Washington College (now Washington and Lee Univ.), in Lexington, Va., and Union Theological Seminary in Hampden-Sydney, Va. He served in Holly Springs from 1855 to 1872, and was closely involved with the local educational effort. Paine was likely born in Ireland about 1805.

According to records of Princeton Seminary, James, Henry's older brother, was born near Londonderry, December 25, 1803, with the family immigrating to America in 1820. The cause of the family's removal from the old country is not known, but as historian Arthur Young has said, almost all came in this period because of the decline of the linen industry and persecution of Presbyterians. Some of the family's ancestors were in the siege of Londonderry and perished as martyrs in the Protestant cause, and if this were not enough, they were also lineal descendants of Scotland's greatest hero and reformer, John Knox. Arthur Young is cited in Billy Kennedy, *The Scots-Irish in the Hills of Tennessee* (Belfast, Northern Ireland: Ambassador Press, 1995): 23; see *The Presbyterian* (Apr. 28, 1860); Joseph M. Wilson, *The Presbyterian Historical Almanac, 1861*, Vol. III (Philadelphia: Joseph M. Wilson, 1861): 104; Edward Howell Roberts, *Biographical Catalogue of Princeton Theological Seminary, 1815-1932* (Princeton: prv. pub., 1933): 51.

[19] Waddel was also professor of ancient languages at the LaGrange Synodical College, sponsored by the Presbyterian Church. Located twenty-four miles north of Holly Springs, it educated young men from Holly Springs, including Henry M. Paine, the minister's son. Judge Watson was among the board members and also gave a course on Evidences for Christianity. Waddel, who later was chancellor of the University of Mississippi, performed the wedding for Arthur Fant, Watson's law partner, to Miss Lizzie Anderson, daughter of John McCartney Anderson and Sarah Joanna Thornton, December 21, 1871. It was the first marriage to be solemnized in the recently completed Holly Springs Presbyterian Church.

[20] John N. Waddel, *Memorials of Academic Life: Being an Historical Sketch of the Waddel Family* (Richmond: Presby. Comm. on Pub., 1891): 364-65, 366-68.

[21] Belle's mother wrote her husband, Mar. 9, 1862, that: "This morning Willie is crazy about Sunday school-was distressed last Sunday because he was absent. I have just finished Belle's dress (her red dress) to wear to Sunday school."

[22] The minister's daughter.

[23] Because Sunday school and divine service were longer than at present, an interval between the two allowed participants to rest between services. Citing a news clipping from 1869, John Mickle reported that "Hours for Sunday services at the Protestant Churches then were: Sunday school 8-1/2 o'clock, morning services 10-1/2 o'clock, evening, 8 o'clock." SR (Dec. 15, 1932).

[24] Cora E. White was born June 29, 1843, in Fayette, Miss. At six, her mother died, and she was adopted by her uncle-in-law and aunt, Judge and Mrs. John W. Harris, of Covington, Tenn. ("Pa" in the pages of her journal.) In 1861, she married William T. Watson, son of Mr. and Mrs. J. W. C. Watson of Holly Springs ("Father" and "Mother" in the diary). Will Watson was killed in battle, April 10, 1863, and ten months later, her foster-mother Mrs. Harris died, and Cora made her home with her husband's family in Holly Springs-so that the Holly Springs household consisted of Mrs. Watson, her daughter, Elizabeth (called "Lizzie" or "Sister" by all), and his two younger sons, Edward and James ("Eddie" and "Jimmie"). Cary Johnson, 1-2; Mickle, SR (Dec. 10, 1931): 2.

²⁵ Sophia Boyd Hays, widow of Presbyterian minister, the Rev'd John Sidney Hays, penned an account of similar difficulties while attempting to make a journey in the same part of the country in 1862. On June 6, having sought a pass from General Sherman to cross Federal lines at LaGrange, which was summarily refused, she cried, "Petty, contemptible tyranny!" But on the 25th of the same month she again asked for a pass, which this time was granted by General S. A. Hurlbut, whom Boyd described as "a profane, drinking, gambling character-destitute of principle." When she was finally able to begin her journey south from LaGrange about 6:00 a.m. on July 8, Boyd passed the U. S. outposts easily, as Hurlbut's men had moved toward Holly Springs, engaging Confederate forces at "Cold Water." She found the countryside desolate on the way to Holly Springs, where she stopped briefly to inquire the road to Abbeville, and after obtaining a pass through Confederate lines, boarded a train at Abbeville, where she rode to West, Miss., arriving at 2:00 a.m., July 10. The next morning she rode a horse to her farm near Koscuisko. *Diary of Sophia Boyd Hays*, 2: 115, 129, 135, 141; cited in an unpublished paper by Donald R. Taylor, 11-14. The diaries of Sophia Boyd Hays are held by her great-niece, Mrs. Frank Buchanan of Koscuisko.

²⁶ A skirmish between Confederate and Union soldiers was reported in Holly Springs on this date. "Holly Springs Control Exchanged 59 Times During Civil War Days," SR (Apr. 28, 1983).

²⁷ Another result was a change in travel patterns. For example, Sophia Hays recorded details of a trip from Koscuisko, Miss. to establish a new home in LaGrange, Tenn., in the spring of 1859. She and her party traveled by rail from Jackson to Vicksburg, where they booked passage on the steamboat *Nebraska*, just arrived from New Orleans. The river was at flood stage, and as they made the dangerous trip north Sophia saw many farms under water, the residences deserted. They arrived at Memphis on the second day and presumably completed the journey to LaGrange on the Memphis & Charleston Railway. Two and a half years later, on Dec. 26, 1861, Sophia returned to Koscuisko on the Mississippi Central, boarding at Grand Junction, three miles east of LaGrange and traveled through Holly Springs, leaving the train at West (named for Gen. A. M. West, a line official who later made his home in Holly Springs) about seven or eight miles from her farm, near Koscuisko. Taylor, 4, 5, 8.

²⁸ Hamilton, 61-62.

²⁹ That is, a train of railroad cars.

³⁰ Bessie Craft Driver's and John Craft's grandmother.

³¹ Holly Springs citizens kept swine within the city limits. Belle's mother wrote from Strickland Place to her husband on April 20, 1862 that "My sow has 4 pigs. She eats all my young chickens and ate up one hen that was setting and broke up another and ate up the eggs."

³² On Nov. 15, 1862, Mildred Strickland wrote her husband that the "Yanks have left, are up about Lamar. They searched the house, took nothing-took a great many hams in town."

³³ Gaines Foster writes that "the war not only complicated the household work of

women but also forced many to face personal danger as they rarely had before." He remarks that, "women wrote of their anxieties when the men departed and they waited alone for the arrival of northern troops." Gaines M. Foster, *Ghosts of the Confederacy: Defeat, the Lost Cause, and the Emergence of the New South, 1865-1913* (New York: Oxford Univ. Press, 1987): 32.

[34] The Mason House, now called "Hamilton Place," stands at the foot of Memphis Street, where the road through town turned west briefly before resuming its southward course. Built in 1840, the Mason Place was the first Holly Springs home of Carrington Mason's father, William F. Mason, a builder of the Mississippi Central Railroad. It was the first two-story brick home in the village. The house, at 105 E. Mason Ave., was originally of Federal design, and in the 1850s was enlarged with fluted Greek columns added to the front, making it the city's first grand Greek Revival structure. In 1920, the house burned, and in its reconstruction the upper story and Greek columns were removed. See Margaret Nickle, "Hamilton Place," SR (Apr. 24, 1980): 11; Schuler, 92-93; Baum, 77, 112.

[35] Maria Mason's account is reprinted in Pruitt, 56. On June 1, 1862, Mildred Strickland, had written her husband: "The news was received here last night that the Federals were at Grand Junction. Expect them to be here soon." Cited in *Southern Tapestry*, 65. Sophia Hays described similar scenes LaGrange, Tenn., where on June 13, 1862, a Federal cavalry passed through. She related the entrance of Sherman's army two days later on Sunday, June 15: "The rattling of the drums, the sound of the fife, companies marching, the clatter of cavalry, the swearing of the soldiers, & all manner of unpleasant sounds. Oh, this horrid desecration of our soil & our sabbaths." Hays, 2:112. Ironically, a little over a hundred years later, in September 1962, U. S. troops and armaments again came down the same Holly Springs streets, en route to Oxford to quell riots opposing the desegregation of the University of Mississippi.

[36] The William F. Mason Place, a beautiful mansion incorporating Gothic features, built in the 1850s, known today as "The Magnolias," was the second home of William F. Mason in Holly Springs. It stood on the road to Oxford, at what is now 305 South Craft St. Pruitt, 48, 49; Mrs. N. D. Deupree, "Some Historic Homes of Mississippi," 347-47; Mary Wallace Crocker, 161, Kempe, 89-90, Schuler, 94; Conway and Moulder, 27; Baum, 77; Miller-Smith, *Marshall County*, 37.

[37] As late as the 1930s, the Rev'd Raymond McBlain, rector of Christ Church, kept a cow, which grazed in Mrs. Edgar Francisco Jr.'s pasture on the edge of Strickland's Woods.

[38] Mildred Strickland wrote that "General Hamilton had a room at my house and headquarters at Mr. McCarroll's and I was never treated more kindly and more civilly than I was by Genl. Hamilton. All the officers that I have met (which have been a good many) have been universally kind to me." Later, she reported that "I received a letter from Gen. Hamilton with this letter of yours enclosed, saying he would not for the world deprive me of a letter from my husband and that it was taken from the saddle bags of a prisoner." In this letter Mildred tells of plans to go to LaGrange for some runaway slaves and says, "I think Gen. Hamilton will let me get Hop's Negroes." Mildred Strickland to W. M. Strickland, Jan. 5, 1863; Mar. 19, 1863.

[39] Walter Place stands at 300 W. Chulahoma Ave., and has been magnificently restored by current owners, Mr. and Mrs. Michael Lynn. J. Frazier Smith: *White Pillars: The Architecture of the South* (New York: Bramhall, 1946): 95-97, Mary Wallace Crocker, 164-65; Baum, 76. After Van Dorn's raid, when Grant returned to Holly Springs, he occupied the William Henry Coxe Place-again, by invitation of the owner.

[40] Fonta W. O'Dell's grandmother.

[41] Child's play in Holly Springs consisted of simple games. Mary Virginia Grigsby Foley, who was ten when her father came to Holly Springs as the Presbyterian minister, told how she played with dolls in an attic playhouse and enjoyed outside games such as croquet. "We played mumble-peg and hop-scotch, marbles and bean bags. Lightning bugs caught put in glass jars were fun at night. (No bicycles, motorcycles, tennis or skateboards.) The children also enjoyed a sand pile outside their front yard. *Memories of Childhood in Holly Springs* (Medford, Ore.: prv. pub., 1981): 6, 56.

[42] Sherwood Bonner described how Holly Springs was first occupied by in 1862. She said that war came "with the sound of music and the beating of drums, into a silent town. From behind closed blinds we listened to the tread of their advancing feet or peeped timidly at the blue ranks marching by. Before sundown the pleasant groves of [the town] were dotted with white tents, the stars and stripes fluttered from a high flag-pole, and from the park the inspiring strains of 'Yankee Doodle' seemed to mock our impotent anger and bitter humiliation." Sherwood Bonner, "From '60 to '65," *Lippincott's* 18 (Oct. 1876): 500-501. Sometimes bands could amuse. Cordelia Lewis Scales, a young woman of about eighteen wrote from "Oakland," her plantation near Hudsonville, seven miles north of Holly Springs on Jan. 27, 1863, that a Yankee colonel had taken a liking to her and "made the band come up and play Dixy for me." Cited in Hamilton, 155.

[43] A slave of the Watsons.

[44] Brigadier General James R. Chalmers (1831-1898), a close associate of J. W. C. Watson and J. W. Clapp. Chalmers served in Nathan Bedford Forrest's campaigns in Mississippi, Tennessee, and Kentucky. The end of the war found him in command of all Mississippi cavalry in service in Mississippi and West Tennessee. Hamilton, 100-101.

[45] Mildred Strickland reported a similar experience, Jan. 5, 1863: "I have a little fellow staying with me who is out of the army now and to whom I shall always feel grateful for his kindness. His name is Mr. Resor from Ills."

[46] Ralph E. Morrow, *Northern Methodism and Reconstruction* (East Lansing: Mich. State Univ. Press, 1956).

[47] Seizure of churches was common. At College Hill, near Oxford, Federal soldiers occupied the Presbyterian Church and would not permit the congregation to worship; however, when the chaplain held services for the troops, he put away the hymnbooks for fear that his men would abuse them. Maud Morrow Brown, "The War Comes to College Hill," *Journal of Mississippi History* 16 (January 1954): 22-30. In Memphis, Grant's men commandeered the Second Presbyterian Church-at the instigation of a former pastor, the Rev'd Robert C. Grundy.

Grundy, who came to Memphis from Maysville, Ky., in 1857, opposed secession, and the presbytery, despite his objections, dissolved his relationship to Second Church. The elders had stood by their pastor in spite of his views but good relations ended when he opposed melting the church bell for a cannon. A few months later when Memphis fell into Union hands, Grundy urged President Lincoln to put churches in liberated territory into loyalist hands. Second Church and others like it were seized, and northern chaplains held services in Second Church for convalescent soldiers and restored Grundy to the pulpit. Appeals by Second Church to the military authorities failed, so that the elders carried their cause to Lincoln. According to the Rev'd A. B. Curry, the church's historian, "This truly great man wrote in his own hand on the back of their petition...orders for the restoration of the property." Finding himself unwelcome in Memphis, the disgruntled Grundy secured a call to Cincinnati. George M. Apperson, "Lincoln, the Churches, and Memphis Presbyterians," *American Presbyterians: Journal of Presbyterian History* 72 (Summer 1994): 97-107; A. B. Curry, *History of the Second Presbyterian Church, Memphis, Tenn.* (Memphis: Adams, n.d.): 9-11.

[48] Belle's mother had earlier written to Major Strickland: "I want to see you so much, but sometimes when I look around and see healthy, strong men walking lazily along the street, I almost feel a little glad that you went." The next year she wrote, "Every man ought to be pressed into service now....The men should go." A few days later she wrote: "I always thought that you would be in no danger, but I have given up now and never expect to live with you again. I believe that every man now in the field will be killed, and then we are to live here with these cowards." Still later, she wrote of the men who still remained in Holly Springs: "I hate to see men take it so easy....Our men don't do right. The town is filled with men now that ought to be in the army." Mildred Strickland to W. M. Strickland, Apr. 1, 1861. Undated letters, Feb., 1862, and Jun. 8, 1862.

[49] John B. Boles, *Black Southerners, 1619-1869* (Lexington: Univ. Press of Ky., 1984): 110, 185.

[50] Josephine McGowan Cox, "My Father Told Me," McGowan Family Papers (unpub., mss., n.d.): 49. Virginia Woodson Carter Historical Room of the Holly Springs Presbyterian Church. Mildred Strickland wrote her husband, Jan. 16, 1863: "I don't think the Yanks will be here any more. There is nothing to come for now."

[51] As John W. Blassingame has remarked, "One of the key figures in the white child's socialization was the ubiquitous black mammy to whom he frequently turned for love and security. It was the black mammy who often ran the household, interceded with his parents to protect him, punished him for misbehavior, nursed him, rocked him to sleep, told him fascinating stories, and in general served as his second, more attentive, more loving mother." *The Slave Community: Plantation Life in the Antebellum South* (Rev. ed., New York: Oxford Univ. Press, 1979): 266.

[52] Slaves had already left Holly Springs to join the U. S. army. In August 1862, Mildred Strickland reported that "Ned saw Yellow Ben [a former slave] in uniform riding around-saw the others. They would not hear to coming home, they've got everything nice to eat, $8 a

month in gold. That day they had received their shoes and pants. They all seemed satisfied, have no idea of coming back. When Ned goes in the neighborhood and tells this tale they will nearly all leave."

[53] Slave disappearances had been a problem for some time. A year earlier, Mildred Strickland reported that "The servants all slipped off Saturday night soon after supper. Sunday morning Miss Carrie and I milked the cow and cooked breakfast. The hardest work is nursing Minnie. About dinnertime Sunday old Sallie walked in crying about Fannie. I was astonished to see Sallie for I was sure she had gone too. She says she had no idea of going, but I cannot trust her, think she was left. Mine went on the last train. They took the cart and oxen-I am sorry for that....If you ever see Joe and Hardin, if you don't kill them, you will not be the husband I think you are. They have gone to Memphis." A few days later she wrote: "I am going to Memphis this week and will hire someone to try and get [Hardin] out. I only want to kill her for she deserves nothing else." Mildred Strickland to W. M. Strickland, Jan. 16 and 25, 1863.

[54] Another Mississippian recalled the shock of women who awoke to find slaves gone, and no fire, no water, no breakfast. "Ah, then and there were hurryings to and fro' and gathering tears and tremblings of distress and cheeks all pale, their Waterloos had come-face to face with a question never before presented in life. How to get a breakfast." Annie E. Harper papers, Mississippi Department of Archives and History, Jackson, Miss., cited in Foster, 31. When she learned that a former slave who had worked for wages had died suddenly, Mildred Strickland wrote to her husband on May 4, 1863 that: "Miss Carrie met me at the gate with the melancholy news of Sallie's death, which you know is a great shock to me...for although she was old, she did my work, and now it will fall on me. She died suddenly with apoplexy-you can see I cannot spell, but it matters not now, as I will seldom have occasion for writing. I shall have to throw every accomplishment aside and go to the wash tub."

[55] Skirmishes between Confederate and Union troops were reported at the Tallahatchie Bridge south of Holly Springs on August 7-8, 1864. "Holly Springs Control Exchanged 59 Times During Civil War Days," SR (Apr. 28, 1983).

[56] John Boles remarked that "again and again it was not the field hands who left first, but the house servants-the cooks, valets, and maids the whites most trusted" and observed that "Few things disconcerted slave owners more than their slaves forsaking them and fleeing to the Union armies." Boles, 185.

[57] Boles records that on August 25, 1862, the U. S. War Department had authorized General Saxton to accept "volunteers of African descent" into the army, an edict reinforced by Lincoln's Emancipation Proclamation of Jan. 1, 1863. Thereafter black soldiers became commonplace, numbering 178,895, of whom 133,000 came from the former slave states. Boles, 193.

[58] Pickett, a young widower, had been rector of an Episcopal Church in Paducah, Ky., and fled with most of his congregation when Federals captured that city. He accepted a call to Christ Church and chose to remain with his flock at Holly Springs even when a

wealthy congregation in Louisville, Ky. promised him five times the salary that his small parish could offer. By John Mickle's recollection: "He not only preached splendid sermons, but was the best pulpit reader I ever heard. He recognized that the Bible throughout is couched in dramatic language, and the rituals of the Episcopal Church so rich and lofty that they require dramatic treatment and he was wonderfully gifted." SR (Dec. 10, 1931): 14. Mickle also wrote that "I have never heard Rev. J. T. Pickett's equal in reading the service for the burial of the dead. In the committal prayer he was dramatic." SR (Oct. 30, 1930).

[59] *The Episcopal Church in Mississippi, 1763-1992* (Jackson: Episcopal Diocese of Mississippi, 1992): 40.

[60] Ingraham was buried in Hill Crest Cemetery in the family plot of the Martins, who were loyal members of Christ Church and who appear frequently in these pages.

[61] Many admired Pickett, but author Kate (Sherwood) Bonner did not hold orthodox beliefs and disliked the strictness of her rector's preaching. In her novel *Like unto Like* (1878), which was modeled upon Holly Springs scenes and characters, she created a rector, who was a superficial and uninteresting personality. *Prodigal Daughter*, 147.

[62] Women adjusted to doing their own work. Belle's mother reported Feb. 2, 1863 that "we are getting along very well now. We clean the house ourselves. Sallie cooks and old Abram is here to cut my wood. I was obliged to send for him, for there is no one else to hire. We get along a great deal better without the servants and if you only could come home, I know you will enjoy yourself better than you ever did. We keep everything in the house so clean and nice and Minnie is no trouble in the world. I could not get along without Miss Carrie. She gets down on her knees and scrubs the hall and dining room, rubs the hearth, and helps me sew. She is worth two or three Negroes." But in the same letter, Mildred confessed that "It is a right serious thing to lose all one's Negroes."

[63] Slaves, who typically protested their status by working as slowly and as inefficiently as possible, became unruly when the prospect of liberation drew near. Meanwhile, the overseer was the weakest link in the chain of plantation management. In the summer of 1862, Mildred Strickland besought her husband: "Do write me, if you can, what to do with the servants. They are unmanageable. I fear Megginson [the plantation overseer] is not tight enough. I sent Janette to the farm yesterday, brought Ann in. Had Hardin [a house servant] whipped-did not help her much." About a month later, she wrote: "I had to send for Megginson to come in to whip Ann. She would not mind me and fretted me so much I could not stand it." Blassingame, 276; Mildred Strickland to W. M. Strickland, Jun. 1, 1862; undated letter, summer 1862.

[64] Other slaves.

[65] As Gaines Foster observes, for Southern white women, "emancipation altered their status by diminishing executive responsibilities in the home and increasing the difficulty and drudgery of the workday." *Ghosts of the Confederacy*, 31.

[66] Belle's early experience with U. S. troops had been less cordial. Her mother reported to Major Strickland, Jan. 16, 1863, that "Belle and Willie did not like the Yankees. Belle especially told one she would have her head cut off before she would kiss him."

[67] See David Hackett Fischer, *Albion's Seed: Four British Folkways in America* (New York: Oxford Univ. Press, 1989): 256-64; 652-55.

[68] Aunt Mollie Thomson Hudson's slave.

[69] Daughter of Hugh and Elizabeth Collier Craft.

[70] The Hulls were next door neighbors. The colonnaded Hull Place eventually became part of the North Mississippi Presbyterian College. It originally stood at the northeast corner of E. College and N. Randolph Sts. In 1903, the house was moved to southeast corner of Randolph and Falconer, to make way for a new administration building at Mississippi Synodical College. "The Annex," as the old house came to be called, was used for classroom purposes. After the college closed in 1939, the Hull house was demolished. SR (Dec. 18, 1930): 4.

[71] See Alexis McCrossen, *Holy Day, Holiday: The American Sunday* (Ithaca: Cornell Univ. Press, 2000).

[72] Mary Virginia Grigsby Foley, whose father was minister of the Presbyterian Church from 1897 to 1904, gave this account of Sunday mornings in Holly Springs: "Breakfast, of course, then Sunday school followed by the church service, and a large Sunday dinner prepared by our cook and her helpers. This was followed by brief naps, then the reading of *The Herald and Presbyter* and *The Christian Observer*. How well I remember them! Suitable reading for both young and old. Then the study and recitation of the catechisms, the Child's Catechism for the very young and the Shorter (misnomer, certainly) Catechism for the more mature." *Childhood in Holly Springs*, 23.

[73] In 1858, Emma Finley, of Holly Springs, also Presbyterian, reflected upon her attempt to keep the Sabbath at home. "Sunday 24th Oct. The unfavorable appearance of the morning prevented our attendance at church today, & with holy readings and quiet conversation we have tried to keep the day holy." *Our Pen Is Time*, 33.

[74] A skirmish between Union and Confederate soldiers was reported that day at Lamar, Miss., eleven miles northeast of Holly Springs. "Holly Springs Control Exchanged 59 Times During Civil War Days," SR (Apr. 28, 1983).

[75] In December 1858, Emma Finley wrote in her diary that: "Ma, Ginnie and I, were quietly seated by the fire, when Aunt Merina came in saying that they wanted Ma to go up and see Mrs. Hargrove who was very sick of Jaundice. She went and sat up with her- and Wed. evening Ma having returned Ginnie and I rode over. There being no one with them but Martha Bell and the girls thinking their mother worse Ginnie staid and I came home to see if Ma could go up again....Next morning...she went up to Mrs. H.'s leaving me to keep house, sending Ginnie home to see Uncle John. Ma came home that night, and Saturday Ginnie and I spent the day, Sam, Uncle John, and George occupying themselves during our absence laying off our flower garden. We found Lou very low-spirited and her mother drowsy-but seeming no worse....Monday morning before breakfast Hilliard came by saying that Mrs. H. was much worse and they wanted Ma to go up as soon as she could. She left before breakfast taking only a cup of coffee....Gus reached home soon after dinner and about dark George came

for Ginnie to go up and stay with Lou. It was so late that he did not return for supper, but Sam came back and kept us company. Tuesday Ma came home for a short while to cut out work for Line and she, George and Ginnie were all there that night. Wed. morning Gusta and I went up and staid until 12 o'clock. Dr. Nannie who spent the night before - Dr. Rives - Mr. and Mrs. Howard were there. George went back at night and at ten Mrs. Hargrove died,- he then went to town to order the coffin- get the materials for a shroud- and Gusta and I went up to help them make it. The body was buried about four Thursday evening- a number of persons from town and country attended. Ma had been suffering all day with a very bad headache, and tho' it was sprinkling she thought she ought to go home so she, George and Ginnie came- leaving Gus and me, who with Mr. Howard, staid all night. They were very much distressed though more cheerful after the burial than I had expected. They will miss for a long time, I know, the occupant of the corner chair." *Our Pen Is Time*, 43-44.

[76] Other Holly Springs girls had trouble making jelly. Emma Finley recorded, Sept. 2, 1858, that she and her sister "took our citron off after supper & found it cooked to candy. I was mighty sorry but it could not be helped then." *Our Pen Is Time*, 21.

[77] Fischer, 278.

[78] Rosa May Clark, eldest daughter of William and Mary Barton Clark married Richard Henry Tunstall in 1880. Rosa was a gifted organist, and for many years directed the Christ Church choir. She died in 1903. SR (Dec. 10, 1931): 18.

[79] Mary McCrosky was a daughter of Hiram and Jane Lane McCrosky.

[80] One of the family slaves.

[81] William Crump, one of Marshall County's pioneer settlers.

[82] A house servant.

[83] A Holly Springs teacher. Her school was called Beauregard Institute. *Prodigal Daughter*, 14.

III. WE ARE LIVING ON CORNBREAD AND BUTTER

[1] In 1860, the assessed value of Marshall County's real estate had been $14 million. Ten years later, it was $4 million. Personal property plunged from $25 million in 1860 to less than $2 million. *Prodigal Daughter*, 41. Food had begun to become scarce from the winter of 1861-62 onward. Belle's mother had written that "Joe [a slave who tended the Strickland garden] complains so much about Mollie's horses staying here, eating so much corn. But she needs her carriage here, and then Belle enjoys riding in it so much. It is such a nice carriage." That summer Mildred Strickland wrote, "I want to break up housekeeping. I am too much troubled about getting provisions. . . .I cannot get anything hardly to eat, and I am out of nearly everything." That fall she wrote, "I think we will starve. You know I am no manager, and know nothing about managing. There are no men here, no one will help us do a thing." Mildred Strickland to W. M. Strickland, Mar. 9, 1862; Aug. 31, 1862; Nov. 26, 1862.

[2] SR (Nov. 30, 1931).

[3] Marshall County once had many gristmills, some powered by water, others by the labor of men and animals. See *Southern Tapestry*, 25, 87, 97.

⁴ Genesis 41:17-41, King James Version.

⁵ Cox, 47-49. Some U. S. soldiers complained for lack of food. In the aftermath of Van Dorn's raid, one wrote from Moscow, Tenn., twenty miles north of Holly Springs, that for New Year's the men had "baked a big Joney Cake without any salt or grease, and that was all we had, no meat, no crackers, no flower, and no nothing." "O cow," he exclaimed, "the Rebs had all but the joney cake when they took Holly Springs behind us." Leo M. Kaiser, "Letters from the Front," *Journal of the Illinois State Historical Society* 56 (Summer 1963): 158-59.

⁶ The Watsons tried to help needy neighbors. On Jan. 19, 1865, Cora recorded that "Mother and Mrs. John C. Walker went this morning to see some poor families in town. Visited three families. Found them-though very poor-making exertions to support themselves and managing to live without actual suffering. Mother came home and sent Mrs. Humphries some cotton to spin and all the biscuits in the house, and she is going to do something for the others."

⁷ Belle's neighbors, the John R. McCarrolls, reported that during Union raids on Holly Springs the family horses were hidden in the brick kitchen and servants' quarters which still stand behind the main house. Ruth Bitzer Francisco, "126 Years of Family History Treasured at McCarroll Place," SR (Apr. 22, 1960).

⁸ The home of Martha Reese (Mrs. Rufus) Jones, two blocks east and one block north of the Watsons, was commandeered for the surgeon general of Grant's army. In the aftermath of Van Dorn's raid, December 20, 1862, her young son, who had felt the pangs of hunger more than once, took advantage of confusion on the town square, in which Van Dorn's men had broken open the stores and set fire to the buildings, scattering provisions of every kind in every direction, including hundreds of barrels of flour which were left rolling about the streets. By one account, the young Jones boy spirited away a barrel of flower, which he rolled into his mother's storeroom. He anticipated the speedy return of the Federal troops and surmised that they might go hunting, therefore he emptied the flour into a cedar chest and burned the heads, hoops, and staves of the barrel, thus providing against the loss of his biscuit. A few hours later, he made another trip to the ruined stores and saw casks of rice split open and the snowy grains sifting into the dust. He filled a sack with rice, getting about two bushels. Rice would not roll, so he caught an army mule and got the rice up on its back and made his way home through the crowds of soldiers, horses, and wagons unnoticed. In 1859-60, Martha Reese Jones, widow of Rufus Jones, built a house at what is now 501 E. Falconer Ave. Their daughter, Miss Reese Jones, whose name appears elsewhere in these pages, later married Dr. Franklin Brevard Shuford. The home was later purchased by Mr. and Mrs. Thomas Finley, after which it passed into the hands of their daughters, Ruth Finley and Margaret Finley Shackelford, who gave it, with their plantation, "Strawberry Plains," to the National Audubon Society. The Jones-Shuford-Finley House is now Audubon Society's Mississippi office. Mrs. N. D. Deupree, "Some Historic Homes of Mississippi," 344-45; Kempe, 99; Baum, 48.

⁹ See Fischer, 373.

Endnotes

[10] Canton was the junction of the Mississippi Central with the New Orleans, Jackson, & Great Northern Railroad.

[11] Hamilton, 62.

[12] At low water, pilings from the pre-war bridge that was destroyed may still be seen on the east side of the present railroad bridge, where Miss. Highway 7 crosses the Tallahatchie River.

[13] Waddel, 439-40. Kate Bonner gave this account. "In the summer of 1863, at the end of her school term, Kate left Montgomery, Ala., to travel through the ruined countryside back to Holly Springs. The last part of the journey she made on the only vehicle left on the Mississippi Central Railroad, a handcar run by a black man, a cripple, and two former slaves." *Prodigal Daughter*, 15.

[14] Caroline R. Craft, a daughter of Mr. and Mrs. Hugh Craft.

[15] Frances Breckinridge Young (Mrs. Addison) Craft, daughter of the Rev'd John Clarke Young, president of Centre College in Danville, Ky. Addison Craft met her while attending college there.

[16] Bradley served in the Holly Springs Confederate Guards (Gen. W. S. Featherston's company). Hamilton, 149.

[17] Although born in Ireland, Paine was reared in Virginia and studied at Union Theological Seminary in Hampden-Sydney, where the professors furnished powerful intellectual leadership for the causes of slave ownership and secession. He had been known to preach about social issues of the day-a practice eschewed by conservative Presbyterians who advocated the "Spirituality of the Church," which emphasized Christ's teaching that His Kingdom was "not of this world." Robert B. Alexander, a member of the Holly Springs Methodist Church, made these observations about Paine's preaching during the period in 1860 when the Presbyterians and Methodists worshiped together while the new Presbyterian Church was being built: "Heard Mr. Paine preach a political sermon and I thought from his sermon he was a Breckinridge and Lane man, and McCully thought he was a Bell and Everett man." (Breckinridge and Lane represented the southern wing of the Democratic Party and Bell and Everett the Constitutional Union Party.) Six months later, Alexander recorded that "Rev. Paine preached in our church.... Rather a political discourse. Nothing extra." *Diary of Robert B. Alexander* (Jul. 29, 1860 and Dec. 9, 1860). Miss. Dept. of Archives and Hist.

[18] Edwin C. Bearss, "The Armed Conflict, 1861-1865," McLemore, 1:487.

[19] Mary Virginia Grigsby Foley recalled that as late as 1900, "Little children were called 'Master' and 'Miss' as soon as they were born, much like English royalty now." She remembered that "when I was six years old I was 'Miss Mary.' Now at ninety-two I am 'Mary' to old and young alike." The old forms of address are heard in Holly Springs today. *Childhood in Holly Springs*, 6.

[20] A swampy area along the banks of the Tallahatchie River, at the boundary of Lafayette and Marshall Counties, much of which forms the bed for a lake behind the present Sardis Dam.

[21] Belle reversed her letters. The place was Panola, a location to which she refers elsewhere in the diary.

[22] On one night, the glow of fourteen fires was said to have been visible in and around the city-all set, it was said by U. S. soldiers.

[23] Genesis 39:7-18.

[24] "N'Omporte," "A Full Account of Van Dorn's Brilliant Raid," Mobile, Ala., *Advertiser and Register* (Jan. 7, 1863): 2. Kate Bonner called the day *"The Glorious, GLORIOUS Twentieth." Prodigal Daughter,* 13. Cordelia Scales wrote from Hudsonville, Oct. 17, 1863: "Oh! how I did shout when Van Dorn came into Holly Springs. He made them 'skedaddle' . . . . I was so glad I had the pleasure of seeing Mr. Yankee run."

[25] "Recollections of Van Dorn's Raid," SR (Apr. 27, 1978).

[26] Mary Fonta Hopson, "Holly Springs Churches" (unpub. typescript, n.d.): 1, Hugh H. Rather to R. M. Winter, 15 June 1994. The Crump Place, at 127 W. Gholson Ave., is presently the home of Mr. and Mrs. Roger Woods; Mary Wallace Crocker, 158; Kempe, 81-82; Schuler, 88-89; Conway and Moulder, 25; Smith, Baum, 25; Miller-Smith, *Marshall County*, 35.

[27] J. G. Deupree, "The Capture of Holly Springs, Miss., Dec. 20, 1862," *Publications of the Mississippi Historical Society* 4 (1901): 49-61.

[28] Lewis Scruggs had served in the Confederate forces, attaining the rank of major. His friend, Dr. J. D. M. Litchfield was a popular local physician and pharmacist, and in happier days, the two had gone courting together. In April 1859, Emma Finley described a visit from Litchfield and Scruggs for her diary. They had called on Emma and Augusta Finley at their plantation east of Holly Springs. She wrote: "Thursday Gusta had a chill, & inferred therefrom that her indisposition of Tuesday might be laid to the same cause, was quite sick for a while, but with the aid of some buttermilk & toast- and primping felt and looked well enough to receive, with us, the visit of Dr. Litchfield and Mr. Scruggs. These gentlemen were late getting out, but it was not until the candles were brought in, that I knew of their intention to remain for [supper],-made themselves as agreeable as possible & seemed to enjoy very much Auntie's good waffles, biscuit & dried beef. Left half after nine, with our wishes for their safety over the bad road." Augusta Finley later married Scruggs. Litchfield, a widower, had been married to the late Pamela Brooks Lucas (1836-1856), daughter of Peter W. and Clementia Donoho Lucas, a prominent Holly Springs family, with roots in the valley of Virginia. She was the sister of Eveline D. (Mrs. J. W.) Clapp, wife of Major Strickland's law partner. Holly Springs *South* (Feb. 29, 1903); Hamilton, 64, 146.

[29] James J. House ran a livery stable on or near the square.

[30] Scruggs, a popular Holly Springs merchant, was in business with Joseph B. Mattison, later one of the city's newspaper editors. Emma Finley told her journal in September 1858 how the two brought eager viewers to their store to see a section of the transatlantic cable which they displayed. The technology was highly interesting, for rural Holly Springs had not long had telegraph service. Wires had been strung east toward Salem, and on to Alabama, beginning Jan. 7, 1848. Service was disrupted during the war. James J. Selby, "Sundries Events," *Ansearchin' News: The Tennessee Genealogical Magazine* 31 (Fall 1984): 132.

Endnotes

[31] Kate Bonner gave this account of her return to Holly Springs in the summer of 1863: "I should never have recognized in the dreary village the once prosperous, comfortable little town. Rank weeds grew everywhere, and desolation hung over all things like a funeral pall. Where the town-hall had stood was now a shapeless heap of brick and mortar overgrown with nettles and dog-fennel. The door of [our] church...had been torn away, and, looking in, I saw the organ bereft of its pipes, the pulpit of its cushions. The seats were broken up, and not a pane of glass was left in the windows. Even in the graveyard the destroyer had been at work: the gravestones were toppled over, and upon the white columns yet standing were scrawled rude jests and caricatures....The school-house was leveled to the ground, but its red chimneys stood, like faithful sentinels, over the ruined pile....The square was deserted, except by a company of small boys, who were marching round it in soldier-fashion, and a few old men with long white hair, who were dozing in the sun." *Prodigal Daughter*, 15. Mildred Strickland likewise wrote to her husband April 4, 1861, that "The town is entirely deserted." Two years later, on January 25, 1863, in the aftermath of Van Dorn's raid, she complained that "we are entirely cut off from everything here. We never get a paper nor hear anything at all. It looks like a deserted village. The town is ruined forever now." See Arthur B. Carter, *The Tarnished Cavalier: Major General Earl Van Dorn, C.S.A.* (Knoxville: Univ. of Tenn. Press, 1999).

[32] Hamilton, 146.

[33] Daughter of Gray Washington Smith. The family lived at the house now called "Linden Terrace." In the 1850s and 1860s, the house was owned by Dr. Smith, a physician-planter from Lamar, Miss. The house was owned in the 1870s by Gen. Henry E. Williamson (whose name is mentioned elsewhere in these pages), then mayor, and the person responsible for the lindens both at his home and at the public school on Walthall St. The house was acquired by Mississippi Synodical College as a home for its president. Linden Terrace, at 225 E. College Ave., is currently the home of Mr. and Mrs. James R. Dunworth, of Balboa, Panama, and Holly Springs. SR (Dec. 18, 1930): 4; Pruitt, 32-33; Shuler, 93; Kempe, 89; Baum, 36.

[34] Children of Laura Smith and Morgan Hopson Thomson, Belle's first cousins.

[35] Cora Watson, visiting in Covington, Tenn., recorded details of Forrest's Memphis raid: August 25, 1864: "John [a family slave] went about ten days ago to Memphis, and there was 'drafted into the army' by a Negro in the Yankee service named Jake who-John says-is a 'Major-general' (!) They gave him a blue uniform, but the day after 'Mr. Forrest's criller [guerrilla] company' rode in and performed, he took a furlough. Got home to find-or rather, not to find-his wife. He had better have stayed, for he will surely go, and ought to, since he is too completely demoralized ever to be of any more value.... This evening Pa carried little Sallie Barrett home and there saw Lucinda. She went down on a boat to Memphis, but found a perfect panic prevailing there and did not get off. Traveled with Washburn's adjutant, Morgan, who, so far from being killed, was not even in the city....Two days before the raid one of Forrest's men went over the city peddling watermelons, sold one to Washburn, and so found his room. It is rumored in town, tho' Lucinda said nothing to Pa about it, that all our prisoners in the Irving Block were liberated. Our men left Memphis by the Hernando Road."

[36] Susan and Lucy Hull were daughters of John and Anne Crump Hull. Susan married William Lea.

[37] The Govans, whose plantation "Snowdoun" lay in the northeast part of the county near the Strickland plantation, were a family of social standing. Andrew Robinson Govan, who had represented North Carolina in Congress, came to Marshall County at an early day. His wife, Mary Pugh Jones Govan, was an heiress. Their children married well. Eaton Pugh Govan married the daughter of the Rev'd Dr. Francis L. Hawks, an early rector of Christ Church, and Daniel Chevillette Govan took as his wife the daughter of the Rt. Rev'd James H. Otey, the Episcopal bishop of Tennessee. Beautiful Sallie Govan married Christopher Haynes Mott, who was appointed special U. S. commissioner to California. *Southern Tapestry*, 43-44.

[38] Dr. Francis Dancy and his family lived in the cottage on the southwest corner of College St. and Walthall Ave.-now known as the McDermott Place. Baum, 29.

[39] Pruitt, 48-49. Located at 305 S. Craft St., the house, now known as "The Magnolias," was for many years the home of Mrs. Everett Slayden.

[40] Lida Anderson lived in the old Anderson home, where Mrs. John Rylee's house is now on E. College Ave. There is an old dependency still standing in back. Lida Smith Anderson was the second Mrs. James H. Anderson. James H. Anderson, son of Peter Anderson, one of the wealthy men of Holly Springs in its early days, married as his first wife, Jane Watson, daughter of J. W. C. and Catherine Davis Watson. She and their infant died shortly after the latter's birth and were buried in the Watson lot in Hill Crest Cemetery. Lida was a sister of Miss Carrie Smith, Belle's music teacher. The Andersons finally settled in Memphis, but are buried in Hill Crest Cemetery. SR (Dec. 10, 1931).

[41] Mrs. R. R. McWilliams, who lived in the McWilliams-Jones-McCrosky Place on E. College Ave. Mr. McWilliams was a master blacksmith, and his shop evolved into the Jones, McIlwain Iron Foundry. Baum, 35.

[42] Gaines Foster reports that "when northern soldiers came to the front door of another woman, she admitted to being so frightened she could not move. She added that the squeaking of the metal axle on the Yankee supply wagon 'made every Southern woman tremble.'" *Ghosts of the Confederacy*, 32.

[43] Anne Crump Hull, widow of John Hull and sister of William Crump, was a neighbor of the Watsons.

[44] Gaines Foster remarks that Confederate women learned that "their homes and their status as ladies...did not always protect them." He observes that Confederate condemnations of U. S. soldiers who invaded private homes "were often couched in rhetoric that suggested the ultimate violation," i.e., rape or physical abuse of women. He notes that there were relatively few allegations that this actually occurred, rather the accounts specified that "Yankees had forcibly entered and ransacked homes and treated women with wanton disrespect" so that "perhaps entering the home served as discreet imagery for physical violation." *Ghosts of the Confederacy*, 32.

[45] Brodie Strahan Hull, son of John and Anne Crump Hull. He was a young boy at the time.

[46] If Mrs. Hull possessed a set of silver, it may have been hidden, but during the nineteenth century, even in prominent families, the principal quantity of table silver often was made up of spoons-not all having embraced the use of forks. William E. Woodward, *The Way our People Lived: An Intimate American History* (New York: Liveright, 1963): 55, 76.

[47] The courthouse survived Van Dorn's raid, but on August 27, 1864, when Confederates captured Union General J. A. "Scoey" Smith and his men, and placed them in the courthouse, Smith, still in chains, set fire to the building and it burned down. SR (Apr. 24, 1986): 1, 3.

[48] Cordelia Scales, on January 27, 1863, gave this account of pillaging that accompanied the arrival of Federal soldiers in Holly Springs: "The day the army came to Holly Springs, & when the wagon trains were passing thirty or forty Yankees would rush in at a time, take everything to eat they could lay their hands on, & break, destroy and steal everything they wanted to-all of our mules, horses, and wagons were taken, 42 wagons were loaded with corn at our cribs & many more after. I'll tell you what I thought we would certainly starve." Later one thousand "black republicans," the 26th Illinois regiment, camped at the Scales plantation. Cordelia wrote that "Col. Gilmore was in command of the 26th; he made our house his headquarters; he used to let his men go out foraging every day and one day while some of them were out stealing chickens and hogs about four miles from here at [Thompson's] place, a company of our 'gurilliars' overhauled them and killed two and wounded two." Hamilton, 154. A description of the plantation and its mansion may be found in Miller, 74-76.

[49] Many buildings were used as hospitals during the war, including the Jones, McIlwain Foundry, the Female Institute, the Courthouse, the Baptist, and Roman Catholic Churches. Cordelia Scales wrote May 15, 1862 that "It would make your heart bleed to witness the sufferings of the poor Soldiers!.... There are five Hospitals [in Holly Springs].... You can't cross a street or turn a corner, but what...you see wounded or sick soldiers. Some...their leg shot off and walking on crutches, and some with their arms shot off..." Rosa Barton Tyler, "Holly Springs Schools" (unpub. mss., n.d.): 2; "First Baptist Was Used as Hospital During the Civil War," SR (Apr. 23, 1986): Hubert H. McAlexander, "First Baptist Church, 1837-1900," in *A History of the First Baptist Church of Holly Springs, 1837-1987* (Holly Springs: SR, 1987): 6; Sister Joan Kobe, D.W., "History of the Old St. Joseph's Church," unpub. typescript (Oct. 4, 1994): 2, 4; Pruitt 20, 21; Cordielia Lewis Scales to "Dearest Darlie Loulie," Scales letters. Miss. Dept. of Archives and Hist.

[50] The McConnico house stood on the site of Lucius Dancy's house on Peyton Road west of Holly Springs.

[51] In this era, locomotives were named for prominent men, and the third engine placed in service on the Mississippi Central was the "A. J. McConnico." When he died at New Orleans in 1874, all locomotives and stations on the line were draped in mourning. Holly Springs *Reporter* (Dec. 31, 1874), SR (Dec. 15, 1932); Hamilton, 56, 57, 60, 61, 63.

[52] The Minors were early settlers in the county. Dabney Minor came from Virginia in 1836 and was a member of the vestry in St. Andrew's Church (Episcopal), at Salem, in 1839.

Their daughter Lucy married Major Belton Mickle, father of John M. Mickle. SR (Nov. 27, 1930); Hamilton, 5, 132, 146. John Mickle, born September 5, 1860, writing nearly eighty years later, recalled the incident in these words: "The War Between the States followed in seven months after my birth and we moved to Holly Springs for protection from the Yankees, while my father was in the army-and got right in the thick of them. I have lived in Holly Springs ever since. Strange to say I remember quite a little of the War, but no fighting, chiefly lines of blue. I saw the courthouse burn. The most exciting experience I had was when my grandmother snatched me from my bed against which a Yankee held a torch. It is but just to say he was acting without knowledge or consent of his officers." SR (May 4, 1939).

[53] Sometimes attempts to burn homes and churches were countered by acts of heroism. In nearby Oxford, where the Union soldiers camped in the yard of the First Presbyterian Church, an attempt was made to burn the building, but Mrs. Henry Rascoe dashed from her house and put out the fire while the soldiers jeered. The building was saved and continued in use until replaced by the present church in 1880. Maud Morrow Brown, *History of the First Presbyterian Church of Oxford, Miss., 1837-1950* (Oxford: prv. pub., 1952): 10; Maud Morrow Brown, "What Desolations! At Home in Lafayette County, Miss., 1860-1865" (unpub. typescript, n.d.): 105-108. Miss. Dept. of Archives and Hist.

[54] Cora Watson, writing in her diary at Covington, Tenn., gave this report on conditions at Holly Springs: "Saturday, Aug. 27, 1864: Dr. Barrett, I hear in the neighborhood, intends returning to Holly Springs Monday, and will carry a letter for me. His account of matters in H.S. adds fuel to the fire of my anxiety. 20,000 Yanks, there for two weeks, ate up all provisions for man and beast in and around town, cut down the growing corn to feed their horses. Dr. B. says it will be next to impossible to live there. He is here now arranging to move his family-has rented Dr. Hall's new house. Was commissioned by Dr. Reed, a Mr. Williams, and two or three others to procure homes for them here.... Asked him about home. Our family not molested particularly. Seven or eight business houses in Holly Springs burned."

[55] Yale historian Roland Bainton has called the nineteenth century "the missionary century," for it was in this era, with its improved transportation and communication, as well as zeal for imperial expansion and colonization, that the propagation Christianity became a world enterprise. Support for the effort was garnered from people in the pews with thousands of books and pamphlets filled with human-interest accounts of missionaries and their success. Just two decades later, the Rev'd Dr. David C. Rankin, minister of the Holly Springs Presbyterian Church went to be his denomination's assistant secretary for foreign missions, and played a key role in opening Cuba, the Congo, and Korea to his church's witness. The local Presbyterian Women's missionary society was named in honor of Catherine Watson, and Belle's Sunday school teacher, Miss Mary R. Paine, organized a similar society for the children. *Shadow of a Mighty Rock*, 284-91.

[56] Mrs. Carrington [Maria Brodie] Mason, "Van Dorn's Raid into Holly Springs, or Why General Grant's Flank Movement on Vicksburg Failed," Memphis *Commercial Appeal* (May 30, 1901). Not all accepted the influx of soldiers graciously. Belle's mother, a beautiful, spoiled heiress, who was having trouble keeping supplies on hand at Strickland Place, wrote

to her husband, then a captain serving at Corinth, April 20, 1862, to complain that she expected that "these soldiers will stay with me forever. One is well enough to go to camp-nothing the matter with him. The other one is unhealthy. I don't know what is the matter with him, and he eats up everything on the table and would eat more if he had it. I don't want to stay here forever for them. They are so <u>nasty</u> I hate for them to eat at the table when I have company.

[57] Cora Watson described a less pleasant incident later that fall: "Wednesday, Nov. 16, 1864: Old Mr. Crump had General Adams and staff to dine with them yesterday, and imbibed so freely as to have to be sent to bed in disgrace." Cora's diary indicates that the Watsons were kind to military visitors- "Sunday, Nov. 27, 1864: Tonight three boy soldiers, belonging to the company of Reserves stationed here-came in and got supper. Sister gave one a testament."

[58] Betty and Susan Hull were daughters of John and Ann Crump Hull, and Carrie Smith was the daughter of the late Frank Millington Smith and Lida Smith Anderson. Miss Carrie later became Belle's music teacher.

[59] On January 17, 1863, Cordelia Scales wrote of the music which Confederate young ladies sang. When the wife of a Union officer begged her to play for her, Cordelia stated that she knew "nothing but rebel songs," and when urged to perform the songs she knew, she sang "My Maryland," "Bonnie Blue Flag," "Mississippi Camp Song," "Cheer Boys, Cheer" "Life on the Tented Field" and, of course, "Dixie." The woman said, "Oh they are beautiful. I don't blame you for loving them. She made me write them off for her to carry with her."

[60] Additional hospitality was extended to soldiers by the Watsons in the winter of 1864. As Cora remembered: "Dec. 15, We are always so interested in talking to the soldiers-their experiences seem so wild and strange to us, battles and skirmishes and escapes. Every now and then one or two come to ask for something to eat or to stay all night. A week or two since, a robust looking soldier stayed with us who-poor fellow!-four weeks before had lost one hand and the thumb and forefinger of the other, and was thus rendered completely helpless."

[61] Pianos were fairly common in the privileged homes of Holly Springs. Indeed, music teachers had made their appearance on the local scene even before the town was incorporated. Several pianos dating from the Civil War may still be seen in the old homes of the city.

IV. HE WAS MUCH TAKEN WITH THE LADY THAT SANG

[1] Wollenhaupt (1827-1863), studied in Leipzig and emigrated to New York, where he made a reputation as a concert pianist and teacher. He wrote about 100 piano pieces. *Baker's Biographical Dictionary of Musicians.*

[2] Pruitt, 52-55. From 1868 to 1870, after the Carrington Masons moved to Memphis, the Mason (now Hamilton) Place housed Bethlehem Academy. In 1892, the house was

purchased by Dr. S. D. Hamilton. Later, Belle and her husband Judge Bates lived here, and occupied the home when it was struck by lightning and partially burned in 1920. The house was reconstructed as a one-story dwelling. One Holly Springs citizen remembers that prior to the fire the famous piano still sat in the hallway. SR (Dec. 15, 1932).

[3] The Clapps and Coxes were friends and had made an extensive Eastern tour in 1853. But they had their great houses constructed in differing architectural modes. The Clapp Place, a refined blend of Greek and Italianate styles, was sited close to the street on a thirty acre lot, while the Coxe home and its dependencies, all flamboyant Gothic, were set back behind a massive cast iron fence identical to one at the U. S. Military Academy in West Point. *Southern Tapestry*, 49.

[4] The William Henry Coxe home, a Gothic mansion now known as "Airliewood," or the Coxe-Dean Place, was in recent times the home of the Charles Nunnally Dean family. Located at 385 E. Salem Ave., it is now owned by Ms. Barbara Fant Schuler, 95-97; John M. Mickle, "Mayor Dean's Home Long a Show Place," SR (Aug. 7, 1930): 4; Mills Lane, *Architecture of the Old South: Mississippi & Alabama* (New York: Beehive Press, 1989): 160, 163; Mary Wallace Crocker, 168-69; Baum, 73. The Clapp and Coxe houses were on Salem Road, over which Emma would have traveled to and from her plantation at Woodland.

[5] Cited in *Southern Tapestry,* 48.

[6] Dora Barton Clark, a younger daughter of William and Mary Barton Clark, died in 1877. SR (Dec. 10, 1931): 18.

[7] By Mickle's account: "Will Henry Cox, one of a wealthy planters in the Chulahoma neighborhood, had the house built for a town house in the mid-fifties. The most noteworthy historical fact in connection with the house is that it was the official headquarters of Gen. Ulysses S. Grant at the time during the war between the states when he was massing here his army, for his descent upon Vicksburg. Gen. Van Dorn's brilliant dash into Holly Springs and the destruction of the vast amount of army supplies here caused Gen. Grant to change his plan of campaign and proceed against Vicksburg by the Mississippi river. While the Cox place was Gen. Grant's office building so to speak, he and his family occupied as a residence the home of the late Col. H. W. Walter on Chulahoma Ave., now occupied by Mrs. M. A. Greene. Gen. Grant was better liked by the people of Holly Springs than any Federal Commander who operated through here. He was considerate of the people as the exigencies of war permitted. He listened to their troubles, helped them when he could and readily granted guards to protect private homes." SR (Jun. 20, 1929).

[8] In a subsequent article, Mickle gives details about the Coxe Place: "Since it was built about 185[8], the Will Henry Cox place on Salem Ave. has been one of the show places of Holly Springs. Mayor Charles N. Dean now owns the property and makes his home there. The house is said to have cost $[6]0,000, and building could be done much cheaper then than now, with the best materials plentiful and cheap. It is designed in the perpendicular gothic style, which was observed in all particulars. The halls above and below are sixteen feet wide and run the length of the house. There are four rooms on each floor, large and high pitched

with a wing at the back in which are located a beautiful sitting room, with pantries and kitchen. The two parlors on the west side are connected by an archway, the rear and smaller room having a bay window. One or two were added to the rear of the house by later owners. The windows and veranda are in keeping with the gothic style, and add much to the beauty of the house. So far as conveniences went, the house was well provided for that time. It was piped for gas throughout and the chandeliers were artistic in hammered iron. The bathroom with running water was so far as known the first installed in Holly Springs. Water for it was pumped by hand. A system of call bells from all rooms was also arranged. The grounds which Mr. Cox bought in 1858, contained about fifteen acres, the front of it covered with large forest trees, many of which have yielded to time and the elements, but enough are left to give beauty to the place. Much landscaping was done, almost wholly in the way of trees and shrubs. Small cedars, kept properly trimmed, formed hedges for the drive. The tall iron fence and large gates are...a pleasing part of the building scheme of the place....The panels of the fence carried spear heads which were broken off during the war of the sixties. Someone from Holly Springs while in Ohio a few years ago met an elderly man who said that he and another young Federal soldier in a spirit of boyish wantonness had knocked them off, and he was sorry to have marred the beauty of the fence....The original front of the place on Salem Ave., included the sites of the John Gray and Pulliam homes. The large stable was located back of John Gray's house and its architecture conformed with the Gothic style of the house, as did the kitchen and servants quarters in the rear of the house. Gen. Grant made the house his official headquarters while collecting supplies here for his proposed campaign against Vicksburg. During this time Gen. Grant used Col. H. W. Walter's house, now Mrs. M.A. Greene's home on Chulahoma Ave., for his family residence. Gen. Van Dorn's dash into Holly Springs and the destruction of the vast store of supplies caused Grant to change his plan of approach to Vicksburg by rail and go by the Mississippi river....Mr. Cox died in 1865 and his town house was sold to Col. Dixon Comfort Topp of Grenada, who lived there until his death." SR (Aug. 7, 1930). William Henry Coxe was a member of a family who came from Oglethorpe County, Ga. and settled near Chulahoma; there were several brothers, all large planters. Hubert McAlexander to R. M. Winter, Jan. 9, 2001.

[9] *Diary of Henry Craft* (Apr. 5, 1849).

[10] The Female Institute, which had occupied a handsome two-story building of the Tuscan order, large enough to accommodate 140 students and to board 60, stood in a park-like setting laid two blocks from the Watson home. The town's first public school was later built on the site which fronts on the present Walthall St., now filled by the new Holly Springs High School. Kate Bonner described the tree lined grounds of the Female Institute, "where the young folks walked on summer evenings and fed tame squirrels or made love to each other on the 'swinging seats' under the linden trees." *Prodigal Daughter*, 9; "From '60 to '65," 500-501; *A Vanishing America*, 60.

[11] Dental woes caused much suffering, and most dentists were in military service.

[12] Too young to serve in the army, young James Henry Watson had enrolled in the Virginia Military Institute.

[13] The Smiths may have lived in the old Fennell house, which has been moved to 340 E. Van Dorn Ave. and extensively remodeled. See Baum, 21.

[14] Edward Minor Watson once raised the ire of his church's elders when he publicly stated his approval of dueling. The Holly Springs church session appointed a committee, July 2, 1876, to prepare an article "expressive of the views of this Session upon the subject of duelling." Judge Watson was, of course, among the elders. Edward Watson later expressed to the body "his matured conviction that the Duelling Code is wholly contrary to the word of God, and his regret for having given it his endorsement." *Shadow of a Mighty Rock*, 229-30.

[15] The boys obtained the spare bits of gas pipes because Holly Springs was one of the few cities of its size which had been piped for gas. By John Mickle's recollection, "The installation of gas works was a big feather in the cap of Holly Springs in ante-bellum days." The first lights were outside, for Mickle records that "the old minute book of the Mayor and Board of Aldermen shows. . .August 7, 1860, that Messrs. Craft and McGowan were appointed a committee to locate the ten lamp posts..." Later, houses and churches were piped for gas. The gas plant, at the foot of Falconer Ave. in Spring Hollow, was owned and operated by Herman Sneider, who also operated a bakery on the east side of the square. The gas was produced from coal, and a man was employed to ride his horse around town to turn on the street lights at dusk. James Fort Daniel recorded that "a workman, Johnny Garrett, better known as Johnny Gas, and a Negro helper, Green Lucas, were making some repairs on a gas pipe which was clogged with tar. They evidently used a blow torch, which ignited the gas and cause a huge gas storage tank to explode with a terrific loud noise and clouds of black smoke. This explosion caused quite a lot of excitement over town." Daniel records further that "the iron gas posts, which Sneider owned were removed and were replaced by wooden posts owned by the city. The fixtures at the top of these posts used naptha for fuel. The late Jim House, liveryman, had a contract to service these posts. A horse drawn cart with an extra high frame was used in servicing these lights." Gas lights were first used in New York City in the 1820s. Holly Springs did not obtain natural gas until after World War II. SR (Dec. 10, 1931); Marshall County *Messenger* (Apr. 24, 1980): 10.

[16] A slave child with whom the white youngsters played.

[17] Cora Watson was still visiting her uncle at Covington, Tenn.

[18] Shields McIlwaine records how in the winter of 1863 a wartime shopper complained that in Memphis, "all the principal stores are closed and their contents confiscated. . . .Not even a spool of thread can be purchased without registering your name and address, and swearing it is for personal or family use, and no number of articles can be taken from the store without, after selection, going to the Board of Trade, accompanied by the clerk of the store, and then swearing on the Bible that the articles mentioned are for family use, and not to be taken out of the United States." *Memphis Down in Dixie* (New York: E. P. Dutton, 1948):129.

[19] This editor recalls how in the early 1960s his own grandmother, then in her eighties, and educated in a one-room school, was appalled at the amount of paper her young grandson consumed in his school work. In a day that predated serious environmental concerns, she believed it was an unconscionable waste.

Endnotes

[20] Use of these readers was nearly universal. Mildred Strickland, who often asked her husband to try and find items for her and send them home from his military posts, wrote to Major Strickland Feb. 12, 1862, that "Willie says you must get for him and Belle McGuffey's *Second Reader.*"

[21] Major Strickland was able to obtain items for his family from sutlers who followed the army. When Minnie was an infant, Mrs. Strickland wrote him Feb. 25, 1862, to, "try and get me 6 yards of cotton flannel or cotton diaper either." That summer she wrote, "In your travels if you come across shoes, thread, or handkerchiefs, or toothbrushes, buy some."

[22] Travelers could use "trading passes," which allowed them to cross enemy lines. On the evening before Van Dorn's raid, several persons with such documents were apprehended as they were leaving the city. The Confederates took the captive's clothes and papers and entered Holly Springs to spy out the situation. Carter, *The Tarnished Cavalier,* 133-134.

[23] General C. C. Washburn, who had escaped Forrest's raid on Fort Pickering the previous summer by fleeing in his night clothes.

[24] On other occasions, Holly Springs citizens seem to have passed through enemy lines freely for shopping and recreation. Cora Watson reported Wednesday, Jan. 11, 1865 that "Mrs. Hull called this evening. She gave us a very amusing account of Betsy's and Carrie's Memphis trip. Says they spent three or four hundred dollars apiece, and had nothing new when they came home but two worsted dresses. They kept their bureau drawers filled with candies, oranges, and all sorts of nice things. Would go out walking, and when tired call a hack. In short, 'lived high,' luxuriating in Yankee elegancies." See Mary Elizabeth Massey, *Refugee Life in the Confederacy* (Baton Rouge: La. State Univ. Press, 2000).

[25] Many of Mildred Strickland's wartime letters to Major Strickland are addressed "in care of" or "by favor" of this or that person who hand-delivered them. She began a letter April 4, 1861, this way: "Mr. Sims sent me word this evening that he would leave for Pensacola tomorrow morning, and as letters seem to go so much quicker by hand, I conclude it is much better to write by some one." On Mar. 19, 1863, she confided that "I don't write to you as often as I desire, but it is difficult to get persons to take letters; they so often keep the letters in their pockets several days."

[26] The McConnicos were from Shongalo, four miles west of Vaiden, Miss.

[27] John Mickle recorded this story of mail delivery in Holly Springs. "Neither side, during the war, maintained a post office here. There was a small brick store on the corner named Simpson's store. Two cracker boxes were placed here, on where the Confederate soldiers slipped letters in for the various families from the boys on the front and the other box was used by the families to place mail which they wished delivered to the boys on the front. Any soldier on leave would go the cracker box and see if any of the mail was going to any buddy he knew and if so he would deliver it personally. He usually brought some in to deposit in the other box. It was a slow means of getting messages in and out, but those cracker boxes were never molested." *Frisco Railroad Employees' Magazine* (Jul. 1931).

[28] Son of Mrs. John D. Martin.

[29] Samuel Creed Gholson, M.D., a local physician. Born near Farmville, in Cumberland

County, Va., in 1828, he moved to Holly Springs in 1846. He was a graduate of the Medical College of Virginia in 1852 and, three years later, married Miss Mary Hannah Caruthers, the daughter of Holly Springs physician, Dr. Samuel Oliver Caruthers. Gholson died in 1910 and is buried in Hill Crest Cemetery. Hamilton, 105; Robert Lowry and William H. McCardle, *A History of Mississippi* (Jackson: R. H. Henry, 1891): 544.

[30] Minutes of the trustees of the Holly Springs Female Institute.

[31] Laura Smith (Mrs. Morgan H.) Thomson grew up in the house now known as "Linden Terrace," mentioned elsewhere in these pages.

[32] People of the Old South did not use nearly so much refined sugar as Southerners today, but probably used more molasses. See Joe Gray Taylor, *Eating, Drinking and Visiting in the South: An Informal History* (Baton Rouge: La. State Univ. Press, 1982): 43.

[33] *Our Pen Is Time*, 85.

[34] Fannie was the daughter of James Fort, a Holly Springs lawyer, and his wife Martha Craft. Fannie was the great-grandmother of Chesley Thorne Smith, whose photos illustrate this book. James Fort died in the yellow fever epidemic of 1878. Fannie Fort and Belle Strickland were lifelong friends. Hamilton, 157.

[35] Some thirty years after these lines were written, Mary Virginia Grigsby Foley, daughter of the Presbyterian minister, recalled that: "Ready-made clothes were a rarity. Seamstresses came to the house if required but most women made their own clothes. Although members of a moderately salaried minister's family...our dresses made by our mother were very pretty and we were considered by the members of the congregation to be very well dressed....All our little girl's dresses were of nice material, bought by the bolt or yard, and heavily embroidered. A new engagement or wedding called for more embroidery. We all knew how to hem, stitch, feather stitch and button hole. Towels and sheets and pillowcases were all embroidered. We sewed on samplers and made 'crazy quilts' from pieces of our clothing that had been discarded." *Childhood in Holly Springs*, 31.

[36] John Blassingame wrote that "At first, bondage weighed lightly on the shoulders of the black child.... Often assigned as playmates to their young masters, black children played in promiscuous equality with white children." Then when a certain age was attained, strict rules of segregation prevailed, and the former playmates would be expected to labor without remuneration for their white masters and mistresses. *The Slave Community*, 183-84.

[37] Medicine of various kinds were sold by physicians who had offices and drug stores on the square. Healing remedies were also prepared at home. Most had copious amounts of alcohol as a base.

[38] *A Vanishing America*, 63.

[39] Willis Monroe Lea, whose plantation, "Wildwood," lay at the crossing of the Hernando Road with the road to Red Banks (an intersection still known as Lea's Crossing), built an impressive house on his plantation and opened another plantation in the Mississippi Bottom, as the state's Delta region was then called. *Southern Tapestry*, 48.

[40] Sister of John M. Mickle, whose writings are cited in these pages. The widowed

Jane Hull Minor rented various houses in Holly Springs in the 1860s-one of them was the present insurance agency on Van Dorn across the street from Christ Church. Her daughter Lucy Minor Mickle and children lived with her-Lucy's husband being in the army.

[41] "McCarroll's Woods," which covered a large expanse behind the Strickland Place was territory adjacent to the original McCarroll and Strickland farms. Some of this land is still uncut and rich in Civil War relics and lore. On April 4, 1863, Mildred Strickland reported to her husband that, "I walked out to your woods the other day and it distresses me very much the way people haul it away."

[42] Unlike many who practiced medicine in those days, W. M. Lea was qualified for his profession. Lea-for years president of the County Medical Association-had been one of Marshall County's delegates to the Mississippi Secession Convention (along with A. M. Clayton, Samuel Benton, J. W. Clapp, and H. W. Walter). A native of North Carolina, Lea was a graduate of that state's university, and received his M.D. from the University of Pennsylvania. He came to Holly Springs about 1836 where, in partnership with Dr. Charles Bonner, he mixed planting and politics with medicine. News of his popular son's death was received with sorrow. A. M. Clayton, *Centennial Address on the History of Marshall County, Miss.* [delivered to mark the centennial of the American Declaration of Independence], August 12, 1876 (Washington, D. C.: R. O. Plankinhorn, 1880): 27; *Memoirs of Mississippi,* 2:264; Hamilton, 132; *Prodigal Daughter,* 5.

[43] In a similar vein, Cora Watson told her diary on Dec. 28 of the same year that "This evening I walked home with Mrs. Smith and borrowed 'Harper' and 'Peterson' for December, and 'Waverley' and 'Old Mortality.' Tonight we have been reading aloud in the magazines." Libraries in Holly Springs homes, such as "McCarroll Place," which preserve nineteenth century collections, are filled with Scott's novels. Some Southerners, such as Mark Twain, thought that the romantic and chivalric emphases of Scott and the romantic writers retarded the South as it struggled to enter the modern world.

[44] Sallie Govan Mott, widow of Christopher Mott.

[45] W. A. Anderson, longtime master of Chalmers Institute.

[46] St. James 1:19, 20.

[47] Proverbs 25:28.

[48] SR (Dec. 10, 1931).

[49] Miss Matilda Paine, a daughter or niece of the Presbyterian minister.

[50] Samuel S. Hill Jr., *Southern Churches in Crisis* (New York: Holt, Rinehart & Winston, 1966): 75.

[51] Emma Finley spoke for many when she recorded in her diary on various occasions comments such as these about her minister's sermons: "Ginnie, George & Johnie came in to preaching, and after listening to one of Mr. Paine's good sermons..." [Sept. 5, 1858]; "Mr. Paine preached his New Year's sermon today. It was that "the grace of our Lord Jesus Christ be with you all [2 Thessalonians 3:18]. Thanks to, and blessings on the preacher, who has done so much good amongst us .." [Jan. 2, 1859]; "Mr. Paine as usual gave us a very good sermon." [April 1859]. *Our Pen Is Time,* 22, 55, 67.

[52] *Diary of Robert B. Alexander* (Apr. 30, 1854); *Minutes of the Synod of Mississippi* (1865): 58.

[53] Daughters of William Clark, who lived in the house now called "Colonsay Cottege"-until recently the George M. Buchanan residence, at 315 E. College Ave. The property now belongs to St. Joseph's Catholic Church. The arch which frames the door is not original and was taken from a Gothic cottage completed by Heber Craft during the war and later owned by George M. Buchanan. That house sat on the west side of Craft St., on what is known as Buchanan Hill. Baum 31; Hubert McAlexander to R. M. Winter, June 24, 2001.

[54] Consistent with the speech customs of Presbyterians, Belle did not call Mr. Paine's services a "revival." For many years, Old School Presbyterians carefully reserve the word "revival" to the fruits produced at an evangelistic meeting, for the devout objected to ideas that "revivals" could be induced by human effort. The services were "protracted" in the measure and to the degree that interest was sustained.

[55] In 1870, the Holly Springs Presbyterian Church was one of the first public buildings of the city to be piped for interior gas lighting-several of its leading members being among the incorporators of the Holly Springs Gas Light Company. "When Gas Was Used Holly Springs Had It," SR (Dec. 10, 1931).

[56] In a diary entry from Covington, Tenn., Cora Watson-who attended the Methodist Church in that city-describes the procedure of visiting and dining in one's carriage between the morning and afternoon services. By her account: "Sunday, Aug. 14, 1864: At Love-Feast an old man named Black spoke in such an earnest, impassioned manner and with so much pathos that my utmost efforts could not restrain my feelings.... After church, Fannie and Jennie Hall spoke to me. They looked sad, and were in deep mourning for the gallant brother slain at Atlanta. After dining and talking a while, we went and sat in our carriage. Shed Dickinson and Bert Winfrey came to the carriage and talked with Lou and Mollie. Charlie Tucker brought us half of a nice watermelon."

[57] Mildred Strickland to W. M. Strickland, undated letter, Feb. 1862.

[58] Daughter of Mrs. John D. Martin.

[59] A rail link to Memphis (via Grand Junction, Tenn.) was completed February 21, 1856. Even then, travel was not ideal. John Mickle wrote that in the olden days, "the northbound passenger train passed here at 3 o'clock in the morning and people had to go to Memphis by Grand Junction then. The long drawn-out cry in the night of [the] 'railroad' usually waked up the neighbors." SR (Dec. 10, 1931).

[60] The Westminster Shorter Catechism, Q. 160.

[61] Rowland, *Mississippi, Heart of the South*, 1:837.

[62] Joe Gray Taylor writes that children of the Old South might get candy at Christmas, but were unlikely to taste it at other times unless some relative liked to make candy. *Eating, Drinking, and Visiting in the South*, 43.

[63] "Woodland's" Emma Finley wrote in her journal of preparations for a similar trip-to Virginia in 1859 to visit to her ailing grandmother: "All four 'hands' are busy now fitting up the travelers-did our shopping yesterday and Ma is still in town.... Ma says we'll stay

about six weeks, but if the time is pleasant to both I trust it may be lengthened-I don't get to Va. every year!" *Our Pen Is Time*, 98.

[64] The Holly Springs Presbyterian Church reported 134 members in 1863. Due to the disruptions of war, no report was made in 1864. The next year a report was made-1866- only 105 were among the church's faithful-the result of battle's toll and dislocations in the community. Records of the city's other churches tell a similar story of loss.

V. TO THE FOUNDRY FOR SOME TACKS

[1] By Mickle's account, "Jones, McElwaine & Co...did considerable business in the Mid-South, their most notable work being the three-story Moresque Building in New Orleans, which occupied a block facing Lafayette square. It was destroyed by fire about thirty years ago, but previously had been listed in guidebooks as one of the sights of New Orleans. During the civil war the foundry...manufactured small arms for the Confederacy. Prior to the war and during part of it they did considerable work for the Mississippi Central Railroad." SR (Aug. 7, 1930); "Foundry at Holly Springs Supplied Confederate Guns Until Taken, Later Burned," Memphis *Commercial Appeal* (Oct. 18, 1936).

[2] "From '60 to '65," 500-501.

[3] SR (Aug. 7, 1930): 4; "Early Holly Springs Industry as Shown by Official Records," SR (Jun. 9, 1938); Wilson Golden Jr.," The Rebel Armory," SR (Apr. 20 and 27, 1961); Carter, 63, 67; Les Crocker, "An Early Iron Foundry in Mississippi," *Journal of Mississippi History* 35 (May 1973): 113-26.

[4] In December 1858, Emma Finley told of a similar experience at her plantation home near Holly Springs: "In the evening it rained and nearly all of Monday so we had to content ourselves in the house-reading, chatting, and eating apples." *Our Pen Is Time*, 47.

[5] McCarroll was sheriff in 1839 and continued in office until 1869. Ruth Watkins, "Reconstruction in Marshall County," *Publications of the Mississippi Historical Society* 12 (1912): 182-83; Hamilton, 132.

[6] Memphis *Commercial Appeal* (Mar. 27, 1955); SR (Apr. 22, 1960); Kempe, 91; Conway and Moulder, 27, Baum, 24. The bayonet is displayed in the Marshall County Historical Museum. The house stands at 285 E. Van Dorn Ave.

[7] A bodice, or woman's undergarment.

[8] Paine wrote a hymn for the dedication of the Holly Springs Presbyterian Church in 1869.

[9] Sessional records of the First Presbyterian Church of Holly Springs, 2:35. The new hymnal, like the introduction of every new hymnal, occasioned controversy. Disputes centered around whether to include all or only part of the old Scottish Psalter and whether or not to omit the hymn, "Oh thou that driest the mourner's tear," which some charged had been written by a licentious man. In debates before the General Assembly in Memphis, Dr. Benjamin Morgan Palmer had said it was a favorite of his New Orleans congregation and that he would regret very much parting with the hymn, even if the devil wrote it. Meanwhile, Dr. George Howe, of South Carolina, rose to assert that it must be shocking to every Christian

that Satan or any of his servants should be accepted by us as ministers of our worship. The minority report from a committee to study the subject was presented by the Rev'd Charles S. Dod, President of West Tennessee College, who was pastor of the Holly Springs Church (1848-55). In the end, the hymn was retained. *Southern Presbyterian Review* (July 1867): 131-33.

[10] Belle's brother, William M. Strickland Jr., usually called "Buddie" in these pages.

[11] Colonel Thomas W. and Sue Watson Harris lived on Chulahoma Ave., on the site of the house built by Judge and Mrs. L. A. Smith Jr.

[12] Sue Watson Harris, niece of Judge Watson and grandmother of Harris Gholson.

[13] Infant deaths were frightfully common. Mildred Strickland, too, had lost an infant, named Madie, in the spring of 1861 while Major Strickland was away, just at the time daughter Minnie was born. She was comforted with a letter from her neighbor, Mary Clark, who also had lost a child. Strickland letters. William Stebbins collection.

[14] Tableaux were a popular means of raising money. Cordelia Scales of Hudsonville wrote a friend, Nov. 24, 1861, that "We are going to have a grand exhibition Christmas for the benefit of the soldiers...Tableaux, Choruses, dialogues and private theatricals." Hamilton, 150.

[15] Lou Hamner, daughter of Morris and Mrs. Mary W. Hamner. She and sister Sallie were prominent in the church and community life of Holly Springs. After the war they moved away and never returned. The Hamner Place, a two story frame cottage built about 1850, still stands at 280 S. Memphis St.; Baum, 44.

[16] Events such as this were held in churches because the Masonic Hall with its fine auditorium for theatrical productions had been blown up in Van Dorn's raid, December 20, 1862. Miller-Smith, *Marshall County*, 13.

[17] *Shadow of a Mighty Rock*, 115, 221, 310-11.

[18] Cora Watson's diary reveals a similar resolution: "Sunday, Jan. 8, 1865: Mr. Jesse Franklin, Mr. Moore's cousin, belongs to Forrest's command, and has just come home-having been in the late campaigns in Tennessee-his regiment being disbanded for the present for the purpose of recruiting men and horses to take the place of those worn out by the hardships they have endured in the last few months. Hood's army, he thinks, will go into winter quarters at Columbus and West Point in this State. He says our loss in this campaign was between eight and ten thousand men and sixty pieces of artillery. Hood's army, he thinks, will number about 2,500 men now...I have commenced again this year to read the Bible through. Reading about Abraham, Isaac and Jacob, and I got Blent's *Lectures on the Patriarchs* and read some. I find them very interesting and instructive."

[19] The former Miss Carrie S. Craft, daughter of the Hugh Crafts. She married Dr. Richard N. Venable.

[20] This was the Second Battle of Franklin, November 30, 1864.

[21] Son of Kate Walthall and George R. Freeman and uncle of Kate Freeman Clark, the Holly Springs artist.

[22] James J. House made a fortune running the blockade. He bought the home of J. H. Nelson at 390 E. College Ave., known today as "Grey Gables." John Mickle wrote that

House bought the Nelson home, which he described as "an ugly brick house on College Ave., remodeled it, added rooms and had the walls stuccoed. He put in a bathroom- unusual in those days-and a fountain with a large basin in front. Water for bath and fountain was pumped by hand from a cistern." House lived there a few years, then moved to Jackson, Tenn. It was the only postwar mansion in Holly Springs to compare with houses erected before the war. SR (Nov. 20, 1931), *Prodigal Daughter*, 41; Schuler, 94-95; Mary Wallace Crocker, 169-70; Kempe, 85; Conway and Moulder, 25; Baum, 84; Miller-Smith, *Marshall County*, 40. [Hubert H. McAlexander], "Grey Gables" (pamphlet, prv. pub., n.d.); Imogene H. Farnsworth, "Grey Gables" (pamphlet, prv. pub., n.d.).

[23] Travel to and from Memphis was slow. The town's large neighbor, according to the local press, could be reached in twelve hours by four-horse post coach. *Holly Springs Guard* (Jun. 12, 1845 and Dec. 25, 1844). Henry Craft remembered the Memphis-Holly Springs portion of a journey home from Princeton, N. J.: "On Tuesday [I] took my seat on the driver's box of the stage and after a long hot day's ride was welcomed to the house of which I had been thinking so long. *Diary of Henry Craft* (Jun. 25, 1848). A Tennessee historian wrote these words about the old road from Holly Springs to Memphis, once known as the 'Pigeon Roost' road because of the many wild birds that once nested in the trees along the route. "The old road leading from Memphis during pioneer days was made of plank. It was an interesting road then. From Pontotoc pioneers journeyed up to the Fourth Chickasaw Bluffs [at Memphis]. The Chickasaw Indians marched that way in 1832 when they were saying good-bye forever to their ancestral hunting grounds....Many old homes are dotted along the way...[and] the old road went in a meandering way and 'passed everybody's house' on the way to Mississippi." George M. Morland, "Highway No. 78," Memphis *Commercial Appeal* (Oct. 26, 1930).

[24] Shields McIlwane reports that in Memphis, "The Confederates with their cotton money bribed the Yankee officers to buy and smuggle through the lines for them all sorts of army supplies. Dead mules were hauled out of the city beyond the lines with their bellies stuffed full of quinine for the Johnny Rebs. More and more funerals passed out of the city to the 'old family graveyards' in the country-always laden with army supplies. Women's hoop skirts became veritable drugstores when they went 'out into Dixie' on visits. Sherman wrote that Memphis was worth more to the Confederacy since its capture than before." *Memphis Down in Dixie*, 124.

[25] Watson was assistant attorney general during Cleveland's first administration. SR (Dec. 15, 1932); see also "Edward Minor Watson," Hines, 73-74; tribute, *In Memory of Edward Minor Watson* (Holly Springs Bar Association, 1888); SR (Dec. 18, 1930): 4. His son also grew up to a distinguished career. Baptized in 1875 as Staige Davis Watson (the names coming from his maternal great-grandfather and uncle killed in the Civil War), the boy's name was changed to Edward Minor Watson in 1887 after his father's death. The younger Watson was appointed by President Woodrow Wilson to the Territorial Supreme Court of Hawaii. He is buried in Diamondhead Memorial Park, 78-79; Honolulu *Star Bulletin* (Sept. 25, 1938).

[26] See Charles Reagan Wilson: *Baptized in Blood: The Religion of the Lost Cause*, 1865-1920 (Athens: Univ. of Ga. Press, 1980: 68.

VI. EDDIE AND JOHNNY WENT TO SELL EDDIE'S YANKEE HORSE

[1] In better times, people could afford to be selective. Mary Jane Finley (1814-1885), Emma' Finley's widowed mother, who lived on the outskirts of Holly Springs drove a hard bargain in 1859 when it came to horse trading. Emma recorded that: "The carriage horses for which Ma sent on by Mr. Phillips came Monday, & such ugly creatures. They tried them in harness Tuesday- Ginnie & Gus going to the Grand Templars celebration & they worked tolerably well,- but are not good riding horses & so ungainly in appearance that Ma would not keep them." *Our Pen Is Time*, 77-78.

[2] *Memphis Down in Dixie*, 124.

[3] Mildred Strickland had problems disposing of the family's cotton. On Jan. 5, 1863, she told Major Strickland that "Megginson [the overseer] is making money fast, selling cotton and other things. The last I heard from him he had ten thousand dollars in his pocket. He sold a little cotton for me and gave me some of the money." On Mar. 24, 1863, she complained that "He has never accounted to you for those two bales he sold in Memphis," and asked: "Has he paid you for the corn he has sold, and for the corn his stock now use? He goes to LaGrange and exchanges greenbacks for gold, and I spend mine for something to eat."

[4] The effort could not have been easy. Cora Watson sighed on Friday, Feb. 10, 1865: "Cousin Sue spent the day with us, busy altering old finery into fashionable shapes."

[5] The Chalmers building still stands lonely and abandoned near the corner of Chulahoma and Boundary Sts. In 2000 it was placed on the Mississippi Department of Archives and History's list of the state's ten most endangered historic landmarks. Mary Wallace Crocker, 154; Mary Carol Miller and Mary Rose Carter, *Written in the Bricks: A Visual and Historical Tour of Fifteen Mississippi Hometowns* (Brandon, Miss.: Quail Ridge Press, 1999): 89.

[6] The manse stood on the southwest corner of Craft and Chulahoma Sts. It was torn down in 1999. Baum, 110.

[7] "William Albert Anderson," *Mississippi: Sketches*, 3:36-37, Hamilton, 80-82; Inez Berryhill Adams, with Tom Adams, *The Class of 1912* (Lafayette, Calif.: Thomas-Berryhill Press, 1995): 26; John M. Mickle, "Mrs. Anderson's Home Dates from Far Past," SR (Dec. 10, 1931): 1.

[8] John M. Mickle, "Craft-Daniel House a Monument of Skill," SR (Nov. 20, 1930); Mary Wallace Crocker, 160-61. The home at 184 S. Memphis St., has recently been purchased and restored by Mrs. Maxine M. Hall. Mary Wallace Crocker, 160-61, Kempe, 85; Baum, 49.

[9] A Northerner, friend of Belle's mother.

[10] Adams, 29-30.

[11] *Our Pen Is Time*, 58-59. Also popular in Holly Springs were *Godey's Lady Book* and newspapers.

[12] Misses Annie and Mary R. Stewart were milliners, born in Ireland. Both died in the yellow fever of 1878.

[13] William D. Miller, *Mr. Crump of Memphis* (Baton Rouge: La. State Univ. Press, 1917): 17.

[14] By the last year of the Civil War, the Watsons found themselves in pecuniary

straits, but not so much that they could not be of charitable assistance, and although Confederate bills were still the "coin of the realm"-with stiff penalties for possession or use of bills printed by the U. S. Treasury, all knew and respected the value of the "greenback"-which was outranked in value only by gold. Even in these inflationary times a contribution of twenty dollars was munificent.

[15] The Crumps lived east of Holly Springs on a place called Tuckahoe. *Southern Tapestry*, 25. When the order came to destroy stores of cotton lest it fall into Union hands, Mildred Strickland had written to her husband, Jun. 8, 1862: "Some men hate to burn their cotton so much. I bet old Crump will hide some."

[16] Only in Brazil did a significant Confederate settlement survive-peopled by expatriate Southern Presbyterians, and it was small. Descendants of these émigrés may be identified there today. *Southern Presbyterian* (Jul. 12, 1866 and Oct. 24, 1866); E. T. Thompson, *Presbyterians in the South*, 3 vols. (Richmond: John Knox, 1961-1973): 2:110-12, 259, 302-303; Lawrence F. Hill, *The Confederate Exodus to Latin America* (Austin, Tex.: Texas State Hist. Assoc., 1936); James E. Bear, "The Southern Presbyterian Mission in Brazil," (unpub. Th.D. diss.) Union Theological Seminary, Richmond, Va.; Blanche Henry Clark Weaver, "Confederate Immigrants and Evangelical Churches in Brazil," *Journal of Southern Hist*. 18 (November 1952): 446-68; cf. Andrew F. Rolle, *The Lost Cause: The Confederate Exodus to Mexico* (Norman: Univ. of Okla. Press, 1965); Alfred J. and Katherine Abbey Hanna, *Confederate Exiles in Venezuela* (Tuscaloosa: Univ. of Ala. Press, 1960); William B. Hesseltine and Hazel C. Wolf, *The Blue and the Gray on the Nile* (Chicago: Univ. of Chicago Press, 1961).

[17] Walter is quoted in A. B. Moore, *Conscription and Conflict in the Confederacy* (New York: Macmillan, 1924).

[18] On March 28, 1862, Belle's mother wrote to her husband about her great resentment of the behavior of William Henry Coxe and James J. House, who not only remained at home, but took dancing lessons-the better to socialize in the heady times surrounding the early days of the war. She said, "Jim House and Will H. Coxe go to dancing school. How I do hate House-that is all I get mad with you about [i.e., that Major Strickland went to the army while these men stayed home]." Coxe died in September 1865 as he drunkenly tried to force his horse up the stairs of his mansion. *Southern Tapestry*, 64-65, 68.

[19] The utopian dream of immigration to Central or South America to continue the Confederate way of life received its boldest expression in the writings of Matthew Fontaine Maury. The former Confederate naval officer led a failed colonization effort in Mexico. Elizabeth Watson named her school for the naval commander whose sister Mrs. Elizabeth Maury Holland lived near Sylvestria Church, five miles north of Holly Springs. Francis L. Williams, *Matthew Fontaine Maury: Scientist of the Sea* (New Brunswick: Rutgers Univ. Press, 1965): 421-41.

[20] Gaines Foster remarks that "countless Southerners who never left the country filled letters and diaries with discussion of emigration." One of the most remarkable schemes was formulated by the Rev'd Robert L. Dabney, doughty professor in Virginia's Union Theological Seminary. Dabney proposed a colony of prominent Southerners in New Zealand,

which he thought a likely spot since it had "no Negroes" and was "a long way from Yankeedom." As in so many cases, nothing came of his ideas. Cited in *Ghosts of the Confederacy*, 17.

VII. CARING FOR THE SICK

¹ Cordelia Scales wrote May 15, 1862: "I have been busy night and day nursing sick and wounded soldiers...Lou, our house has been nothing but a hospital for the last two months. For five days I did not take my clothes off. I was going night and day. We have had two lieuts. & one Capt....There are...sick and wounded soldiers in...every dwelling house." Hamilton, 150.

² The women of Holly Springs were well aware of such inclinations, and in the summer of 1861, had circulated a resolution urging their men to remain and "continue their watchful care over us and ours," instead of leaving to join the army. A good cross-section of the femininity of Holly Springs was represented among the signers, including Mrs. J. W. C. Watson. Holly Springs *Southern Herald* (Aug. 2, 1861).

³ Mildred Strickland wrote again and again to her husband of concerns that their son William Jr., called "Buddie" by intimates, was in difficulty for lack of a man in the house to oversee his upbringing, e.g.: "Willie must go to school or I can never do anything with him" [Feb. 13, 1862]; "Willie has been gone all evening. I don't know what to do with him." [Mar. 9, 1862]; "I am distressed about Willie. He will stay with the boys and they are so bad. This war will ruin everybody." [Jun. 8, 1862]; "Willie troubles me a great deal. I don't know what will become of him." [undated letter, summer 1862]; "It is such a misfortune that you cannot be here to raise Willie. I am afraid he will be ruined." [Nov. 26, 1862].

⁴ John M. Mickle, "First Literary Club the Philomathesian," SR (Dec. 10, 1931); "Roster is Found of Philharmonic Club," SR (Apr. 28, 1932).

⁵ SR (Dec. 10, 1931): 2. The idea for the Thursday Club originated with Cora Watson, then Mrs. S. E. Carey.

⁶ John Mickle, "Mrs. Helen Anderson Dies in 85th Year," SR (Dec. 31, 1931): 1; *Prodigal Daughter*, 3, 19.

⁷ Mrs. Anderson told graduates of 1930 that at Elizabeth Watson's school, "we finished the course but had no diplomas; so I have never had the honor of having an A.B. affixed to my name, but I think I am entitled to call myself the oldest alumna." Helen Craft Anderson, "Commencement Address," Mississippi Synodical College (May 1930). [Helen Craft Anderson], "Marshall School of Presbyterian Church Advances," Jackson, Miss., *Daily News* (Jul. 5, 1931): 1.

⁸ During Reconstruction, Stephen Watson came to Judge Watson a few days before an election and told him that he did not want to do anything that Judge Watson would not like, but believed that if he voted against the proposed new constitution of 1868, he feared that other Negroes would drive him out of town. The new constitution was sponsored by Republicans and, among other things, disenfranchised whites who had served the Confederate cause. (Stephen Watson was living in a house furnished him, rent free by Judge

Watson.) J. W. C. Watson told him that he could not look upon any one as his friend who would vote to take away from privileges which were to be given all colored persons. Stephen Watson nonetheless voted for the constitution. Watkins, 184-85.

⁹ See Giselle Roberts, "'Our Cause': Southern Women and Confederate Nationalism in Mississippi and Louisiana," *Journal of Mississippi History* 62 (Summer 2000): 97-121.

¹⁰ Major General Napoleon Jackson Tecumseh Dana, a native of Maine.

¹¹ White women dreaded being "elbowed" off sidewalks by Negroes emboldened to such uncharitable acts by the encouragement of "carpetbaggers" and U. S. authorities. During Reconstruction, girls and boys in Mrs. Nelson Gill's school for children of freed slaves were said to have pushed white girls from Holly Springs sidewalks. According to Lizzie A. Fant, this happened when white girls from Bethlehem Academy were returning from school. If the whites met Mrs. Gill, she would place herself in the center of her column, and her pupils would lock arms so as to form a solid wall across the walk. The white girls would have to pass around or come into contact with the black children. They generally chose the former. Sometimes the whites succeeded in forming just as solid a wall as their antagonists, and would face Mrs. Gill until she gave way and let them pass. After the white power structure was reinstated, laws were made to prevent such violations of race and class prerogative. But not all whites believed that these rules were fair or needed. Mary Virginia Grigsby Foley recalled that when girls from Mississippi Synodical College went on outings they walked two by two, "and when we met students of Rust University, the Negro girls were required to get off the sidewalk to let us pass." She wrote, "I think this was grossly unfair, but that seemed to be the average treatment in those days." Watkins, 199; *Childhood in Holly Springs*, 20.

¹² Sometimes these searches were costly. Mildred Strickland reported to Major Strickland April 4, 1863, that "Mrs. Alexander (Bob) was coming out of Memphis with $1800 belonging to a friend. They carried her back and took it from her. I don't know the particulars. You can hear anything in the world here, but that is really true."

¹³ Palmer's ideas approved in Marshall County, Mississippi, and he was invited to preach at the dedication of the new Holly Springs Presbyterian Church on March 28, 1869. He continued to preach Negro inferiority and social subordination after the Civil War, and the ideas found expression in Mississippi's religious press until the 1960s. See Stephen Haynes, "Race, National Destiny, and the Sons of Noah in the Thought of Benjamin M. Palmer," *Journal of Presbyterian History* 78 (Summer 2000): 125-43; *Shadow of a Mighty Rock*, 159, 170-72, 196-97.

¹⁴ John B. Boles has remarked that "slavery simply disintegrated in the crucible of war" and that "The logic of wartime necessity finally forced Jefferson Davis and Robert E. Lee to make the fundamental decision against slavery in a critical choice between sure defeat and possible success." Still the idea went against the oft-repeated statements of slave owners that their bondsmen represented a childlike and inferior race. As General Howell Cobb argued in January 1865: "If slaves will make good soldiers, our whole theory of slavery is wrong." Enlistment of slave soldiers for the Confederacy was authorized by Jefferson Davis on March 23, 1865, but eight days later, on April 3, with his city surrounded by Union troops,

the mayor of Richmond surrendered his city. Then on April 9, at Appomattox, the long war was over. Boles, 195-98.

[15] In keeping with other reformist ministers in the South, the Rev'd James A. Lyon, Presbyterian minister in Columbus, Miss. (who later retired to Holly Springs to live with his daughter, Lucy Deaderick Lyon (Mrs. Eagleton M.) Smith), pursued a crusade to require slave owners to raise their slaveholding "to the biblical standard." In the winter of 1865, Lyon confided that "It would seem strange that there should be any reluctance that would in the slightest mitigate the abhorrence that the world has of Negro slavery. Perhaps," said Lyon, "God's intentions are to bring the institution to an absolute end." R. Milton Winter, "James Adair Lyon: Southern Presbyterian Apostle of Progress," *Journal of Presbyterian History* 60 (Winter 1982): 324-25. Meanwhile, as John Boles observed, "Among the far-reaching results of the process of emancipation was a significant increase in white racial animosity toward blacks." Boles, 198.

[16] In theory, the Confederacy abandoned slavery for independence when in the final months of the war it recruited black troops with promises of freedom. An act authorizing black enlistment passed the Confederate Senate by one vote. As Gaines Foster notes: "A few Confederates, including Davis and Lee, were willing to abolish slavery to win the war, but the recruitment effort hardly constituted a general repudiation of slavery." Still black soldiers did serve the South's cause and their descendants are represented in the Sons of Confederate Veterans. Foster remarks that "few Southerners expressed any guilt over the owning or the mistreatment of slaves, even though they had been raised in a society that encouraged the public confession of sin." *Ghosts of the Confederacy,* 23. See Robert F. Durden, *The Gray and the Black: The Confederate Debate on Emancipation* (Baton Rouge: La. State Univ. Press, 1972).

[17] After the war, Marshall County had a Freedman's Pauper Fund; there was also a poorhouse, and in 1868 it was ordered "that the board of paupers at the poorhouse be reduced to $8 per month for board alone." Watkins, 181. See H. Shelton Smith, *In His Image, But...Racism in Southern Religion, 1780-1910* (Durham: Duke Univ. Press, 1972).

[18] Soldiers from Covington, Tenn.

[19] William Strickland, Jr., Brodie S. Hull and Andrew Govan.

[20] Great parties had been given for Confederate soldiers at the onset of hostilities-before Holly Springs had known the pain of war. Soon after the first Northern raids, when Confederate General Sterling Price made Holly Springs his headquarters for two months in 1862, the town's hostesses vied to entertain the soldiers. As Kate Bonner recalled: "Ah, those golden October days! Who among us can forget them? Houses were thrown open, and around every table gathered gray-coated officers. Young girls taken from the school-room blossomed into belles and coquettes. Picnics, balls and reviews made every day 'run to golden sands.'" "From '60 to '65," 501. In February 1862, Mildred Strickland had written to her husband, "There was a rumor here that Beauregard would make this place headquarters. The ladies were delighted."

[21] Betsy Thomas and Betsy Hull, the latter a daughter of John and Anne Crump

Hull. She married John S. Finley.

[22] A family of slaves who had gained freedom.

[23] Very few black pastors had been ordained before the Civil War, and in many places unsupervised preaching by Negroes was illegal. Naturally, as soon as they obtained freedom, many were eager to sever all ties with their former overseers, ecclesiastical and otherwise. Whites feared the power of black exhorters, as is illustrated in this passage from the writings of J. H. Aughey, a Holly Springs schoolmaster and slavery critic, who later became a Presbyterian minister and was imprisoned during the war at Tupelo for unionist sentiments. The account describes a slave meeting near the home of Dr. Thomas L. Dunlap, a local physician and planter, following a speech in Holly Springs by Jefferson Davis in 1856 when he stayed with the Stricklands. Aughey wrote that "Mrs. Dunlap informed me that she noticed a large gathering of their colored people at one of the cabins. Wishing to learn the cause, she slipped around to the back window, as the night was dark....A well-dressed burly African, in an earnest tone, was haranguing them after this manner:'I tells you, ladies and gentlemen, we is all gwine to be free befo' long. We won't be slaves no longer and be whipped and cuffed by de white folks.' 'How duz you know all day'....'Why did'n' I hear Massa Jeff Davis say so? I done drove him out in de carriage to dat stan', where he'd dressed de people today, en I had to wait to bring 'im back. From what he sed de people uv de Norf is comin' down to set us free and dey'll jes mow deze Southern people down like dey mows de grass.'" John Hill Aughey, *The Iron Furnace, or, Slavery and Secession* (Philadelphia: Alfred S. Martien, 1863); (Lincoln, Neb.: State Journal Co., Printers, 1888; rev. ed., 1905): 392-93. The first Negro congregation in Holly Springs, Asbury Methodist, was established in 1866 and reported 168 members, making it the town's second largest religious organization. It is still the state's largest black United Methodist congregation.

[24] Slaves regularly protested their bondage by feigning disability or inability to do even simple tasks.

[25] A privilege which had been forbidden to almost all bondsmen prior to Emancipation. Judge Watson, along with J. W. Clapp, gave themselves to educational efforts for freed slaves in Holly Springs.

[26] Both sides were responsible for misconduct in the Civil War, and the abuse of alcohol was often the cause. Cordelia Scales wrote one October 14th [no year is given] of "disgraceful conduct" by Louisiana troops at Grand Junction, Tenn. She stated that "the reason of this was that they had been drinking almost all the way up and they had no control over themselves." Apparently their own officers had to kill some of their men, and the people of the village thought they were justified in doing so. Hamilton, 151.

[27] Feminist tendencies in the South were retarded by women's fears of lawless men, especially blacks. This "encouraged white females to turn to their men for protection and thereby hindered any feminine revolt." Foster, 31.

[28] Rather than flee to foreign countries, many Southerners tried to escape the growing prospect of defeat with alcohol or drugs. Observers from both within and beyond

the Confederacy commented on the prevalence of immoderate drinking among demoralized soldiers and others, a situation Federal authorities exploited for their own purposes. Gaines Foster also notes that Southern whites also had an extremely high rate of opium addiction. *Ghosts of the Confederacy*, 17-18.

[29] Mrs. Henry Cohen Long, a milliner.

[30] Mr. Morgan Hopson Thomson, Belle's uncle.

[31] Father of Mrs. Robert Dancy and Mrs. Douglas Baird.

[32] Daughter of Elizabeth Maury Holland and niece of Col. Matthew Fontaine Maury.

[33] The Presbyterians did not have Sunday school in the dead of winter, for the church was unheated.

[34] The Confederate Congress had recessed on March 18, as Lee's army retreated from Richmond.

VIII. HELPING POOR SOLDIERS' FAMILIES

[1] Mary (Mrs. Alexander B.) Lane. The Lanes were pioneer settlers. They came to Hudsonville and moved to Holly Springs in 1840. They lived in the house at 285 E. College Ave., which was in this century the home of the Frank Hopkins family and Mrs. A. E. Bell. It is presently owned by Misses Mary Walker and Frances Gatewood. Baum, 40.

[2] This, again, represented change, for Presbyterian elders had long been loath to allow their church to be used for any secular purpose. As late as 1889, for example, the church-even though most of its members supported the temperance movement-would not allow its building to be used for a meeting of the Women's Christian Temperance Union.

[3] This was the Rev'd Dr. Rachel Henderlite, dean of MSC (1936-1938). *Shadow of a Mighty Rock*, 396-97, 466-67.

[4] Miss Reese Jones was the daughter of Martha Reese (Mrs. Rufus) Jones. She married Dr. Franklin Brevard Shuford, and the couple made their home in her mother's house.

[5] The Rev'd James T. Pickett was noted for his eloquence, and additionally, as Charles Reagan Wilson has written: "As the most ritualistic of Southern Protestants, Episcopal churchmen may have been a logical choice for prominence in the highly ritualized religion of the Lost Cause." *Baptized in Blood*, 36.

[6] Daughter of General and Mrs. Thomas Polk. The Polks lived in a raised cottage on what was then called Oxford Street. The location is today 180 S. Craft St., the home of Mr. and Mrs. Collier C. Carlton. Schuler, 89, Mary Wallace Crocker, 158, Kempe, 94. Thomas Polk was a brother of Louisiana's Episcopal bishop and Confederate general, the "fighting bishop," the Rt. Rev'd Leonidas Polk, and a cousin of James K. Polk, the former U. S. President.

[7] America (Mrs. Samuel) McCorkle, widow of one of the town's founders.

[8] Mrs. Charles G. Nelms, a widow. Her husband, a Holly Springs attorney, was killed at Shiloh. Clayton, 29-30.

[9] John Fennell served with the Home Guards. In the 1850s, he built the house

Endnotes

known as "Hill Top," which stands on Park Ave., at the eastern edge of Spring Hollow.

[10] Dr. Francis William Dancy, an early Holly Springs settler and physician.

[11] James F. Trotter, born in Brunswick County, Va., came to Monroe County, Miss. in 1823 or 1824, where he practiced law. In 1838 he was appointed to the U. S. Senate, and subsequently served on Mississippi's Supreme Court. Later he came to Holly Springs, serving as a judge on the Chancery Circuit for the Northern District. In 1860 he became a professor of law at the University of Mississippi. He died March 9, 1866. James D. Lynch, *The Bench and Bar of Mississippi* (New York: E. Hale & Son, 1881): 205-207; Hamilton 118. John Mickle recalled that "Judge Trotter, great grandfather of Frank Hopkins...must have held court...after the war either in the basement of the Methodist Church or in the old Franklin Female College. His portrait in oil hangs in Mississippi's hall of fame." SR (Nov. 20, 1930).

[12] The Rev'd W. C. Johnson, the Methodist minister.

[13] Peter Walker Lucas came to Holly Springs from Fauquier County, Va. in 1840. He fought with Andrew Jackson at New Orleans in 1812, and when he came to Marshall County, he bought and sold rich lands acquired from the Indians. As president of the Northern Bank of Mississippi and a financier of the Mississippi Central Railroad, he became one of the community's wealthiest men. Lucas built an impressive house on N. Memphis St. His daughter Evelina, married J. W. Clapp, Major Strickland's law partner. Like many other citizens of Holly Springs, Lucas was impoverished by the war. John M. Mickle, "Col. Peter Lucas," SR (Dec. 10, 1931); "Wreckers find It Hard to Raze 90-Year Old Lucas Residence," SR (Mar. 24, 1932); Hamilton, 10-11, 23, 56.

[14] Mrs. Cal Smith was the former Miss Henrietta Lucas, sister of Evalina Donoho Lucas (Mrs. J. W.) Clapp.

[15] Mrs. Thomas died in the yellow fever epidemic of 1878.

[16] John Mickle described A. W. Goodrich as "a portly gentleman, reserved in manner and rather stern in countenance, upon whom children loved to play tricks, and the 'first citizen' of the town." His small house stood across the street from the Presbyterian Church, of which he was an adherent. He was mayor of Holly Springs during the Civil War and at the time of the yellow fever epidemic of 1878, and was the first local person to die from the plague. His funeral was a large one, attended by all the prominent men of the city. It was the last public funeral held until after the epidemic. "Col. Goodrich Famed As City's War Mayor," SR (Dec. 15, 1932); "Small Brick House Relic of Old Days," SR (Nov. 20, 1930): 12; Holly Springs author Sherwood Bonner used Goodrich as a model for Squire Barton in her novel *Like unto Like* (1878). *Prodigal Daughter*, 117, 140.

[17] Goodrich was not always a tease. He was one of a group who requested Presbyterian minister Henry Paine to repeat his stirring sermon on "The Nature and Duration of Divine Punishment." *Our Pen Is Time*, 8.

[18] Captain John Chew, an early Holly Springs settler, active in political affairs.

[19] Mrs. Adrian Mayer

[20] Lieutenant James Sims, who ran the stage line, had served in the Mexican War.

[21] Another local attorney.

[22] Kate Bonner (1849-1883), later became famous as one of Mississippi's first penwoman authors under the name Sherwood Bonner. See Hubert H. McAlexander, *The Prodigal Daughter: A Biography of Sherwood Bonner* (Baton Rouge: La. State Univ. Press, 1981); Miller-Smith, *Marshall County*, 96. Her sister Ruth Martin Bonner was born in 1851. They lived at the beautiful Bonner House on suburban Salem Rd.

[23] Here follows Hubert McAlexander's account of events at the Bonner House, as told in the writings of Kate Bonner: "So the long months stretched on, and by the late winter of 1864-65 the last great body of U. S. troops had left Holly Springs. The citizens had now merely to wait, receiving mixed reports of distant battles with alternations of hope and despair. When the final news came, however, they were unprepared. On an April evening, the Bonners had just received two young women collecting money and plate to be sent to Richmond for the depleted Confederate treasury; and Kate and her sister had walked with them to the brow of the hill beyond, when they saw an aged neighbor coming up the hill almost at a run. The girl was never to forget the next moments: 'In the wild white face that he turned toward us there was such agony as I have never seen.... He looked at us a moment in silence, then in a hollow, harsh voice struck us with the words, "General Lee has surrendered!" and passed on into the falling darkness.'" *Prodigal Daughter*, 16.

[24] Pruitt, 73.

[25] John Mickle recalled that "Just after the War I was following my father and a friend when the bells began to toll at the hour of President Lincoln's funeral. They both looked grave and agreed that the assassination of Mr. Lincoln would bring great trouble upon the South, although it proved to be the work of a few misguided men." SR (May 4, 1939).

[26] Covington, Tenn. author Frances Boyd Calhoun employed delicious irony in her famous children's book, *Miss Minerva and William Green Hill* (1909), when she gave her principal character's black playmate the name Wilkes Booth Lincoln.

[27] Dr. Charles Bonner, whose home has been described by Hubert McAlexander in this way: "A picturesque gate hung between two ancient bois d'arc trees formed the entrance to the Bonner estate, an expanse of land on the highest ground in Holly Springs. Set well back from the road at the end of a broad brick walk stood the two-story house. Piercing its brick mass were long gothic windows, and across the front façade ran a delicately filigreed porch of cast iron, which gave to the whole the appearance of a delicate and fanciful valentine. Within, one entered the first of two halls, a wide entry with huge sliding doors on each side. Behind the right set was the parlor, furnished in the fashionable 'French antique' mode; behind the left led to Dr. Bonner's library. For entertaining, both sets of doors were opened, and the front of the house thrown into one grand room. The rest of the house contained a long dining room, various halls, a dressing room, and five bedrooms. To the rear of the building, amid the gardens and orchards planted by Dr. Bonner, were several brick dependencies, including what Sherwood Bonner would recall as 'the pleasantest place in the world,' the 'great wide kitchen, with its roomy fireplace, where the backlog glowed and the black kettle

swung.'" *Prodigal Daughter*, 7-8; Mary Wallace Crocker, 166-168; Lane, 160, 162; Conway and Moulder, 26; *A Vanishing America*, 76-77; Baum, 72; Miller-Smith, *Marshall County*, 37. The mansion, at 490 E. Salem Ave., is owned by Mr. and Mrs. Fred M. Belk Jr.

[28] Such talk was widespread. Many reported that France was coming to the South's aid, while others hoped for assistance from Great Britain, Austria, Belgium, or an alliance of all the European countries. The wide circulation of these rumors indicates a knowledge that the only hope was for salvation from above or abroad. Foster, 12.

[29] Gaines Foster writes that contemporary observers reported greater unwillingness to forgive and accept defeat on the part of Confederate women, than among their men. Some thought women "were simply more emotional, or 'less forgiving than men.' Others argued that women's experience of the war differed from men's. They had 'more time to brood over the wrongs that had been done them...and had not the excitement of battle to sustain them.'" *Ghosts of the Confederacy*, 31.

[30] Captain Holland had served in Major Strickland's company, the Jeff Davis Rifles. Hamilton, 146-47.

[31] The combined disasters of Richmond's fall and Lee's surrender left little chance for the Confederacy's continued survival. On April 26 Johnston had surrendered, despite opposition from Jefferson Davis, who urged adoption of guerilla tactics as a means to continue the war.

[32] SR (Aug. 10, 1995).

[33] Perrine Hall Fant, who became an elder in the Holly Springs Presbyterian Church. He later moved to Colorado.

[34] McLean clerked in J.W. Fant's Grocery and Dry Goods store on the town square. Hamilton, 48.

[35] The Nunnallys were an old Marshall County family who farmed near Tallaloosa. *Southern Tapestry*, 25.

[36] Hubert McAlexander gives a vivid account of the situation in and around Holly Springs at this time: "As the soldiers began straggling back home, the defeated began to attempt to pick up their old lives. The country had suffered greatly during the four years. Fences were gone, many barns and houses had been destroyed, most of the stock had been confiscated by the Union Army, and the neglected land had become badly eroded. In the town three-fifths of the large central square lay in ruins. Increasing the sense of oppression was the appearance of an army of occupation less than a month after Appomattox. Many citizens talked of leaving, of new opportunities in Texas or Brazil, but most remained and began the work of salvaging what they could and earning a livelihood." *Prodigal Daughter*, 16-17.

IX. A POPULAR MERCHANT SLAIN

[1] Controversy surrounded a decision of Holly Springs Methodists to acquire an organ in the summer of 1865. Robert B. Alexander wrote that when his church "had the vote

taken whether there should be a Melodion in the Church I voted for it." He then recorded that "Some of the Sisters got very hot indeed & jumped up & run out of the Church." *Diary of Robert B. Alexander* (Aug. 11, 1865).

[2] Episcopal clergy were persecuted because The Book of Common Prayer of the Protestant Episcopal Church in the Confederate States specified prayers that were to be read for Confederate President and others in authority. Because the Prayer Book of the Protestant Episcopal Church provided similar prayers for the President of the United States, Federal authorities believed that Confederate clergy should amend their services accordingly when their churches were in territory occupied Northern forces. General Sherman is said to have interrupted a service at Calvary Church, Memphis, to correct "in a loud voice" the words omitted by the rector during the service of Morning Prayer. Next, he ordered the rector to read the complete ritual or close the church's doors. Perhaps the best-known incident of this sort occurred when Brigadier General William Nelson Pendleton, who had been Lee's chief of artillery and after the war was rector of Grace Memorial Church in Lexington, Va., was ordered by Federal troops occupying Lexington to reinstate the prayer for the President of the United States. Pendleton refused and was arrested. The news spread throughout the South and made Pendleton-and the Episcopal Church-heroes in the eyes of Southern sympathizers. Presbyterian ministers were at liberty to frame their prayers as best suited the occasion, but nonetheless felt pressure from conflicting interests. James A. Lyon, of Columbus, Miss., an ardent Unionist, angered Confederates by praying "for the success of the armies," without saying which one. Some Episcopal clergy found a way out of their dilemma by celebrating the rite of Holy Communion each Sunday, omitting Morning Prayer, as the former liturgy included no intercessions for the civil magistrate. This was the course chosen from the war's beginning by the dean of St. Mary's Cathedral, Memphis, a Unionist. Susan Pendleton Lee, *Memoirs of William Nelson Pendleton* (Philadelphia: J. B. Lippincott, 1893): 422-23; Winter, "James Adair Lyon," 325-26; McIlwaine, 122.

[3] Helen Craft Anderson, "Recollections of Van Dorn's Raid," reprinted in the SR (Apr. 27, 1978); Raymond B. McBlain, "Christ Church: Its History and Traditions" (unpub. typescript, Oct. 25, 1936): 4; Charles N. Dean, "A Century Ago" [A History of Christ Church, Holly Springs] (Holly Springs: Christ Church, [1958]): 2.

[4] Activities of desperados had troubled Holly Springs before. On Nov. 15, 1862, Mildred Strickland wrote her husband that "Mr. Daniel's kitchen and smoke house, and Bishop's house, kitchen and smoke house were burnt up the other night. The Yanks were afraid everyone would think it was them. It was not them."

[5] Nelson, a member of Christ Church parish, clerked in Hugh Winborn's store on the southwest corner of Memphis St. and Van Dorn Ave., which now houses the Graham Miller Store. The structure served the Presbyterians as their first brick house of worship (1848-60) when the present church was built. John Mickle described Nelson's murder at the Miller corner as "one of the most cowardly and brutal murders that ever stained the annals of Marshall county.... It was immediately following the surrender in April 1865, when disbanded Confederate soldiers were going home. Whether the robbers were Confederate

soldiers, guerillas or unconnected desperados was never known. Mr. Nelson...lived...on E. College Ave., and the robbers got him and started for the store. On the way up he dropped the key of the store in the weeds, and didn't have it when they demanded it at the store. They beat him over the head with their pistols and he ran west on Van Dorn Ave., or Church St., as it was called. They fired on him and he fell. He was carried to the Lewis house, which stood across the alley back of Stafford's Café, and was later known as the Nabors place. He died that night. I was a small boy and lived at what is the Moore Apartments across from Christ Church, and I saw some of the rioting. We saw horsemen riding back and forth before what is Stafford's Café [the site is now occupied by the Ralph Doxey Building] and firing into the doors and windows. The robbers supposed a shoemaker in there had whiskey and wanted him to unbar his door. Few soldiers had returned and the white male population was composed of old men and young boys. W. J. L. Holland of Morgan's command had ridden in from his home on Coldwater that afternoon to call on Misses Susan and Betsy Hull (sisters of Brodie Hull). Word was sent to Holland, the only soldier in town, about the raid. Those old soldiers were brave fellows, and he started out single-handed to meet them, armed only with a six-shooter-cap and ball at that. He found them gathered just off the square on S. Center St., preparing to leave town. 'What command do you belong to, gentlemen,' he called out. They replied with a volley, one shot piercing his hat, and then galloped out S. Center [a street leading down south by the cemetery and out of town]. Mr. Holland was later editor of the *Reporter*, and met a hero's death in the yellow fever visitation in 1878. The Mississippi Press Association monument marks his grave in Hill Crest Cemetery." SR (Dec. 10, 1931): 13.

[6] In 1873, a pipe organ was installed. It had previously been used at Calvary Church in Memphis. John Mickle remembered it as a "sweet-toned instrument." This organ was traded for the present instrument during the rectorship of the Rev'd Peter Gray Sears, D.D., in 1898. The present organ in Christ Church, a tracker, was installed by Henry Pilcher & Sons in 1898, its opus 318, and except for electrification of the bellows in 1926, is preserved as built. The organ case is oak, and has forty stenciled façade pipes. It is one of the oldest instruments of its type still in use in the area. *Shadow of a Mighty Rock*, 486-87. The centennial of this instrument's continuous service to the parish was celebrated with a month long series of concerts by members of the American Guild of Organists and the Organ Historical Society in October 1998. Holly Springs *Reporter* (Dec. 31, 1874); SR (Dec. 15, 1932).

[7] Mickle wrote that: "The little reed organ, now used by the Sunday school served until about 187[3], when the parish bought the old organ from Calvary Church, Memphis." SR (Dec. 10, 1931).

[8] Hugh Winborn died in the yellow fever of 1878. Hamilton, 158.

[9] John Mickle remarked that "Civil life following the war was sometimes as trying and dangerous as the war itself." Perhaps referring to these men, Mickle recalled that "A gang of outlaws had established a still and camp in Tallahatchie bottom and were committing many outrages." SR (Mar. 10, 1933).

[10] Gaines Foster writes that "Some Southerners, males and females experienced

such agony and despair that they began to question their faith in God." Mary (Mrs. Charles Colcock) Jones, widow of a Presbyterian minister in Liberty County, Ga., wondered if God had indeed "forgotten to be gracious." Cited in *Ghosts of the Confederacy*, 13.

[11] Possibly the Rev'd O. O. Church, professor of mathematics and ancient languages in Franklin Female College.

[12] Davis was captured on May 10 at Irwinsville, Ga. It was reported in the Northern press that he made his attempt to flee dressed in women's clothes, a charge that Davis made great effort to refute.

[13] The soldiers returning from the war "considered the civilians as 'spiritless' as themselves." "One veteran observed that during the first months after Appomattox all seemed 'steeped in a fatal lethargy, unwilling or unable to resist or forward anything.' Even the women, formerly the mainstay of Confederate morale, gave in to despair." Foster, 13.

[14] Watkins, 173.

[15] With the passage of the Congressional Military Reconstruction Acts of 1867, Major General Edward O. C. Ord was appointed U. S. military commander of the Fourth Military District, comprising all of Mississippi and Arkansas (one of the five districts into which the Confederacy was divided). Based in Holly Springs, he proceeded to register a new electorate, which included Negro males and excluded whites who had served in public positions before the war and who subsequently violated their oaths of office by supporting the Confederacy.

[16] Gaines Foster notes that in the first years after the war, "Southerners heaped their greatest abuse on [Benjamin] Butler-a tendency suggesting that respect was as much or more at issue than rape or the destruction of property. Called 'the beast, the wretch, the reviler of women,' Butler had in addition to his other transgressions threatened to treat loyal Confederate females in New Orleans as women of the street." *Ghosts of the Confederacy*, 32.

[17] *Prodigal Daughter*, 17.

[18] Mildred Strickland had written her husband June 8, 1862 that Mrs. Walter Goodman, wife of the president of the Mississippi Central Railroad, "says the Yankees will have to get tired and go home for we will never scare them back."

[19] John Mickle recorded that "when Gen. Ord of the Federal Forces was assigned to the post at Holly Springs, he lived at Bonner House. It was not the harsh occupation of war time, but a peacetime arrangement with Dr. Bonner." Bonner arranged the rental about a year after his initial gesture of reconciliation to the Union occupation troops in May of 1865. Mickle recorded that "I never saw Gen. Ord afoot, but he was a commanding figure on horseback. He kept about six horses, a pair of carriage horses and the rest saddlers. Afternoons I would see the party ride by-Gen. Ord, his daughter, Birdie, and Miss Ruth Bonner, who was subsequently Mrs. David McDowell." "Name 'Bonner House' Stirs Old Memories," SR (Nov. 20, 1930); *Prodigal Daughter*, 17.

[20] Isaac C. Levy and Sol Rhine had been merchants on the town square before the war. The Levy store, founded in 1858, continued until the 1960s. John Mickle wrote that "I. C.

Levy, then located on the site of the Pythian-Odd Fellow building, was the senior store of the town, having been founded before the war, and is the only one [established before the Civil War] still in existence." SR (Dec. 15, 1932). (Linwood's Department Store, owned by the Graham Miller family, now occupies the building and continues the tradition of Levy, operating the town's oldest clothing emporium in its historic location.) Life in Holly Springs was difficult for Jews during the Civil War, for it was while operating in the area that General Grant issued a controversial order banning Jews from trading with the U. S. army.

[21] Former Confederate leaders often had to cast about before finding a means of making a living. Many were prevented from practicing their old professions. Some moved away from Holly Springs, including J. W. Clapp, who went to Memphis and J. B. Mattison, who took his family to Indiana. And, as Gaines Foster noted: "Anyone considering emigration faced many obstacles: federal hostility, opposition by Confederates as Lee and Wade Hampton, the high cost of travel, and negative reports by émigrés-not to mention the dangers and hardships of pioneering. Perhaps most talked of going to Mexico or Brazil in the same vein as a Georgia minister who dreamed of escape to "some soft green island, far out in the Pacific, a stray from the Tahitian group...where no Yankee ever had come..." Cited in *Ghosts of the Confederacy*, 17.

[22] Ordered by U. S. authorities to display no Confederate insignia, veterans covered their Confederate buttons with mourning cloth but left them on their coats. Ibid., 15.

[23] Charles Reagan Wilson notes that the South's defeat prompted sermons and essays on the book of Job, urging Southerners to accept their burdens without murmerings. *Baptized in Blood,* 72. Such represented a revolutionary turn of mind in the theology of Henry Paine.

[24] Mildred Strickland made this report, Jan. 16, 1863, of damage to their place near Hudsonville: "The gin house was burned but the cabins were not. Blanche [a slave] is gone. Some few stock, hogs, and some corn left in the field. The fences are not burned. The whole country is ruined."

[25] By late 1863, only five of fifty plantations along the road between LaGrange and Holly Springs were still occupied. Land erosion which began during the war continued for three-quarters of a century, and the area never regained prominence as a planting community. Bettersworth, "The Home Front, 1861-1865," in McLemore, 1:510.

X. MISS LIZZIE EXPANDS HER EDUCATIONAL EFFORTS

[1] James H. Watson did attend the University of Virginia and became an attorney, practicing with his father in Holly Springs. SR (Dec. 10, 1931).

[2] Holly Springs *South* (Jan. 12, 1881; Dec. 13, 1894); SR (Dec. 15, 1932): 10. John Mickle remembered that "Railroad travel in the early years entailed an unbelievable amount of trouble, vexation and danger. The railroad had no telegraph after the war, or possibly before, and passengers dared not leave the depot less they miss the train, which might be delayed for hours by a washout. The diminutive locomotives were gorgeous in brass trim-

mings, with enormous smoke stacks. Wood was the fuel and a train of sparks flew from the funnel, and were a source of many fires along the road side, but they were pretty at night. Locomotives were named after prominent local men, the name heavily lettered in brass; the only one I recall was the A. M. Clayton. There may have been method in this, as there was an impression that some of these big men presented the road with a locomotive, though I can't imagine 'Uncle Mosby' being that reckless with his cash." "Old I. C. Depot Once Center of City Life," SR (Nov. 6, 1930). Mildred Strickland wrote her husband in February 1862: "I don't want you to travel on the cars now. There are so many accidents."

[3] William Howard Russell, *My Diary North and South*, ed. by Fletcher Pratt (New York: Harper & Bros., 1954): 158; Meanwhile, in August 1858, Emma Finley reported a more pleasant trip, travelling with a party of her teen-aged friends: "Into the cars we crawled &- took- a last look-away we go- 'shooting over bridges, rumbling over ridges' & leaving the rain, thunder, & lightning in the rear somewhat....changed cars at the Junction & made slow speed past the renowned Salisbury, Corinth, Pocahontas & arrived at Burnsville near 3 a.m." *Our Pen Is Time*, 9.

[4] James Moore Crump (1843-1865), son of William and Elizabeth Hull Crump, married Miss Caroline Hatch Smith, Belle's music teacher.

[5] As it turned out Miss Amelia McCarroll, the Stricklands' next-door neighbor, married Walter John Leak in 1866, and Leak's half-sister Jane married Major Strickland the following year.

[6] See *Prodigal Daughter*, 28. Corrinne Leggett lived at "Edgewood," near Hudsonville.

[7] Mickle wrote that Butler's Drug Store, established soon after the war, "was the club of the town-most everybody of every walk of life, drifted in there more or less." He records that "Mrs. Butler was a democrat and her father, Dr. John S. Burton, a republican, and their political spats were always interesting." The telegraph office was back of the drug store, and on election night a crowd would gather there and flow over into the drug store to listen to the news. Dr. Butler died soon after the yellow fever epidemic and his wife carried on the business. SR (Feb. 16, 1932): 4; Baum, 105.

[8] In 1859, Butler had married Miss Malvina Burton in a ceremony described in great detail by Miss Emma Finley: "Sat. June 11th. Home again from Mal's wedding! How handsomely she was dressed! How fine-looking the groom notwithstanding his very long whiskers & moustache,- the lower part of his face I cannot answer for either since it was completely hidden....Determined on seeing the ceremony performed we commenced preparing before sundown, 8 1/2 being the hour in the invitation. We found only a few at Mrs. Burton's on our arrival but they poured in so rapidly that soon my little space was uncomfortably decreased. In order, I suppose, that all might witness it, the ceremony was not performed until nearly ten, when there was a commotion about the door, when Mrs. Burton entered leaning on John's arm, then the waiters- Winnie Lea, Rowena Knox, Pridge Arthur & Bettie Govan, Messrs. Clopton, Govan & the Arkansas gents- I do not know their names. Mal looked more serious than I expected. Poor John Smith! He could not wait to see it, but left

a few days before for N.Y. Mr. Paine, on concluding made Mal a present of a beautifully bound book- in damask- "Hints for Young Married People"- He has some more of the same sort, & it will be quite an inducement for him to marry you,- after congratulations & dancing a while supper was announced. How the folks, all, did eat & enjoy,-the coffee was good, chicken salad, excellent, ice cream, cakes, jellies & all so delicious, that I would run through my vocabulary complimentary long before I finished the eatable list. Mrs. Burton was quite sick,- scarcely able to be up." *Our Pen Is Time*, 89, 90. Malvina Burton Butler was the great-grandmother of Hugh H. and Edward Rather. The Burton house, now called *"Fleur de Lys,"* at 248 S. Memphis St., is the home of Ms. Marjorie Harriet Tyson. Baum, 44; For another account of a grand wedding in Marshall County during this period, see *Southern Tapestry*, 45.

[9] In the 1860 Census, Tepe gave his birthplace as Wurttemburg, Germany. He is buried in Hill Crest Cemetery.

[10] SR (Dec. 10, 1931). Hamilton, 146.

[11] Mildred Strickland reported to her husband on April 4., 1863 that "Belle is dressing Minnie in a little red dress and red sash, new shoes and stockings. She looks very sweet indeed. They are going to take a walk."

[12] Mrs. Dabney Minor-Jane Hull Minor, sister-in-law of Anne Crump Hull.

[13] Greenery, more than cut flowers, was used to decorate for weddings in this period. John Mickle recalled that Dr. Pickett of Christ Church, "was regarded as very high church when he first came, and on Easter Day when he had the church decorated with flowers one good lady would not stay to service with the church so 'decorated.'" He noted that she later was very active in such work! SR (Dec. 10, 1931): 14. A generation later, elaborate decorations do not seem to have become the rule, as may be inferred from this newspaper comment: "Easter Day was generally observed at the churches. Father Althoff [Roman Catholic] having been absent Palm Sunday, the ceremony of blessing the palms was combined with the Easter service. . . . At Christ Church, Rev. P. G. Sears, rector, the cross, altar, font, reading desk and chancel rail were draped in heavy mourning Good Friday, but removed Saturday for Easter." SR (Apr. 2, 1891).

[14] Blassingame, 165, 167-68. Though civil law in the Black Belt states did not recognize slave marriages, slave couples often had weddings solemnized by clergymen or their owners. Slaveholders emphasized the secular celebration over the religious, typically hosting a big supper and dancing, and scheduling the nuptials to coincide with festive seasons, such as Christmas. Charles S. Sydnor, *Slavery in Mississippi* (New York: Appleton-Century-Crofts, 1933): 62-63; Blake Touchstone, "Planters and Slave Religion," John B. Boles, ed., *Masters and Slaves in the House of the Lord: Race and Religion in the American South, 1740-1870* (Lexington: Univ. Press of Ky., 1988): 124.

[15] In October 1858, Emma Finley told of arrangements for the marriage of two slaves at her plantation near Holly Springs: "There is to be a wedding tonight,-the happy couple James & Julia Ann;- the <u>wardrobe</u> is almost completed, & cakes, pies, chickens, meats generally are in a state of preparation. *Our Pen Is Time*, 32.

[16] *Memoirs of Mississippi*, 1:556-57; *Mississippi, Heart of the South*, 1:789; SR (Jul. 4, 1929): 1; SR (Sept. 4, 1930); 4; Hamilton, 84-93.

[17] Sophia Hays carried out a similar mission. When she learned that both her brothers had been wounded in battle in Virginia, she left Mississippi July 12, 1862 for Richmond to bring them home. There Sophia found Robert Boyd so ill that it was some time before she could get him and his brother home. Nonetheless she achieved her goal, displaying strength and courage that few in that era would have believed a young widow could muster. Hays, 2:147-48; Taylor, 9.

[18] Mildred Strickland wrote of the heady days when the soldiers marched off to war. She told her husband, Feb. 25, 1862: "Brown's Company leaves here tomorrow. Will Watson has been elected captain. I do want them all to go so much." Then of a "shirker" she remarked, "I know John L. will not go."

[19] William T. Watson rests in Hill Crest Cemetery, Holly Springs, but his grave and the graves of his parents no longer have headstones.

[20] A year earlier, Cora Watson gave this description of the family's Christmas celebration: "Sunday, Dec. 25, 1864: Christmas-Sis. Lizzie called me from writing in my journal last night to help pull the children's candy. We made two kettles full, and Sis. Lizzie iced some cakes, and we filled the children's stockings. We were up until almost one o'clock. We cannot buy any nice things for them, and have to content ourselves with hazelnuts, homemade cakes, and candy. Ed said he would be satisfied if we made up in quantity what we lacked in quality. This morning at day the children were up catching us 'Christmas gifts.' They were delighted with what Santa Claus had brought them. We were up so late last night that we slept correspondingly late this morning, and did not have breakfast until 10 o'clock."

[21] Christmas could be a time of indolence and dissipation. Mildred Strickland worried as she wrote to her husband, Nov. 26, 1862, about the prospect of celebrating the holiday: "I dread Christmas with the Negroes very much. I don't expect they will do a thing after Christmas. They will all know about Lincoln's [Emancipation] proclamation. They are bad enough in time of peace, but I dread for Christmas to come." John Blassingame noted that "Weekends, Christmas holidays, and the months when corn was still standing in the fields were the favorite times for running away." *The Slave Community*, 200.

[22] Allen Cabaniss, "Christmas," *The Encyclopedia of Southern Culture*, Charles Reagan Wilson and William Ferris, eds. (Chapel Hill: Univ. of N. C. Press, 1989): 680.

[23] On Dec. 22, 1858, Emma Finley noted receipt of invitations to "a big party in town Friday night [Christmas Eve]," but lamented that "it is doubtful if any of us attend." She wrote later: "Is it possible that I have permitted Christmas Day to pass, and have waited nearly a week before recording it? Even so. We spent Friday preparing cakes, etc. for the occasion; most of us consider ourselves too large, or too old, to adhere to the 'hang up stocking' practice-only our pet Toby prepared for Santa Claus and the next morning with many cries of delight emptied his stockings of nuts, cakes, candy, and a 'big clump of sugar.'" *Our Pen Is Time*, 50.

Endnotes

[24] Mary Virginia Grigsby Foley remembered Yuletide customs a generation later. "Christmas services were held on the Sabbath nearest Christmas Day, with no service on the day itself. Christmas was lots of fun, though quite simple compared to holidays now. We did not have trees in our homes, but hung up our stockings by the fireplace. Trees were used in the churches, though, and programs were given by the children. Candles were lighted on the boughs of the evergreen tree (very dangerous!). One year the tree caught on fire, due to the lighted candles. Everyone rushed out and no one was hurt. The fire was quickly extinguished. We had pleasant but simple gifts. One great treat was an orange in the toe of each stocking. Oranges were not to be had at all seasons of the year as they are now and were really a treat." Christmas was 'calling day.' The parlor was opened, fires lighted, and the entire house bright and cheery, with many goodies about, particularly beaten biscuits, chicken salad, and fruit cake.... And we all wore our best Sunday clothes. Many visitors from our congregation and elsewhere called and the little tray on the table in the hall would be filled with calling cards. A queer custom was shooting fire crackers, Roman candles and skyrockets, all of which are generally used on the Fourth of July. Our Northern cousins thought this custom absolutely reprehensible." *Childhood in Holly Springs*, 29-30.

[25] Major Strickland was visiting Mrs. Francis Terry Leak, a widow who lived just across the county line in what was then Tippah County, near Salem. Mrs. Leak's daughter Jane married Major Strickland in 1867.

[26] "Probably not one North American in ten thousand had ever seen or tasted a banana in 1870," writes Charles Morrow Wilson, in his biography of the banana, *Empire in Green and Gold: The Story of the American Banana Trade* (New York: Henry Holt & Co., 1947). Until the advent of refrigerated boxcars, the delicate fruit could hardly be served outside the vicinity of New Orleans. The Mississippi Central Railroad and its connections through Holly Springs would eventually become the trunk line for transporting the yellow fruit to the cities of the North.

[27] John Mickle wrote that "The most glamorous social event since the close of the War Between the States was undoubtedly the big tournament that took place in July 1866 at Mrs. Powell's grove-known in later years as the Chesterman place.... I have never know a tournament in Marshall county on such a scale, and the object, to raise funds for a monument to the Confederate dead-the strongest appeal that could have been made. The aroma of the Old South was just the breath of the war behind, the knights were heroes of a hundred battles; and woman still stood on her pedestal-worshiped of all men." By the account of the Memphis *Daily Argus* (Jul. 20, 1866): "At or near 10 o'clock, the marshals, headed by Gen. W. S. Featherston, mounted on the most showy charger on the ground, and the knights made their appearance and entered the enclosure. The knights, after parading around the ring to the music of the band, retired to await the calling of their names." Various events allowing the town's men and boys to display equestran skills, with the young ladies of the community acting as judges. A grand ball and supper completed the events that night at Franklin Female College. The two-day event raised $1,722 for the Monumental Association. (The money was unfortunately loaned and lost.) *SR* (Dec. 20, 1934): 4.

[28] A next door neighbor.

XI. ELIZABETH WATSON AND FENELON HALL

[1] Although the Watsons had discussed immigration, most were, as Gaines Foster has observed, "far too realistic to let bitter memories get in the way of rebuilding their society." *Ghosts of the Confederacy*, 5. The family turned its energies to positive efforts, and their contributions to the life of their community were significant.

[2] Margaret Burr DesChamps, "Presbyterians and Southern Education," *Journal of Presbyterian History* 31 (January 1953): 117. Richard A. Bolling, *The Presbyterian Church in Mississippi Since 1861* (prv. pub., n.d.): 10; Rosa Barton Tyler, "Holly Springs Schools" (unpub. research paper, Holly Springs, n.d.), 7. A copy of a textbook, Nicholls' *Introduction to the Study of the Holy Scriptures*, published by the American Sunday School Union, belonging to Helen Craft and dated, "Fenelon Hall, 1866" is displayed in the Holly Springs Presbyterian Church. The book also bears the signature of her friend Kate Bonner, the Holly Springs author. In 1869, Clark taught in Franklin Female College, serving with the Rev'd Henry Paine, who had resigned from the Presbyterian Church. SR (Dec. 15, 1932).

[3] Among the changes in Belle's life was her father's marriage to Jane Leak. The family was again living in the Strickland Place, although Belle maintained close ties with the Watsons, whose home was nearby.

[4] In 1867, Major Strickland had married Jane Leak, whom Belle calls "Mama."

[5] Cora Watson assisted her sister-in-law with the school, but did not find the effort rewarding. On Feb. 23, 1865, she wrote that: "Uncle Stephen's delay in returning has made us short of wood, and Sister had school in the sitting room to-day. If there is any sore trial of patience, it must be teaching the young ideas to shoot."

[6] Kate Bonner described scenes on the town square prior to the war: "The planter and the merchant, as the one ordered and the other measured jeans and linsey for the hands; the young men in broadbrimmed hats and negligent neckties, who lounged at the street corners and arranged the details of fox-hunts and game suppers; the village great man and the village loafer-all had the same common interest." Girls and women did not often go to the square unchaperoned. But war relaxed these restrictions somewhat. Thus, during Reconstruction, when ladies did go to the square, sights were sometimes unpleasant. In 1869, Bonner told her diary how she felt when she chanced to see the minister's son, a popular attorney and something of a rake (for whose attentions she had vied) in a saloon near the square. Henry M. Paine had once inspired her to write: "Surely God never made a nobler-looking man," but his conversion to the Republican Party and election as county attorney on the "radical ticket," coupled with her sight of him in a low-grade house of entertainment, "the Can-Can," made its negative impression: "Looking in, I saw a sight that is stamped on my brain-Mr. Paine with his coat off, & a glass raised to his lips. He turned his face almost as I did mine and its expression-wild, defiant, glaring, he flushed, and with blood-shot eyes-I shuddered as though I saw some wild animal." "From '60 to '65," 500-501; *Prodigal Daughter*, 21, 37.

Endnotes

[7] Belle's mother wrote of this unfortunate incident June 29, 1862 while shopping on the square: "I went downtown, had a good many things in my hands to carry, went to McGowan's. Belle asked me to let her carry my purse. I gave it to her. She went behind the counter, was looking in some boxes and things, laid the purse down somewhere. Someone must have picked it up. It had $35 in it and my tax receipts. I looked everywhere for it and am so distressed about it."

[8] Janette and Aunt Harriet were former slaves. Harriet was a member of the Presbyterian Church, one of only a handful of Negroes formally affiliated with the white controlled churches of the city.

[9] The Stricklands seemed predisposed to this condition, for which not even aspirin yet existed as a treatment.

[10] Amelia (Mrs. D. C.) Calkins, active in the Philharmonic society. The couple came to Holly Springs after the Civil War.

[11] "Old Timers" and advocates of global warming maintain that there was more snow in days gone by. Be that as it may, it did seem to snow often during the period Belle records. James J. Selby, who recorded events in Holly Springs 1839-56, described winter conditions this way: Jan. 17, 1841: "A very cold day with Snow"; Jan. 26, 1844: "The first snow this year"; Mar. 30, 1845: "The Second Snow"; Nov. 29, 1845: "A heavy snow and very extreme cold weather"; Feb. 8, 1846: "The Second Snow this Winter"; Feb. 18, 1846: "The Third snow this winter"; Feb. 21, 1846: "The Fourth Snow this winter"; Dec. 1, 1848: "A very rainy day and the first snow"; Dec. 10, 1849: "The first snow"; Dec. 4, 1850: "The first Snow, and a very great Sleet, tremendous Cold Weather"; James J. Selby, "Sundries Events," *Ansearchin' News: The Tennessee Genealogical Magazine* 31 (Summer 1984): 85; (Fall 1984): 125, 129; (Winter 1984): 183-85.

[12] A modicum of tenderness for Negroes could prevail. In the summer of 1862, Mildred Strickland wrote to her husband, "Phebe is worse. I sent for Dr. Dougherty. He says it is a bad case of diphtheria-then there is no hope for her. You don't know how much I am distressed about her. She will never be very valuable, but she has played with my children, and goes with me everywhere I go and I grieve for her almost like a child."

[13] Southern church services were so oriented around preaching that Belle was not amiss in declaring that a funeral was "to be preached." In some communions the practice continues to the present.

[14] Henry Craft told his diary April 1, 1849, how he accompanied Mrs. Daniel Baker, wife of the former Holly Springs minister and her daughter Theodora as far as Memphis, as they went to Texas to join Dr. Baker. Upon arrival at the steamboat he said: "I felt as if I was parting with some of my best friends when I turned away from them. I could not bear to say good-bye and so I left them without a word of parting." Emma Finley described the latter procedure: "Tuesday morning was the time appointed for the departure of Lou Hargrove & her father- but they were both unwell & the morning unfavorable so they did not get off. Hearing of it, Ginnie & I rode out to tell them good-bye & we had been prevented from doing

so earlier. Dr. & Mrs. Rives were there too; Lou was much disappointed from the detention & feared they would not get started for a week- if then,- consequence of having every-thing ready,- & her mind set on that day. The next morning, however, they were really off & Mr. Marcus saw them as far as Memphis. Lou was very uneasy & went immediately to the "Ingomar" to lay down; they have not since heard from them." *Our Pen Is Time*, 72-73.

[15] At the time of Miller's retirement, Belle Strickland Bates was church clerk and penned these words about her pastor: "He has been with us in our prosperity and in our adversity, in our joys and in our sorrow. In him we have unbounded confidence." See McAlexander, *First Baptist Church*, 6-8; *Memoirs of Mississippi*, 2:437. Belle Bates later wrote her church's history which was published in the local newspaper. See "Baptists Celebrate 90th Year Here," SR (Oct. 9, 1930). Most of the document is printed in Lois Swaney, *A History of the First Baptist Church* (prv. pub., 1974), A window in the present First Baptist Church honors the memory of Belle Strickland Bates.

[16] Robert Lowry and W. H. McCardle, *A History of Mississippi* (Jackson: R. H. Henry, 1891): 544; Hamilton, 105.

[17] The precariousness of preaching schedules is well-illustrated by this account from the memoirs of the Rev'd John N. Waddel, who left the University of Mississippi in 1857 to serve the Presbyterian Synodical College at LaGrange, Tenn., maintaining his preaching arrangements in and near Oxford, Miss., while also serving churches near his new location. He wrote that "my many warm friends in the churches of Oxford and Hopewell, to whom I had been warmly and deeply attached. . .seemed very unwilling that I should dissolve the pleasant relations which had existed for nine years in uninterrupted harmony. It was, therefore, settled that I should still supply these churches with preaching, going down every Saturday by rail, and returning on Monday morning by the early train, in ample time for my duties in the [LaGrange] college. Then as my labors became unusually heavy in the fact that I was obliged to add a horseback ride out to the country to my railroad ride, whenever it became time for that appointment [at Hopewell], I gave up the country church, and continued to supply Oxford twice in the month and the LaGrange church twice per month, in which latter church Dr. [John Hannah] Gray preached during the alternate Sabbaths. But the labors of the year 1858 were very heavy indeed on me, so much so, indeed, that at its close I felt it was gradually undermining my health. . . .I felt obliged, under these circumstances, to give up Oxford. I thenceforward confined my labors to the church at LaGrange, still dividing the supply of that pulpit with Dr. Gray, and riding down to Lamar. . .south of LaGrange a few miles, every alternate Sabbath, and preaching to the few excellent Presbyterians who resided in that neighborhood." *Memorials of Academic Life*, 331-32.

[18] The Wootens had a plantation near Tallaloosa in the western part of the county. *Southern Tapestry*, 25.

[19] Kate Walthall Freeman, whom Sherwood Bonner described as "nearer to perfection than any woman I knew," a person of "manifold perfections" was regarded as the social and cultural leader of Holly Springs. In Bonner's novel *Like unto Like*, Mrs. Freeman was

said to have been the model for the thrifty, clever Mrs. Oglethorpe, who "timed the music of the [town's] orchestra." Kate Freeman's daughter Cary was a blond belle, and had many suitors. *Prodigal Daughter*, 19.

[20] John M. Mickle, "First Literary Club, The Philomathesian," SR (Dec. 10, 1931): 16, *Prodigal Daughter*, 19-21.

[21] In a subsequent article, Mickle added to his description local literary clubs: "In my recent story of the clubs I neglected to state that the Philomathesian Society, the first literary club here, was founded by Miss Lizzie Watson and Mrs. Cora Watson as a pleasant way for young ladies who had studied under Miss Lizzie Watson during the war of the sixties, to continue their literary work. Miss Lizzie Watson was the daughter of the late Judge J. W. C. and Mrs. Catherine Watson. As practically all schools were closed during the war Miss Watson taught a girls' school in the Watson home. Mrs. Cora Watson's husband, Willie Watson, was killed in battle. She later married Sam E. Carey, and they had two daughters, Nellie and Elizabeth. She was the first president of the present Thursday Club. Prior to the war it was considered highly improper for ladies to appear in even amateur theatricals, but the war emancipated woman to some extent, and the Holly Springs Dramatic Association, organized in the early seventies, was enriched by their talent. The present Masonic building had just been completed on the site of the old one, and the second floor, as before, was a theater, and the association leased it and spent $2,500 on the stage and scenery. The scenery was painted by Gulick of the Memphis Theatre, an artist of ability. Gulick would only work at night and so 'loved his drams' that the men had to relay each other to keep him sober. 'The Hall' as completed was perhaps the finest outside of the largest cities in the state, with thirteen sets of scenery and a curtain. The association was organized with about twenty gentlemen and fifteen ladies, others joining later. Maj. Strickland was active president. Col. H. W. Walter honorary president, Heber Craft vice-president, I. C. Levy manager and treasurer, James T. Fant prompter, Kinloch Falconer secretary, and W. I. McGowan property man." "Dramatic Club Here in Early Seventies," SR (Dec. 10, 1931).

[22] *Our Pen Is Time*, 67, 48.

[23] "Church Music," *Presbyterial Critic* (September 1856): 239-40.

[24] Emma Finley recounted a visit of suitors to her sister Augusta in 1858 that showed how much rain could interfere with simple travel and getting about. "While we were at supper that night someone knocked and on going to the door George found Dick Holland and Mr. Lewis Scruggs. About ten they arose to go but on going out found it raining- stopped until the shower should be over, but it poured from that time 'til-I don't know how long- they not getting off. The next morning after breakfast it still sprinkled and rained and they waited and waited until Scruggs could stand it no longer, and whispered to Johnie to have the horses brought. When they were ready-off the two started without umbrellas, and before they were out of the lane the hardest shower there had been, since they came, overtook them-and I think in the end they paid right dear for the visit." On another occasion, Emma wrote: "It had been our intention to go on with Uncle John to Aunt Martha's- after preaching- but it was so

cloudy we had to give up the idea; and tho' Sam and George started, and went nearly half way, they turned back and reached home just in time to save themselves a good ducking." *Our Pen Is Time*, 44-45.

XII. PRESIDENT JOHNSON IMPEACHED

[1] Mildred Strickland's wartime letters frequently alluded to her husband's friendship with Jefferson Davis. On April 4, 1861, she said: "I want to write to Davis, but he may give you some appointment that you nor I would not like."

[2] John M. Mickle, SR (Dec. 10, 1931): 11; Baum, 106.

[3] Mickle wrote that in olden times, mud would often be so deep in winter on Depot St. that the big, horse-drawn bus which ran between the town square and the railroad station would have to detour out on the Salem Road to reach its destination. SR (Dec. 10, 1931). Mickle wrote that "some say [that Van Dorn came] "by the depot up Church (or Depot) St., and the name has been changed to Van Dorn Ave. in commemoration of the event." SR (Jun. 18, 1931).

[4] Ted Ownby, *American Dreams in Mississippi: Consumers, Poverty, and Culture, 1830-1998* (Chapel Hill: Univ. of N. C. Press, 1999), 7-16.

[5] Emma Finley had trouble finding goods from which to make clothes. She gave this account of a trip to the Holly Springs square, April 11, 1859, to buy cloth: "Ma, Gus, George, Johnie, & I all went to the city chiefly to lay in our supply of summer goods....We found trading difficult, goods very high-nothing exactly to our taste-settling finally-Gus on a double skirt - uppers open organdie & I ___ double blue beige. Gus & Ginnie got very pretty bonnets too-I am to fix up my last summer's-Disagreeable work this-to me- hunting up new fashions." Calico was an enduring favorite, as Emma reports in her entry for May 4 of the same year: "My new calico was voted to be [the] "very thing" & thimble, needle & thread were immediately called into use." *Our Pen Is Time*, 71, 72.

[6] Mickle remembered that "When the Mississippi Central railroad...was preparing to enter Holly Springs in the early fifties they planned to cut through town and locate the depot at the Arthur place, now the McDowell place on Salem Ave., but such a storm of protest came that the change was made to the present site of the Illinois Central station." SR (Nov. 6, 1930). The old station which is still preserved today was much-enlarged in 1886, and was converted into a private dwelling in the 1960s. A small brick structure dating from before the Civil War stands north of the passenger station and houses offices of a short line railroad which has reclaimed the Mississippi Central name. Mickle comments that the term "depot" was "what they used to call the railroad station, until 'high hats' introduced 'station.'" SR (Dec. 15, 1932); Pruitt, 72-73; Baum, 75, 105.

[7] Holly Springs had white minstrel performers. John Mickle records that "The Amphionic Minstrel Club was started in 1860 and revived for a time after the war. Charles S. Mattison, Frank Mattison's uncle, led the orchestra with his sweet violin. Some other members were Charles Bracken, brother of the late Mrs. F. A. Lucas, Charles Estep, George M. Govan, Heber Craft and 'Hannie' Robinson." SR (Dec. 10, 1931).

Endnotes

⁸ Bill Barlow, "Minstrelsy," *Encyclopedia of Southern Culture*, 1018-20

⁹ Mickle recalled that Rust College put on the cantata "Ruth and Naomi" in the music hall of the Masonic Hall on the town square, with white spectators seated in the gallery for the occasion. SR (Nov. 20, 1930).

¹⁰ The Rev'd Thomas Grace, pastor of Sts. Peter and Paul Roman Catholic Church in Memphis wrote in August 1857 to the Very Rev'd William Henry Elder, of Natchez, Catholic Bishop of Mississippi, that "there are three or four Catholic families in Holly Springs with some few others in the vicinity, fifty miles from Memphis. Along the line of the rail road & scattered over two or three communities some few more are found." Grace urged Catholics in Holly Springs to "get up a Church no matter how small…in which Divine Service may be had." John Mickle tells the story of the beginning of St. Joseph's Church this way: "When the present Christ Church was to be built, in the mid-fifties, Mr. Farrell inaugurated a movement among his fellow Roman Catholics and bought the first Christ Church building and moved it to its present location and it has been since St. Joseph's Church." SR (Dec. 15, 1932).

¹¹ Mickle, who was five years younger than Belle, gives this description of the local Catholic Church, including his own account of a service there: "The Roman Catholic congregation was at its high tide here from 1855 to 1890. There was a fair sized congregation, a resident priest and a school for girls-Bethlehem Academy-that was well attended. There were some fine priests here then at St. Joseph's Church, and outstanding was Father Wise, a jolly Irishman, beloved alike by Catholic and Protestant. He survived the yellow fever at Yazoo City and died there a few years ago and his funeral was attended by all classes. Father Oliver was another fine man, and the only native Mississippian ever stationed here. He later went to Jackson, Miss., and built the new Roman Catholic Church there. At his death by special permission of the city authorities, his body was buried beneath the altar. When I was about five years old I went with my mother to St. Joseph's Church one Sunday, much against my will, though I said nothing. I had heard that Catholics stoned and burned Protestants, and I decided that when the first stone crashed I would run to Joseph Farrell, the only person I knew there. I did not know that in the dark ages religious controversialists burned each other. The nuns kept a watchful eye on their charges at Bethlehem Academy, but cloistered beauty was ever a strong challenge for youth, and the boys found means of slipping notes and candy to the girls. The boys never acted as rough as at the uptown schools, due to gallantry, I believe. There were none but women at the convent. The girls themselves, were not altogether 'prunes and prisms,' for I remember passing there in the dusk one evening and saw about twenty of them in the yard, with an unusual occurrence, no nun in sight, and all-horrors-smoking cigarettes, and that in the eighties, and turned the lights defiantly toward the street. That was only a feminine gesture against restrictions, though." SR (Nov. 6, 1930).

¹² A teacher in Chalmers Institute. See *Prodigal Daughter*, 20.

¹³ *An American Postal Portrait* (Washington: U. S. Postal Service, 2000).

¹⁴ Katie McGuirk was the daughter of Col. John McGuirk, a druggist, who came Holly Springs before the war and was said to have enlisted more soldiers for the Confed-

eracy than anyone in the area. The McGuirks lived in the house on W. Chulahoma Ave. now known as "Alicia." McGuirk purchased the cottage from the Rev'd Daniel Baker, the Presbyterian minister, enlarging the original two room log cottage to its present dimensions. The McGuirk children Walter, Kate, and Will were popular among the local youth. Col. McGuirk was Roman Catholic and Mrs. McGuirk, an Episcopalian. They were married in Christ Church. Katie became Mrs. C. Fulton Smith and lived in Holly Springs for some years before moving to Memphis in the 1890s. SR (Dec. 10, 1931):1; Baum, 23.

[15] Though the Episcopal Church in Mississippi was regarded as moderately "high" in its conception of churchly prerogatives and drew many of its members from the wealthier class, it then practiced very little of the colorful ceremony and almost none of the social and doctrinal tolerance for which it is known today. Penitential holy days were more likely to be kept than the celebratory feasts, and Episcopal ministers were known for their strictness. For example, when Tennessee bishop, the Rt. Rev'd James H. Otey first arrived in Memphis, November 12, 1852, he rented a hall over an oyster room and across from a dancing school, and preached a sermon entitled "The Tendency of Worldly Amusements." In Holly Springs, Kate Bonner, who was reared in Christ Church, complained about "bullying denunciations from the pulpit," and in 1879 when her seven year old daughter Lilian was baptized, Kate objected to the Rev'd Mr. Pickett's telling the child that "we were all, at birth, outcasts and under sentence of wrathful judgment." McIlwaine, 101; *Prodigal Daughter*, 147.

[16] Major Strickland's second wife was an Episcopalian, and Major Strickland worshiped in Christ Church after his marriage to Jane Leak. However, he remained a trustee of the Baptist Church, and so on March 29, 1893, was one of the purchasers of a lot for a new Baptist Church at the corner of Spring St. and Church (now E. College) Ave. McAlexander, *First Baptist Church*, 8. He was baptized and confirmed at his home, November 15, 1905, by the Rt. Rev'd Theodore DuBose Bratton, Episcopal bishop of Mississippi, his sponsors being his wife and daughter Perle. He was buried in 1908 from Christ Church.

[17] Emma Finley described a Holly Springs Easter in April 1859 in different, but amusing terms. Bad weather had prevented Emma and her sisters from attending services. They were at "Strawberry Plains" (a plantation north of the city belonging to their uncle and aunt, Ebenezer and Martha Trimble Greenlee Davis), where an all-day rain on Saturday had made it impossible to return home. On Sunday, slaves arrived from "Woodland," the Finley plantation, to retrieve the stranded party. To make the ten-mile journey it was necessary to go through town, and all were embarrassed as the church doors opened and the congregation poured out just as the Finley carriage passed. Considering that only Episcopalians and Roman Catholics observed Easter in this period, it was likely at Christ Church that the incident of which Emma spoke took place: "Saturday we could not come home as it rained all through the day, but next morning early Edmund came, and with five precious souls inside & "black eyed Susie" & Edmund & Tidy, Nan's body servant- in front, we bid the folks all goodbye- & set out for home (The only adventure, our having to all crawl out that the little mules might get the carriage out of a mud-hole.) Passed through town just as everybody was

leaving church,- cut a fine figure no doubt- laden as we were with bag & baggage, children, & servants-eggs being chief inducement for the little ones to come, they ransacked the place for them & enjoyed to the <u>bottom of the basket</u>,- visiting the little Canadian pony, gathering flowers- music- pictures-amused them thro' the day." *Our Pen Is Time*, 70.

[18] Ibid., 65.

[19] SR (Jul. 4, 1929). The first Episcopal service in Woodville, Miss., was Oct. 4, 1823, at the courthouse. After the church was organized, the novelty of Protestant services with a liturgy attracted large crowds. Mississippians were so unfamiliar with the Episcopal form of organization that the legislature, when asked to charter the church, changed some of the terminology, shifting the titles of "warden" and "vestryman" to "trustee," as the term was used in other denominations. "St. Paul's Episcopal Church, Woodville, Miss." (prv. pub., n.d.): 2.

[20] Colonel Dixon Comfort Topp, a planter who came to Holly Springs after the war, purchased the Coxe Place on Salem St. that had been Grant's military office during the Vicksburg campaign. Topp had survived the war with his fortune intact, but after the war, he, also suffered financial distress. To relieve his poverty, he followed the example of his neighbor Dr. Charles Bonner a decade before and agreed to another Federal occupation of the Coxe place, this time taking a boarder in the summer of 1875 the commander of the U. S. forces in Holly Springs. This latter arrangement (unlike the first) was voluntary and wholly beneficial to the house's owner, and a series of dinners and balls signaled the town's desire, if not for reconciliation, at least for gaiety in the midst of the "Yankee" occupation of their city. *Prodigal Daughter*, 84; Hamilton, 48.

[21] Mr. Frank's store-Captain Sam Frank, another Jewish merchant. The Franks lived in a cottage at the northwest corner of Salem Ave. and Walthall St., presently the home of Mr. and Mrs. Victor Baker. Pruitt, 38.

[22] When Bishop Elder arrived to consecrate the church in November 1857, he found the re-fitting incomplete but lent encouragement and hallowed the work. Anticipating the bishop's arrival, Father Grace wrote that "owing to the hard times little progress has been made towards the completion of the Church in Holly Springs. In moving the church edifice to the lot, it was found necessary to take off the roof; the whole of the plastering, the gallery & other woodwork had also to be removed. The roof has been reshingled, but besides this little has been done. There is a prospect of better times now, and no efforts will be spared to bring the church to an early completion-of which you will be advised." This letter tells all we know about the little church's original appearance. It had plaster walls-a luxury not every Church or home in that era possessed. There was also a slave gallery-the only one among the town's pioneer-era churches. The gallery was omitted or used for other purposes by the Catholic parish. The little church served well, for in less than three years, the Catholic community in Holly Springs increased to more than 300-far exceeding the size of the Episcopal parish which the little church had formerly served. Holly Springs was now headquarters of the Mississippi Central Railroad, and its shops, along with the iron foundry, were all based in the community. The congregation was visited once a month by a priest from Memphis.

Soon a rectory was purchased and a parochial school organized-one of five such Catholic institutions in the state.

[23] All the promise of St. Joseph Church's auspicious beginnings was swept away by the coming of the Civil War. By September 1861, the Sisters of Charity who had come to Holly Springs to assist the school were nursing the wounded in the courthouse. On April 4, 1862 it was reported that there were 600 in the hospital at Holly Springs. The lone priest, Father Basilio Elia, was unable to visit all the Catholic wounded or administer the consoling rites of his Church to them as they died. After Shiloh, trainloads of wounded started arriving in Holly Springs and Oxford-so many that Bishop Elder himself came from Natchez to help. Unfortunately, Holly Springs was not to remain a quiet refuge for the wounded. In November 1862, Grant's army occupied the town. The Sisters were alerted, and except for a few patients too ill to be moved, all hospitals were evacuated. Van Dorn's raid on Holly Springs, destroyed 4-6 million dollars of Federal supplies and left the small Union guard with little to do but wreak havoc upon local citizens and property. Cyrus F. Boyd, a soldier of the 15th Iowa Infantry, recorded, December 22, 1862, that "soldiers could be seen [pillaging] everywhere...in every house and garret and cellar, store and church..." He tells of the desecration of "a fine large Roman Catholic Church." Because of unfamiliarity with the town, it is likely that Boyd mistook Episcopal church for the Catholic (recall that small-town churches did not have signs as is the custom today), but because this source for local history is not well-known, the account printed in full: "A lot of soldiers were in the building, some were taking the organ to pieces and had the pipes out blowing on them and throwing them away. Up in the pulpit was a squad playing cards and another lot were scattering the library over the floor. One daring and reckless soldier climbed to the pinnacle of the temple and took off the little silver image of 'Jesus' that stood there. It was at a giddy height but he got it-said to be worth several hundred dollars." Father Elia's congregation for the most part dispersed as both the iron foundry and the railroad shops that had employed his people went out of operation. Unable to reach Natchez, he refugeed to Memphis, and from time to time visited the Catholics who remained in Holly Springs. By 1863, Elia had moved his labors elsewhere. It was years before Holly Springs had another resident priest. After the war, the town was slowly revived, but the railroad shops moved to Water Valley, and much of the Catholic population followed. Notwithstanding, a petition containing thirty-six names was presented to Bishop Elder in January 1866, requesting "a college for young ladies." Elder asked the Sisters of Charity at Nazareth, Ky. to operate the school. The following September, H. W. Walter told Elder that local Catholics had collected $3,500. Eight nuns arrived in September 1868 and set to work. Bethlehem Academy immediately enrolled fifty pupils. It was first located in the former Carrington Mason home at the foot of Memphis St. As it grew, the school moved to the Pointer Place on Salem Ave. (That house is long gone, but a memory in the name of the little road that runs south from Salem Ave. by the railroad tracks-Bethlehem St.) Old St. Joseph's Church in Holly Springs has recently been restored as a shrine to the sisters who gave their lives nursing victims of yellow fever in 1878. The old church houses a

museum with artifacts illustrating the early development of Catholicism in North Mississippi. James J. Pillar, *The Catholic Church in Mississippi, 1837-1865* (New Orleans: Hauser Press, 1964): 97-100, 140, 143, 196, 212, 222-26, 229, 235, 240, 245, 258-59, 280, 286. Sister Joan Kobe, D.W. "History of the Old St. Joseph's Church," (unpub. typescript, Oct. 4, 1994); SR (May 30, 1996); Memphis *Commercial Appeal* (Aug. 10, 1996); Baum, 71.

[24] The church was completed in 1869 with the installation of Bohemian grisaille glass windows, the gift of Presbyterians in the North. SR (Dec. 10, 1931 and Dec. 15, 1932); *Prodigal Daughter*, 20.

[25] Foster, 39-40. Books and tourist brochures for Holly Springs have always urged pilgrims to visit Hill Crest Cemetery, which, because of the generals buried there, one author has proclaimed "the Little Arlington of the South." Pruitt, 101-104.

[26] These are the graves of Susan Davis, wife of E. N. Davis, died March 25, 1838; Richard Harbert Eppes, son of Wyatt and Mary T. Eppes, died June 17, 1838; David L. Davis, son of E. N. Davis, died September 3, 1838; and Susan Thomas, died November 19, 1838. Bill Gurney, Bobby Mitchell, and David Pryor, *Cemeteries of Marshall County, Miss.* (Ripley, Miss.: Old Timer Press, 1983): 35, 38, 39.

[27] John M. Mickle, "Hill Crest is Most Appropriately Named," SR (Nov. 20, 1930): 4; Memphis *Commercial Appeal* (Aug. 16, 1936); Marshall County *Messenger* (Apr. 24, 1980): 10.

[28] For a listing of Strickland graves in Hill Crest Cemetery, see *Cemeteries of Marshall County*, 3, 22, 43. Major Strickland and his two wives rest in the plot referred to above, along with six of their children, including daughters Mildred ("Minnie") and Perle, both mentioned in these pages. William M. Strickland Jr., referred to as "Buddie" in Belle's diary (1853-1927) rests with his wife Lorena Lumpkin Strickland and a daughter Eva Belle Strickland Hudson in a nearby plot. Belle Strickland and her husband Charles Bates rest in the Bates plot.

[29] Mary Virginia Grigsby Foley gave this description of the front yard and gate at the Presbyterian manse: "I remember our yard which, compared to lawns and plantings of today, seems very unattractive. Our front yard was divided in two by the narrow walk leading from the porch steps to the fence gate. Everyone had fences of one description or another. One side of our front yard was covered with grass and was not unattractive. We had one lovely pecan tree in the middle of it. We had a lattice fence at the rear. The other side of the yard was totally bare of any form of verdure and the sun had baked it until it was hard as cement. Why this plot of land was never sodded I will never know. However, it served a purpose for which it made a most excellent setting for our favorite hop-scotch game. Where the two sides of our fence met our father had erected a board seat. It was our favorite seat, and always in demand. I think the first child through breakfast claimed it." *Childhood in Holly Springs*, 7.

[30] A decade before, Emma Finley told her diary that she would stay home while her younger sister enjoyed a party in the company of her beau: "At home having a very quiet, pleasant time,- Gusta having left us two hours or so ago for town in expectation of attending the party tonight at Masonic Hall. Yesterday evening tickets were sent out to all of us, and on

Gus' was an invitation from Mr. Lewis Scruggs to accompany her. Very glad of the chance to frolic some, she bundled up this morning and set off. Hope they'll have a fine time." *Our Pen Is Time*, 36; Augusta Finley and Lewis Scruggs were married April 11, 1865.

[31] A new courthouse was completed with local tax levies in 1870.

[32] The First United Methodist Church of Holly Springs is the oldest brick church in the county still in use. When Belle worshiped in it, the stairs leading from the ground floor to the sanctuary were open to the elements, standing in the recess of an open front porch. In 1869-70, the porch was enclosed, creating the lovely entrance foyer through which worshipers now enter. An interesting feature of the church is the Old Parsonage, added in 1862, to the rear of the building. There is a private passageway from the upstairs bedroom of the parsonage through which the minister could pass directly into the pulpit. Ruby Sigman, "History of the Methodist Church of Holly Springs," (unpub. typescript, 1942); Watkins, 182; also *History of the First Methodist Church, Holly Springs, Miss.*, (prv. pub., n.d.). The remodeling of the church is described by John M. Mickle SR (Dec. 15, 1932); see Baum, 55, 58.

[33] According to Mickle, the Strickland and Fant law office was upstairs in what was once known as the C.A. Jones building south of the present Tyson Drug Company, just off the courthouse square. SR (Dec. 15, 1932); Baum, 105. An interesting Civil War incident is connected with Major Strickland's office. A member of the 101st Illinois Regiment's drum and bugle corps named F. L. Bristow told the Memphis *Appeal* in December 1906: "As leader of the post band, I had my headquarters in the deserted office of a lawyer named Strickland, at one corner of the business square in Holly Springs, in front of which we played reveille, guard mount, taps, etc., as our daily military duties.... On the night of the 20th of December, 1862, in our fancied security, we peacefully retired to our soldier beds in Strickland's law office ... .Suddenly we were awakened by the rapid and continuous firing of muskets in the near distance. Quickly six of us Yankee 'musicianers' sat upright in our beds, and stared at each other with eyes, ears and mouths wide open. 'What on earth is it?' each one of us instinctively asked of the others, as the firing continued, accompanied by terrible Comanche yells and howls. At last, I found courage to say, 'Boys, I will go out doors and see what is up.' I cautiously opened the door, walked to the corner of the office, looked down the street toward the railroad depot, and saw what seemed to be a heard of wild buffaloes, snorting, mad, all headed toward me at the rate of a mile a minute, yelling, bellowing and shooting, bullets whistling around my heard, and only giving me time to run back into the room, lock the door and breathlessly say to my terrified companions, 'By George, boys, the rebs have got us sure and certain this time.' Before my comrades could make reply our ears were horrified by the following emphatic orders, never before nor afterward issued to us, by friend or foe: 'Come down from there, you d-d Yankees! Lay down those arms and surrender, sir!' Such orders, coming from a thousand Johnny Reb throats, had to be obeyed by those of our regiment, aroused suddenly from sound sleep, and wondering what was the necessity for so much fuss, firing, yelling, cussing, and commanding. So Holly Springs, Miss., with its many millions of dollars worth of supplies of all kinds for Gen. Grant's army, was captured by Gen.

Earl Van Dorn's command on December 20, 1862."

³⁴ In this era, ministers did not take regular vacations and, if the minister was ill, assisting another minister in special service, attending a meeting of the church governing bodies, etc., the pulpit was simply closed for the day. The Sabbath school would meet, and the members would then visit one of their neighbor churches for divine service.

XIII. DECORATING THE SOLDIERS' GRAVES

¹ Other historians place the ritual's origin in Georgia. But in all accounts the role of women is emphasized. One Southern woman compared her sisters to the biblical Mary and Martha, who "last at the cross and first at the grave, brought their offerings of love." *Baptized in Blood*, 28.

² This act inspired Francis Miles Finch's poem, "The Blue and the Gray."

³ Foster, 42-44.

⁴ *Baptized in Blood*, 36. Well into the twentieth century, the girls of Mississippi Synodical College walked in procession to Hill Crest Cemetery on Confederate Memorial Day to lay flowers upon the soldiers' graves. Chesley T. Smith to R. M. Winter, Jan. 11, 2001.

⁵ Loud's was a music store on the town square. John Mickle cited the *Mississippi Paladium* for 1851 in which Loud's advertises pianos, melodeons, guitars, and new music." SR (Dec. 10, 1931). Citing the *Empire Democrat* (Apr. 6, 1855), Mickle noted that among the new songs which the store listed among its stock of sheet music, he recognized only two: "Long, Long Weary Day" and "When the Swallows Homeward Fly." SR (Dec. 10, 1931).

⁶ Emma Boling was the daughter of Spires Boling. She married Dr. Lea A. Stephenson a local dentist, who in 1871 built what is now called the Baird cottage on the southeast corner of Salem and Walthall. It is presently the home of Ms. Betsy Kent.

⁷ Walter Brownlow Posey, *The Presbyterian Church in the Old Southwest* (Richmond: John Knox, 1952), 46-47; Allen Cabaniss notes that such sermon lengths were hardly amazing, citing the example of Bishop Forbes, an Anglican, who once preached for five hours; Allen Cabaniss, "Review of *The Presbyterian Church in the Old Southwest*," *Journal of Mississippi History* 14 (July 1952): 210.

⁸ *Diary of Robert B. Alexander* (Sept. 11, 1859).

⁹ The Rev'd Samuel Irwin Reid was born in Elizabethtown, Pa., in 1845 and received a master's degree from Washington and Jefferson College in Pennsylvania in 1845. He studied at Western Theological Seminary, Pittsburgh and was ordained by Transylvania Presbytery in Kentucky. Coming to Mississippi, he was minister of the Oxford and Hopewell churches (1846-48), before undertaking home mission work for Chickasaw Presbytery, which he added to his labors as a teacher in Chalmers Institute, Holly Springs (1855-69). *Ministerial Directory of the Presbyterian Church, U. S., 1831-1941* (Austin, Tex: Von Boeckmann-Jones, 1942): 602.

¹⁰ Reid did not move to Illinois. He remained in Mississippi, serving for many years as pastor of small churches in the northern part of the state. Reid, his wife Mary Jane, who died in the yellow fever epidemic of 1878, and five children who died in infancy, rest in Hill Crest Cemetery, Holly Springs.

[11] For generations gypsies, associated with a circus, claimed the Main Street Presbyterian Church in Columbus, Miss., as their home, and sent their dead back there for burial.

[12] Charles Reagan Wilson, "Traveling Shows," *Encyclopedia of Southern Culture*, 1247. John Mickle wrote that the Holly Springs *Reporter* for Oct. 31, 1872 announced that "The Great Eastern Menagerie, Museum, Circus and Caravan will exhibit in Holly Springs Saturday, Nov. 16." Mickle commented that "it was a large show for that day, and set up on the High School grounds-no buildings there then. It traveled overland, using mules for draft animals." SR (Dec. 15, 1932).

[13] Baum, 99.

[14] Wilson has written that "The coming of traveling shows signaled an unusual period of gaiety, when normal moral restrictions might be loosened and humdrum daily life enlivened." "Traveling Shows," 1247.

[15] In a deed recorded September 29, 1874, Major W. M. Strickland's name appears among others of the town's leaders in a conveyance of land for a Confederate monument in the Holly Springs Cemetery. The document is reproduced in *The Marshall County Heritage News* 6 (2000): 26.

[16] "Hill Crest Is Most Appropriately Named, SR (Dec. 20, 1930): 4; John M. Mickle, "Mrs. Helen Anderson Dies in 85th Year," SR (Dec. 31, 1931): 1; SR (Mar. 8, 1958); A description of the cemetery and listing of the graves may be found in *Cemeteries of Marshall County*, 1-47.

[17] Dancing, while practiced in Bible times, was condemned by preachers in the American South until the early decades of the 20th century. Belle gives no hint that she knows of such condemnations, but a decade earlier, Emma Finley did. On June 25, 1859, she told her secret book: "They tell us that Mr. Paine discoursed last Sunday on dancing to the wide gate & broad way [St Matthew 7:13, 14]- but not having heard the sermon I cannot discuss it. Our town has been very gay and there may have been danger of running into excess." Dancing seemed to have been the principal recreation during young people's outings in Emma's day, and despite clerical frowns, most seem to have pursued this pleasure without qualms of conscience. Judge Watson, of course opposed dancing, but his law partner J. W. Clapp told Emma and her friends that he had his own secret vice. By Emma's account, on one of their outings, her friends "rolled ten pins- & most danced after supper, but Mr. Clapp says he won't tell on them- he plays cards!" *Our Pen Is Time*, 9-10, 93-94.

[18] Edward McDowell, of Holly Springs, living in Galveston, Tex., wrote Cora Watson May 29, 1868, that "I was quite taken by surprise when I read…of the fact that there had been a Masquerade Ball in H. S…But of course you wouldn't have gone because you are so- sopious! I don't think that young people whose families are of the persuasion which do not sanction such indulgences, ought to become 'religious' until they are of a certain age (which, you know, means about 30). But of course we differ widely on this point." Cora Carey Letters, Miss. Dept. of Archives & Hist.

[19] William H. Foote, *Sketches of North Carolina: Historical and Biographical* (New York:

Endnotes

Robert Carter, 1846); 524; Hubert H. McAlexander, "Flush Times in Holly Springs," *Journal of Mississippi History* 48 (February 1986): 6. Christy Ann Farnham, *The Education of the Southern Belle* (New York: N.Y. Univ. Press, 1994); Hamilton, 64-74.

[20] Clayton, 8.

[21] *Prodigal Daughter*, 11.

[22] The J. A. Hale dental office.

[23] Nineteen year-old Emma Finley's comments in the autumn of 1858 indicate envy that even though she could ride a horse, she was not allowed to handle a gun: "Tuesday morn early we were up for a ride before breakfast, & the next morning much to our delight we came upon some wild turkeys. We came back in a hurry & posted off somebody to kill them, but they made their escape with the loss only of a few feathers. Now if girls could only shoot!" *Our Pen Is Time*, 23. As some indication of how unusual these infractions must have been, Mary Virginia Grigsby Foley, recorded this incident: "My father made his round of pastoral calls on a bicycle. I was not allowed to have a bicycle as it was considered very unladylike for me to ride one. However, sometimes when everyone was otherwise engaged, I surreptitiously purloined this forbidden vehicle and enjoyed a short ride. Oh yes! I had learned to ride it. Streets and sidewalks were not conducive to very fancy riding however. Sooner or later this heresy was discovered and the practice forbidden. *Childhood in Holly Springs*, 56.

[24] During the war, older women sometimes carried pistols for their own protection. On October 29, 1862, Cordelia Scales wrote from her plantation near Hudsonville that "I never ride now or walk without my pistol." She joked about the unusual and unladylike nature of this action with the wry comment, "Quite warlike, you see," telling her correspondent that "you would take me for a Gurilla" [that is, a guerilla fighter]. Hamilton, 151.

[25] Mrs. Addison Craft was the former Frances Breckinridge Young, of Danville, Ky. Her father was the Rev'd Dr. John Clarke Young, president of Centre College in that city. Addison Craft, brother of Helen and Heber Craft, also mentioned in these pages, had distinguished himself in the war and was prospering as a young attorney in Holly Springs. The Addison Crafts later built the large and lovely home called "The Pines" across the street from the Presbyterian manse on the street leading out of the city to Oxford, which came to be named in their honor. John Mickle wrote that "for many years Maj. Craft was the unofficial host of the city." SR (Nov. 20, 1930): 2:1; *Prodigal Daughter*, 41; Baum, 86. The house, at 251 S. Craft St., is now the home of Mr. and Mrs. Robert D. Farnsworth.

[26] Although no large communion ordained women in the nineteenth century, women played key roles in the church, especially the minister's wife, whose presence was especially prominent in pastoral visiting. See Leonard I. Sweet, *The Minister's Wife: Her Role in Nineteenth-Century American Evangelicalism* (Philadelphia: Temple Univ. Press, 1983).

[27] A daughter of Mr. and Mrs. Hugh Craft, who lived next door to the Presbyterian Church. As Belle's comments indicate, she later served as organist of the Presbyterian Church.

CIVIL WAR WOMEN

XIV. A DIFFICULT ERA IN A PROUD COMMUNITY

[1] A U.S. force consisting of three companies was stationed in Holly Springs in 1865. By 1875 there was still a garrison of 200 in the city. At this time there were only two other garrisons in the state, one at Vicksburg consisting of 100 soldiers, and the other at Jackson, with 120. Watkins, 173-74.

[2] SR (Nov. 20, 1930); Watkins, 159-81.

[3] On Sunday, September 1, 1872, the Holly Springs session recorded that Bibles and diplomas were awarded publicly nine boys and girls, "a reward for having committed to memory the Assembly's Shorter Catechism, and for having recited it accurately to the pastor, in the presence of the Session." A generation later, on June 2, 1914 the elders of the Holly Springs Presbyterian Church ordered "that special emphasis be placed upon the study of the Catechisms in the Sunday School, and that the teachers be requested to insist upon their pupils' committing to memory the Shorter Catechism questions given in the *Earnest Worker* each Sabbath, and that Mrs. Jno. E. Anderson be requested to complete in her Class the Shorter Catechism, as this is part of the regular grade work of the Class." Members of the congregation remember having to memorize at least part of the catechism as a confirmation requirement as recently as the 1970s.

[4] *Prodigal Daughter*, 20-21, 28, 140-41; Hamilton, 47, 51, 79, 145, 147, 158.

[5] A black servant of the Stricklands.

[6] Belle's comments represent the harsh feelings which nearly all whites shared in this era. The parade she describes recalls the noisy demonstrations and torch-light parades held by the "Loyal Leagues" which were organized for the double purpose of teaching the former slaves how to vote and of holding their vote solid for the Republican ticket. These processions to and from the town square were said to be a mile long. The "Yankee flag" to which Belle refers was, of course, the stars and stripes. Ironically, it was Judge Watson who led the first effort to educate the freed slaves. The Hinds County *Gazette* of July 13, 1866 states that Watson and Kinloch Falconer were superintendent and teacher respectively in a school they established for former bondsmen. Watkins, 176-77, 197.

[7] Citing a newspaper of 1869, John Mickle noted that "A revival has been in progress at Chulahoma Methodist Church, Rev. G. B. Baskerville pastor, for three weeks." SR (Dec. 15, 1932).

[8] In 1866 Major Strickland and others had formed the Holly Springs Savings and Insurance Company, to insure livestock, life, health, fire protection, marine risks, river risks, freight, money, goods, wares, and merchandise. *Laws of Mississippi* (1866): 76; Hamilton, 45.

[9] So far as we know, Belle's wish was never gratified.

[10] *Childhood in Holly Springs*, 23-24.

[11] *Our Pen Is Time*, 20.

[12] Citing the Holly Springs *Gazette* (Nov. 8, 1850), John Mickle recalled that S. P. Cutler, resident dentist, has rooms over Malloy & Wilkins new store. He said, "I remember him, and his office in my boyhood was in a two-story frame building on the site of the

southwest corner of the Post Office lot. He advertises 'teeth extracted, plugged and nerves destroyed without pain.'" He remarked that "The plugging and nerve destroying without pain had become a lost art in dentistry by the time I came on." *SR* (Dec. 10, 1931).

[13] Othniel A. Pendelton Jr., "Temperance and the Evangelical Churches," *Journal of the Presbyterian Historical Society* 25 (March 1947): 14-45;

[14] Roger Burlingame, *The American Conscience* (New York: Knoph, 1957): 211-12

[15] Holly Springs *Southern Banner* (Apr. 9, 1841); J. W. Clapp, "Temperance: An Address Delivered at the Request of the Holly Springs Temperance Society at the Methodist Church...(Mar. 8, 1842); "Address on the Presentation of a Bible to the Sons of Temperance," Holly Springs, Miss., (Dec. 25, 1847), *Public Addresses by J. W. Clapp*, collected by his granddaughter. John D. Williams Library, Univ. of Miss.; *Shadow of a Mighty Rock*, 280-81.

[16] As the Rev'd James Weatherby of the Female Institute declared in a speech before the Sons of Temperance on Christmas Day, 1848, in the Presbyterian Church-(This date was chosen no doubt because Southern men often drank to excess at Christmas even if they abstained on all other days.):"Why have the Ladies manifested such a partiality for your order, and taken such a lively interest in your Institution? The lesson is obvious. Who most suffer from the brutality of a drunken brother, son, or husband? The sister-the mother-the wife. Now when the youthful maiden hears that her brother has become a Son of Temperance, her heart thrills with delight, and she feels that he is now safe. . . .When the widowed Mother, whose anxious heart has watched the movements of her beloved son, and feared that he might be persuaded to enter the dead-falls so numerous around us, how is her heart relieved, and with what sensations of joy does she receive the glad tidings, that her son has become a Son of Temperance. . . . The wife. . .who with a tearful eye and troubled spirit has watched hourly for the midnight return of the partner of her joys and sorrows, from the haunts of dissipation and the dens of iniquity-How does this beloved wife rejoice. . .that her Husband has enlisted under the Banner of the Sons of Temperance. . . ." Holly Springs *Gazette* (Jan. 24, 1848); Encouragement of the temperance movement was an avenue by which women took first steps toward participation in the larger world of politics; see Barbara Leslie Epstein, *The Politics of Domesticity: Women, Evangelism, and Temperance in 19th Century America* (Middletown, Conn.: Wesley Univ. Press, 1981).

[17] Nineteen year-old Emma Finley's diary of 1858-59 indicates that spirits were part of Holly Springs table fare, and that the young apparently enjoyed both wine and liquor at their meals, for the temperance movement was not yet at its peak. On an outing to Red Sulphur Springs, in Hardin County, Tenn., a group of Holly Springs young people and their elders were treated to the following; "Soup- Lamb- Chicken, ham with usual vegetables & breads- preserves & apple pies, melons, cakes, nuts, & Maderia, Port- Claret & Whiskey." The next morning the young people "hurried down to breakfast, finding a julip at our places." On the way home, the young people "made do" with champagne for breakfast. As Emma explained, "The snack upon which we had all depended was not-to-be-found,- thanks to the forgetfulness of some one. Mollie's breakfast was divided round though, with some of the

children's cakes,-& with a bottle or two of champagne wasn't very bad to take." At a dinner with Mr. and Mrs. Cal Smith, Emma reported that the meal "would have tempted the palate of the most fastidious,- soup-turkey-chickens-vegetables-wine-cakes-peaches & cream, nuts & raisins." And at a reception in the home of Mr. and Mrs. Walter Goodman, president of the Mississippi Central Railroad, honoring their son and his new bride, Emma told that the table featured "Pyramids and pagodas of cake, temples of candy, decanters of sparkling wine,- with all the minor dainties & decorations usual in grand suppers." *Our Pen Is Time*, 11-12, 15-16, 30, 86.

[18] Daughter of General H. E. Williamson, who bought the house mentioned elsewhere in these pages, now called "Linden Terrace." Mal Williamson married Harry C. Smith, uncle of L. A. Smith Sr.

[19] The Rev'd William M. Pettis was rector of Christ Church from 1866 to 1869.

[20] Thousands of distilleries dotted America in the nineteenth century. They were purely local industries, some with no more than a dozen customers. William E. Woodward writes that "the distiller-whose real occupation was farming, or running a store, or a blacksmith shop-had a still in his back yard. There was no tax on liquor, none at all, and anybody who had the inclination might make and sell it." Woodward, 193.

[21] Spring Hollow was the site of a trading post operated by Alexander Calvin McEwen, whose order that supplies be sent to "the Holly Springs" about 1835, is said to have given the town its name. McAlexander, "Flush Times," 2-4. Later, legends grew up about the lush valley where natural springs flowed forth their streams of pure water, so that citizens of the town came to believe that Indian princesses had once bathed among holly trees which encircled a glade of rare loveliness. It was Annah Robinson Watson, daughter-in-law of Judge and Mrs. J. W. C. Watson, who gave literary expression to the tale in a poem called "The Story of Latoka," published in *One Hundred Years, 1836-1936: History of Marshall County, Miss.* (Holly Springs: Garden Club of Marshall County, 1936): 34; Mrs. Watson was recognized as "Poet Laureate of the United Daughters of the Confederacy"; see "Mrs. Annah Watson Dies; Noted as Poet," Memphis *Commercial Appeal* (May 1, 1930). Boling's house has recently been purchased by the City of Holly Springs as a museum for display of paintings by Ida B. Wells, who achieved fame because of her efforts in the anti-lynching movement of the 1890s. She was born on the place in the home of her father, who was a laborer for Spires Boling. The Boling house stands on land once owned by W. S. Randolph, a founder of the town. James Fort Daniel recalled a three-story building at the north end of Spring Hollow which "housed a grist mill, a flour mill and a distillery. This building was known by two names, Johnson's Mill and the Boling Mill." Daniel states that the large spring on the east side of the hollow was called the Boling Springs. Marshall County *Messenger* (Apr. 24, 1980): 10; Baum, 52.

[22] By John Mickle's account: "Down in the spring hollow behind the water works was a three-story distillery, later known as Johnson's mill after it had been converted into a cotton gin and gristmill. In my boyhood a boy, son of the proprietor fell into a swill tub and was so badly scalded that he died two days later. Mickle states that Boling also operated a

"gallon house," or wholesale liquor distributorship, in the Masonic building (which later housed Crawford's Drug Store) on the square. SR (Dec. 10, 1931, Dec. 15, 1932)

[23] Nelson G. Gill, who came from Illinois, was the county's main carpetbag leader. A masterful speaker, he would address freed slaves for hours at a time. He was postmaster, and for a time had charge of the Freedmen's Bureau. He organized the Negroes into "Loyal Leagues," and other political clubs, and instructed them how to vote. During election campaigns, Gill led torchlight parades and cut a striking figure astride a horse wearing a red sash, while his black constituents marched in columns a mile long. Because the Gills appeared to treat blacks as social equals, they were despised by the white establishment and incurred the wrath of the Ku Klux Klan. After serving briefly in the state legislature, he was defeated for sheriff by Democrat Henry C. Myers. Watkins, 168-69, 175.

[24] George B. Myers was born in North Carolina in 1830 and came to Marshall County in 1848. He was wounded in the Confederate army, causing the loss of an arm. He was elected circuit clerk in 1867, and, except for two years, when he was removed by the military governor, held this office until his death in 1879. Watkins, 164.

[25] Mrs. Gill was a Missourian, and was incorrectly thought to be a mulatto, a mistake probably due to the fact that she wore her hair short, in tight corkscrew curls. She taught in her husband's school and was an important force in shaping Reconstruction-era attitudes and opinions of many blacks. One summer she had a large number of photos made, and required each of her pupils to buy one at the cost of twenty-five cents. Gill divorced her while they were living in Holly Springs and married her sister. Watkins, 169.

[26] Ruth Watkins gives a version of this or a similar event: "On one occasion, the Republicans had arranged a very extensive program. About ten speakers had been provided to address the Negroes, and Gill was the last speaker on the list. The speaking took place in the center of the square at Holly Springs, where a stand had been erected for the occasion [the courthouse having been destroyed in 1864]. Col. Geo. B. Myers accompanied by Henry Dancy and a few others went over to hear Gill's speech. None were armed. Gill made a false statement, and Col. Myers, without any thought of consequences, jumped on the platform and declared it to be a lie, and struck Gill. Mr. Dancy and others ran to assist Col. Myers … and a little battle with sticks and brickbats ensued. Mr. Dancy threw a brickbat at one of the men on the platform and it broke his leg. Things were quieted down by the presence of armed white men from the stores around the square. The injured man was taken to Dr. Compton's drug store to have his leg set. Mr. Dancy was immediately informed that this man had reported him, and he left town for a short time. Several men were wounded, but no one was seriously injured." By Watkins' reckoning, the event took place in the summer of 1869. "Reconstruction in Marshall County," 186-87.

[27] Turner H. Lane, a deacon in the Presbyterian Church

[28] John Mickle wrote that "The War of the Sixties had drained the town of all men and boys able to bear arms, and women and children were left unprotected. Tough characters, hangers on of both armies, swarmed in, and on petition of the women, the Confederate

military authorities released Mr. [Billie] Jones [the long-time town marshal] and he was sent back to protect them. The Federal authorities did not arrest or interfere with him. SR (Mar. 3, 1932).

[29] Psalm 55:6.

[30] *Shadow of a Mighty Rock*, 209, 277, 284-85, 312, 322, 343, 455.

EPILOGUE

[1] *Shadow of a Mighty Rock*, 27-37.

[2] Minutes of the trustees of the Holly Springs Female Institute; Clayton, 8.

[3] Mickle wrote that "Holly Springs claims some world-famous characters as its past citizens. Commodore Matthew F. Maury, who served with the old navy when war broke out and who went into the Confederate navy, made charts of navigation which are used at the present time the world around. Russia offered him a handsome fee after the war to come abroad and reorganize her navy. He often visited his sister, Mrs. [Elizabeth Maury] Holland, who resided near Holly Springs." John M. Mickle, "Grant Remembered at Holly Springs," *Frisco Railroad Employees' Magazine* (July 1931). Betsy Holland was the mother of Holly Springs newspaper editor W. J. L. Holland.

[4] Wesleyan College, Macon, Ga., appears to have been the first collegiate institution for women (1836). Woodward, 169. Vassar was first woman's college to offer same curriculum as a men's college. *Prodigal Daughter*, 43.

[5] John M. Mickle, "Masonic Hall One of City Landmarks," SR (Oct. 23, 1930): 4.

[6] Minutes of North Mississippi Presbytery, 2:139.

[7] The memory of Maury Institute is recalled in Maury Street, beside what was the east side of the campus.

[8] "Marshall School of Presbyterian Church Advances," Jackson, Miss. *Daily News* (Jul. 5, 1931): 1.

[9] Fred R. Graves, *The Presbyterian Work in North Mississippi* (Sumner, Miss: Sentinel Press, 1927): 52-57. In 1938, at the Holly Springs Garden Club Pilgrimage, a pageant was presented, tracing the growth of Elizabeth Watson's school into the Maury Institute and the Mississippi Synodical College. See Programme, "Mississippi Synodical College Presents in Pageant, 'A Dream of Education,' April 18-19, 1938."

[10] A full history of Mississippi Synodical College may be found in *Shadow of a Mighty Rock*, 274-77, 296, 312-19, 324-25, 339-40, 347-48, 359-63, 385-86, 397, 403-405; see Miller-Smith, *Marshall County*, 64-69.

[11] Judge Bates edited the Marshall County *Register* in the 1880s.

[12] L. A. Smith Jr., "Holly Springs Bar," *1836-1936 History of Marshall County, Miss.* (Holly Springs: Garden Club of Marshall County, 1936): 39.

[13] SR (Feb. 20, 1936); Mitchell, 43.

[14] Mrs. Dancy was the former Nell Carey, daughter of Mrs. Cora Watson and Col. S. E. Carey.

Endnotes

[15] Edgar W. Francisco Jr., son of Mr. and Mrs. Edgar W. Francisco Sr., who lived next door at "McCarroll Place." (Mr. Francisco Sr. had married Betsy Leak, daughter of Walter John and Amelia McCarroll Leak. Walter John Leak was Perle Strickland's uncle. His half-sister Jane was the second Mrs. William M. Strickland.)

[16] Hindman Doxey.

[17] Dr. Bitzer was pastor of the Holly Springs Presbyterian Church. His daughters Ruth and Mary later wed the wedding ceremony's ushers, Messrs. Francisco and Doxey!

[18] SR (Oct. 2, 1926).

[19] SR (Nov. 20, 1930). In March 1970, the Marshall County Historical Museum, found a permanent home in the administration building of the former Mississippi Synodical College, one block from the old Strickland Place and next door to the site of the Watson Place. SR (Feb. 15, 1990): 3. The building is a registered National Historic Landmark, a Mississippi Historic Landmark, and National Presbyterian Historic Landmark.

[20] "Famed Old Strickland Place Will Lure Pilgrimage Crowds," Memphis *Commercial Appeal* (Mar. 2, 1941).

[21] Memphis *Commercial Appeal* (Apr. 10, 1938, Apr. 11, 1948, Apr. 24, 1965).

INDEX

Abram, a slave, 237
Ada, 214
Ada, a former slave, 95
Adams, Gen., 65, 247
Adams, Inez Berryhill, 81
Airs, Capt., 91
Alexander, Miss, 3
Alexander, Mrs. Bob., 261
Alexander, Robert Burrell, 31, 54, 177, 241, 267-268
Alfred, a slave, 20
Alfred, a servant's child, 80, 197
Alfred, uncle of Cora Watson, 28
Ames, The Rev'd Edward R., 16
Anderson, Helen Craft (Mrs. William Albert)
  (see also Miss Helen Craft), 8, 78, 88, 119, 181-182, 260
Anderson, Henry M., 165, 174, 179
Anderson, James H., 244
Anderson, Jane Watson (Mrs. James H.), 244
Anderson, Mrs. John E., 290
Anderson, John H., 78
Anderson, John McCartney, 231
Anderson, Lee Ann Ridley Haggard
  (Mrs. John H.), 23, 78, 188
Anderson, Lewis, 34
Anderson, Lida Smith (Mrs. James H.), 35, 65, 66, 117, 244
Anderson, Peter, 244
Anderson, Sarah Joanna Thornton
  (Mrs. John M.), 231
Anderson, William Albert, 25, 52, 78-79, 84, 88, 193, 208, 253, 258
Ann, a slave, 237
Anna, 164

Armstrong, Gen., 103
Arthur, President Chester A., 215
Arthur, Pridge, 272
Athey, Batey, 157
Aughey, The Rev'd James H., 263
Autry, Lt. Col. James Lockhart, 226
Badow, Gerard, x, 217-221
Badow, Perle Strickland (Mrs. Gerard), 217-222
Baker, The Rev'd Dr. Daniel, 277, 282
Baker, Elizabeth (Mrs. Daniel), 277
Baker, The Rev'd German, 228
Baker, Miss Theodora, 277
Baptist, Mrs. Edward, 64
Barrett, Dr., 246
Barrett, Sallie, 243
Barrett, Sophronia Falconer (Mrs. Columbus), 205
Baskerville, The Rev'd G. Boothe, 145, 166, 180, 197-199, 290
Basset, Mrs., 7
Bates, Maj., 92, 94
Bates, Belle Strickland (see Strickland, Belle), 285
Bates, Judge Charles Lee, 216, 217, 285, 294
Beauregard, Gen., P. G. T., 123, 262
Bee, 18
Belk, Fred, 167
Belle, a slave, 20, 166, 168
Benjamin, Sec. Judah P., 123
Bennett, Lieut., 13
Benton, Gen. Samuel, 34, 224-225, 253
Berryhill, The Rev'd Charles Z., 79, 81
Berryhill, Estelle ("Aunt Essie"), 81
Bishop, 268
Bitzer, The Rev'd Dr. George L., 220, 295

295

CIVIL WAR WOMEN

Bitzer, Mary (Mrs. Hindman Doxey), 295
Bitzer, Ruth (Mrs. Edgar W. Francisco, Jr.), 295
Blackburn, The Rev'd Gideon, 176
Blair, Frank, 83
Blanche, a slave, 271
Boling, Emma, 175, 287
Boling, son of Spires Boling, 207, 208, 292
Boling, Spires, 207, 208, 287, 293
Bonds, Con, 230
Bonner, Dr. Charles, 42, 114, 125, 253, 266-267, 270, 283
Bonner, Miss Kate ("Sherwood"), 32, 59, 88, 109, 151, 234, 237, 241, 243, 249, 262, 265, 276, 278-279, 282
Bonner, Ruth Martin (Mrs. David McDowell), 109, 145, 150, 266, 270
Booth, John Wilkes, 113, 115, 226, 120, 124
Bowles, Col., 192
Bowles, Dell, 180, 212
Bowles, Willie, 192, 212
Boyd, Cyrus F., 284
Boyd, Robert, 274
Bracken, Charles L., 107, 280
Bracken, Mrs., 107
Bradley, John, 29, 94, 241
Bragg, Gen., 123
Branscome, Amp, 28, 92, 93, 117
Branscome, George, 28, 117
Bratton, The Rt. Rev'd Theodore DuBose, 282
Bristow, F. L., 286
Brooks, The Rev'd Joseph, 177
Brown, Dr. George, 220
Brown, Mrs. George, 221
Burton, Dr. John S., 272
Burton, Mrs. John S., 272-273
Burton, Mary Malvina Shields Butler (Mrs. Jasper F.), 65, 272-273
Butler, Gen. Benjamin F., 270
Butler, Dr. Jasper F., 131-132, 272
Byrne, Ransom H., 171
C., Ida, 104
Cage, Mrs., 124
Calkins, Amelia (Mrs. D. C.), 142, 147, 153, 156-157, 187, 188, 193, 277
Cameron, Mr., 126
Campbell, Mr., 91
Canby, 123
Cannon, Mr., 8
Carey, Cora Watson (Mrs. S. E.) (see also Cora White Harris Watson), 217, 260, 294
Carey, Miss Elizabeth, 279
Carey, Nellie (Mrs. Lucius Dancy), 279, 295
Carey, Maj. S. E., 217, 279, 294
Carrie, Miss, friend of Mildred Strickland, 236, 237
Carrier, Mr., 57-60
Carroll, Gov. William, 176
Carter, Mr., a lecturer, 159, 160,
Carter, Mr., 192
Caruthers, Dr. Samuel Oliver, 49
Chalmers, Brig. Gen. James R., 16, 234
Charles, cousin of Cora Watson, 127
Cherry, Mrs., 125
Chew, Capt. John, 108, 109, 265
Chism, Alex, 74
Chism, Lee, 74
Church, The Rev'd O. O., 122, 270
Clapp, Miss Clementine, 10, 12, 112
Clapp, Evelina Donaho (Mrs. J. W.), 6, 227, 242, 265
Clapp, Judge Jeremiah Watkins, xvii, 5, 6, 42, 43, 62, 93, 120, 204, 227, 228, 253, 263, 265, 271, 288, 291

Clapp, Will, 6
Clark, Miss Dora Barton, 43, 51, 55, 64, 68, 135, 147, 156, 164, 170, 248
Clark, Miss Kate Freeman, 222, 256
Clark, Mary Barton (Mrs. William), 23, 63, 69, 151, 167, 168, 206, 248, 256
Clark, Miss Rosa May, 23, 43, 51, 55, 64, 68, 117, 135, 141, 147, 156, 157, 164, 197, 198, 206, 239
Clark, Prof. William, 10, 33, 72, 139, 140, 151, 168, 169, 178, 186, 192, 208, 210, 214, 230, 248, 276
Clayton, Judge Alexander Mosby, 134-135, 184, 253, 272
Clayton, Miss Clara, 131, 134, 135
Cleburne, Gen. Pat, 70
Cleveland, President Grover, 74, 258
Clopton, Mr., 272
Cobb, Gen. Howell, 261
Cockrell, Gen. Francis Marion, 70
Coffman, Miss Katie, 47
Coffman, Mrs. 138
Compton, Dr. William M., 293
Connelly, William, 33
Connor, Capt., 92
Cooper, Mrs. Robert Franklin, 222
Cox, Col., 92
Coxe, William Henry, 42-43, 234, 248, 249
Craft, Maj. Addison, 151, 213, 226, 259, 289
Craft, Caroline R. ("Miss Carrie") (see also Mrs. R. N. Venable), 29, 33, 48, 49, 58, 108, 109, 241, 256
Craft, Cornelia Crittenden ("Miss Nina"), 222
Craft, Elizabeth Collier (Mrs. Hugh), 29, 63, 79, 88, 105, 116, 124, 167, 241, 256, 289
Craft, Frances Breckinridge Young (Mrs. Addison), 29, 151, 187, 210, 213, 241, 289
Craft, Heber, 151, 185, 226, 279, 280, 289
Craft, Miss Helen (see also Mrs. W. A. Anderson), 32, 58, 78, 79, 89, 91, 126, 151, 276, 289
Craft, Henry, xvii, 43, 226, 257, 277
Craft, Hugh, 2, 3, 63, 79, 88, 241, 256, 289
Craft, Miss Lizzie Belle, 222
Craft, Mary Bowman (Mrs. Heber), 151
Craft, Miss Mollie, 16
Craft, Sallie, a slave, 101, 236
Craft, Miss Stella, 22, 45, 58, 108, 109, 116, 188, 193, 210, 290
Crawford, S. R., 42
Crump, Maj. Brodie S., 101, 102
Crump, Helen Edmundson (Mrs. Brodie S.), 111
Crump, Mayor Edward Hull, 32, 85
Crump, Elizabeth Hull (Mrs. William), 36, 258, 272
Crump, Capt. James Moore, 52, 65, 97, 123, 130, 272
Crump, Mollie Nelms (Mrs. Edward Hull Crump), 111
Crump, William, 23, 35, 52, 97, 98, 111, 239, 244, 247, 258, 272
Crump, William Jr., 67
Cummings, Eliza, 173
Cutler, Dr. S. P., 202, 290
Dabney, The Rev'd Dr. Robert Lewis, 259
Dagg, Mr., 35
Dana, Maj. Gen. Napoleon Jackson Tecumseh, 90, 96, 261
Dancy, Miss Fannie, 89
Dancy, Dr. Francis William, 89, 97, 105, 122, 244, 265
Dancy, Miss Hattie, 8, 10
Dancy, Henry, 293
Dancy, Miss Mary Jane, 89, 131
Dancy, Mason, 74
Dancy, Nell Carey (Mrs. Lucius), 217, 294
Dancy, Rebecca Elizabeth (Mrs. Francis William), 34, 89, 109

Index

Daniel, Mrs., 268
Davis, Mr., a soldier, 117
Davis, David L., 285
Davis, Ebenezer Nelms, 282, 285
Davis, President Jefferson, 8, 70, 98, 123, 159, 224, 261, 263, 267, 270, 280
Davis, Martha Trimble Greenlee (Mrs. Ebenezer Nelms), 279, 282
Davis, Staige, 9
Davis, Susan Sill (Mrs. Ebenezer Nelms), 285
Dawson, Capt., 17
Dawson, Mrs., 137
Deupree, J. G., 32
Dickinson, Mr., 18
Dickinson, Miss Nannie, 2, 3, 7, 10, 12, 13, 18, 23, 226
Dickinson, Shed, 254
Dod, The Rev'd Dr. Charles S., 256
Dougherty, Dr. J. R., 277
Doxey, Hindman, 182, 219, 295
Doxey, Wall, 182
Driver, Bessie Craft (Mrs. James), 222
Dunlap, Dr. Thomas L., 263
Dunlap, Mrs. Thomas L., 263
Dunlap, Thornwell, 133
Edmondson, Miss Jennie, 225
Edmund, a slave, 282
Eggleston, Mr., 64
Elder, The Very Rev'd William Henry, 281, 283- 285
Eli, a servant's child, 197
Elia, The Rev'd Basilio, 284
Ellen, a slave, 47, 60, 74
Eppes, Mary T., 285
Eppes, Richard Harbert, 285
Eppes, Wyatt, 285
Estep, Charles, 280
Ethridge, Mrs. 222
Evans, Miss, 106
Everett, Mr., a lecturer, 160, 162
Ewell, Willie, 92-93
Ewen, Maj., 212
Falconer, Mr., 202
Falconer, Howard, 151, 194, 195, 213, 214, 226
Falconer, Col. Kinloch, 151, 194, 279, 290
Falconer, Sophronia, (see also Mrs. Columbus Barrett), 202, 205
Falconer, Thomas, 194
Fannie, a slave, 236
Fant, Arthur, xvii, 231
Fant, Miss Helen, 222
Fant, James Thornton, xvii, 151, 170, 173, 183, 192, 195-198, 207, 209, 226, 279, 286
Fant, Lester Glenn, 42
Fant, Lizzie Anderson (Mrs. Arthur), 231, 261
Fant, Perrine Hall, 117, 267
Farrell, Mr., 281
Farrell, Joseph, 281
Farris, Mr., 41
Featherston, Gen. Winfield Scott, 241, 275
Fenelon, Francois, 139
Fennell, John, 106, 264
Fennell, Mrs. John, 105
Finley, Augusta, (Mrs. Lewis Scruggs), 49, 227, 239, 242, 258, 279-280, 285-286
Finley, Miss Emma, 7, 42, 43, 49, 82, 152, 168, 202, 227-229, 238-239, 242-243, 253, 254, 258, 272-274, 277-280, 282-283, 285-286, 288-289, 291-292
Finley, George James, 152, 227, 238, 254, 255, 279-280
Finley, John Samuel, 254, 279
Finley, Mary Jane Greenlee (Mrs. John Tate), 238-239, 254, 258, 280
Finley, Mary Rachel ("Miss Mit"), 131, 133
Finley, Miss Mary Virginia ("Ginnie"), 202, 238-239, 277
Foley, Miss Mary Virginia Grigsby, 201, 234, 238, 241, 252, 254, 258, 261, 275, 285, 289
Forrest, Col. Jesse, 85, 256
Forrest, Gen. Nathan Bedford, 16, 30, 31, 34, 103, 117, 123, 243, 256
Fort, Capt., 67, 116
Fort, Miss Fannie B., 49, 252
Fort, James T., 104-107, 109, 110, 252
Fort, Martha Craft (Mrs. James T.), 121, 252
Foster, The Rev'd Colly A., 169-170
Francisco, Edgar Wiggin, Jr., 219, 295
Frank, a slave, 101
Frank, Capt. Sam, 170, 186, 283
Franklin, Mr., 68, 71
Franklin, Jesse, 256
Freeman, Miss Cary, 151, 279
Freeman, George R., 256
Freeman, Kate Walthall (Mrs. George R.), 151, 256, 278-279
Freeman, Russell, 74, 205
Freeman, Yates, 72, 74
Frost, E. D., 125
Garrett, Johnny, 250
Gates, Col. 70
George, cousin of Cora Watson, 127
Gholson, Cynthia, a slave, 101
Gholson, Henry Fort, 219
Gholson, Mary Hannah Caruthers (Mrs. Samuel Creed), 149,252
Gholson, Dr. Samuel Creed, 48, 108, 149, 251
Gibbons, Miss Emma, 213
Gill, Nelson G., 207, 293
Gill, Mrs. Nelson G., 207, 208, 261, 293
Gilmore, Col., 245
Glover, Dr., 114
Goodloe, Mrs. Rosa, 230
Goodman, Walter A., 13, 292
Goodman, Mrs. Walter A., 270, 292
Goodrich, Col. A. W., 108, 109, 229, 265
Govan, Mr., 272
Govan, Andrew, 94
Govan, Andrew Robinson, 34, 94, 151, 244
Govan, Miss Bettie, 151, 273
Govan, Daniel Chevilette, 244
Govan, Eaton Pugh, 244
Govan, George M., 280
Govan, Mary Pugh Jones (Mrs. Andrew Robinson), 108, 136, 244
Govan, Mrs. Pugh, 137
Govan, Sallie (see also Mrs. C. H. Mott), 244, 253
Govan, Willie, 138
Grace, The Rev'd Thomas, 281, 283-284
Grant, Julia Dent (Mrs. Ulysses S.), 15
Grant, Gen. Ulysses S., xvi, 2, 9, 14, 15, 31, 33, 109-110, 112, 127, 191, 234, 240, 248, 249, 271, 284, 286
Gray, Mrs., 27
Gray, Jimmy, 34
Gray, The Rev'd John Hannah, 278

297

Gray, Lena, 34
Green, The Rt. Rev'd William Mercer, 228
Greenway, Mr., 18
Greer, James, 74
Grierson, Col. Benjamin Harrison, 41
Grigsby, The Rev'd Dr. Sherwood Leon, 289
Grundy, The Rev'd Robert C., 234-235
H., Leonora, 113
Hackleton, Prof. J. H., 225
Hal, 121
Hall, Fanny, 254
Hall, Jenny, 254
Hamilton, Gen. C. S., 15, 233
Hamilton, Dr. S. D., 248
Hamner, Miss Lou, 66, 104, 256
Hamner, Mary (Mrs. Morris), 104, 256
Hamner, Morris, 256
Hamner, Miss Sallie, 69, 104, 112, 256
Hampton, Dick, 143-144
Hannah, 18
Hannah, a slave, 24, 28, 30, 79, 79
Hardin, a slave, 236, 237
Hargrove, Lou, 238-239, 278
Hargrove, Mrs., 238-239
Harrell, Miss Mary, 150-153, 155-157, 159, 163, 164, 166, 168, 173, 175, 179, 181, 183, 184, 186, 187, 189, 192, 200, 203, 208, 210, 211, 213
Harriet, a slave, 142, 277
Harris, Judge John W., 12, 82, 231, 243
Harris, Mrs. John W., 231
Harris, Mason, 64, 67, 91, 124
Harris, Sue Watson (Mrs. Cal), 64-65, 67, 69, 72, 74, 79, 80, 89, 94, 96, 108, 110, 124, 256-258
Harris, Col. Thomas W., 224, 229, 256
Harrison, Miss Hallie, 137
Hawks, The Rev'd Dr. Francis Lister, 244
Hays, The Rev'd John Sidney, 231
Hays, Sophia Boyd (Mrs. John Sidney), 231, 233, 274
Henderson, Capt., 114
Henry, a slave, 23, 28, 29, 45
Hester Ann, a former slave, 95
Hill, Sen. Bill, 106
Holland, Miss Diana, 97, 104, 105, 109, 125, 264
Holland, Capt. Dick, 115, 267, 279
Holland, Mrs. Elizabeth Maury, 259 264, 294
Holland, W. J. L., 269, 294
Hood, Gen. John B., 67, 73, 75, 256
Hopson, Miss Mattie, 219, 221
House, James Jarrell, 72-74, 83, 96, 105, 111, 113, 212, 227, 242, 256-257, 259
Howe, The Rev'd George, 255
Hudson, Capt., 125
Hudson, Eva Belle Strickland, 285
Hudson, Miss Fonta, 15, 24, 34, 53, 69
Hudson, John Lewis ("Uncle Hudson"), 46, 80, 85, 91, 274
Hudson, Mary Fontana Thomson (Mrs. John Lewis, "Aunt Mollie"), 7, 12, 15-18, 20, 21, 23, 24, 34, 35, 43, 46-48, 60, 61, 64, 65, 69, 83-85, 97, 136, 228, 239
Hughes, Mollie, 189, 205
Huling, Judge Frederick W., 224

Hull, Anne Crump (Mrs. John), 20, 35, 36, 45, 53, 102, 104, 110, 111, 121, 136-137, 238, 244, 251, 261-262, 273
Hull, Bettie or Betsy (Mrs. John S. Finley), 14, 16, 22, 29 36, 39, 41, 65, 73, 94, 104, 106, 109, 134, 251, 262, 269
Hull, Brodie Strahan, 36, 74, 94, 130, 242, 262, 269
Hull, John, 238, 244, 262
Hull, Miss Lucy, 16, 34, 244
Hull, Miss Susan, 16, 34, 36, 39, 104, 134, 244, 269
Humphries, Mrs., 240
Hunter, Mr., 91
Hurd, The Rev'd Samuel, 215
Hurlbut, Gen. S. A., 231
Huyett, Col., 87
Iback, Mr., 19
Ingraham, The Rev'd Dr. Joseph Holt, 7, 20, 237
Jackson, Gen. Andrew, 265
James, a slave, 273
Janette, a slave, 142, 197, 277, 290
Jennie, a slave, 49
Joe, a slave, 236, 239
John, a slave, 243
Johnnie, 18
Johnson, President Andrew, 115, 159, 195-196
Johnson, Cyrus A., 33-34
Johnson, The Rev'd W. C., 265
Johnston, Gen. Joseph E., 73, 83, 111, 112, 114, 123, 267
Jones, Mr., 210
Jones, Constable Billie, 294
Jones, Miss Helen, 149
Jones, Margaret Mason (Mrs. William A.), 84
Jones, Martha Reese (Mrs. Rufus), 109, 111, 227, 240, 264
Jones, Mason, 84
Jones, Reese (Mrs. F. B. Shuford), 104, 105, 109, 112, 240, 264
Jones, William A., 84
Jordan, Capt., 85
Judy, a slave, 27
Julia Ann, a slave, 273
K, Dr., of Durhamville, 73
Katie, 137
Keen, Mrs. Allin, 222
Kennedy, Miss, 212
Knox, Miss Rowena, 272
Lamar, L. Q. C., 135, 151
Lane, Mary (Mrs. Alexander B.), 102, 264
Lane, Turner H., 210, 293
Latimer, Miss Fannie, 137
Lea, William, 244
Lea, Willis, 50
Lea, Dr. Willis Monroe, 7, 43, 51, 252
Lea, Miss Winnie, 272
Leak, Ada, 200
Leak, Betsy (Mrs. E. W. Francisco Sr.), 295
Leak, Ella (Mrs. Warren Moore), 167, 199, 203, 206, 211, 213
Leak, Frank, 157, 167, 169, 199
Leak, Col. Francis Terry, xi
Leak, Mrs. John, 202
Leak, Martha Jane Malone (Mrs. Francis Terry), 137, 148, 195, 197-199, 202, 203, 212, 275
Leak, Walter John, 295

298

Index

Lee, Gen. Robert E., 91, 92, 103, 109-112, 115, 117, 123, 261, 264, 266
Leggett, Miss Corinne, 131, 133-135
Levy, Isaac C., 126, 270-271, 279
Lewis, Mr., of North Carolina, 137
Lewis, Mrs., blockade runner, 89
Lewis, Miss Annie, 164, 170, 185, 187-189, 211
Lincoln, President Abraham, 9, 70, 83, 93, 112, 113, 115, 120, 235, 274
Lippincott, J. B., 185
Litchfield, Dr. J. D. M., 33, 242
Litchfield, Pamela Brooks (Mrs. J. D. M.), 242
Little, Miss Julia, 2, 7, 69, 131, 133
Lizzie, a slave, 20
Lloyd, Mr., 28
Logan, Gen. John A., 11
Long, Mrs. Henrietta Cohen, 96, 113
Lowenstein, B., 126
Lucas, Clementia Donaho (Mrs. P. W.), 242
Lucas, Col. Peter Walker, 107, 108, 204, 242, 265
Lucinda, 243
Lucy, a slave, 15, 47, 49, 60, 74
Lyon, The Rev'd Dr. James Adair, 262
McCarroll, Amelia (Mrs. Walter John Leak), 3, 114, 131, 164, 168, 169, 272, 295
McCarroll, Miss Bettie, 43, 97, 138, 142, 144, 146, 160, 170, 171, 174, 175, 177, 188, 193, 209
McCarroll, Elizabeth (Mrs. John R.), xiv, 61, 97, 156, 169, 174, 185, 187, 202, 240
McCarroll, John, 2, 74
McCarroll, Sheriff John R., xiv, 51, 61, 233, 240, 253, 255
McCarroll, Miss Mary, 61-62, 194, 202, 211
McCarroll, Miss Sallie, 43, 205
McClellan, Dr., 18
McConnico, Andrew J., 37, 245, 251
McConnico, Miss Mollie, 47
McCorkle, America (Mrs. Samuel), 105, 106, 264
McCrosky, Hiram, 239
McCrosky, Jane Lane, 239
McCrosky, Miss Mary, 23, 239
McCulley, Mr., 108, 241
McCulley, Mrs., 1, 2, 108
McCulley, Miss Pet, 108
McCullough, Col., 116
McDowell, Edward, 288
McDowell, Miss Lillian Kirk, 282
McEwen, Alexander Calvin, 292
McGehee, Hugh, 133
McGowan, Capt. Robert Jr., 42, 224
McGowan, W. Irwin, 25-27, 279
McGuffey, The Rev'd William H., 46, 251
McGuirk, Col. John, 94, 281-282
McGuirk, Katie, 167, 281-282
McGuirk, Walter, 282
McGuirk, Will, 282
Mackay, Mr., 116
McLean (or McLain), Bob, 117, 267
McWilliams, R. R., 244
McWilliams, Mrs. R. R., 35, 244
Mal, slave of Mrs. Hull, 45
Malone, Miss Amanda, 164
Malone, Dr. Ellis, 7

Malone, T. J., 194
Mammy, slave of Mollie Hudson, 17, 18, 20-21
Manning, Miss Mittie (or Mattie), 145, 189
Marcus, Mr., 278
Margrove, Mr., 78
Martin, Gen., 66
Martin, Miss Eliza, 56, 60
Martin, Johnny, 27, 47, 72, 74, 77-79
Martin, Sarah Dickens (Mrs. John Davidson), 1, 27-29, 44, 45, 47, 52, 56, 60, 90, 164, 226, 237, 251, 254
Mary, Aunt, 168
Mason, Carrington, 14, 233, 247, 284
Mason, Maria Brodie (Mrs. Carrington), 14, 38, 41, 66, 104, 155, 160, 170, 175, 233, 246, 247
Mason, T. B., 46
Mason, William F., 15, 34-35, 41, 233
Mattison, Charles S., 280
Mattison, Joseph B., 222, 242, 271
Mattison, Katherine L. (Mrs. Frank), 222
Maury, Commodore Matthew Fontaine, 215, 259, 264, 294
Maury, Gen., 123
Maximilian, Emperor, 91
Mayer, Mrs. Adrian, 109, 265
Mayer, Johnny, 109
Mayers, Willie, 113
Megginson (Maj. Strickland's overseer), 237, 258
Mickle, Maj. Belton, 123, 230
Mickle, Miss Jennie, 48, 50, 130, 252
Mickle, John Martin, 25, 42, 74, 79, 88, 93, 132, 161, 181, 182, 229-230, 236, 246, 251-253, 265, 266, 268-271, 273, 275, 279, 281, 286-288, 289, 290, 292, 293, 294
Mickle, Lucy Minor (Mrs. Belton), 109, 111, 123, 246, 253
Miller, The Rev'd E. D., 147, 149, 150, 187, 278
Miller, Margaret Elizabeth Ford (Mrs. E. D.), 147, 187
Minor, Dabney, 245-246
Minor, Jane Herndon Hull (Mrs. Dabney), 37, 104, 109, 124, 246, 253, 273
Mollie, 137
Molloy, Daniel B., 1-3, 6-8, 226
Monk, a former slave, 95
Moore, a wounded soldier, 68, 71
Moore, Mr., 18
Moore, Miss Lillie, 144-146, 149, 150, 154, 155, 172, 185-188, 193, 203, 211
Morgan, Adj., 243
Morgan, Mr., 197
Morgan, Gen. John H., 46
Mott, Sallie Govan (Mrs. Christopher H.), (see also Miss Sallie Govan) 51, 65, 253
Mullaly, 167, 168
Munford, Mr., 44
Myers, Emma, 172
Myers, George B., 207, 293
Myers, Henry C., 230, 293
Myers, P., 157
Ned, a slave, 235
Neilson, Mr., 170, 171
Nelms, Charles G., 264
Nelms, Mrs. Charles G., 105, 106, 264
Nelson, James Henry, 6, 23, 120-123, 228, 256-257, 268-269
Nelson, Maria Courtney (Mrs. James Henry), 122
Nelson, Tom, 74, 122
Nelson, Willie, 122
Newsome, Carey, 116
Newton, Lieut., 192
Newton, Miss Carrie, xvi, 81

CIVIL WAR WOMEN

Nunnally, Mr., 117, 267
Nuttall, Lou, a slave, 101
Oliver, Father, 281
Ord, Gen. Edward O. C., 124, 270
Orr, Miss Birdie, 270
Otey, The Rt. Rev'd James H., 244, 282
Owen, Mr., 170, 171
Owen, Miss Donna, 170
Owen, Miss Olena, 170
Paine, David Baxter, 33
Paine, Elizabeth Baxter (Mrs. Henry H.), 213, 230
Paine, The Rev'd Henry H., 7, 10, 12, 20, 27, 30, 33, 44, 49, 54-56, 58, 60, 62, 63, 70, 71, 75, 83, 92, 93, 106, 111, 112, 126, 137, 140, 182, 183, 186, 213, 229-231, 241, 253, 255, 265, 273, 276, 288
Paine, Henry Martyn, 151, 186, 231, 276
Paine, Henry Rowland, 33
Paine, The Rev'd James, 231
Paine, Miss Mary Rowland, 12, 151, 212, 213, 246
Paine, Matilda ("Miss Tillie"), 53, 175, 181, 211, 253
Paine, Miss Rosa, 143
Palmer, The Rev'd Dr. Benjamin Morgan, 91-92, 255, 261-262
Peats, Maj. F. F., 11-12
Peel, Mrs. Faye, 222
Pendleton, Gen. William Nelson, 268
Perkins, Hardin, 137
Pettis, The Rev'd William M., 206, 292
Phebe, a slave, 277
Phillips, Miss Emily, 7, 205
Phillips, Miss Fannie, 140, 144, 164, 172-174, 179, 189, 195, 198, 201
Pickett, a servant, 154
Pickett, The Rev'd Dr. James Thomas, 19, 20, 67, 104, 105, 119, 151, 236-237, 264, 273, 282
Pointer, Dr. P., 42, 284
Polk, Miss Emily, 105, 265
Polk, President James Knox, 265
Polk, The Rt. Rev'd Leonidas, 169-170, 264
Polk, Gen. Thomas G., 264
Polk, Mrs. Thomas G., 264
Powell, George, 227
Powell, Mrs., 275
Powers, Capt., 207
Powers, Maj., 207
Preher, Adam, 171
Price, Gen. Sterling, 38, 262
Pryor, Mr. Sam, 97
Quantrell, R., 73, 121
Raiford, Mrs., 48
Randolph, W. S., 292
Rascoe, Mrs. Henry, 246
Rather, John Edward, 219
Read, (or Reed?) Miss Lucilla, 24, 140, 183
Read, Mr., 23
Rebecca, cousin of Johnny Martin, 47
Reed, Mr., stabbing victim, 208
Reed, Dr., 246
Reid, Mary Jane (Mrs. Samuel Irwin), 287
Reid, The Rev'd Samuel Irwin, 177, 287
Rhine, Solomon, 126, 270
Rives, Dr., 278
Rives, Mrs., 278
Rives, William, 83
Robbie, 199
Roberts, Mr. and Mrs., 107
Robinson, Hannie, 280
Roddy, Gen., 103
Ross, Mr., 198

Rutland, Miss Alice, 164, 170, 200
Rutter, Adj., 41
Ryan, The Rev'd Abram, 180
Sallie, a slave, 236, 237
Saulsberry, a former slave, 95
Saxton, Gen., 236
Scales, Cordelia Lewis, 234, 242, 245, 247, 256, 260, 263, 289
Scales, Joe, 3
Scruggs, Lewis, 33, 242, 279, 286
Sears, The Rev'd Peter Gray, 269, 273
Selby, Capt., 92
Selby, James J., 277
Seward, Sec. William H., 93, 112, 115
Shaw, Mattie, 114
Sheridan, Gen. Philip Henry, 98
Sherman, Gen. William Tecumseh, 31, 67, 70, 96, 98, 111, 114, 123, 127, 226, 231, 257, 268
Shuford, Dr. Franklin Brevard, 151, 240, 264
Simms, Mr., 85
Simms, Mrs. 111
Sims, Lieut. James, 109, 265
Sims, William L., 33
Smith, Mr., 180, 251
Smith, Annie, 106
Smith, Billie, 74
Smith, Cal, 292
Smith, Caroline Hatch ("Miss Carrie") (Mrs. James Crump), 25, 39, 44, 47, 50-53, 60, 65-67, 105, 112, 150, 244, 251, 272
Smith, Eagleton M., 213
Smith, Frank, 44, 51, 56
Smith, Gladys Ridley (Mrs. E. Deaderick), 219, 221
Smith, Dr. Gray Washington, 44, 102, 121, 243,
Smith, Mrs. Gray Washington, 25, 105, 253
Smith, Henrietta Lucas (Mrs. Cal), 107, 265, 292
Smith, Gen. J. A. ("Scoey"), 245
Smith, John, 272
Smith, Kirby, 116
Smith, Lucy Deaderick Lyon (Mrs. Eagleton M.), 213, 262
Smith, Miss Mollie, 34, 58
Smith, Miss Susan, 112
Sneider, Herman, 250
Sowell, John, 42
Speed, Attorney Gen. James, 124
Stanford, Prof., 140, 141, 143-146, 148, 169, 171
Stanley, Mr., 18
Stanton, Sec. Edwin M., 6, 124
Steinway, Henry E., 41
Stephens, Vice-President Alexander Hamilton, 83, 91, 123
Stewart, Miss Annie, 83, 113, 258
Stewart, Miss Mary R., 83, 113, 258
Stillman, Mr., 107
Strickland, Mr., a jeweler, 107
Strickland, Miss Belle, ix, *passim*
Strickland, Frank, x, 220
Strickland, Jacob, 220
Strickland, Mrs. Jacob, 220
Strickland, Jane Leak (Mrs. William Mathew), x, xi, 140, 144, 145, 147-150, 156, 168-170, 194- 197, 199, 205, 272, 275, 276, 282, 285, 295
Strickland, Sir John, xvii
Strickland, Miss Lorena, ix
Strickland, Miss Madie, 256
Strickland, Martha Mildred Thomson (Mrs. William Mathew), x, xiv, xv, xvi, 55, 223, 225-228, 231-233, 235-239, 243, 247, 251, 253, 256, 258-262, 269-271, 273, 274, 277, 280, 285
Strickland, Lorena Lumpkin ("Rena") (Mrs. William M. Jr.), ix, 285

300

Index

Strickland, Miss Mary Thomson, ix
Strickland, Squire Mathew, xvii
Strickland, Miss Mildred ("Minnie"), 1-3, 7, 8, 15, 19, 20, 46, 50, 53, 57, 63-65, 69, 131, 133, 136, 144, 153, 157, 199-201, 205, 226, 236, 237, 251, 273, 285
Strickland, Perle (see also Mrs. Gerard Badow), x, xv, 217-222, 282, 285, 295
Strickland, Will (Belle's cousin), 193
Strickland, Maj. William Mathew, x, xiv-xvii, 1, 7, 10, 19, 46, 47, 49, 50, 53, 55, 60, 63-64, 69, 80, 85, 98, 120, 123, 136-138, 140, 142, 144, 145, 148, 150, 151, 156, 159-163, 166, 169- 171, 174, 175, 177-179, 181, 182, 184, 186, 188, 191-193, 195, 197-201, 203, 205, 210, 223, 225-227, 230-233, 235-239, 242, 243, 246, 251, 253, 256, 258-261, 263, 265, 267, 269, 270, 272-277, 279, 280, 282, 285, 286, 288, 290
Strickland, William Mathew Jr. ("Buddie"), ix, 1-3, 7, 10, 12, 16-18, 21, 22, 24, 44, 45, 47, 49, 52, 56, 58, 63, 64, 72, 74, 80, 88, 89, 91, 94, 98, 125, 126, 130, 137, 138, 152, 154, 156, 163, 178, 197, 203, 205, 223, 224, 231, 237, 251, 260, 262, 285
Stuart, Miss Elizabeth, 216
Stuart, Gen. J. E. B., 216
Sue, a slave, 49, 69, 89
Susie, a slave, 282
Taylor, Dick, 123
Tepe, Prof. F. A., 65, 88, 132-133, 273
Thomas, a Union commander, 75
Thomas, Miss Bettie, 14, 36, 93, 94, 262
Thomas, Charles, 117
Thomas, E. A., 95, 107-108
Thomas, Mrs. E. A., 265
Thomas, Miss Laura, 108
Thomas, Miss Susan, 104
Thomas, Susan, 285
Thompson, Mrs. Netty Fant, 222
Thomson, Dr. James Madison, 224
Thomson, Jimmy Gray, 34
Thomson, Laura Smith (Mrs. Morgan H.), 48, 243, 252
Thomson, Miss Lena, 34
Thomson, Lewis, 7, 91, 228
Thomson, Morgan Hopson ("Hoppy"), 96, 103, 109, 234, 243, 264
Thomson, Sara Merrill (Mrs. Lewis), 227, 228
Tidy, a slave, 282
Topp, Col. Dixon Comfort, 42, 249, 283
Topp, Ella (Mrs. Dixon Comfort), 170
Travis, Miss, 202, 213
Trenholm, George A., 104, 106-108
Trotter, Miss Bettie, 109
Trotter, Judge James F., xvii, 105, 106, 109, 265
Tucker, Mr., 28, 210
Tucker, Charlie, 254
Tyler, F. A., 9
Tyler, Mrs. Rosa Barton, 151, 230
Van Dorn, Gen. Earl, 2, 31, 32, 38, 41, 61, 160, 175, 234, 240, 242, 243, 245, 248, 249, 251, 280, 284, 287
Vaughan, Mabel, 82
Venable, Carrie Craft (Mrs. R. N.) (see also Miss Carrie Craft), 70, 84, 96, 256
Waddell, The Rev'd Dr. John Newton, 10-12, 29, 231, 278
Waite, Gordontia, 229
Walker, Janette Thomson (Mrs. John C.), 227, 228, 240
Walker, John C., 67, 113, 124, 228
Wallace, Katie, 167
Walter, Col. Harvey Washington, 15, 85, 226, 234, 248, 249, 253, 259, 279, 284
Walter, Irene (Mrs. Oscar Johnson), 216
Walthall, Mr., 102, 131
Walthall, Ben, 109
Walthall, Maj. Gen. Edward Cary, 22
Walthall, Sarah Southall Wilkinson (Mrs. Barret White), 22, 23, 28, 34
Warren, Mrs. James Buchanan, 222
Warwick, Earl of, xvii
Wash, slave of Mollie Hudson, 17-18
Washburn, Gen. C. C., 47, 102, 243, 251
Watson, Annah Robinson, 292
Watson, Catherine Frances Davis (Mrs. J. W. C.) x, 9, 13, 15, 18-20, 22, 23, 25, 28, 30, 33, 34, 36, 37, 44, 45, 47, 48, 50, 57, 58, 60, 66, 68, 72, 74, 79, 80, 82, 84-86, 94, 104, 121, 122, 125, 144, 148, 149, 150, 156, 188, 189, 231, 240, 244, 246, 260, 279
Watson, Cora E. White Harris (Mrs. Wm. T.), x, 1-3, 7, 10, 12, 13, 17, 18, 21, 23, 28, 30, 44, 45, 47, 63, 64, 66, 68, 72-74, 77, 79-83, 85, 86, 89, 90, 94, 97, 101-117, 121, 122, 126, 127, 129, 130, 132, 135, 141, 143, 146, 150, 163, 197, 206, 208, 212-214, 229, 231, 240, 243-244, 246, 247, 250, 251, 253, 254, 256, 258, 260, 274, 276, 279, 288, 294
Watson, Edward Minor, 1, 7, 14, 23, 27-31, 34, 37, 45, 47, 49-52, 58, 60 63, 64, 67, 69, 73, 74, 77-80, 82-85, 87-89, 98, 122, 126, 130, 132, 192, 226, 231, 250, 257, 274
Watson, Edward Minor II (see also Staige Davis Watson), 257
Watson, Elizabeth Davis ("Miss Lizzie"), x, 2, 3, 7, 8, 19, 21-23, 24, 30, 33, 34, 43-48, 50-52, 56, 57, 60, 61, 63-66, 69, 71-75, 78-82, 97, 98, 104, 105, 107, 109, 111, 112, 114-116, 126, 129, 130, 132, 139-141, 150, 155, 157, 164, 165, 167-169, 172, 179, 181-184, 186, 187, 191, 192, 195, 196, 200, 202, 203, 206, 208, 209, 212-217, 223, 231, 247, 259, 274, 276, 279, 294
Watson, Elizabeth Finch, 9
Watson, James Henry, 44, 57, 58, 85, 117, 129, 137, 187, 231, 249, 271
Watson, John, 9
Watson, John Staige Davis, 229
Watson, Sen. John William Clark, xiv, xvii, 1, 2, 5, 8-10, 16, 19, 34, 45-48, 56-60, 65, 74, 85, 93, 98, 117, 126, 127, 129, 133, 136, 137, 173, 191, 205, 229-231, 244, 250, 256, 257, 260, 261, 263, 279, 288, 290
Watson, Richard L. ("Dick"), 226
Watson, Staige Davis, (see also Edward Minor Watson II), 9, 257
Watson, Stephen (a slave), 16, 45, 89, 95, 260-261, 276
Watson, William Taylor, x, 33, 229, 231, 274, 279
Weatherby, The Rev'd James, 291
Wells, Ida B., 292
West, Absalom Madden, 194, 227, 231
Wilfong, Mrs., 18
Wilkerson, Dr., of Somerville, 67
Wilkerson, Dr. Cary, 222
Williams, Mr., 246
Williams, Mr. Nat, 109
Williamson, Mr., 131
Williamson, Gen. Henry E., 243, 292
Williamson, Mrs. Henry, 93
Williamson, Mal (Mrs. Harry C. Smith), 206, 292
Wilson, President Woodrow, 257
Winborn, Hugh, 120, 268, 269
Winfrey, Bert, 254
Wise, Father, 281
Wollenhaupt, Hermann Adolf, 41, 175, 247
Wooten, Miss Nettie, 150, 156, 188, 192, 212
Worsham, Col., 17
Wright, Gen. Marcus, 114
Wynne, Dr., 42
Yellow Ben, a slave, 235
Young, The Rev'd Dr. John Clarke, 241, 289